Student Engagement in Higher Education

Student Engagement in Higher Education is an important volume that fills a longstanding void in the higher education and student affairs literature. The editors and authors make clear that diverse populations of students experience college differently and encounter group-specific barriers to success. Informed by relevant theories, each chapter focuses on a different population for whom research confirms that engagement and connectivity to the college experience are problematic, including low-income students, racial/ethnic minorities, students with disabilities, LGBT students, and several others. The forward-thinking practical ideas offered throughout the book are based on the 41 contributors' more than 540 cumulative years of full-time work experience in various capacities at two-year and four-year institutions of higher education. Faculty and administrators will undoubtedly find this book complete with fresh strategies to reverse problematic engagement trends among various college student populations.

Shaun R. Harper is an assistant professor of Higher Education Management at the University of Pennsylvania. Formerly, he was executive director of the Doctor of Education Program at the University of Southern California, Rossier School of Education.

Stephen John Quaye is an assistant professor in the College Student Personnel Program at the University of Maryland and a department editor for *About Campus*.

Student Engagement in Higher Education

Theoretical Perspectives and Practical Approaches for Diverse Populations

EDITED BY

SHAUN R. HARPER AND STEPHEN JOHN QUAYE

FOREWORD BY ESTELA MARA BENSIMON

AFTERWORD BY GEORGE D. KUH

Routledge
Taylor & Francis Group

NEW YORK AND LONDON

First published 2009
by Routledge
270 Madison Ave, New York, NY 10016

Simultaneously published in the UK
by Routledge
2 Park Square, Milton Park, Abingdon, Oxon OX14 4RN

Routledge is an imprint of the Taylor & Francis Group, an informa business

Typeset in Minion Pro by Prepress Projects Ltd, Perth, UK
Printed and bound in the United States of America on acid-free paper by Edward Brothers, Inc.

Library of Congress Cataloging in Publication Data
Student engagement in higher education: theoretical perspectives and practical approaches for diverse populations/editors Shaun R. Harper and Stephen John Quaye; foreword by Estela Mara Bensimon.
p. cm.
Includes bibliographical references and index.
1. Student affairs services—United States. 2. Student activities—United States. 3. College students—Services for—United States. 4. Multicultural education—United States. I. Harper, Shaun R., 1975– II. Quaye, Stephen John, 1980–
LB2342.92.S78 2008
378.1'97–dc22
2008002146

ISBN 10: 0–415–98850–0 (hbk)
ISBN 10: 0–415–98851–9 (pbk)
ISBN 10: 0–203–89412–X (ebk)

ISBN 13: 978–0–415–98850–6 (hbk)
ISBN 13: 978–0–415–98851–3 (pbk)
ISBN 13: 978–0–203–89412–5 (ebk)

We dedicate this book to Margaret Cyrus,
Etta R. Hollins, and other authentic agents
for social justice.

Contents

About the Editors

Shaun R. Harper is an Assistant Professor of Higher Education Management at the University of Pennsylvania, Graduate School of Education. Formerly, he served as an assistant professor and executive director of the Doctor of Education Program at the University of Southern California, Rossier School of Education. He maintains an active research agenda that examines race and gender in higher education, Black male college achievement, the effects of college environments on student behaviors and outcomes, and gains associated with educationally purposeful student engagement. In September 2007, Harper was featured on the cover of *Diverse Issues in Higher Education* for his National Black Male College Achievement Study, the largest-ever empirical research project on Black male undergraduates. He is the author of more than 40 peer-reviewed journal articles, book chapters, and other academic publications. His other books and monographs include *Responding to the Realities of Race on Campus* (Jossey-Bass, 2007), *Creating Inclusive Campus Environments for Cross-Cultural Learning and Student Engagement* (NASPA, 2008), and *Using Qualitative Methods in Institutional Assessment* (Jossey-Bass, 2007).

Harper has presented more than 100 research papers, workshops, and symposia at national higher education and student affairs professional conferences. In 2004, the National Association of Student Personnel Administrators (NASPA) awarded him the Melvene D. Hardee Dissertation of the Year Award. In addition, the American College Personnel Association (ACPA) presented him the 2005 Emerging Scholar Award and the 2006 *Annuit Coeptis* Award for early career achievement. In 2008 the National Association of Academic Advisors for Athletics presented him its Outstanding Contribution to Rearch Award. Harper has prior professional experience in student activities, sorority and fraternity affairs, graduate admissions, and academic program administration. He is currently Director of Research on the NASPA Board of Directors. Harper has also served as a trustee for the Association of College Unions International, a member of the advisory committee for the National Conference on Race and Ethnicity in American Higher Education, and on the editorial boards of the *Journal of College Student Development*, the *American Journal of Education*, *NASPA Journal*, and *NASAP Journal*. He earned his bachelor's degree in Education from Albany State, a historically Black university in Georgia. His master's degree in College Student Affairs Administration and Ph.D. in Higher Education Administration are from Indiana University.

Stephen John Quaye is an assistant professor in the College Student Personnel Program at the University of Maryland, and a department editor for *About Campus*. His research concentrates on the influence of race relations on college and university campuses, specifically the gains and outcomes associated with inclusive racial climates, cross-racial interactions, and color-conscious pedagogical approaches. He has presented nearly two dozen research papers, workshops, and symposia at national higher education and student affairs conferences. In addition, he is the author of various book chapters, peer-reviewed articles, and other scholarly publications, some of which have appeared in the *Journal of College Student Development*, the *Journal of Research Practice*, and *Liberal Education*. Quaye is on the editorial boards of the *Journal of the Professoriate*, the *Journal of Research Practice*, and *NASAP Journal*, and has served as associate editor of *Higher Education in Review*. He is co-editor (with Peter Magolda) of the forthcoming book *Educational Awakenings: Creating Learning Partnerships during Graduate School*. His previous experience in student affairs includes residence life, multicultural affairs, and learning assistance. Formerly, he was a graduate student and research assistant in the Center for Higher Education Policy Analysis at the University of Southern California, Rossier School of Education. Quaye earned his bachelor's degree in Psychology from James Madison University, his mater's degree in College Student Personnel from Miami University, and his Ph.D. in Higher Education from The Pennsylvania State University.

About the Contributors

Sarvenaz Aliabadi earned her Ed.D. in Higher Education Administration from the University of Southern California, Rossier School of Education. Her bachelor's and master's degrees are in Environmental Science, both from the University of California, Riverside. Aliabadi is currently an administrator at the University of California, Los Angeles, in the Office for the Protection of Research Subjects. She previously taught Integrated Coordinated Science at the high school level. She is a member of National Association of Student Personnel Administrators, and her research interests include the effects of crime and crime statistics on college students' behaviors, specifically with regard to students' safety over time.

Gregory Anderson has been teaching, mentoring, training teachers, and leading programs for two decades. For much of that time, he worked overseas in a variety of faculty and administrative positions. He returned to the United States in 2001, joining the faculty of the University of Southern California. Anderson has been the director of the Student Success Center at De Anza College for the past two years. In this position, he integrates instructional support programs that serve 12,000 students yearly. Anderson has been elected to leadership positions on state and national organizations and has received awards for teaching, mentoring, and leadership. His Ed.D. is in Higher Education Administration from the University of Southern California, Rossier School of Education.

Tony Arguelles received his Ed.D. in Higher Education Administration from the University of Southern California, Rossier School of Education. He is an instructor at a community college and teacher at a Los Angeles high school. Arguelles has previous professional experience serving as a vice principal, assistant principal, and dean of students. His research interests include cognitive and psychosocial development, student learning, community college students, and non-traditional students.

Ramona Barrio-Sotillo is a tenured faculty member at Glendale Community College. As a professor and counselor she has experience teaching classes in student success, including College Orientation, Freshman Seminar, and Career Planning. As a counselor, she has guided many students from underrepresented and low-income communities to achieve their academic goals, including transfer to major universities. In 2005, she was named Latina Woman of the Year by the Glendale Latino Association for her work with Latino students in the community. Her Ed.D. is in Educational Leadership with a focus on Community College Leadership from the University of Southern California, Rossier School of Education.

Karen Y. Carmichael is the Associate Director of the Learning Resource Center at Loyola Marymount University. Previously, she has served the Center as assistant director and mathematics specialist. She also has experience in teaching mathematics at both secondary and undergraduate levels. Carmichael's primary research interest is underrepresented minority student achievement in science and mathematics. Her Ed.D. in Higher Education Administration is from the University of Southern California, Rossier School of Education.

Cristina Castelo-Rodriguez is an Associate Professor of Counseling at Los Angeles Pierce College. She has also worked as a high school counselor. Rodriguez' research interests include race and gender in higher education and minority student college achievement. Her Ed.D. is in Higher Education with an emphasis in Community College Leadership from the University of Southern California.

Jarrett T. Gupton is a Ph.D. candidate in Urban Educational Policy with an emphasis on Higher Education at the University of Southern California, Rossier School of Education. Gupton is a research assistant in the Center for Higher Education Policy Analysis at the University of Southern California, Rossier School of Education. His research interests include access to higher education for low-income students, diversity in higher education, the sociology of education, and qualitative methods. Gupton's master's degree in Higher and Postsecondary Education is from Arizona State University.

Todd J. Harper is an Assistant Professor of Music at the University of La Verne. Harper received the Doctor of Musical Arts degree from the University of Southern California, where he graduated with honors from the Thornton School of Music. His dissertation, titled "Hugo Distler and the Renewal Movement in Nazi Germany," examines the juxtaposition of Distler's personal beliefs and his political/professional obligations to the Nazi Party. Harper taught music in California public schools for six years and was honored for excellence in teaching in *Who's Who Among America's Teachers*.

W. Paul Harrington is Director of Admissions at Westerly School in Long Beach, California. Formerly, he worked as a resident director in the student affairs division and an administrator for the School of Education at Loyola Marymount University. He also has extensive professional experience at the pre-kindergarten through high school levels as a teacher and administrator. Harrington's Ed.D. in Higher Education Administration is from the University of Southern California, Rossier School of Education.

Frank Harris III is an Assistant Professor of Postsecondary Education at San Diego State University. Previously, he served as Associate Director of the Center for Urban Education at the University of Southern California, Rossier School of Education. Harris' scholarship focuses on college men and masculinities, gendered trends in postsecondary learning environments, and equity in educational outcomes for historically underrepresented and underserved student populations. In 2007, Harris earned the national dissertation of the year awards from the American Educational Research Association (Division J) and the Association of Student Judicial Affairs. His Ed.D. in Higher Education Administration is from the University of Southern California, Rossier School of Education.

Viannda M. Hawkins is an academic advisor in the College of Letters, Arts, & Sciences at the University of Southern California, where she also is the coordinator of Pre-Law Advising Services. Hawkins currently serves as the staff advisor for several student organizations at USC. Formerly, she served as a graduate assistant in various departments within the Division of Student Affairs at USC, including the Center for Black Cultural and Student Affairs and the Center for Academic Support. Hawkins earned her Ed.D. in Higher Education Administration from the University of Southern California, Rossier School of Education.

Jeffrey A. Hoffman is Associate Dean of Students at the Art Center College of Design in Pasadena, California. Previously he served as Director of Marketing and Programs at California State Polytechnic University, Pomona. In his current role, he provides leadership for the Department of Student Life programs and services as well as a variety of Division of Student Affairs initiatives. Hoffman received his master's degree in Student Affairs in Higher Education from Colorado State University and is a doctoral candidate in Higher Education Administration at the University of Southern California, Rossier School of Education. He currently serves on the Board of Trustees for the Association of College Unions International (ACUI).

Tzufang Huang earned her Ed.D. in Educational Psychology from the University of Southern California, Rossier School of Education. She is currently a postdoctoral research associate in the USC Information Sciences Institute. Her bachelor's degree in Mass Communication with a concentration in Broadcasting is from Fu Jen University in Taiwan. Huang's master's degree in Communication Management is from the USC Annenberg School for Communication. Her research interests include international student affairs management, computer-based assessment, the learning effectiveness of computer games, and effective instructional design for online learning, multimedia learning, and bilingual education.

Helen S. Kim works at the University of Southern California, Marshall School of Business. Formerly, she served as a program coordinator in alumni relations at USC. Her research interests include the rise of niche degree programs and the impact of market forces on the landscape of higher education. Her Ed.D. in Higher Education Administration is from the USC Rossier School of Education.

Dennis A. Kramer II earned his master's degree in Postsecondary Administration and Student Affairs at the University of Southern California, Rossier School of Education. His thesis examined the academic socialization process of male student-athletes participating in revenue-generating sports. Kramer is currently a doctoral student in Higher Education at the University of Georgia. His scholarly interests are related to the collegiate experiences of student-athletes, higher education economics, and the utilization of sports and popular culture to increase institutional prestige and access to higher education. Kramer also works with the Knight Commission on Intercollegiate Athletics.

Heather J. Larabee is an Assistant Dean and Director of Campus Activities at the University of Southern California. She oversees the Graduate and Undergraduate Student Senates, the Program Board, over 600 student organizations, campus-wide events, and leadership development programs. Prior to joining USC, she worked at the University of Tennessee, Knoxville, and Francis Marion University. Larabee received the 1996 NACA C. Shaw Smith New Professional Award. Her Ed.D. in Higher Education Administration is from the USC Rossier School of Education.

Jaime Lester is an Assistant Professor of Higher Education at George Mason University. Formerly, she was an assistant professor in the Department of Leadership and Counseling at Old Dominion University. Lester received her Ph.D. in Urban Education Policy with an emphasis in Higher Education from the University of Southern California, Rossier School of Education. At USC, she was a research assistant in the Center for Higher Education and Policy Analysis where she worked primarily on the Transfer and Retention and Urban Community College Students (TRUCCS) project. Lester maintains an active research agenda that examines gender equity in higher education, retention and transfer of community college students, socialization of women and minority faculty, and leadership. She has published articles in the *Community College Journal of Research and Practice, Community College Review, Journal of Higher Education*, and *NEA: Thought & Action*. Lester recently published the book *Gendered Perspectives on Community College* (Jossey-Bass, 2009), and has another forthcoming on family-friendly policies in higher education.

Moreen E. Logan earned her Ed.D. in Higher Education Administration at the University of Southern California, Rossier School of Education, where she also completed her master's degree. Logan has been the medical student educator for the Introduction to Clinical Medicine Program at the USC Keck School of Medicine since 1998. She is also a registered nurse at Torrance Memorial Medical Center. Her research interests include medical student professional behaviors, critical reflection in medical education, and clinical skills training.

Caitlin J. Mahaffey is the Assistant Director for Communications and Student Services for the undergraduate program in Health Promotion and Disease Prevention Studies at the University of Southern California, Keck School of Medicine. She has previous professional experience teaching writing at USC and the California Institute of Technology. Mahaffey's research interests include spirituality and student development, interfaith dialogue on campuses, and the ways in which religion affects students' experiences of campus life. Her master's degree in Postsecondary Administration and Student Affairs is from the USC Rossier School of Education.

Lindsey E. Malcom is an Assistant Professor in the Graduate School of Education at the University of California, Riverside. Her research interests include minority student achievement in the sciences and related fields (STEM), with an emphasis on community college transfer as a pathway to STEM; the relationships between college financing strategies and academic outcomes for minority STEM majors; and the organizational cultures of Hispanic-serving institutions. Malcom received her Ph.D. in Urban Education Policy with an emphasis in Higher Education from the University of Southern California, Rossier School of Education. She also has a B.S. from the Massachusetts Institute of Technology and an M.S. from the California Institute of Technology, both in Planetary Science.

Brandon E. Martin is an Associate Athletics Director at the University of Southern California. As a senior athletics administrator, he manages the day-to-day operations for seven Division I sports. He also serves as the liaison with the USC Admissions Office and the Student Affairs Division. Coupled with his athletic duties and pursuits, Martin is an assistant professor of Clinical Education at the USC Rossier School of Education. He maintains an active research agenda related to the factors that facilitate academic success among African American male student-athletes, the effects of college environments on student-athlete outcomes, management and leadership in college athletics, and gains associated with student-athlete engagement in out-of-class activities. Martin earned the Ed.D. in Higher Education Administration from the Rossier School of Education.

David Angel Martínez is Department Chair and Professor of Engineering at College of the Canyons. Formerly, he was Assistant Director of the Center for Engineering Diversity at the University of Southern California. Martinez has also served as Associate Director of Education and Outreach for the UCLA Center for Scalable & Integrated Nano-Manufacturing, a role in which he was responsible for technology-based research, graduate recruitment, student retention, and advising engineering students. He has a master's degree in Operations Research Engineering. His Ed.D. is in Higher Education Administration from the USC Rossier School of Education.

Kaneesha Miller is the Associate Dean of Outreach and Recruitment for East Los Angeles College, one of the nine colleges composing the Los Angeles Community College District. Miller has over eight years of experience in student affairs within the California Community College system. She is also an adjunct assistant professor at the University of Southern California. Her Ed.D. is in Higher Education Administration from the USC Rossier School of Education.

Kenechukwu (K.C.) Mmeje is the Director of the Scholars Program at the University of Southern California, a grant-funded initiative that encourages first-generation, underrepresented, and low- to moderate-income students to transfer from two-year colleges to elite research universities. At USC, he has also served as the Student Affairs Advisor and Special Projects Coordinator for the Office of the Vice President of Student Affairs, and as the Assistant Director of Student Judicial Affairs. Mmeje also has previous professional experience in undergraduate recruitment and admissions. He is currently pursing his Ed.D. in Higher Education Administration at the USC Rossier School of Education.

Kuro Nagasaka is a doctoral candidate in Higher Education Administration at the University of Southern California, Rossier School of Education. He is an international student from Japan. Nagasaka earned the master's degree in Postsecondary Administration and Student Affairs from the USC Rossier School of Education prior to enrolling in the Ed.D. program. His research investigates transfer rates at community colleges, retention rates across institution types, and developmental outcomes among undergraduates, specifically international students.

Christopher B. Newman is a doctoral student in Higher Education and Organizational Change and a research assistant in the Choices Project at the University of California, Los Angeles. He previously served as a recruiting and admissions counselor for the University of Southern California, Rossier School of Education. Newman's research interests include Black and Latino student college achievement, the effects of individual identity development on student outcomes, and institutional assessments of diversity policies and initiatives. His master's degree in Leadership Studies is from the University of San Diego.

Andrew H. Nichols, a Bunton-Waller Graduate Fellow and Edward & Susan Wilson Graduate Scholarship recipient, is a doctoral candidate and research assistant in the Center for the Study of Higher Education at The Pennsylvania State University. Formerly, he worked in residence life and the Topping Student Center at the University of Southern California. Nichols' research agenda examines the influence of race and ethnicity on student outcomes, experiences, and behaviors; diversity and equity in higher education; and race relations on predominantly White campuses. He received a master's degree in Postsecondary Administration and Student Affairs from the USC Rossier School of Education and a bachelor's degree in Psychology from Vanderbilt University.

Mark A. Pearson is a research assistant at the University of Southern California, Rossier School of Education, where he is pursuing the Ed.D. in Educational Psychology. For five years, Pearson worked as assistant director of the Center for Black Cultural and Student Affairs at USC. He is the founder of the developing University Metropolitan Day School, a charter school in California for which he recently received a grant from the Walton Foundation. Pearson's research interests include organizational development and performance and change management, as well as equity in urban education. His master's degree in Public Administration is also from USC.

Elizabeth Peterson received her bachelor's degree in Music Education and her master's degree in Vocal Performance from the University of South Dakota. She began her professional career at California State University, Chico, as a resident director and then a residence community coordinator. Peterson then moved to Los Angeles to work as an area coordinator and the Women's Center Advisor at Occidental College. Currently she is the Selection and Training Coordinator at the University of Southern California, Office for Residential Education.

Imelda Quintanar is an academic counselor for the Educational Opportunity Program at California State University, Dominguez Hills. In this role, Quintanar is responsible for the implementation of retention programs aimed at ensuring that students persist toward graduation at the university. She also has previous professional experience in student affairs and advising, recruitment, and designing and implementing parent orientation initiatives, such as Spanish Parent Orientation. Quintanar received her Ed.D. in Higher Education Administration from the University of Southern California, Rossier School of Education.

Candace Rypisi is the Director of Student–Faculty Programs at the California Institute of Technology. In this role, she provides leadership for 14 different undergraduate research programs. Formerly she served as the director of the CalTech Women's Center, the director of the Cornell Women's Resource Center, and a program coordinator at the Office of Women's Programs and Services at Colorado State University. Rypisi is a doctoral candidate in Higher Education Administration at the University of Southern California, Rossier School of Education. Her research interests include gender equity in higher education, institutional change, and leadership.

Margaret W. Sallee is an Assistant Professor of Higher Education at the University of Tennessee. She received her Ph.D. in Urban Education Policy with an emphasis in Higher Education from the University of Southern California, Rossier School of Education. Her master's degree in Higher Education and Student Affairs is from The Ohio State University. Sallee's research interests include the impact of gender on graduate student socialization, work–life balance issues for faculty, and the challenges of ensuring access and equity at the institutional and national levels.

Leah A. Schueler is Assistant Dean of Students and Director of Housing and Residence Life at Hollins University in Roanoke, Virginia. Her previous professional experience has included the fields of residential life/residential education, academic advising, student services, and undergraduate teaching. Her Ed.D. in Higher Education Administration is from the University of Southern California, Rossier School of Education.

Scott C. Silverman is Coordinator for First-Year Programs in the Office of Student Life at the University of California, Riverside. He has recently completed his Ed.D. in Higher Education Administration at the University of Southern California, Rossier

School of Education. His dissertation, "Creating Community Online: The Effects of Online Social Networks on College Student Experiences," is based on hundreds of surveys and focus groups with undergraduate students around the country.

Susan Sims is the Executive Officer of the University of California, Los Angeles, Summer Sessions and Special Programs. Formerly, she has held positions in international education and has served as Assistant Director of the Center for Near Eastern Studies in the International Institute at UCLA and as the Assistant Director of the Professional Program in Arts Management in Hong Kong, a program of the UCLA Anderson School of Business. Sims received her Ed.D. in Higher Education Administration from the University of Southern California, Rossier School of Education.

Scott A. Smith is Associate Director of Student Publications at the University of Southern California. He also serves on the university's Accessibility Task Force and has managed services for the Division of Student Affairs Information Technology. Smith's research interests include the effects of architecture and campus design on student development and retention, the role of emerging technology in higher education, religion and spirituality among college students, disabilities services, and student publications. His master's degree in Postsecondary Administration and Student Affairs is from the USC Rossier School of Education.

Michelle R. Stiles is Director of Budget and Financial Services at University of California, Los Angeles Extension. Stiles has received two Staff Innovation Awards while at Extension. She has previous professional experience in the areas of business, finance, and budget in non-profit, public, and private higher education environments. Additionally, Stiles has experience developing services for academic libraries and public regional library systems. Her Ed.D. in Educational Leadership is from the University of Southern California, Rossier School of Education.

Rameen Ahmadi Talesh is Associate Dean of Students at the University of California, Irvine. He recently completed his Ed.D. in Higher Education Administration at the University of Southern California, Rossier School of Education. Talesh has previous professional experience in student affairs and residential life administration in both public and private institutions in California. His dissertation focused on leadership perspectives of senior student affairs officers in implementing the Clery Act. His other research interests include living/learning communities and leadership. Talesh earned his master's degree in Public Administration from California State University, Northridge.

Tracy Poon Tambascia is Vice President of Student Affairs and Dean of Students at the Art Center College of Design in Pasadena, California. Formerly, she served as the Dean of Students at Whittier College in Whittier, California. Her previous professional experiences in student affairs include working with diverse student populations, grant writing and administration, and developing leadership programs. Tambascia's Ed.D. is in Higher Education Administration from the University of Southern California, Rossier School of Education.

Foreword

At present, the primary focus of my research is institutional change, specifically the role of educational practitioners as agents of place-based change—at the classroom, department, school, or institutional levels. In this foreword, I discuss the role of institutional agents in relation to the following questions about student engagement: How does engagement happen? Where does it happen? What does engagement produce, and for whom? As an outsider to the community of scholars that regularly generates scholarship on student engagement, I tend to ask basic questions that may be taken for granted by experts on the subject. Furthermore, I tend to view engagement from the perspective of practitioners rather than of students. Instead of asking "in what ways do students become engaged?" or "how often do students engage in one activity versus another?", I am more inclined to explore "in what ways do practitioners enable engagement?" and "for whom does the culture of an institution inhibit engagement?"

A foreword generally serves the purpose of commenting on a book and its authors. This one is not written in the traditional style, primarily because the editors invited me to write about engagement from my own perspective. Nevertheless, I have observed the spirit of a traditional foreword to some extent by embedding "engagement-in-practice" in my account of how this book came to be written.

How Engagement Happens: Expectations, Expertise, and Serendipity

I cannot think of a better example of how engagement happens than the process by which this book took shape. In addition to dealing with different aspects of engagement, this is an actual case study that illustrates how engagement happens, where it happens, and what it accomplishes. At the time of writing, most chapter authors were enrolled in the University of Southern California (USC) Rossier School of Education's newly established Doctor of Education (Ed.D.) program. Their published contributions originated from an assignment they were required to complete for the *College Student Development Theory* course taught by Dr. Shaun Harper during his tenure on the USC faculty. Only a handful of the authors came from the School's much smaller Doctor of Philosophy (Ph.D.) program. At the time this project was conceived, the ratio was 20 or more Ed.D. students for every Ph.D. student at the Rossier School.

The Ed.D. and Ph.D. programs have dissimilar purposes and are therefore guided by different expectations. The Ph.D. is for students who aspire to academic careers, mostly as tenure-track faculty members at research universities. Accordingly, they are assigned as research assistants to a professor in one of the School's three research centers with the expectation that they will be socialized into academic culture—developing a research agenda, presenting at conferences, and ideally publishing their findings, either independently or with their faculty mentors, before completing the program. In contrast, Ed.D. students are prepared to become educational leaders (usually in senior-level administrative positions) and are required to write applied dissertations on topics of practical relevance. The Ed.D. students who contributed to this book also worked full-time, mostly in mid-level administrative capacities at a wide range of colleges and universities, while pursuing their doctorates at the Rossier School.

The clarity of expectations is pertinent to how engagement happens for three reasons. First, the fact that the majority of authors were doctoral students who became involved in a rigorous and intensive research assignment that culminated in a published book chapter underscores the power of high expectations and educationally purposeful opportunities for engagement. The instructor's expectations as well as the students' willingness to meet them made productive engagement possible. Second, engagement was facilitated by the instructor's expertise and considerable investment of effort to create a collaborative and intellectually productive activity. Third, the course activities themselves were not necessarily based on "engagement theory" with the expressed goal of apprenticing students to the art and science of academic writing for publication. Judging from this instance, I suspect that meaningful engagement often happens serendipitously.

What Does Engagement Produce and for Whom?

In very simple terms, productive engagement is an important means by which students develop feelings about their peers, professors, and institutions that give them a sense of connectedness, affiliation, and belonging, while simultaneously offering rich opportunities for learning and development. For this to happen, students must invest time and effort into academic activities and practices (e.g., studying in the library, establishing relationships with faculty, and taking advantage of academic support services) that correlate highly with positive educational outcomes, such as those described in Chapter 1 and in the Afterword.

In keeping with the belief that engagement produces positive outcomes, I raise the following question: In what ways did students benefit from their engagement in this book writing project? This leads to a second question that I believe is less frequently posed in the literature on engagement: In what ways will the editors (two untenured assistant professors at major research universities) benefit from the effort invested in structuring a graduate course as a means of engaging graduate students in an intensive and extended writing project? As I have not asked the chapter authors or editors what they gained from their involvement in this project, my conclusions are purely speculative. However, they are informed by my knowledge of higher education leadership and administration, academic culture, and the typical promotion and tenure process. These observations are also shaped by my personal knowledge of the chapter authors, many of whom were also students in courses I taught at the Rossier School—nearly all have since earned their doctorates.

Starting with the authors, they work at different types of postsecondary institutions, hold an array of administrative positions, and are remarkably diverse in terms of ethnicity. Most are experienced educational leaders, including vice presidents for student affairs, deans, and directors of major offices and programs. A few are tenured faculty at community colleges. All are seasoned practitioners who are involved in the business of engagement and write on this topic from the standpoint of experienced insiders who are doing and thinking about many of the practices they wrote about. Indeed, their individual and cumulative years of professional work in various roles in higher education render them qualified to write on the topics they chose—Dr. Harper's course provided a forum for the engagement of their collective wisdom and experience. In my view, this is an extraordinary example of engagement-in-practice. I see three distinct benefits accrued through engagement-in-practice: (1) gaining access to insider knowledge; (2) developing into reflective practitioners; and (3) experiencing leadership as a collaborative practice.

Insider Knowledge

Whether enrolled in a Ph.D. or an Ed.D. program, very few doctoral students have the opportunity to gain firsthand experience with the complexities, messiness, and frustration that are normal in academic writing and publishing. For newcomers to the profession, the processes by which ideas and research findings evolve into journal articles, chapters, and books are often a mystery. Consequently, one of the important outcomes for the participating authors is likely to have been the demystification of academic writing and access to specialized knowledge and tools that normally are available only to those who have the good fortune of being invited individually by a professor to participate in a research project or are tapped for research assistant positions.

Because insider knowledge contributes to one's understanding of academic culture, it is as essential for the Ed.D. student who is an experienced administrator as it is for the Ph.D. student who will join the professoriate upon degree completion. It is particularly important for those who may not see themselves as scholars. Insider knowledge can increase students' self-efficacy, confidence, sense of empowerment, and long-term commitment to the sharing of professional knowledge via publications.

Reflective Practice

In higher education, we often speak about the value of reflective practice. A reflective practitioner is one who understands the difference between simply knowing theories and effectively employing them in practice. Reflective practice also involves being able to see an abstract concept. There is tremendous difference between knowing about engagement from reading articles and books and the insight that comes from having to write about it. Writing compels us to think about the meanings of things we often assume are givens. It is one of the most effective ways to find out what we do not know or what we need to understand better. Writing can reveal multiple layers of deeper meaning that lie beneath the veneer of engagement.

Reflective practice requires valuing inquiry, knowing how to structure opportunities for discovery and sense making, and having the patience to engage in it. The book project is likely to have increased students' appreciation for deeper inquiry into a topic they had read about and facilitated in their administrative careers. As practitioners, they learned how to organize and conduct collaborative inquiry as a means of acquiring additional expertise on engagement, a topic that is too often assumed to be well understood.

Everything the authors experienced throughout this project—planning, reading, talking, arguing, compromising, writing and rewriting over and over again—is likely to have increased their ability to solve problems and enthusiasm for undertaking new collaborative initiatives. Needless to say, writing a book chapter will not magically transform every individual into a reflective practitioner, but the learning experience it provides is sure to be of enduring value to those who participated in this powerful exercise while pursuing their doctorates.

Collaborative Leadership and Organizational Learning

Just as collaboration is essential for organizational learning and creative problem-solving, collegial relations are a requirement for successful leadership in academic organizations. The chapters in this book are jointly authored by two or more former doctoral students who undoubtedly gained valuable insight on working together effectively in the process. I cannot think of a more effective professional development exercise for present and future administrative leaders than to engage in a project that depends on their capacity for collaborative thinking and doing. Such experiences reveal the value of diverse viewpoints in the creative process, as well as practical approaches for resolving conflict and achieving consensus.

In essence, by writing about engagement the chapter authors engaged in a collaborative and productive activity that is likely to have developed their knowledge of reflective practice, teamwork, and cognitive complexity, as well as the inherent value of inquiring into practices, ideas, or concepts that may seem to require little explanation. Not having spoken with the authors about what they learned from the project and how this experience has influenced their professional practices, I am drawing conclusions on the basis of my own stored knowledge about engagement, individual and organizational learning, leadership, inquiry, and collaborative practice.

The Editors: Time Well Spent?

What did the editors gain from investing time and effort into teaching about college student development through a model exercise in educationally purposeful engagement? More specifically, in what ways will two untenured assistant professors benefit from this activity and the wonderful book that has emerged from it? Given the reward structure in research universities, was this a sound investment of time? One possible benefit is that this project made a very large class more manageable. By organizing students into writing teams, the number of papers that had to be read and graded was reduced considerably. In addition, the concept of engagement is central to Shaun Harper's research, and therefore he successfully combined teaching with his scholarly interests.

Simultaneously, his doctoral advisee and former teaching assistant, Stephen Quaye, was advantaged by participation in an exercise where teaching, research, and student engagement converged in such creative ways. This experience will surely enhance his work as a new assistant professor at the University of Maryland. In all likelihood, both Shaun and Stephen derived a great deal of intrinsic satisfaction from seeing such a large project come to fruition. A benefit for the field of higher education is that this project can provide other faculty members a model of how the scholarships of discovery, teaching, and practice can be combined effectively.

But what about benefits from the perspective of tenure and promotion? How much does the effort to structure an experiential activity in intellectual engagement actually count? Will it be accepted as evidence of scholarly accomplishment? Promotion and tenure criteria and guidelines vary from institution to institution, so what is expected at USC may not be equivalent to what is expected at the University of Pennsylvania and the University of Maryland where Shaun and Stephen are assistant professors. Variations notwithstanding, the most widely advised form of engagement for untenured faculty members in schools of education is writing single-authored articles for peer-reviewed, Tier-I academic journals. Normally, demonstration of impact is primarily based on citation indexes.

The narrow definition of scholarly excellence that is applied in promotion and tenure decisions at research universities is not likely to encompass a project such as this. Although it might serve as an example of teaching excellence, it would never count as much as an article in a top-tier journal, which is unfortunate. Essentially, in research universities the reward system is a disincentive for the development of powerful practices to facilitate student engagement.

Concluding Thoughts

This book illustrates how expectations, expertise, and serendipity created a meaningful engagement experience for instructors and students. Hence, engagement cannot be left to happen on its own and it cannot be treated as a "techno-rational" process in which students become involved in discrete activities that quantify time on task without consideration being given to the quality of the experience. For engagement to happen in intellectually and culturally responsive ways, faculty members need to learn the theoretical foundations and practices of engagement needed in different types of institutions and with diverse student populations. But most of all we should reward the facilitation of engagement and count it as legitimate and valuable academic activity, as demonstrated in this important book and the powerful process that led to its development.

Estela Mara Bensimon

Professor and Director, Center for Urban Education, USC Rossier School of Education

Acknowledgments

We salute in advance the thoughtful educators and administrators who will use this book to guide bold, imaginative institutional efforts to engage diverse student populations—those who will do the authentic work of aligning espoused values concerning equity, diversity, and inclusiveness with the deliberate actions necessary for actualizing those ideals. We also owe an enormous amount of gratitude to Donahue W. Tuitt for his participation in the earliest stages of this project. Also deserving of recognition are Kimberly A. Truong and Tryan L. McMickens, doctoral research assistants at Penn GSE, who located missing references and microscopic editorial oversights. In addition, we wish to thank the following important persons for their support at various stages in the development of this book: Brenda Lutovsky, Michael L. Jackson, Arlease Woods, Lori S. White, Marybeth Gasman, Ryan J. Davis, Beverly Lindsay, Corliss P. Bennett-McBride, Samuel D. Museus, Anthony R. Keith, Shon Fuller, Linda Serra Hagedorn, and Lori D. Patton. Lastly, we acknowledge Dean Karen Symms Gallagher and Professors David Marsh, Stuart Gothold, and Myron Dembo for their visionary leadership in boldly transforming doctoral education at the University of Southern California, Rossier School of Education, the birthplace of this book idea.

Shaun R. Harper
University of Pennsylvania

Stephen John Quaye
University of Maryland

February 2008

Chapter 1

Beyond Sameness, with Engagement and Outcomes for All

An Introduction

Shaun R. Harper and Stephen John Quaye

As American higher education continues to become increasingly diverse, so will the needs of and challenges faced by our students. It is possible that creating engaging campus environments was easy when the overwhelming majority of students was male, heterosexual, Christian, and economically affluent. That is, at some point in history, doing the exact same thing for everyone likely produced the same or similar results. Perhaps staff in the student activities office, for example, had it easier when one set of programs was appealing to all students. Or maybe professors got away with less planning when there were fewer cultural perspectives to be considered in readings, curricular development, and class discussions.

A dependency on sameness is no longer appropriate, as contemporary cohorts of students at colleges and universities are different; the ways they experience and respond to our campuses are varied. Thus, educators and administrators must be strategic and intentional about fostering conditions that compel students to make the most of college, both inside and outside the classroom. In their acclaimed 1991 book, *Involving Colleges: Successful Approaches to Fostering Student Learning and Development Outside the Classroom*, George D. Kuh and colleagues concluded:

> *Involving Colleges* are committed to pluralism in all its forms, and they support the establishment and coexistence of subcommunities that permit students to identify with and receive support from people like themselves, so they can feel comfortable in becoming involved in the larger campus community. (p. 369)

This declaration and subsequent related perspectives guided the conceptualization and writing of our book. Although we differentiate involvement from engagement later in this chapter, transforming today's campuses into "involving colleges" for all students is very much the vision with which this work was undertaken.

We use the publication of this book as an occasion to amplify the specific challenges faced by diverse groups of undergraduates and to offer guidance for accepting institutional responsibility for the engagement of all students. Our hope is that readers will be moved to respond with deliberation through conversations, collaborative planning, programs, services, curricular enhancements, and assessment. A cursory scan of the table of contents will confirm that this book is not exclusively about "minority students." Instead, authors focus on a range of populations for whom the published research confirms that engagement, belongingness, and connectivity to the college experience are in various ways problematic. Emphasis is also placed on enhancing outcomes and development among different populations, such as women and men.

The practical implications presented at the end of each chapter are in response to issues noted in the literature, informed by relevant theories, and based on the collective professional wisdom of those who have written. The 41 authors bring to this book more than 540 cumulative years of full-time work experience in various capacities (faculty, student affairs educators, academic affairs administrators, etc.) at a wide range of two-year and four-year institutions of higher education. That experience notwithstanding, we neither claim to furnish all the answers nor contend that this book contains prescriptive solutions for all engagement problems facing every student population. Instead, experienced educators, seasoned administrators, and emerging scholars have collaborated to produce a resource for the field of higher education and the student affairs profession that will hopefully ignite dialogue, agency, and strategic thinking and action on behalf of undergraduates who are known to typically miss out on the full range of benefits that educationally purposeful engagement affords.

The remainder of this chapter sets the stage for the population-specific chapters that follow. We begin by making clear what we mean by "student engagement" and synthesizing what decades of empirical research says about the associated gains, educational benefits, and outcomes. Next, the importance of shifting the onus for engagement from students to educators and administrators is discussed as we advocate strategy, intentionality, and reflective action. The role of theory in this book and in engagement practice is then justified. The chapter concludes with a plea for seriousness about aligning espoused values for diversity with institutional actions—we urge an abandonment of empty buzzwords related to multiculturalism on college and university campuses.

Understanding the Nature and Importance of Engagement

Student engagement is simply characterized as participation in educationally effective practices, both inside and outside the classroom, which leads to a range of measurable outcomes. This operational definition is borrowed from Kuh, Kinzie, Buckley, Bridges, and Hayek (2007), who also note:

> Student engagement represents two critical features. The first is the amount of time and effort students put into their studies and other educationally purposeful activities . . . The second component of student engagement is how the institution deploys its resources and organizes the curriculum, other learning opportunities, and support services to induce students to participate in activities that lead to the experiences and desired outcomes such as persistence, satisfaction, learning, and graduation. (p. 44)

We are persuaded by a large volume of empirical evidence that confirms that strategizing ways to increase the engagement of various student populations, especially those for whom engagement is known to be problematic, is a worthwhile endeavor. The gains and outcomes are too robust to leave to chance, and social justice is unlikely to ensue if some students come to enjoy the beneficial byproducts of engagement but others do not.

Engagement and Student Outcomes

"The impact of college is largely determined by individual effort and involvement in the academic, interpersonal, and extracurricular offerings on a campus" (Pascarella & Terenzini, 2005, p. 602). Researchers have found that educationally purposeful engagement poroduces gains, benefits, and outcomes in the following domains: cognitive and intellectual skill development (Anaya, 1996; Baxter Magolda, 1992); college adjustment (Cabrera, Nora, Terenzini, Pascarella, & Hagedorn, 1999; Kuh, Palmer, & Kish, 2003); moral and ethical development (Evans, 1987; Rest 1993); practical competence and skills transferability (Kuh, 1993, 1995); the accrual of social capital (Harper, 2008); and psychosocial development, productive racial and gender identity formation, and positive images of self (Evans, Forney, & Guido-DiBrito, 1998; Harper, 2004; Harper & Quaye, 2007; Torres, Howard-Hamilton, & Cooper, 2003). In addition, Tross, Harper, Osher, & Kneidinger (2000) found that students who devote more time to academic preparation activities outside of class earn higher grade point averages. Although all these benefits are important, the nexus between engagement and persistence has garnered the most attention.

Engagement and Retention

Roughly 35 percent of undergraduates at four-year institutions actually attain bachelor's degrees within four years; only 56 percent graduate within six years (Knapp, Kelly-Reid, & Whitmore, 2006). Equally problematic is that only about half of matriculants at two-year and community colleges earn associate's degrees and certificates within six to eight years (Hoachlander, Sikora, & Horn, 2003). Although the reasons for student persistence through degree attainment are multifaceted and not easily attributed to a narrow set of explanatory factors (Braxton, Hirschy, & McClendon, 2004), we know one thing for certain: Those who are actively engaged in educationally purposeful activities, both inside and outside the classroom, are more likely than are their disengaged peers to persist through graduation. This assertion has been empirically proven and consistently documented by numerous higher education researchers (e.g., Astin, 1975, 1993; Bean, 1990, 2005; Berger & Milem, 1999; Braxton, Milem, & Sullivan, 2000; Bridges, Cambridge, Kuh, & Leegwater, 2005; Milem & Berger, 1997; Pascarella & Terenzini, 2005; Peltier, Laden, & Matranga, 1999; Stage & Hossler, 2000; Tinto, 1993, 2000, 2005).

Vincent Tinto, the most frequently cited scholar on college student retention, contends that engagement (or "academic and social integration," as he has called it) is positively related to persistence. In fact, his research shows that engagement is the single most significant predictor of persistence (Tinto, 2000). He notes that many students discontinue their undergraduate education because they feel disconnected from peers, professors, and administrators at the institution. "Leavers of this type express a sense of not having made any significant contacts or not feeling membership in the institution" (Tinto, 2000, p. 7). In his classic 1993 book, *Leaving College: The Causes and Cures of Student Attrition*, Tinto argues that high levels of integration into academic and social communities on campus lead to higher levels of institutional commitment, which in turn compels a student to persist.

Similarly, Bean (1990, 2005) proposes that students leave when they are marginally committed to their institutions. Institutional commitment is strengthened when undergraduates are actively engaged in educationally purposeful endeavors that connect them to the campus and in which they feel some sense of enduring obligation and responsibility (Bean, 2005; Swail, Redd, & Perna, 2003; Tinto, 1993). Those who hold leadership positions in student organizations, for example, assume responsibilities in their groups and know that others depend on them for service, guidance, and follow-through on important initiatives. Thus, they feel committed to their respective organizations and the institution at large, and are less likely than are disengaged students to leave. The same could be applied to a student who feels like an important contributor to learning and discussions in her or his classes. While the relationships between engagement, student outcomes, and retention are powerful, it is important to acknowledge the conditions under which these are likely to occur.

Distinguishing Educationally Purposeful Engagement

Nearly 25 years ago, Alexander W. Astin defined student involvement as "the amount of physical and psychological energy that the student devotes to the academic experience" (1984, p. 297). Astin's conceptualization of involvement refers to behaviors and what students actually do, instead of what they think, how they feel, and the meanings they make of their experiences. His theory of student involvement is principally concerned with how college students spend their time and how various institutional actors, processes, and opportunities facilitate development. "The extent to which students can achieve particular developmental goals is a direct function of the time and effort they devote to activities designed to produce these gains" (p. 301). This theory is among the most frequently cited in the higher education literature.

Although conceptually similar, there is a key qualitative difference between involvement and engagement: It is entirely possible to be involved in something without being engaged. For example, a student who is present and on time for every weekly meeting of an organization but sits passively in the back of the room, never offers an opinion or volunteers for committees, interacts infrequently with the group's advisor or fellow members outside of weekly meetings, and would not dare consider running for an office could still legitimately claim that she is involved in the group. However, few would argue this student is actively engaged, as outcomes accrual is likely to be limited. The same could be said for the student who is involved in a study group for his psychology class, but contributes little and asks few questions when the group meets for study sessions. Action, purpose, and cross-institutional collaboration are requisite for engagement and deep learning (Kinzie & Kuh, 2004; Kuh, Kinzie, Schuh, Whitt, & Associates, 2005; Kuh et al., 2007).

The National Survey of Student Engagement (NSSE), an instrument through which data have been collected from more than 1,458,000 undergraduates at nearly 1,200 four-year colleges and universities since 2000, is constructed around these five benchmarks of effective educational practice:

1   **Level of academic challenge**—Working hard to meet professors' expectations, analyzing and synthesizing ideas, applying theories and course concepts to practical situations, studying and academic preparation activities, and composing papers of various length.

2   **Active and collaborative learning**—Asking questions and contributing to class discussions, making class presentations, working with peers on projects during class, collaborating with classmates outside of class to prepare assignments, participating in community-based projects as part of class activities, and discussing ideas from readings or course concepts with others outside of class.

3   **Student–faculty interaction**—Talking through career plans with professors and advisors, discussing ideas from readings or assignments with faculty outside of class, collaborating with faculty on committees and assorted campus activities, and working on research projects with professors.

4   **Enriching educational experiences**—Interacting across difference, taking foreign language courses, completing a culminating senior-year experience (e.g., a senior thesis), and participating in a range of value-added activities, including student organizations and campus events, community service or volunteer work, study abroad programs,

internships, faculty-supervised independent study experiences, and learning communities.

5 **Supportive campus environment**—Students' perceptions of the support needed to succeed academically, thrive socially, and cope with non-academic matters, as well as the self-reported quality of relationships with other students, faculty, administrators, and staff at the institution. (NSSE, 2007)

Student engagement in the activities associated with each NSSE benchmark is considered educationally purposeful, as it leads to deep levels of learning and the production of enduring and measurable gains and outcomes (Kuh et al., 2005). This focus on student learning and outcomes creates another distinction between involvement and engagement. We offer one additional defining characteristic: the dual responsibility for engagement. In the next section, we argue that students should not be chiefly responsible for engaging themselves (as it has been proven that many do not anyway), but instead administrators and educators must foster the conditions that enable diverse populations of students to be engaged.

Shifting the Onus for Engagement

Put simply, weak institutions are those that expect students to engage themselves. Kuh (2001) suggests student engagement is a measure of institutional quality. That is, the more engaged its students are in educationally purposeful activities, the better the institution. Similarly, Pascarella (2001) maintains, "An excellent undergraduate education is most likely to occur at those colleges and universities that maximize good practices and enhance students' academic and social engagement" (p. 22). Given this, we deem it essential for educators to view engaging diverse populations as "everyone's responsibility," including their own. And presidents, deans, and other senior administrators must hold themselves and everyone else on campus accountable for ensuring institutional quality in this regard. A clear signal of institutional deficiency is when there are few ramifications for those who either blatantly refuse or unintentionally neglect to enact the practices known to produce rich outcomes for students.

From Negligence to Intentionality

Quaye and Harper (2007) describe the ways in which faculty neglect to incorporate multicultural perspectives into their class discussions and assigned materials. The onus is often placed on racial/ethnic minority students to find books that appeal to their unique cultural interests and to bring up topics related to race in class discussions. There is little accountability for ensuring that professors are thoughtful and strategic about creating classroom experiences that enable students to learn about difference. Interactions with diverse peers inside and outside of class has been positively linked to benefits and outcomes in the following domains: self-concept (intellectual and social), cultural awareness and appreciation, racial understanding, leadership, engagement in citizenship activities, satisfaction with college, high post-baccalaureate degree aspirations, and readiness for participation in a diverse workforce (antonio et al., 2004; Chang, Astin, & Kim, 2004; Chang, Denson, Sáenz, & Misa, 2006; Gurin, Dey, Hurtado, & Gurin, 2002; Harper & antonio, 2008; Hu & Kuh, 2003; Pascarella, Edison, Nora, Hagedorn, & Terenzini, 1996; Villalpando, 2002). "Knowing that students and society could ultimately benefit from new approaches to cross-cultural learning, but failing to take the necessary steps to intentionally create enabling conditions [inside and] outside the classroom is downright irresponsible" (Harper & antonio, 2008, p. 12).

The negligence described here is partially explained by the "magical thinking" that often undergirds practices of student engagement:

> The [magical thinking] rationale provides no guidance for campuses on assembling the appropriate means to create environments conducive to realization of the benefits of diversity or on employing the methods necessary to facilitate the educational process to achieve those benefits. Under this rationale, the benefits will accrue as if by magic. (Chang, Chang, & Ledesma, 2005, pp. 10–11)

Negligence is synonymous with magical thinking; simply providing services for students is not sufficient to enrich their educational experiences. Rather, we defend a position of intentionality in which educators are conscious of every action they undertake and are able to consider the long-range implications of decisions.

Across various campuses, race relations among students are generally poor and campuses are becoming increasingly segregated (Hurtado, Milem, Clayton-Pederson, & Allen, 1999). Underrepresented students often report there is infrequent interaction between them and their peers in dominant groups, and that there is a lack of attention paid to improving the climate (Ancis, Sedlacek, & Mohr, 2000; Cabrera et al., 1999; Harper & Hurtado, 2007; Hurtado, 1992). When campus climates are hostile and antagonistic toward certain students, disengagement, dropping out, and maladjustment are likely outcomes.

As Chang et al. (2005) and Harper and antonio (2008) note, an erroneous assumption is often made that students will naturally learn about their peers simply by coming into contact with those who share different views, experiences, and identities. For example, simply increasing the numbers of lesbian, gay, bisexual, transgender, and questioning (LGBTQ) students on campus will not automatically create more opportunities for heterosexual students to interact with them. Rather, as the authors of the chapter on LGBTQ students in this book maintain, educators must facilitate structured opportunities for dialogues to transpire. Necessary are meaningful strategies that enable institutions to realize the benefits of engaging diverse populations. These solutions must be grounded in students' actual experiences, reflective of their unique backgrounds and interests, and designed with both broad and specific implications in mind.

The insights presented in this book are consistent with Strange and Banning's (2001) design vision for postsecondary institutions. They call for campuses that are "intentionally designed to offer opportunities, incentives, and reinforcements for growth and development" (p. 201). Such a philosophy of engagement responds to the multifaceted and complex needs of diverse populations. When an institution provides reinforcements for students, it means educators have envisioned and enacted the types of learning opportunities that will contribute to student development and engagement. This of course requires knowing who students are and understanding their prior knowledge and experiences, the types of educational contexts from which they have come, and what they view as necessary for enabling engagement (Harper, 2007). Devoting attention to those students who are not as engaged in educationally purposeful activities is an important way to be deliberate in one's practices.

Understanding before Acting

Creating optimal learning environments in which all students feel connected is difficult, but nonetheless important. Educators must have the requisite skills and expertise to analyze the campus environment and determine where gaps in engagement and achievement exist. More importantly, they must resist the urge to act without considering the effects of potential solutions and, instead, must spend time understanding the obstacles facing disengaged students. Baxter Magolda and King (2004) suggest educators should participate in self-reflection prior to attempting to develop methods to resolve the issues confronting students. This self-reflection enables the person to contemplate how the limitations and strengths she or he possesses either facilitate or impede student engagement.

A faculty member who is interested in providing avenues for racial/ethnic minority students to be engaged in predominantly White classroom contexts might decide to incorporate readings that reflect the scholarly contributions of racial/ethnic minority writers. On the surface, this practice seems logical and consistent with research that demonstrates the influence of culturally relevant literature on student learning (Ladson-Billings, 1995). However, what this professor might fail to consider is the reactions of White students to these readings. How might the faculty member deal with White students who believe the course is primarily focused on students of color and accuse the instructor of attempting to indoctrinate them with a politically liberal agenda? After thinking about this practice, the faculty member might still decide to proceed in the same manner, but the outcomes will be different since she or he has considered not only the needs of racial/ethnic minority students, but also the reactions of and growth opportunities for White students in the course.

Repeatedly emphasized throughout this book is the importance of listening to students in order to understand how to enhance their educational experiences. As the authors of the chapter on religious minority students report, since September 11, 2001, several campus environments have become unsafe for and hostile toward Muslim and Arab students. Seeking to improve engagement among these students, institutional leaders might plan campus-wide programs that include cross-cultural dialogues, Arab and Muslim speakers, and panels composed of religious minority students sharing their experiences on campus. As educators strive to determine why these hateful behaviors persist, they may gradually learn that religious minority students are experiencing prejudice not only from their peers, but also from professors in their courses. The decision to incorporate a wide array of programs aimed at students is often missing in trainings for faculty and staff on teaching about difference in all its forms. In the current example, if educators failed to ask Arab and Muslim students about their needs and developed interventions to improve their experiences based on assumptions about the issues students face, such efforts would be devoid of a complex understanding of the challenges confronting these students and would likely be, at best, marginally effective.

This example demonstrates the importance of analyzing problematic trends and outcomes from students' vantage points. One of the most effective ways to improve student engagement is to invite those who are the least engaged to share their knowledge and experiences (Harper, 2007). As the authors of *Learning Reconsidered* recommend: "All institutions should establish routine ways to hear students' voices, consult with them, explore their opinions, and document the nature and quality of their experience as learners" (ACPA & NASPA, 2004, p. 33). When educators speak with students from diverse backgrounds, they will begin to see patterns in their stories emerge and gain a more nuanced understanding of their needs. In addition, educators can observe the particularities in students' experiences and begin to develop customized services to improve student outcomes.

Barriers to achievement and engagement can result from making decisions without qualitative input from students (Harper, 2007). Strange and Banning (2001) discuss how a project for renovation of a campus building should include insights from multiple people (including students) prior to the construction. Allowing future users of the facilities to comment on its accessibility and openness to multiple groups enables students to feel included in the decision-making process. This sense of ownership can facilitate engagement for various campus members. Some chapters in this book explore the impact of space and campus design on student engagement. For instance, providing opportunities for students with disabilities and racial/ethnic minority students to share their opinions about the physical design of a building as well as select potential artwork for the walls confirms that educators are taking their needs into consideration prior to proceeding. This practice will facilitate the construction of buildings that align with students' needs and interests, thereby leading to a campus environment that is emblematic of the varied experiences, backgrounds, and perspectives of its students.

In an era in which student engagement is receiving increasing attention, providing undergraduates with numerous, sustained opportunities to participate actively in determining the appropriate methods for enriching their academic and social experiences in higher education cannot be overstated. Several scholars (e.g., Baxter Magolda & King, 2004; Harper, 2007; Harper & antonio, 2008; Kuh et al. 2005, 2007; Strange & Banning, 2001) propose educational practices that are student-centered, well planned and researched, and guided by student input and assessment data. As Freire (1970) notes, acting without reflecting on why people are oppressed can lead to further oppression. He advises that educators utilize praxis—combining reflection with action. Throughout the book, authors write in this manner and advocate inviting students into dialogues on improving their engagement.

Using Theory to Guide Practice

One of the primary premises of *Student Engagement in Higher Education* is that informed decisions are made when educators utilize relevant theories to guide practice. Thus, theories related to identity development, racial/ethnic awareness, stereotypes, deconstructing Whiteness, universal design, and others are tied to the needs of the populations considered in each chapter that follows. "Theory is a framework through which interpretations and understandings are constructed. Theory is used to describe human behavior, to explain, to predict, and to generate new knowledge, [practices], and research" (McEwen, 2003, p. 166). In this book, authors use it to frame the issues students face and to inform the strategies they propose. In essence, there is interplay between theory and practice, as theory is used to recommend tentative solutions to educational disparities, keeping in mind that those approaches should be continually assessed and revised given the specific learners and institutional context. Similarly, alternative theories are available as one evaluates the effectiveness of interventions intended to improve engagement.

The use of theoretical frameworks in each chapter is consistent with current student affairs expectations. In *Learning Reconsidered*, student affairs educators and faculty members sought to redefine student learning in higher education and build a common knowledge base on the most pressing challenges confronting today's college students (ACPA & NASPA, 2004). A new definition of learning that integrates elements of student development and academic learning was proposed. The authors maintain that learning focuses on holism and merging students' classroom knowledge with the co-curricular activities in which they participate. The authors of *Learning Reconsidered* conclude:

> The bottom line is that student affairs preparation must be broad based, interdisciplinary, grounded in theory, and designed to prepare forward-thinking, confident, and competent educators who will see the big picture and work effectively with other institutional agents to ensure that colleges and universities become learning communities in which students develop the skills they need to enter the rapidly changing world in which we now live. (ACPA & NASPA, 2004, p. 32)

In this statement, readers see elements of theory and practice synergistically bound. For the various populations described in our book to become engaged, they must become the focus of educators across various institutions. Furthermore, those wishing to enrich students' educational experiences must not only devise imaginative ideas for responding to engagement disparities, as the authors in this book do, but also be informed educators who utilize theories that have received empirical support from researchers—a complementary goal of this book.

For decades, there has existed a superficial separation between faculty and student affairs educators, as the former were thought to be responsible for students' classroom learning, whereas the latter group focused on students' involvement in co-curricular activities (ACPA, 1994). Even though student affairs educators have sought to challenge and transform this demarcation between students' academic and personal selves, there still continues to be an expectation that professors focus on theory and research, while student affairs educators devote their time toward practice (ACPA & NASPA, 2004; Harper & antonio, 2008). The authors in *Student Engagement in Higher Education* reject this false dichotomy and show how educators in both areas are responsible for facilitating a holistic learning environment. The authors model this by using, for example, psychological, environmental, and student development theories to guide the interventions proposed at the end of each chapter. They share some ideas for how faculty and student affairs educators can build on each other's expertise to improve the educational experiences of students.

An example helps illustrate this point. Some educators endeavor to increase White students' interests and participation in race-related activities and discussions. Yet there continues to be an overrepresentation of students from minority groups in campus programming aimed at facilitating an appreciation of differences (Saddlemire, 1996). What often happens is that students from dominant groups do not see the connection between these issues and their experiences (Broido, 2000; Jones, 2008). This book contains ideas for using theoretical perspectives pertaining to power and privilege to understand White students' unwillingness to collaborate with their racial/ethnic minority peers to improve the campus climate. By understanding different theories, educators can take the necessary time to consider the students at their particular institutions and what research indicates about them. In addition, those who teach in classrooms can work to understand why dominant group members often resist talking about issues of difference. The use of theories can provide a foundation for campus programming and classroom-based dialogues.

We recognize that educators are often busy and must react quickly to crises that occur on campus. Decisions can still be made promptly and effectively if one keeps current with theory and reflectively strives to understand the changing needs and demographics of today's college students. Linking theory with practice is not simple; it requires a willingness to rethink one's assumptions about classroom and out-of-class learning and embrace a holistic approach to education that places students' needs at the forefront. One of the central aims of the book is to offer a wealth of examples in which theoretical insights converge with practical solutions.

Beyond Buzzwords: Getting Serious about Engaging Diverse Populations

Diversity, multiculturalism, pluralism, equity and equality, inclusiveness, and social justice are among the many buzzwords used to espouse supposed institutional values. By the time this book is published, another term will likely have made its way into the vocabulary of empty promises in higher education. Colleges and universities use these terms liberally in mission statements, on websites, and in recruitment materials. Consequently, various groups of students show up expecting to see evidence of what they have been sold. The most obvious contradiction to these espoused values is the carelessness with which engagement is treated. That is, many students with special needs arrive, but few engagement plans are in place to ensure their success and persistence. Racial/ethnic minorities and White student participants in Harper and Hurtado's (2007) study expressed extreme disappointment with the institutional rhetoric concerning diversity and inclusiveness. The misalignment of espoused and enacted institutional values must be addressed if students across various groups are to equitably accrue the full range of benefits associated with educationally purposeful engagement—there must be a greater demonstration of institutional seriousness.

"At-risk students" is perhaps one of the most unfair terms used in American education, in K–12 and higher education alike. This suggests that some students are inherently in jeopardy of not succeeding. It is our view that students are placed at risk of dropping out of college when educators are negligent in customizing engagement efforts that connect them to the campus. When students enter with characteristics and backgrounds that suggest they need customized services and resources, we maintain that educators and administrators should be proactive in assessing those needs and creating the environmental conditions that will enable such students to thrive. Students are placed at risk when measures to encourage engagement treat all students the same and population-specific efforts are not enacted. Concerning the engagement of diverse populations of college students, our position is very much consistent with the title of Manning, Kinzie, and Schuh's (2006) book, *One Size Does Not Fit All*. In the chapters that follow, authors advocate moving beyond sameness to customize educational practices and maximize engagement and outcomes for all.

References

American College Personnel Association (ACPA) (1994). *The student learning imperative: Implications for student affairs*. Washington, DC: Author.

American College Personnel Association (ACPA) & National Association of Student Personnel Administrators (NASPA) (2004). *Learning reconsidered: A campus-wide focus on the student experience*. Washington, DC: Authors.

Anaya, G. (1996). College experiences and student learning: The influence of active learning, college environments, and cocurricular activities. *Journal of College Student Development, 37*(6), 611–622.

Ancis, J., Sedlacek, W., & Mohr, J. (2000). Student perceptions of campus cultural climate by race. *Journal of Counseling and Development, 78*(2), 180–185.

antonio, a. l., Chang, M. J., Hakuta, K., Kenny, D. A., Levin, S., & Milem, J. F. (2004). Effects of racial diversity on complex thinking in college students. *Psychological Science, 15*(8), 507–510.

Astin, A. W. (1975). *Preventing students from dropping out.* San Francisco: Jossey-Bass.

Astin, A. W. (1984). Student involvement: A developmental theory for higher education. *Journal of College Student Personnel, 25*(2), 297–308.

Astin, A. W. (1993). *What matters in college? Four critical years revisited.* San Francisco: Jossey-Bass.

Baxter Magolda, M. B. (1992). Cocurricular influences on college students' intellectual development. *Journal of College Student Development, 33,* 203–213.

Baxter Magolda, M. B., & King, P. M. (Eds.) (2004). *Learning partnerships: Theory and models of practice to educate for self-authorship.* Sterling, VA: Stylus.

Bean, J. P. (1990). Why students leave: Insights from research. In D. Hossler & J. P. Bean (Eds.), *The strategic management of college enrollments* (pp. 147–169). San Francisco: Jossey-Bass.

Bean, J. P. (2005). Nine themes of college student retention. In A. Seidman (Ed.), *College student retention: Formula for student success* (pp. 215–244). Washington, DC: ACE and Praeger.

Berger, J. B., & Milem, J. F. (1999). The role of student involvement and perceptions of integration in a causal model of student persistence. *Research in Higher Education, 40*(6), 641–664.

Braxton, J. M., Hirschy, A. S., & McClendon, S. A. (2004). *Understanding and reducing college student departure.* ASHE-ERIC Higher Education Report (Vol. 30, No. 3). San Francisco: Jossey-Bass.

Braxton, J. M., Milem, J. F., & Sullivan, A. S. (2000). The influence of active learning on the college departure process: Toward a revision of Tinto's theory. *Journal of Higher Education, 71*(5), 569–590.

Bridges, B. K., Cambridge, B., Kuh, G. D., & Leegwater, L. H. (2005). Student engagement at minority serving institutions: Emerging lessons from the BEAMS project. In G. H. Gaither (Ed.), *What works: Achieving success in minority retention. New Directions for Institutional Research* (No. 125, pp. 25–43). San Francisco: Jossey-Bass.

Broido, E. M. (2000). The development of social justice allies during college: A phenomenological investigation. *Journal of College Student Development, 41*(1), 3–18.

Cabrera, A. F., Nora, A., Terenzini, P. T., Pascarella, E. T., & Hagedorn, L. S. (1999) Campus racial climate and the adjustment of students to college: A comparison between White students and African American students. *Journal of Higher Education, 70*(2), 134–202.

Chang, M. J., Astin, A. W., & Kim, D. (2004). Cross-racial interaction among undergraduates: Some consequences, causes, and patterns. *Research in Higher Education, 45*(5), 529–553.

Chang, M. J., Chang, J. C., & Ledesma, M. C. (2005). Beyond magical thinking: Doing the real work of diversifying our institutions. *About Campus, 10*(2), 9–16.

Chang, M. J., Denson, N., Sáenz, V., & Misa, K. (2006). The educational benefits of sustaining cross-racial interaction among undergraduates. *Journal of Higher Education, 77,* 430–455.

Evans, N. J. (1987). A framework for assisting student affairs staff in fostering moral development. *Journal of Counseling and Development, 66,* 191–193.

Evans, N. J., Forney, D. S., & Guido-DiBrito, F. (1998). *Student development in college: Theory, research, and practice.* San Francisco: Jossey-Bass.

Freire, P. (1970). *Pedagogy of the oppressed.* New York: Continuum International.

Gurin, P., Dey, E. L., Hurtado, S., & Gurin, G. (2002). Diversity and higher education: Theory and impact on educational outcomes. *Harvard Educational Review, 72,* 330–366.

Harper, S. R. (2004). The measure of a man: Conceptualizations of masculinity among high-achieving African American male college students. *Berkeley Journal of Sociology, 48*(1), 89–107.

Harper, S. R. (2007). Using qualitative methods to assess student trajectories and college impact. In S. R. Harper & S. D. Museus (Eds.), *Using qualitative methods in institutional assessment. New Directions for Institutional Research* (No. 136, pp. 55–68). San Francisco: Jossey-Bass.

Harper, S. R. (2008). Realizing the intended outcomes of *Brown:* High-achieving African American male undergraduates and social capital. *American Behavioral Scientist, 51*(7), 1–24.

Harper, S. R., & antonio, a. l. (2008). Not by accident: Intentionality in diversity, learning, and engagement. In S. R. Harper (Ed.), *Creating inclusive campus environments for cross-cultural learning and student engagement* (pp. 1–18). Washington, DC: NASPA.

Harper, S. R., & Hurtado, S. (2007). Nine themes in campus racial climates and implications for institutional transformation. In S. R. Harper & L. D. Patton (Eds.), *Responding to the realities of race on campus. New Directions for Student Services* (No. 120, pp. 7–24). San Francisco: Jossey-Bass.

Harper, S. R., & Quaye, S. J. (2007). Student organizations as venues for Black identity expression and development among African American male student leaders. *Journal of College Student Development, 48*(2), 133–159.

Hoachlander, G., Sikora, A. C., & Horn, L. (2003). *Community college students: Goals, academic preparation, and outcomes.* Washington, DC: U.S. Department of Education, National Center for Education Statistics.

Hu, S., & Kuh, G. D. (2003). Diversity experiences and college student learning and development. *Journal of College Student Development, 44*(3), 320–334.

Hurtado, S. (1992). The campus racial climate: Contexts for conflict. *Journal of Higher Education, 63*(5), 539–569.

Hurtado, S., Milem, J., Clayton-Pedersen, A., & Allen, W. (1999). *Enacting diverse learning environments: Improving the climate for racial/ethnic diversity in higher education.* ASHE-ERIC Higher Education Report (Vol. 26, No. 8). Washington, DC: The George Washington University, Graduate School of Education and Human Development.

Jones, S. R. (2008). Student resistance to cross-cultural engagement: Annoying distraction or site for transformative learning? In S. R. Harper (Ed.), *Creating inclusive campus environments for cross-cultural learning and student engagement* (pp. 67–85). Washington, DC: NASPA.

Kinzie, J., & Kuh, G. D. (2004). Going deep: Learning from campuses that share responsibility for student success. *About Campus, 9*(5), 2–8.

Knapp, L. G., Kelly-Reid, J. E., & Whitmore, R. W. (2006). *Enrollment in postsecondary institutions, fall 2004; graduation rates, 1998 & 2001 cohorts; and financial statistics, fiscal year 2004.* Washington, DC: National Center for Education Statistics.

Kuh, G. D. (1993). In their own words: What students learn outside the classroom. *American Educational Research Journal, 30*(2), 277–304.

Kuh, G. D. (1995). The other curriculum: Out-of-class experiences associated with student learning and personal development. *Journal of Higher Education, 66*(2), 123–155.

Kuh, G. D. (2001). Assessing what really matters to student learning: Inside the National Survey of Student Engagement. *Change, 33*(3), 10–17.

Kuh, G. D., Kinzie, J., Buckley, J. A., Bridges, B. K., & Hayek, J. C. (2007). *Piecing together the student success puzzle: Research, propositions, and recommendations.* ASHE Higher Education Report (Vol. 32, No. 5). San Francisco: Jossey-Bass.

Kuh, G. D., Kinzie, J., Schuh, J. H., Whitt, E. J., & Associates (2005). *Student success in college: Creating conditions that matter.* San Francisco: Jossey-Bass.

Kuh, G. D., Palmer, M., & Kish, K. (2003). The value of educationally purposeful out-of-class experiences. In T. L. Skipper & R. Argo (Eds.), *Involvement in campus activities and the retention of first-year college students. The First-Year Experience Monograph Series* (No. 36, pp. 19–34). Columbia, SC: University of South Carolina, National Resource Center for the First-Year Experience and Students in Transition.

Kuh, G. D., Schuh, J. H., Whitt, E. J., Andreas, R. E., Lyons, J. W., Strange, C. C., Krehbiel, L. E., & MacKay, K. A. (1991). *Involving colleges: Successful approaches to fostering student learning and development outside the classroom.* San Francisco: Jossey-Bass.

Ladson-Billings, G. (1995). Toward a theory of culturally relevant pedagogy. *American Educational Research Journal, 32*(3), 465–491.

Manning, K., Kinzie, J., & Schuh, J. H. (2006). *One size does not fit all: Traditional and innovative models of student affairs practice.* New York: Routledge.

McEwen, M. K. (2003). The nature and uses of theory. In S. R. Komives & D. B. Woodard (Eds.), *Student services: A handbook for the profession* (4th ed., pp. 147–163). San Francisco: Jossey-Bass.

Milem, J. F., & Berger, J. B. (1997). A modified model of college student persistence: Exploring the relationship between Astin's Theory of Involvement and Tinto's Theory of Student Departure. *Journal of College Student Development, 38*(4), 387–400.

National Survey of Student Engagement (NSSE) (2007). *Experiences that matter: Enhancing student learning and success, annual report 2007.* Bloomington, IN: Indiana University Center for Postsecondary Research.

Pascarella, E. T. (2001). Identifying excellence in undergraduate education: Are we even close? *Change, 33*(3), 19–23.

Pascarella, E. T., & Terenzini, P. T. (2005). *How college affects students, Volume 2: A third decade of research.* San Francisco: Jossey-Bass.

Pascarella, E. T., Edison, M., Nora, A., Hagedorn, L. S., & Terenzini, P. T. (1996). Influence of students' openness to diversity and challenge in the first year of college. *Journal of Higher Education, 67*, 174–195.

Peltier, G. L., Laden, R., & Matranga, M. (1999). Student persistence in college: A review of research. *Journal of College Student Retention, 1*(4), 357–375.

Quaye, S. J., & Harper, S. R. (2007). Faculty accountability for culturally-inclusive pedagogy and curricula. *Liberal Education, 93*(3), 32–39.

Rest, J. R. (1993). Research on moral judgment in college students. In A. Garrod (Ed.), *Approaches to moral development* (pp. 201–213). New York: Teachers College Press.

Saddlemire, J. R. (1996). Qualitative study of White second-semester undergraduates' attitudes toward African American undergraduates at a predominantly White university. *Journal of College Student Development, 37*(6), 684–691.

Stage, F. K., & Hossler, D. (2000). Where is the student? Linking student behaviors, college choice, and college persistence. In J. M. Braxton (Ed.), *Reworking the student departure puzzle* (pp. 170–195). Nashville, TN: Vanderbilt University Press.

Strange, C. C., & Banning, J. H. (2001). *Educating by design: Creating campus learning environments that work.* San Francisco: Jossey-Bass.

Swail, W. S., Redd, K. E., & Perna, L. W. (2003). *Retaining minority students in higher education: A framework for success.* ASHE-ERIC Higher Education Report (Vol. 30, No. 2). San Francisco: Jossey-Bass.

Tinto, V. (1993). *Leaving college: Rethinking the causes and cures of student attrition* (2nd ed.). Chicago: University of Chicago Press.

Tinto, V. (2000). Taking retention seriously: Rethinking the first year of college. *NACADA Journal, 19*(2), 5–10.

Tinto, V. (2005). Moving from theory to action. In A. Seidman (Ed.), *College student retention: Formula for student success* (pp. 371–333). Washington, DC: American Council on Education and Praeger.

Torres, V., Howard-Hamilton, M. F., & Cooper, D. L. (2003). *Identity development of diverse populations: Implications for teaching and administration in higher education.* ASHE-ERIC Higher Education Report (Vol. 29, No. 6). San Francisco: Jossey-Bass.

Tross, S. A., Harper, J. P., Osher, L. W., & Kneidinger, L. M. (2000). Not just the usual cast of characteristics: Using personality to predict college performance and retention. *Journal of College Student Development, 41*(3), 325–336.

Villalpando, O. (2002). The impact of diversity and multiculturalism on all students: Findings from a national study. *NASPA Journal, 40*, 124–144.

Chapter 2
International Students at Four-Year Institutions
Developmental Needs, Issues, and Strategies

Gregory Anderson, Karen Y. Carmichael, Todd J. Harper, and Tzufang Huang

The forces of globalization are driving students to pursue higher education outside their own country, especially in the United States. Though U.S. international enrollment was temporarily affected by the attacks of September 11, 2001, worldwide trends show international student enrollment increasing each year (Bain & Cummings, 2005; Cummings, 1991). Institutions in the United States enroll the largest number of international students (about 28 percent) in the world (Bain & Cummings, 2005; Organization for Economic Cooperation and Development, 2002). This population's proportion of the U.S. undergraduate student body has increased significantly in the past 50 years (Tseng & Newton, 2002). The nearly 600,000 international students (Schoch & Baumgartner, 2004) composed almost 5 percent of the total enrollment in U.S. postsecondary institutions in 2002 (Cigularova, 2005), a figure that would be larger if non-degree-seekers and recent immigrants were included. International students have thus become an important, though insufficiently recognized, population at U.S. colleges and universities. Generally paying full tuition, their contribution to the U.S. economy is estimated to be nearly $13 billion (Schoch & Baumgartner, 2004). Such revenue is vital for postsecondary institutions' fiscal health and the economic competitiveness of this nation, and international students also enhance cultural pluralism and strengthen America's reputation overseas.

Many international students come to the United States with carefully crafted dreams, though most find the path to fulfillment of those dreams filled with obstacles. Students from overseas must cope with many difficulties without sufficient support from families, schools, or communities (Tseng & Newton, 2002). One international student, Rose, shared this story:

> I first attended another university and then transferred to my current university. I experienced serious homesickness, loneliness, and isolation at the first school. I faced a variety of racial/ethnic issues and could not find which group I actually should belong to. In the building I lived in, only one other person and I were Asian. All others were White, and they never invited me to participate in their activities. I also got culture shock and doubted if I should attempt to further integrate myself into American culture. I had academic difficulties as well as many other life difficulties but did not get enough help from my department and school. Once, for instance, I needed help adjusting to writing assignments from professors. Though I searched the campus, I couldn't find any help—to this day I don't even know if there is a writing center on that campus. Based on these situations, I decided to transfer to my current university.
>
> After transferring here, I found that this university did provide more diverse types of assistance and multicultural activities to help me overcome negative psychological feelings, culture shock, as well as academic and living difficulties. I also had a chance to find [my] identity through several student associations. I now enjoy my studying and my life in the U.S.
>
> Based on my experiences, I suggest that higher education institutions should pay more attention to their services for international students. Colleges and universities should help international students accommodate to a new environment by good services and strategies. At my current school, for example, I get an informative email weekly about current issues, campus events, necessary documents, and other things that all international students need to know. I feel that it is necessary for American colleges and universities to assess needs, identify issues, and solve problems that international students face to ensure their success.

In this chapter, we focus on the plight of students, like Rose, who come to U.S. institutions of higher education. We define international students as people from other countries who come to the United States for the primary purpose of obtaining a degree (Bahvala, 2002; Robertson, Line, Jones, & Thomas, 2000). International students share common characteristics and challenges in the transition process to a new environment regardless of their various cultural, social, and political backgrounds. They must continually adjust to a variety of cultural, academic, social, and linguistic differences (Bahvala, 2002; Mori, 2000).

We first explore a variety of distinct challenges that compound the existing developmental barriers that international undergraduates face. These difficulties include psychological, academic, sociocultural, general living, and career development issues—all of which affect academic and social performance. We next demonstrate how Schlossberg's Transition Theory (Schlossberg & Robinson, 1996) and Louis' (1980) Surprise and Sense Making Theory frame our examination of international students' needs and issues. Based on these needs and theories, we conclude with practical strategies for colleges and universities to enhance their services for international students.

Distinct Needs and Issues of International Undergraduates

Rose's story above illuminates the unique challenges and barriers that international students face, which negatively affect their engagement and academic and social development. In order to understand how to improve their experiences at U.S. higher education institutions, it is important to detail further the issues with which they contend.

Psychological Issues

The most common challenges faced by international students are psychological in nature. International students often face homesickness, loneliness, depression, stress, anxiety, alienation, isolation, and the loss of identity, status, and self-value after they come to a new country (Tseng & Newton, 2002). They must adjust through a process of psychological transition. The length of the process depends on the individual student's condition, including proficiency in English, previous experience in cultural adjustment, support systems, and general self-efficacy (Tseng & Newton, 2002). Most international students, no matter how well equipped, still experience a period of homesickness, isolation, and loneliness due to unfamiliarity with their surroundings. Feelings of hopelessness and helplessness also frequently develop, sometimes leading to depression (Bahvala, 2002). Because many international students hold high expectations of their abilities and the quality of their lives in the United States, they may feel frustrated, indignant, and insufficient after they understand the realities and face difficulties and failures (Bahvala, 2002). International students who had high achievements in their home countries are particularly prone to suffer these psychological feelings (Yi, Lin, & Kishimoto, 2003).

Incomplete or unsatisfactory psychological adjustment often leads to a variety of negative physical symptoms, such as loss of appetite and sleep, gastrointestinal problems, low stamina and energy, and headaches (Bahvala, 2002; Tatar & Horenczyk, 2000). These psychosomatic illnesses can eventually impair students' performance, harm their quality of life, and impede their acculturation to American society. Tseng and Newton (2002) pointed out eight ways for international students to adapt to a new environment, overcome or avoid negative feelings, and maintain a good psychological condition:

> Know self and others; make friends and build friendships with peers; expand individual worldview; ask help and handle problems; establish cultural and social contacts; build relationships with advisors and instructors; become proficient in the English language; and use the tactic of "letting go." (pp. 595–596)

These guidelines are only helpful if the educational institution sufficiently supports students. The strategies listed later in this chapter provide more concrete guidance for colleges and universities that expect high achievement from students, including those from overseas.

Some researchers have also suggested that communication and time spent with their U.S. peers have a positive effect on international students' psychological adjustment (Cigularova, 2005; Pruitt, 1978; Rohrlich & Martin, 1991; Searle & Ward, 1990; Zimmermann, 1995). However, international students prefer to seek support most from those who speak their language and come from the same country, less from other international students, and least of all from host national students (Cigularova, 2005; Findsen, 1987). Thus, the most effective solution to psychological challenges, developing quality relationships with host national students, is also the least likely to actually occur. Colleges and universities that recognize these challenges should facilitate international students' engagement in campus activities. They should also encourage the development of relationships with host national students by organizing various cultural events and recruiting international students to act as volunteers. Cultural training for domestic students may be helpful to facilitate their interaction with international students (Cigularova, 2005).

Academic Issues and Needs

International students usually regard their academic success as their first priority (Bahvala, 2002; Yi et al., 2003) and emphasize academic achievement over socializing with Americans (Bahvala, 2002; Ingman, 1999). Having earned honors and demonstrated their intellectual capacities in their home countries, many international students expect similar performance levels not only for themselves but also for their families' tradition and honor (Bahvala, 2002; Mori, 2000). International students' perceptions of their academic performance can either facilitate or hinder their adaptation to a new environment. Students are likely to feel more confident if they achieve high academic success in a new environment (Bahvala, 2002; Tseng & Newton, 2002). To satisfy their academic goals, international students need to cope with a variety of academic difficulties.

Language and communication represent the first academic difficulty. The language barrier sometimes impedes students' abilities to communicate effectively, which results in educational frustration and failure (Wang & Frank, 2002). The second difficulty is adapting to a different educational culture. Educational culture differences appear in the atmosphere of classroom instruction and learning, instructional styles, academic tasks, learning skills, faculty and student interaction, and group work (Burrell & Kim, 2002).

Some Middle Eastern, European, and Asian students are surprised by the open and relaxed ways of classroom instruction and learning in the United States, such as eating in class or questioning the professor directly, because they perceive such behaviors as disrespectful (Bahvala, 2002; Burrell & Kim, 2002; Chen, 1999; Selvadurai, 1998). In addition, some American teachers include classroom discussions, student presentations, independent library research, essays and term papers, and frequent quizzes and exams in their courses (Bahvala, 2002). In many Asian countries, however, teachers' uninterrupted lectures are the norm, while students' roles are limited to passive listening and infrequent, summative evaluation (Bahvala, 2002). Students from those countries, therefore, find it difficult to adjust to the academic culture (Burrell & Kim, 2002). American instructors are faulted for not teaching all knowledge (Bahvala, 2002). Students need to find many references in libraries and study by themselves (Burrell & Kim, 2002; Elsey, 1990). Moreover, many international students have never written a research paper and are suddenly required to work within unfamiliar structures and styles (Burrell & Kim, 2002; Crowe & Peterson, 1995; Kinnell, 1990). They cannot rely on rote learning, but need to incorporate various learning skills to successfully manage new academic expectations (Burrell & Kim, 2002).

In addition to these in-class issues, Burrell and Kim (2002) point out that international students must acknowledge certain distinct features of U.S. faculty culture and learn how to interact effectively with their professors. Good understanding and interactions can benefit international students as well as faculty members. Group work and project assignments are another area in which cultural differences may arise. Because students, domestic and international, bring their cultural backgrounds into group work, different expectations, language choices, and modes of expression can result in learning difficulties for international students (Burrell & Kim, 2002). However, as we suggest in the strategies section below, these difficulties can be turned into learning opportunities.

A final academic challenge is differences in library structures and services. Libraries in many international students' countries are organized and staffed differently. Besides the primary language of texts, available and accessible databases, norms about assistance, hours of service, and accessibility of resources may all differ (Wang & Frank, 2002). In many countries, card catalogs and closed stacks are still commonly used. Some international students, lacking skills at information technologies, experience additional difficulties in performing research (Wang & Frank, 2002). Academic librarians, therefore, play an important role in assisting international students.

Sociocultural Issues

Beyond the psychological and academic barriers described above, a variety of sociocultural issues affect the adjustment of international students. These issues sometimes coincide with the needs listed earlier and should be addressed in an overlapping manner. International students experience culture shock, cultural fatigue, racial discrimination, and difficulty in adjusting to new customs, norms, regulations, eating habits, and differences in educational systems (Toyokawa & Toyokawa, 2002; Tseng & Newton, 2002).

Culture shock is the most obvious but least understood of the sociocultural issues. As the global reach of media homogenizes fashion choices and other superficial features of youth, students at U.S. colleges and universities may appear quite similar—on the outside (Stromquist & Monkman, 2000). Inside, however, international students often experience varying degrees of culture shock. Winkelman (1994) defines culture shock as "a multifaceted experience resulting from numerous stressors occurring in contact with a different culture" (p. 121). An international student could experience culture shock upon arrival at the airport in the new country when faced with the sights, sounds, and immensity of the place, but this culture shock can also continue throughout their undergraduate tenure (Winkelman, 1994). Researchers describe four phases of culture shock: the honeymoon phase, the crises phase, the adjustment, reorientation, and gradual recovery phase, and the adaptation, resolution, or acculturation phase (Ferraro, 1990; Kohls, 1984). In the crises stage, mounting frustrations cause the person to feel powerless and alone. It is during this phase that students generally want to return home (Winkelman, 1994). Thus, interventions must occur before students feel their most vulnerable—confused, isolated, homesick, and lonely—to assist in their persistence at the institution.

Another pressing concern for this population is racial discrimination and prejudice. Incidences in which international students are subject to verbal or physical attacks may further confuse them and threaten their sense of safety (Tatar & Horenczyk, 2000). These threats to student safety must be counteracted, since feeling comfortable and welcome in the college or university environment improves persistence and increases self-efficacy and self-esteem (Gloria & Ho, 2003). Learning about, acknowledging, and celebrating cultural differences become more important the more culturally different students on campus there are (Kuh, Schuh, Whitt, & Associates, 1991). Thus, campuses need to take steps to value diversity and ensure that faculty, staff, and students recognize their responsibilities in addressing any hate and discrimination targeted at international students (Hurtado, Milem, Clayton-Pedersen, & Allen, 1998; Kuh et al., 1991; Land & Land, 1992).

Student learning and personal development are enhanced when out-of-class activities complement the institution's educational purposes (Pascarella, Edison, Nora, Hagedorn, & Terenzini, 1996). Thus, the impact of the college experience on students is increased the more engaged they are in various aspects of college life (Kuh et al., 1991). Participation in out-of-class activities provides international students with opportunities to meet people and make friends—crucial aspects of successful transition (Tomich, McWhirter, & Darcy, 2003; Toyokawa & Toyokawa, 2002). International students who engage in out-of-class activities develop social networks and become adept at negotiating U.S. social skills, values, and customs, which may increase their self-efficacy and confidence (Toyokawa & Toyokawa, 2002). The benefits to the host institution of better-adjusted students are equally powerful—higher rates of retention, improved global reputation, and reduced resources spent on conflict resolution (Toyokawa & Toyokawa, 2002).

Residential Transition Challenges

Many international students choose to live close to students from the same country or similar backgrounds so they can develop strong social relationships in the new environment (Al-Sharideh & Goe, 1998). They often believe that with this secure interpersonal network, it will be easier for them to reach out to other students to build additional social networks. Too often, however, the outreach does not occur, and students remain entrenched in their own linguistic and national groups, disengaged from broader campus life (Al-Sharideh & Goe, 1998). Residence halls are an ideal location for programs designed to foster social relationships among small groups of students that include international students and Americans. Within these communities, there is a support structure built into daily activities to assist with housing challenges international students may encounter (Al-Sharideh & Goe, 1998). International students also face additional obstacles that affect living in the United States, related to (1) counseling and health services, (2) tuition costs, (3) documentation issues, (4) safety threats, and (5) dietary restrictions.

Counseling and Health Services

Access to counseling and health services can be a problem if subtle barriers are in places that hinder the student's feeling of ownership and acceptance (Mori, 2000). International students are usually hesitant to seek services on their own; therefore, it is crucial for college or university personnel to take proactive approaches to increase the visibility and the accessibility of counseling facilities (Bahvala, 2002; Mori, 2000). In addition to accessibility, many international students have negative attitudes toward seeking professional psychological help. Much like U.S. attitudes of previous decades that stigmatized mental health treatment, many international students have grown up in cultures that disapprove of counseling (Yang, Wong, Hwang, & Heppner, 2002; Zhang, 2000).

Tuition Costs

Spiraling tuition and relocation costs hit international students hard. Nearly 80 percent of international students pay for their education with help from family members or overseas agencies (Davis, 1998); however, financial concerns still challenge international student adjustment (Bahvala, 2002; Chen, 1999; Mori, 2000; Sam, 2001). Many international students still desire financial aid or part-time employment to reduce financial burdens on their families. In the 2002–2003 academic year, about 70 percent of international undergraduate students paid full tuition without financial aid (Schoch & Baumgartner, 2004). Conversely, only 24 percent of full-time U.S. undergraduates paid full tuition (Berkner et al., 2005).

Documentation Issues

Documentation issues and bureaucratic hurdles have been a longstanding backdrop to international students' academic endeavors in the United States (Scott, 1994). Recently, these challenges have become more stringent in light of contemporary international political and economic shifts. Challenges include procuring documentation to comply with federal and state regulations and special concerns about documentation needed for insurance, housing, advisement, and communications (Morio, Kawaguchi, Suda & Eto, 2000; Scott, 1994). Since the creation of the Department of Homeland Security and the newly configured Immigration and Customs Enforcement division, the bureaucratic process for new and returning international students has become more difficult to navigate. Furthermore, the Patriot Act mandates that schools produce student visa petitions, known as I-20s, for all international students enrolled in U.S. institutions, and it instituted a Student and Exchange Visitor and Information fee. As a result of these changes, a significant number of students have been denied visas, making them unable to study in the United States (Altbach, 2004). These documentation issues both make it difficult for international students to attend U.S. higher education institutions and affect their engagement once on campus (Scott, 1994).

Safety Threats

On November 12, 2001, *Newsweek* magazine declared today's college students "Generation 9-11." The cover story described a national student demographic dealing with fear for their safety, concern over economic security, and uncertainty about their personal and professional futures (Kantrowitz & Naughton, 2001). Immediately following the tragedy of September 11, 2001, international students at U.S. colleges and universities felt a mounting sense of fear for their personal safety. When students fear for such basic issues as personal safety, fulfilling higher needs, such as self-realization, is unlikely (Maslow, 2005).

Both physical safety as well as identity threat issues are important. According to the Integrated Threat Theory of Prejudice (Stephan & Stephan, 1996), the four basic classes of threats that lead to a high level of discomfort for international students are negative stereotypes, intergroup anxiety, realistic threats, and symbolic/cultural threats that concern differences in morals, values, standards, beliefs, and attitudes. Among these four classes, the least understood are symbolic threats, which endanger the "way of life" of international students (Spencer-Rodgers & McGovern, 2002). These symbolic threats include academic integrity issues, classroom interaction patterns, and religious overtones in many colleges and universities. Both subtle and explicit threats undermine student success and require active attention by the host institution (Stephan & Stephan, 1996).

Dietary Restrictions

The psychological, academic, sociocultural, and living challenges detailed above present real obstacles for international student success. Even if these challenges are addressed, more subtle difficulties exist. One of these issues is the intercultural understanding required to offer dietary options on and around college and university campuses. Many international students may find university cuisine to be unpalatable, nutritionally inadequate, and even culturally and religiously offensive (Chen, 1999). Although larger communities or urban areas may offer a variety of authentic and comforting types of food, colleges and universities in smaller towns and more rural areas may find that meeting the dietary needs of their international student population can be extremely difficult (Cigularova, 2005).

Career Development Issues

Addressing the professional development needs of international students poses challenges for U.S. colleges and universities. To provide effective career services for international students, it is important to understand their cultural contexts, as well as how these contexts affect their worldview (Yang et al., 2002). Hwang and Heppner (2001) note that for international students, choosing a career that is desirable to their family is often more important than finding one that corresponds to their own interests. A career development professional aware of this can become more effective at advising.

Many international students in the United States feel the need to secure employment, either for pre-professional experience, or to supplement their financial situation. Most international students hold either an F-1 (student) or a J-1 (exchange visitor) visa, and the Immigration and Customs Enforcement division of the Department of Homeland Security permits students in both categories to be employed part-time (concurrent with their education) and full-time (subsequent to their education). It is important that educators at higher education institutions consider the career needs of international students, including information on employment opportunities and U.S. work permit policies; assist with major and career decisions; and help with job preparation skills, such as the job search, résumé and cover letter writing, and interviewing procedures (Yang et al., 2002). These services need to be brought to the student through a variety of methods including one-on-one counseling, workshops, mock interviews, and career assessment (Yang et al., 2002).

Theoretical Framework

Two theories guide our understanding of international students' needs and development: Transition Theory (Sargent & Schlossberg, 1988; Schlossberg & Robinson, 1996; Schlossberg, Waters, & Goodman, 1995) and the framework of Surprise and Sense Making (Louis, 1980). Both of these theories provide student affairs educators with valuable assistance in choosing when and how to intervene with international students. Though neither theory focuses specifically on international students, they both apply to that population. The populations for whom they were developed and the contexts to which they have been applied demonstrate their value in developing creative strategies.

Transition Theory

Transition Theory focuses on psychosocial perceptions of change and is mostly utilized by adult education and student affairs professionals. Transitions are defined as the psychological processes that humans undergo when accommodating significant changes in their lives (Sargent & Schlossberg, 1988). These changes are not necessarily related to age, as is commonly thought (Reeves, 1999). Schlossberg et al. (1995) divide these transitions into three types: anticipated events, unanticipated events, and non-events. For international students, anticipated events would include entering a new living situation, such as a residence hall. Being expected to live in completely different ways, such as sharing a communal shower, could represent an unanticipated event. Whereas events can be both negative (problems) and positive (possibilities), non-events are usually problems (Schlossberg & Robinson, 1996). An example of a non-event could be an honors student from Asia receiving poor marks in a philosophy course because her previous academic strategy of memorization failed to translate to the new environment that demanded critical thinking and active engagement. According to Sargent and Schlossberg (1988), humans have a variety of skills and deficits that help or hinder their negotiation with life-changing events. When properly managed, transitions can provide a positive opportunity; the role of student affairs educators is to enable this to occur.

Three stages are involved in the management of transitions: abandoning the old situation, arriving in the neutral area, and beginning afresh (Sargent & Schlossberg, 1988). To advise international students at each of these stages and help them master (and benefit from) the processes, advisors should consider "four S's": situation, support, self, and strategies (Sargent & Schlossberg, 1988). The first three describe when the student analyzes or assesses her or his situation, and the last one is when the student actually confronts the process. The strategies in this chapter are designed to help international students analyze their own transitions, develop effective coping strategies, and, subsequent to the event or non-event, learn from the process.

Surprise and Sense Making

Like Transition Theory, the framework of Surprise and Sense Making is also based on a psychosocial understanding of humans. However, the theory addresses changes within the context of individuals entering an organization (Louis, 1980). Louis developed this approach in response to previous structural theories on workplace turnover and socialization. To her, previous theories overemphasized expectations as the key feature of organizational entry. Louis suggested that organizations can help newcomers adapt by recognizing certain features of the entire entry process.

Before arriving, newcomers should learn the culture of the organization, including differences in the application of skills and strategies. The honors student whose academic strategies proved ineffective, for example, would need assistance to realize that her performance was due not to any lack of ability but rather to the need to develop new tools. In addition, students new to an organization need schemes or maps to help them perceive their new environment (Louis, 1980). Institutions can help international students adjust by providing concrete tools and guidelines that are transparent and clear. These tools should be written and designed simply and directly, avoiding assumptions about incoming students' academic and social schemas. We recognize that the ability of institutions to prepare students before arrival is somewhat limited. However, in our strategies, we propose some ways to address the needs international students face prior to their arrival on campus.

Once international students arrive in the United States, even the best-prepared of them can experience a series of surprises, such as the culture shock described earlier in the chapter. Louis (1980) describes these events in a manner similar to Transition Theory, suggesting that "both pleasant and unpleasant surprises require adaptation . . . it will be important to include both overmet and undermet expectations in considering surprises that contribute to newcomers' entry experiences" (pp. 238–239). Though pre-arrival materials can help international students develop new schemas, educators should also provide ongoing assistance throughout students' collegiate tenures.

At the surprise stage, which can occur throughout the early semesters of international students' experiences in the United States, students need tools to help them benefit from the changes and to ease their entry process. At the precise moment that students encounter events that provoke surprise, their internal reaction is out of the hands of anyone but themselves. It is only after the stage of surprise that educators can once again intervene. In this stage, called sense making, interpretation is critical. What Louis (1980) calls "local interpretation schemes" (p. 242) offer an area ripe for educators to invest resources, since each institution's norms of behavior are worth teaching to international students, who often subscribe to different norms.

Engagement Strategies

Building on Louis' (1980) theory, many of our strategies below note the importance of developing empathy and respect among domestic students. Embedded in our strategies is the strong rejection of the "sink-or-swim, learn-on-your-own philosophy" (Louis, 1980, p. 247). Each strategy described here intentionally recognizes the responsibility of educators in enabling international students to succeed at their studies and achieve their goals. Based on both theories, the strategies below emphasize practices that facilitate effective preparation, ongoing adjustment, engagement, and learning through reflection.

Cross-Cultural Mentoring

Educators should provide mentoring programs for international students. For this population, feelings of isolation, culture shock, and the stresses of living far from familiar support structures present obstacles to achievement. Because racial/ethnic minority students attending predominantly White institutions have similar feelings during their first year of college (Allen, 1992), upper-class racial/ethnic minority students would be ideal candidates to serve as mentors to international students. These mentors would provide necessary cross-cultural interactions and create valuable social networks, enabling international students to form interpersonal relationships as well as academic support groups. Additionally, interactions with mentors provide opportunities for international students to practice their English language skills, enhancing communicative competency. To inform international students of the mentoring program, information would be shared during orientation programs, upon admission to the college or university, and again through residence hall programming. Administrators should recruit current international students who participated in the program as first-year students to discuss the benefits with new students during a panel presentation at orientation.

Family-Style Peer Mentoring

Negative psychological feelings, such as loneliness, homesickness, and anxiety stemming from culture shock, plague many international students upon their arrival in the United States. To lessen these feelings, institutions should help entering international students develop significant relationships among upper-class students who would act as guides or peer advisors. International students would then have a person with whom they could cultivate a relationship. Ideally, these relationships would develop into family-like structures. In each "family," upper-class students would serve as mentors for incoming students. The mentors would contact incoming students before they arrive in the United States, thus reducing anxiety about their new life and increasing their social and academic networks. As first contact, program directors would send a letter of welcome that provides the name, major, and class year of their family mentor, as well as share information on what to expect on move-in day, how to secure transportation to campus from the airport, resources for finding housing, and a list of family events scheduled throughout the academic year. Such family events could include campus entertainment activities, sporting events, and lectures. Through these interactions, international students would have support and the opportunity to develop friendships with both domestic and other international students. These relationships would develop each year, creating generations within the family and a support system that would demand few institutional resources and provide immense institutional benefits.

Residence Hall Staffing

More international students should serve as resident assistants (RAs). Efforts to recruit and hire international RAs can include current resident assistants arranging advisory sessions particularly for international students. In addition, with lists from the registrar (with personal information removed), international student offices can email likely candidates, perhaps even in their own languages, regarding the opportunity to serve as RAs. Having international RAs provides several benefits. First, daily interactions between domestic and international students will break down barriers, even outside the residence hall. For instance, a first-year student from rural Wyoming whose RA was Indian might find himself better able to communicate with his Pakistani chemistry teaching assistant. Second, U.S.-born undergraduates would gain respect for international students who attain high levels of responsibility despite language and culture barriers. Third, greater diversity among RAs would help international students envision themselves as leaders who have valuable ideas and experiences to contribute to their host institutions. Finally, non-Western approaches could provide alternative solutions for common problems, such as excess noise or abuse of controlled substances. We should make one more note about recruiting international residence hall staff: International students have various backgrounds. At one of the author's institutions, for example, a tall blonde woman who spent her first 13 years speaking Chinese and living in Singapore provided precisely the kind of international student leadership modeling described above.

Residence Hall Programming

Residence hall staff can provide more opportunities for co-curricular activities through which students can learn valuable lessons in leadership, interpersonal communication, and other psychosocial growth areas. To inform residents of the needs of international students as well as to promote the benefits of their presence, departments of residence life should offer relevant programming. This programming should include activities that develop empathy among domestic students regarding the challenges international students face in a new country. For example, several upper-class international students could share the challenges faced and their resolutions. Domestic students may view the challenges illustrated in these sessions as routine, though they are often novel for international students. At these sessions, upper-class leaders can explain to the first-year students how people with different levels of experiences in cultures and norms perceive, interpret, and react to the same stimuli. Similarly, other intercultural exchanges and presentations such as dance, music, art, cuisine, and literature would add to the richness of residence life and provide opportunities for cultural understanding and appreciation. Finally, international students and RAs should be part of the planning of these activities.

Dietary Options

Postsecondary educators can foster intercultural understanding and improve the institution's reputation by offering abundant dietary options for international students. One option would be the formation of cuisine advisory committees, with members recruited from food science, marketing, or other related majors, who could suggest alternatives to the food service menu. These alternatives—whether ingredient choices or preparation methods—could not only improve the diet of international students but also reduce acquisition costs and help create empathy among domestic students. Second, food options outside university food services should be provided for international students. Whereas undergraduates across the United States often eat off-campus because they are simply tired of college or university food services, some international students find on-campus dining to be completely unpalatable—whether Muslims who need their meats Halal or students of various nationalities who expect food to be highly spiced. These students should be offered access to appropriate kitchen facilities or shuttles to areas where they can acquire suitable ingredients. To help defray the costs of these efforts, food fairs or other fund-raising efforts can sponsor activities.

Pre-Orientation

Cultural adjustment, as described above, requires more guidance and support than that offered in typical orientation programs. Therefore, institutions should develop a three-stage orientation program. In the first stage, pre-orientation, which occurs prior to the student's arrival, each new student would receive a DVD containing an introduction to the college or university. Representative members of the college or university community, including both current and recently graduated domestic and international students, would introduce useful resources. For example, divisions within student affairs departments, such as the office of international students, and those within academic affairs, such as library and computing services, would be highlighted. It is also important to include counseling services and a discussion of how counseling is viewed in the United States. Further, to ease students' anxiety levels about arrival to the new country, it would be beneficial to include information on necessary paperwork, visas, and I-20 documentation, as well as information on transportation to campus from the airport. Although all the representatives would speak English on the DVD, subtitles in recipients' languages would be included, thus allowing parents to understand the process. This DVD could be produced as collaboration among residence life, orientation staff, the office of international students, and even the school of cinema. To increase commitment by accepted candidates, the admissions office would include the appropriate DVD with acceptance letters.

Orientation of Domestic Students to International Students' Needs

Although pre-orientation and ongoing efforts are integral to helping international students develop academic and social networks, the other side of orientation is equally important: Domestic students should learn about the challenges that international students face and the benefits they provide, the second stage of the orientation program. Thus, current efforts at diversity training that focus on racial/ethnic, sexual orientation, and gender differences should be expanded to include the needs and issues of international students. This training could be accomplished through role playing, discussion, speaker presentations, and reflection activities. International students could present information about their cultures to domestic students. Topics might include gender roles, art, history, and family life. Such activities would enhance both domestic and international students' awareness, communication, and cultural sensitivity (Meyer, 2001). These training efforts would be particularly effective if international students themselves were involved in their planning and execution.

Ongoing Orientation: A Semester-Long Course

Since issues faced by international students continue beyond the first week of classes, ongoing orientation is essential. The length and severity of culture shock depend on various individual factors, and many international students continue to encounter difficulty in adjusting to American culture and the educational system. Meyer (2001) suggests that students need to achieve a balance between participation in the new culture and maintenance of their own cultural identities. To address these issues, institutions should institute ongoing orientation by offering a course to provide strategies for overcoming culture shock. The course would offer concrete social and academic skills training to benefit international students and help participants develop relationships with students from different countries, including the host country. In addition, to help the international student successfully interact with professors during office hours, examples of how to do so are necessary components. This introduction to academic life should be followed by an exercise in which students visit at least two different professors during their office hours and write reflections on that experience. Although the course should be free and non-credit, it must be understood that it is necessary and will be beneficial to the academic and social growth of international students.

One-Stop-Shop

Even for domestic students, the complex bureaucratic organization of a large college or university can be frustrating and intimidating. This challenge is exacerbated when language, customs, and the stressors of living in a new country exist. Institutions should consider creating a new office or enhancing the existing office of international student services to be a place where students can lounge, interact, and address the problems they face. This place would be considered a home for students, a One-Stop-Shop. It would be a place where students find answers or receive referrals to an appropriate department or campus resource from knowledgeable staff. For example, a student in need of degree navigation advice would not only be directed to the appropriate campus office, but also be told the advisor with whom to talk within that office. Staff could even call or email the contact person, introducing the student and her or his needs. These practices would confirm to international students that educators in the college or university understand their needs and are eager to provide support. Finally, this One-Stop Shop should be decorated with an international flair, such as artwork representing different countries, so that students recognize it as a welcoming place. Ideally, this One-Stop-Shop would be a place where international students can relax, re-energize, and connect with other students facing similar struggles.

Distribution of Information

Institutions can facilitate the adjustment and engagement of international students by distributing information that encourages them to engage in campus life. Campus information should have inclusive language and images. International students may assume that an event or job opportunity is unavailable to them if diverse images are not depicted. Moreover, information must be made available in various forms and not limited to flyers. Alternative forms include pamphlets and brochures, university mailings, email, listserv and web-based updates, and the campus newspaper. The college or university should consider providing access to information in different languages. Staff in orientation services, international student services, residence life, and health services could conduct a needs-based assessment to pinpoint where communication efforts break down and address these specific gaps.

Mental and Physical Health Services

For international students, college adjustment issues are compounded by the stressors of living in a new country; therefore, psychological problems such as depression may surface. Brochures containing information on available counseling services along with how counseling is viewed by members of the host country are essential to reduce the stigma associated with counseling. Equally important, culturally appropriate counseling should include educators fluent in students' primary languages and cultural norms, as well as gender-appropriate professionals available upon request. Health services professionals should strive to present information prominently as well as translate key medical terms into different languages. In addition, a video could be played on a continuous loop that addresses major questions in different languages that students can watch while waiting for service. To staff this program and minimize costs, graduate students within the college or university's counseling department could be used as professionals, since a practicum is often a requirement for certification. If there is no such graduate school, unpaid internship opportunities could be made available to graduate students in counseling programs at neighboring institutions. This approach benefits all concerned parties—the international student receives culturally appropriate counseling, graduate students improve their cross-cultural skills, and the college or university serves both populations.

Career Center Services

One goal of postsecondary institutions is to prepare students for professional life after college. Career centers play an important role in enabling students to achieve this aim. At present, most institutions emphasize assisting domestic students seeking employment, often neglecting the needs of international students. Career center staff should reach out to international students by tailoring services to meet their needs. For example, in partnership with the office of international students and various international student associations, the career center could sponsor workshops on work regulations along with guidelines on finding employment in the United States. In addition, senior-level international students with internship experiences could serve as peer counselors in the career center. Finally, the center could build a database of alumni employed in the United States and abroad who are former international students.

Conversation Partners

Foreign language ability is retained through regular use. However, domestic students acquiring languages other than English have few chances to use what they learn. Campus employers can hire international students to tutor domestic students in learning different languages. Employment provides the opportunity for international students to gain interpersonal, leadership, and professional skills, as well as learn the culture and norms of the American workplace. Finally, interactions with students and employers would foster cross-cultural relationships. With support from the modern languages department, students enrolled in beginning language courses could be required to meet several times during a semester for structured conversation with a native speaker. Whereas prior strategies discuss international students as seekers of resources, this one suggests they become providers of resources.

Assessment and Evaluation

Ongoing assessment, through multiple quantitative and qualitative methods, should be instituted to determine the effectiveness of support services for students from other countries. Deliberate evaluation efforts are particularly important for this group of students because of the cultural gaps that divide the service providers and the students in need of service. Rather than basing institutional change on anecdotal evidence, institutional members should provide structured opportunities for students to complete surveys and participate in interviews about their experiences on campus. The vice-president of student affairs should spearhead this assessment in conjunction with efforts by the institution's director of multicultural affairs. Not only would assessment and evaluation provide valuable data that institutions could use to enhance their programs, but an essential message would be sent to international students that educators are committed to improving their engagement and persistence.

Data Disaggregation

Postsecondary institutions should disaggregate data on undergraduate admissions. Currently, many top institutions publicize incomplete and even misleading admissions data. Some, for example, distinguish only the following groups: Asian,

African American, White, Latino/a, and Other. Given these choices, how would Kuwaiti, Brazilian, Mongolian, or Jamaican students label themselves? Other institutions carefully disaggregate undergraduate admissions data by U.S. region or even state, but then lump all international students together into one ill-defined group. To respect diversity, institutions should distinguish student groups. Asian international student needs, for instance, differ from those of Asian Americans. Collecting and displaying data divided at least by world regions would send a message to prospective students and others that the college or university recognizes international students' unique needs and values their contributions.

Conclusion

In this chapter, we identified issues that affect international students' academic success, engagement, and psychosocial development at U.S. colleges and universities. We hope that, after reading this chapter, faculty, administrators, and student affairs educators are aware of these issues and are thus better equipped to respond to them. If America is to maintain its preeminence as a destination for learners from around the world, institutions must strive to enhance the developmental outcomes of international students. While we recognize the diverse student populations across the nation's colleges and universities, no institution of higher education can afford to neglect the issues that confront international students. Inviting students from around the world to participate in U.S. higher education includes the ethical responsibility to serve them well. As the twenty-first century continues to blur boundaries and draw the peoples of the world closer, efforts that facilitate intercultural understanding will lead to enriched opportunities for international students and the institutions that serve them.

References

Al-Sharideh, K. A., & Goe, W. R. (1998). Ethnic communities within the university: An examination of factors influencing the personal adjustment of international students. *Research in Higher Education, 39*(6), 699–725.

Allen, W. R. (1992). The color of success: African-American college student outcomes at predominantly White and historically Black public college and universities. *Harvard Educational Review, 62*(1), 26–44.

Altbach, P. G. (2004). Globalisation and the university: Myths and realities in an unequal world. *Tertiary Education and Management, 10*(1), 3–25.

Bain, O., & Cummings, W. K. (2005). Where have the international students gone? *International Educator, 14*(2), 18–26.

Bahvala, A. (2002). Common stressors for international students in the USA. Retrieved July 3, 2005, from the Alumni Internet Access and Training Program website: http://alumni.iatp.org.ua/publications.

Berkner, L., He, S., Lew, S., Cominole, M., Siegel, P., & Griffith, J. (2005). *2003–04 National Postsecondary Student Aid Study (NPSAS:04): Student financial aid estimates for 2003–04.* Washington, DC: U.S. Department of Education, National Center for Education Statistics.

Burrell, K. I., & Kim, D. J. (2002). International students and academic assistance: Meeting the needs of another college population. In P. L. Dwinell & J. L. Higbee (Eds.), *Developmental education: Meeting diverse student needs* (pp. 81–96). Morrow, GA: National Association for Developmental Education.

Chen, C. P. (1999). Common stressors among international college students: Research and counseling implications. *Journal of College Counseling, 2*(1), 49–65.

Cigularova, D. K. (2005). Psychosocial adjustment of international students. *Colorado State University Journal of Student Affairs, 14,* 17–24.

Crowe, C., & Peterson, K. (1995). Classroom research: Helping Asian students succeed in writing courses. *Teaching English in the Two-Year College, 22*(1), 31–37.

Cummings, W. K. (1991). Foreign students. In P. G. Altbach (Ed.), *International Higher Education: An Encyclopedia Vol. 1* (pp. 107–125). New York: Garland.

Davis, T. (Ed.) (1998). *Open doors: 1997/98 report on international educational exchange.* New York: Institute of International Education.

Elsey, B. (1990). Teaching and learning. In M. Kinnell (Ed.), *The learning experiences of overseas students* (pp. 46–62). Bristol, PA: Society for Research into Higher Education and Open University Press.

Ferraro, G. P. (1990). *The cultural dimension of international business.* Englewood Cliffs, NJ: Prentice-Hall.

Findsen, B. C. (1987). *The process of international graduate student adjustment.* Unpublished doctoral dissertation, North Carolina State University, Raleigh, NC.

Gloria, A. M., & Ho, T. A. (2003). Environmental, social, and psychological experiences of Asian American undergraduates: Examining issues of academic persistence. *Journal of Counseling and Development, 81*(1), 93–105.

Hurtado, S., Milem, J. F., Clayton-Pedersen, A., & Allen, W. R. (1998). Enhancing campus climates for racial/ethnic diversity: Educational policy and practice. *The Review of Higher Education, 21*(3), 279–302.

Hwang, M. H., & Heppner, M. J. (2001). *Korean career choices: Cross-cultural validity of measures and inventories.* Paper presented at the annual meeting of the American Psychological Association, San Francisco, CA.

Ingman, K. A. (1999). *An examination of social anxiety, social skills, social adjustment, and self-construal in Chinese and American students at an American university.* Unpublished doctoral dissertation, Virginia Polytechnic Institute and State University, Blacksburg, VA.

Kantrowitz, B., & Naughton, K. (2001, November 12). Generation 9-11. *Newsweek,* pp. 46–56.

Kinnell, M. (1990). The marketing and management of courses. In M. Kinnell (Ed.), *The learning experiences of overseas students* (pp. 13–45). Bristol, PA: Society for Research into Higher Education and Open University Press.

Kohls, R. (1984). *Intercultural training: Don't leave home without it.* Washington, DC: Society for Intercultural Education, Training and Research.

Kuh, G. D., Schuh, J. H., Whitt, E. J., & Associates (1991). *Involving colleges: Successful approaches to fostering student learning and personal development outside the classroom.* San Francisco: Jossey-Bass.

Land, E., & Land, W. (1992, November). *A proposal for the implementation of programs for culturally diverse students on a predominantly White university campus.* Paper presented at the meeting of the Mid-South Educational Research Association, Knoxville, TN.

Louis, M. R. (1980). Surprise and sense making: What newcomers experience in entering unfamiliar organizational settings. *Administrative Science Quarterly, 25*(2), 226–251.

Maslow, A. H. (2005). A theory of human motivation. In J. M. Shafritz, J. S. Ott, & Y. S. Jang (Eds.), *Classics of organization theory* (6th ed.). Belmont, CA: Thompson Wadsworth.

Meyer, J. D. (2001). A conceptual framework for comprehensive international student orientation programs. *International Education, 31*(1), 56–78.

Mori, S. (2000). Addressing the mental health concerns of international students. *Journal of Counseling and Development, 78*(2), 138–144.

Morio, I., Kawaguchi, Y., Suda, H., & Eto, K. (2000). Educating overseas students: Just another responsibility or a chance to grow for faculty? *European Journal of Dental Education, 4*(3), 128–132.

Organization for Economic Cooperation and Development (2002). *Education at a Glance: OECD indicators 2002 and 2004*. Paris: Author.

Pascarella, E. T., Edison, M., Nora, A., Hagedorn, L. S., & Terenzini, P. T. (1996). Influences on students' openness to diversity and challenge in the first year of college. *Journal of Higher Education, 67*(2), 174–195.

Pruitt, F. J. (1978). The adaptation of African students to American society. *International Journal of Intercultural Relations, 2*(1), 90–118.

Reeves, P. M. (1999). Psychological development: Becoming a person. In M. C. Clark & R. S. Caffarella (Eds.), *An update on adult development theory: New ways of thinking about the life course. New Directions for Adult and Continuing Education* (No. 84, pp. 19–27). San Francisco: Jossey-Bass.

Robertson, M., Line, M., Jones, S., & Thomas, S. (2000). International students, learning environments and perceptions: A case study using the Delphi technique. *Higher Education Research & Development, 19*(1), 89–102.

Rohrlich, B. F., & Martin, J. N. (1991). Host country and re-entry adjustment of student sojourners. *International Journal of Intercultural Relations, 15*(2), 163–182.

Sam, D. L. (2001). Satisfaction with life among international students: An exploratory study. *Social Indicators Research, 53*(3), 315–337.

Sargent, A., & Schlossberg, N. K. (1988). Managing adult transitions. *Training and Development Journal, 42*(12), 58–60.

Schlossberg, N. K., & Robinson, S. P. (1996). *Going to plan B: How you can cope, regroup, and start your life on a new path*. New York: Simon & Schuster.

Schlossberg, N. K., Waters, E. B., & Goodman, J. (1995). *Counseling adults in transition: Linking practice with theory* (2nd ed.). New York: Springer.

Schoch, L., & Baumgartner, J. (2004). *Net contribution to U.S. economy by foreign students*. New York: Institute of International Education.

Scott, R. A. (1994). Campus developments in response to the challenges of internationalization: The case of Ramapo College, New Jersey (USA). *Higher Education Management, 6*(1), 71–89.

Searle, W., & Ward, C. (1990). The prediction of psychological and sociocultural adjustment during cross-cultural transitions. *International Journal of Intercultural Relations 14*(4), 449–464.

Selvadurai, R. (1998). Problems faced by international students in American colleges and universities. *Community Review, 16*, 153–158.

Spencer-Rodgers, J., & McGovern, T. (2002). Attitudes toward the culturally different: The role of intercultural communication barriers, affective responses, consensual stereotypes, and perceived threat. *International Journal of Intercultural Relations, 26*(6), 609–631.

Stephan, W. G., & Stephan, C. W. (1996). Predicting prejudice. *International Journal of Intercultural Relations, 20*(3–4), 409–426.

Stromquist, N. P., & Monkman, K. (Eds.) (2000). *Globalization and education: Integration and contestation across cultures*. Lanham, MD: Rowman & Littlefield.

Tatar, M., & Horenczyk, G. (2000). Counseling students on the move: The effects of culture or origin and permanence of relocation among international college students. *Journal of College Counseling, 3*(1), 49–62.

Tomich, P. C., McWhirter, J. J., & Darcy, M. U. A. (2003). Personality and international students' adaptation experience. *International Education, 33*(1), 22–39.

Toyokawa, T., & Toyokawa, N. (2002). Extracurricular activities and the adjustment of Asian international students: A study of Japanese students. *International Journal of Intercultural Relations, 26*(4), 363–379.

Tseng, W., & Newton, F. B. (2002). International students' strategies for well-being. *College Student Journal, 36*(4), 591–597.

Wang, J., & Frank, D. G. (2002). Cross-cultural communication: Implications for effective information services in academic libraries. *Libraries and the Academy, 2*, 207–216.

Winkelman, M. (1994). Cultural shock and adaptation. *Journal of Counseling and Development, 73*(2), 121–26.

Yang, E., Wong, S. C., Hwang, M., & Heppner, M. J. (2002). Widening our global view: The development of career counseling services for international students. *Journal of Career Development, 28*(3), 203–213.

Yi, J. K., Lin, J. G.., & Kishimoto, Y. (2003). Utilization of counseling services by international students. *Journal of Instructional Psychology,* 30(4), 333–342.

Zhang, N. (2000). *Acculturation and counseling expectancies: Asian international students' attitudes toward seeking professional psychological help.* Unpublished doctoral dissertation, Ball State University, Muncie, IN.

Zimmermann, S. (1995). Perceptions of intercultural communication competence and international student adaptation to an American campus. *Communication Education, 44,* 321–335.

Chapter 3
Beyond Accommodation
Removing Barriers to Academic and Social Engagement for Students with Disabilities

Andrew H. Nichols and Stephen John Quaye

Students with disabilities contend on a daily basis with the pernicious effects of stereotyping. Like students of color, those who can be identified at a glance as physically different experience assumptions about inferior intellectual capacity. (McCune, 2001, p. 9)

People are afraid of disability issues and don't know how to talk about them, either because they don't know what to ask or they don't want to appear biased or prejudiced in some way. (Aune & Kroeger, 1997, p. 351)

Students with disabilities encounter specific barriers that impede their academic and social engagement; however, their needs are often overlooked in comparison to other student populations. These students are sometimes thought of as "a 'forgotten minority' of student affairs practice in higher education" (Junco & Salter, 2004, p. 263). In society, and particularly in academia, people rarely mention, and even less frequently openly discuss, disabilities and their impacts. Consequently, the needs of these students are largely ignored and rarely met by college and university officials, administrators, and faculty. Additionally, students without disabilities may feel uncomfortable or awkward interacting with and approaching students with visible disabilities. To reduce these tense encounters, students may distance themselves, consciously or unconsciously, from their peers with disabilities, thus contributing to the alienation and isolation of this population. Likewise, students with invisible disabilities (e.g., learning disabilities, Attention Deficit Hyperactivity Disorder [ADHD], psychological disabilities, and chronic disease and/or illness) also face their share of challenges. The possibility of being labeled frauds or pretenders by peers, faculty, or staff could cause these students not to disclose their disabilities. Fear of rejection or the complications caused by hiding disabilities can create undue stress and hardship as students pursue their education (Barga, 1996). These harsh realities, and others, create environments where students with disabilities find it difficult to become academically and socially engaged.

In this chapter, we discuss issues that impede the academic and social engagement of students with disabilities and explore means to remove these barriers. After a brief overview of demographical information and enrollment trends among students with disabilities, we present a literature review explicating the barriers students with disabilities encounter, a theoretical framework that clarifies and expands one's understanding of these students' needs, and practical strategies designed to engage these students, produce positive outcomes for this population, and improve their educational experiences.

Enrollment Trends and Demographics of Students with Disabilities

According to the Americans with Disabilities Act of 1990, a person with a disability (1) has a physical or mental impairment that substantially limits one or more major life activities, (2) has a record of such an impairment, or (3) is regarded as having such an impairment (42 USC 12101[2]). This legislation, along with Section 504 of the Rehabilitation Act of 1973, prohibits public entities (e.g., public colleges and universities) or any government-funded institution (e.g., private colleges and universities receiving federal funds), activity, or program from discriminating against qualified persons on the grounds of disabling conditions. To be considered qualified, a person must "meet the essential eligibility qualifications, with or without reasonable accommodation, in spite of the restrictions imposed by the disability" (Thomas, 2000, p. 250). Moreover, these laws require that reasonable accommodations be made in appropriate circumstances to prevent discrimination based on disability. Because the majority of colleges and universities depend on some type of federal funding, these institutions must adhere to these laws; however, compliance is not always that simple.

Demographic information and enrollments of students with disabilities are difficult to determine. The difficulty in obtaining accurate figures on students with disabilities stems from their legal right not to report their disability to colleges and universities. As a result, statistics on students with disabilities are subject to fluctuation. If students do not disclose their disability, it prevents postsecondary institutions from accessing information about them that may be useful in providing them accommodations and services. In many instances, college and university staff and faculty cannot proactively respond to the needs of these students, but can only be reactive when needs are brought to their attention.

Students with disabilities composed roughly 9 percent of the total student population in the United States in 2000. Enrollments for this student population increased from 3 percent in 1978 to 6 percent in 1996 (National Center for Education Statistics [NCES], 1999). Although some might be inclined to visualize students with noticeable physical impairments when thinking of students with disabilities, many invisible disabilities exist among today's students. The American Council on Education reports that 40 percent of incoming first-year students with disabilities report having a learning disability (Henderson, 2001). Statistical trends reflect a rise in the percentage of learning disabilities and a decline in the percentage of physical disabilities among college first-year students at four-year institutions (Henderson, 2001).

In proportion to their representation within the student population, White and Native American students are more likely than Black, Hispanic/Latino/a, and Asian students to report having a disability. Nearly 72 percent of students with disabilities are White, 11 percent are Black, 10 percent are Hispanic/Latino/a, 3.3 percent are Asian, 2.1 percent are Native Americans, and 1.6 percent represent other racial/ethnic groups. The gender gap for students with disabilities is larger than that of their peers: 60 percent of students with disabilities are women, whereas 56 percent of students without disabilities are women. Students with disabilities also tend to be older. Whereas 57 percent of all undergraduates without disabilities were between the ages of 15 and 23, only 42 percent of undergraduate students with disabilities fell within this age range; 41 percent were above 29 years of age, but only 26 percent of their same-race peers without disabilities were 30 or older. In graduate education, the opposite was true; graduate students with disabilities tended to be younger. Moreover, students with disabilities, both undergraduate and graduate, were more likely to enroll part-time and live off campus (NCES, 2004).

A wide array of disabilities is prevalent among today's students. Nearly 30 percent of students with disabilities reported having an orthopedic or mobility impairment in 2000. The next two most common disabilities, mental illness/depression and health impairments, composed 17 percent and 15 percent of disabilities, respectively. Visual impairments, learning disabilities, and various other disabilities accounted for roughly 12 percent, 11.5 percent, and 15 percent of all student disabilities, respectively. The diversity of disabilities existing among students makes satisfactory accommodation a comprehensive task. In order to adequately provide care, proper resource investment and commitment from college and university officials is warranted. Approximately 26 percent of students with disabilities report receiving the necessary accommodations; however, 22 percent state that these accommodations are not available (NCES, 2003, 2004).

Generally, public institutions are more likely to provide the necessary services than private institutions. Moreover, larger colleges and universities tend to provide more services than smaller institutions. The availability of services and accommodations directly correlates with the enrollment patterns of students with disabilities. Students with disabilities are more likely to attend public colleges and universities; roughly 75 percent attend these institutions. Students with disabilities also more readily attend two-year institutions instead of four-year institutions: in fact nearly half attend two-year institutions (NCES, 2003, 2004). This phenomenon could exist for two reasons. First, students who might be concerned with how their disability could affect their postsecondary education may feel that enrolling in these institutions may be less of a risk, financial and otherwise. The risk-versus-reward ratio may be more favorable. Second, students with disabilities may be more likely to attend institutions that seem receptive to their needs and provide the appropriate services, and these institutions, over the years, have adapted to the needs of their student constituency. Regardless of where they enroll, students with disabilities must still overcome barriers that inhibit their engagement in academic and social endeavors.

Barriers to Academic and Social Engagement

Before the passage of Section 504 of the Rehabilitation Act of 1973, access to higher education was limited for students with disabilities (Evans, Assadi, & Herriott, 2005; Palombi, 2000; Paul, 2000). Because these students were largely ignored prior to the 1970s, limited research and analysis have been devoted specifically to examining their academic and social experiences. Much of the existing literature focuses mainly on the legal responsibilities of higher education institutions to students with disabilities, theoretical discussions of disability paradigms, issues concerning access, equity, and accommodation, and the career implications for this population. Certainly, these topics are important and worthy of exploration; however, this section focuses primarily on barriers that impede the academic and social engagement of students with disabilities on college and university campuses.

Academic Barriers

Academically, researchers have found that students with disabilities may graduate at lower rates than their peers without disabilities (Bursuck, Rose, Cowen, & Yahaya, 1989; Durlak, Rose, & Bursuck, 1994; Merchant & Gajar, 1997). The results from the 1989–1990 Beginning Postsecondary Student Longitudinal Survey support this claim. The survey revealed that 65 percent of students without disabilities persisted, in comparison with only 53 percent of students with disabilities (NCES, 1999). A student was counted as persisting if he or she was still enrolled in 1994 or had already obtained a diploma. Because graduation rates were measured over a five-year span, it was difficult to determine if these students were simply not graduating or were just taking longer to finish their degrees. In fact, some evidence indicated that the latter was the case (Greenbaum, Graham, & Scales, 1995; Jorgensen et al., 2003; Vogel & Adelman, 1992). Regardless, both scenarios suggest that students with disabilities encounter academic barriers that prevent them from persisting to degree completion, at least in a timely manner.

Social Barriers

These students also encounter obstacles that inhibit their social engagement. They are the targets of environmental, prejudicial, and interpersonal factors that lead to non-acceptance in social endeavors (Fine & Asch, 1988). Non-acceptance and the inability to socially engage with peers hinder the social development of these students. Both

Allison and Anderson (as cited in Paul, 2000) found that students with disabilities encountered social problems that inhibited their engagement. More specifically, English (1993) reported that these students felt moderately integrated in academic endeavors but socially disengaged. Without participating in out-of-class activities, these students are less likely to develop the teamwork, decision-making, planning, leadership, and personal skills that are necessary for career success (Kuh, Schuh, Whitt, & Associates, 1991; Schuh & Laverty, 1983). Additionally, when students are engaged in out-of-class activities, they are also more satisfied with their college experience (Kuh et al., 1991). Not only do students with disabilities confront social barriers associated with "the minority group paradigm" (Jones, 1996, p. 349), they are also faced with other barriers associated with their respective disabilities. All of these obstacles shape an environment that makes social engagement a daunting task for students with disabilities.

Institutional, Physical, and Attitudinal Barriers

Academic and social engagement for students with disabilities is absolutely critical to their educational experience. Without some form of engagement in both arenas, it will be quite difficult for these students to have positive, meaningful, and productive tenures at institutions of higher learning. If students are going to achieve holistic engagement, institutional, physical, and attitudinal barriers must be removed.

Institutional Barriers

> When things get institutionalized, they don't meet the needs at all of someone with a disability. I just don't fit the mold. (quoted in Aune & Kroeger, 1997, p. 349)

The remarks from this student with a disability illustrate a significant shortcoming of institutionalization. In many instances, institutionalized organizations fail to address the specific needs of minority participants. This failure results in the construction of institutional barriers. These barriers are "aspects of the university that . . . hindered students' progress toward their goals" (Stage & Milne, 1996, p. 434). In an attempt to eliminate institutional barriers for students with disabilities, many colleges and universities have developed offices of disability services. However, even though these offices are specifically committed to meeting the needs of students with disabilities, they tend to be understaffed and underfunded (Measel, 1999).

Institutional barriers exist at colleges and universities of all types and sizes. Small institutions may have limited resources and funds to provide necessary accommodations for students with disabilities, whereas large institutions may find it difficult to meet the individualized needs of students with disabilities (Stage & Milne, 1996). The two main institutional barriers that hinder academic engagement are problems students encounter in acquiring quality academic support resources and the lack of qualified professionals that specifically work with students with disabilities (Aune & Kroeger,

1997). The only institutional barrier to social engagement discussed in the literature focused on scheduling conflicts with out-of-class activities and programs.

In the late 1990s, about 98 percent of postsecondary institutions provided students with disabilities with at least one academic support service (NCES, 1999). Some research indicated that these students were satisfied with their support services (Elacqua, 1996; West et al., 1993); however, this was not always the case. According to Stage and Milne (1996), students with disabilities reported that tutors provided by the school were often underqualified: They often were untrained, lacked experience working with students with disabilities, and were pedagogically unprepared to teach these students. In addition, tutors were also undependable. As one participant commented, "When tutors don't come through and I'm depending on them, that's a real problem" (Stage & Milne, 1996, p. 435). In a study of career development among college students with disabilities, Aune and Kroeger (1997) found that some students were dissatisfied with many of the career services provided by their institutions. Even when students reported being generally satisfied, they mentioned aspects that needed improvement. Similarly, West et al. (1993) reported that although students were mostly satisfied with the services offered by their institutions, many still indicated there was a lack of adaptive aids and other accommodations. Despite reports of general satisfaction with accommodations and services, Elacqua (1996) noted that students with disabilities felt that acquiring the necessary accommodations was often stressful. Even if accommodations are provided, these students may be less inclined to access them if the process is complicated and burdensome.

Another institutional barrier involves college and university staff who lack knowledge and training on the legal rights and needs of students with disabilities. According to Greenbaum, Graham, and Scales (1995), "The most common institutional barrier to success cited by students with disabilities was lack of understanding and cooperation from faculty and administrators" (p. 468). In most circumstances, these types of barriers can be eliminated with the proper information and training. Aune and Kroeger (1997) found that some staff members were oblivious to the fact that they were responsible for providing equal access to students with disabilities. Furthermore, these administrators were unaware that it was not only their duty to produce reasonable accommodations, but it was also their responsibility to notify students that the accommodations were available upon request. Despite their lack of knowledge, they did express interest in learning more about students with disabilities, specifically those with learning disabilities. Faculty members have also demonstrated that they are, at times, unaware of their responsibilities to students with disabilities. Baggett (1994) revealed that professors lacked experience instructing students with disabilities, were unaware of students' legal responsibilities, and were unfamiliar with the university services provided for students with disabilities. Similarly, Aksamit, Morris, and Leuenberger (1987) reported that faculty had limited knowledge of the effects of disabilities and the services available to students with disabilities. Some professors do not understand that it is their responsibility to alter their teaching methods, requirements, and curricula to accommodate students with disabilities. In many cases, faculty members were not sure how to revise their coursework to accommodate students with disabilities and still maintain fair evaluation standards (Stage & Milne, 1996).

Although the literature does not highlight many institutional barriers affecting social engagement, Hodges and Keller (1999) identified scheduling conflicts with out-of-class activities to be problematic for some of the students with disabilities. Since most co-curricular gatherings and student organization meetings convene in the evenings, students who lived off campus found it difficult to participate. Students who lived at home because of conditions related to their disability were hampered by commute times, inadequate transportation, and time constraints. These circumstances made it rather difficult for students to become engaged in out-of-class activities and student organizations. One student said the following:

> I wanted to, at times, get involved in some of the activities they [the college or university] have, but I just don't have the opportunity. Usually when they have a meeting or some activity going on, it always seems to fall on the days I am not here . . . I just can't come back for things. (quoted in Hodges & Keller, 1999, p. 683)

Similar to commuter students in general, students with disabilities who need to live off campus or at home find few opportunities for social engagement.

Physical Barriers

Physical barriers only affect students with mobility concerns; however, these accessibility issues cause significant problems for them. Even though physical impairments can make college life difficult for students who have them, research on the impacts of physical disabilities on college students has been limited (Hodges & Keller, 1999; Junco & Salter, 2004; Neubert, Moon, & Grigal, 2004). When physical barriers exist, navigation around campus becomes a cumbersome task (Strange & Banning, 2001). When accommodations are not made or are insufficient, students with disabilities may perceive the institution to be unconcerned with their needs (Strange & Banning, 2001). Actions such as creating curb ramps instead of spending the time and money to properly install curb cuts may send messages of "not caring enough to do it correctly," "not valuing the user," or "just responding minimally to the needs of the physically challenged" (Strange & Banning, 2001, p. 16). Conversely, when institutions make the appropriate architectural accommodations, students feel valued, respected, and appreciated (Strange, 2000).

The physical barriers that students with disabilities encounter may indirectly influence their academic performance. In a study by West et al. (1993), students with disabilities expressed satisfaction with the services provided by their institutions, but also reported that inaccessibility of campus buildings and grounds was a problem. Anderson (as cited in Paul, 2000) examined the experiences of students with and without disabilities and found that students with disabilities expressed concerns about physical barriers within university buildings that impeded their mobility. Problems with transportation around campus can cause students to be late to classes, meetings, and study sessions. Moreover, the frustration caused by mobility issues may result in students missing classes altogether. From interviews with 52 first-year students with mobility impairments, Zadra (1982) found that simple accommodations such as rest areas would be beneficial. He also reported that ambulatory students underestimated the importance of architectural accommodations, not realizing how instrumental ramps and handrails were to their mobility. Simply having accessible curb cuts, ramps, elevators, restrooms, computer and science laboratories, and parking spaces can dramatically improve a student's ability to navigate across campus and within buildings. By creating a more accessible and accommodating physical environment, students with physical disabilities can channel the extra energy normally used maneuvering across campus into other endeavors. Improvements in academic engagement may be attained by providing students with disabilities the amenities that persons without disabilities commonly take for granted (Zadra, 1982).

Physical barriers also impede the social engagement of students with disabilities. For students living with a disabling condition, extra time is often required for daily life activities (Kinney & Coyle, 1989). These time constraints make it difficult for these students to participate in many out-of-class activities. For example, students needing personal care providers, assistive animals, physical therapy, and medical treatment may spend hours of their day tending to those needs. In a study by Hodges and Keller (1999), a student who needed a personal care provider said:

> Having an attendant come in every morning, I have to get up three hours early every morning. At night, if I want to stay up and hang out with friends, I can't. [My attendant] comes at 10:00 [p.m.], and I have got to go to bed or sleep in my wheelchair, which I have done. (p. 683)

This student was eager to engage socially with his peers, but was unable to do so because of his medical condition. In such cases as this, time constraints caused by a physical disability are roadblocks to social engagement.

In addition to time constraints, students with disabilities must also deal with the specific effects of their physical disabilities. West et al. (1993) found that architectural barriers limit opportunities for involvement. The inability to simply move around campus and access facilities expediently and efficiently may prevent students with disabilities from participating in co-curricular activities or attending student organization meetings. Similarly, students with mobility impairments may be excluded from beneficial activities such as intramural sports and other programs involving physical action. Limitations in mainstream media resources may also restrict the social opportunities for students with physical disabilities (Senge & Dote-Kwan, 1995). For example, students with visual impairments are unable to utilize common methods of communication such as email, flyers, newspapers, and posters used to advertise events and activities. Although disability-specific barriers to social engagement are difficult to resolve, higher education constituents must begin to diversify intervention strategies and provide individualized solutions for students with physical disabilities.

Attitudinal Barriers

Attitudes are learned tendencies to think in a habitual manner toward individuals and groups (Gething & Wheeler, 1992). Attitudes shape the way people perceive and treat themselves and others; yet, in many instances, individuals are not consciously aware that they possess these dispositions. Attitudes can be positive or negative and are directed both internally (toward oneself) and externally (toward others). Research on campus climates reveals that people tend to hold negative attitudes, both conscious and unconscious, toward students with disabilities (Hahn, 1988; Katz, Huss, & Bailey, 1998; Livneh, 1988). Kelly, Sedlacek, and Scales (1994) found that college students without disabilities developed stereotypical opinions of students with disabilities. In addition to dealing with the negative attitudes of others, students with disabilities must also battle their own internal attitudes concerning their disabilities. For example, students with speech impediments may feel self-conscious about their speaking abilities and, consequently, be reluctant to speak publicly in academic settings, even if they have mastered the subject matter and could positively contribute to the class. They may be constantly worrying about what their peers or professors may think. These types of attitudinal barriers make academic and social engagement challenging. In this section, we discuss the academic and social impacts of internal (self-imposed) attitudes and external attitudes (the stereotypes and beliefs of others) on the engagement of students with disabilities.

The academic success of students with disabilities is affected by their own perspectives of themselves and the attitudes of others, specifically faculty members and peers. Even though some studies indicate that students with disabilities regard themselves in the same manner as their peers without disabilities (Fichten, Robbillard, Judd, & Amsel, 1989; Kelly et al., 1994; Kriegsman & Hershenson, 1987), other researchers make different claims. In a 2000 survey (Henderson 2001), first-year students with and without disabilities were asked whether they considered themselves "above average or in the top 10 percent of people" in a number of areas. Students with disabilities rated themselves below the top 10 percent of their peers in 12 of 18 categories: cooperativeness, drive to achieve, intellectual self-confidence, academic ability, self-understanding, competitiveness, social self-confidence, physical health, emotional health, writing ability, popularity, and mathematical ability. Aune and Kroeger (1997) reported that students with disabilities, especially those managing new disabilities, dealt with anxiety and self-acceptance issues. All of the students in a study by Stage and Milne (1996) reported being self-conscious about their disability to some degree, and this self-consciousness made them hesitant to reveal their disabilities. Moreover, these internal dispositions caused the students to adjust their behaviors in academic environments. As one student said, "It will be a cool day in hell when I raise my hand, because that's just a fear of mine, of being wrong" (p. 433). The influences that internal attitudes have on their behavior and academic identities ultimately affect the academic performance of these students.

The attitudes of students without disabilities and other members of the university community also influence the academic performance of students with disabilities. Several studies indicate that students without disabilities tend to hold stereotypical opinions of students with disabilities (Fichten & Amsel, 1986; Fichten et al., 1989; Kelly et al., 1994) and evaluate them in negative ways (Babbitt, Burbach, & Iutcovich, 1979; Fichten et al., 1989; Fichten, Robillard, Tagalakis, & Amsel, 1991; Robillard & Fichten, 1983). Addressing the contradictory findings of other researchers that students without disabilities do not hold negative views toward their peers with disabilities (Belgrave, 1985; Belgrave & Mills, 1981; Tagalakis, Amsel, & Fichten, 1988; Weinberg-Asher, 1976), Fichten et al. (1989) determined that the "prevalence of positive descriptions of individuals with disabilities may be due to the social desirability, sympathy, or self-presentation biases" (p. 244). That is, fear of public scorn or admonishment may prevent people from openly expressing any negative dispositions they have toward this population. If students hold negative attitudes toward their peers with disabilities, they may be inclined to harshly evaluate their academic potential and criticize their work. Additionally, if students without disabilities commonly believe that students with disabilities are incapable of high-quality work, they may be less inclined to approach them for collaborative activities and study groups. If students with disabilities are unable to take advantage of the opportunity to learn from interactions with their peers, their academic experience may be diminished and less rewarding (Kelly et al., 1994).

In addition to contending with the negative attitudes and stereotypes from peers, students with disabilities may also encounter similar dispositions on the part of faculty. Although some research has indicated that faculty are willing to accommodate students with disabilities (Houck, Asselin, Troutman, & Arrington, 1992; Matthew, Anderson, & Skolnick, 1987; Nelson, Dodd, & Smith, 1990; Satcher, 1992), Sweener, Kundert, May, and Quinn (2002) found that faculty were reluctant to accommodate this population. If students with disabilities perceive these negative attitudes among faculty, they are less likely to expresses their needs, request accommodations, and establish relationships with faculty (Nutter & Ringgenberg, 1993).

Not only do attitudes affect the academic performance of students with disabilities, but they also inhibit their social engagement. Both self-directed attitudes and the attitudes of others influence the way students with disabilities interact in social environments. Many students with disabilities have difficulty reconciling their own attitudes about social interactions. For instance, Hodges and Keller (1999) determined that students with disabilities shaped their collegiate expectations of social engagement based upon past negative experiences in high school. They expected their peers to react negatively to their presence and to be exclusive. Students who were adjusting to new disabilities also expressed anxiety and apprehension about developing social connections. If students with disabilities enter college with low expectations for social engagement, disengagement is a likely outcome (Hodges & Keller, 1999). Low expectations due to prior negative experiences may result in students being uncomfortable in the pursuit of social engagement. In Stage and Milne's (1996) study, one student described his experience in the following way:

> I still walk under a dark cloud. I still am a little touchy on the subject of being learning disabled. And you know when you have to deal with any of your peers that you are not as good as they are, you're a little hesitant. (p. 432)

Even though this student's condition was not new, he still found it difficult to accept his learning disability. His self-consciousness and feelings of inadequacy thwarted his ability to become comfortable establishing personal relationships. Once such students overcome their own reservations and establish social connections with peers, they must then decide whether or how to disclose their disability. The possible reactions of disbelief, unacceptance, and exaggerated sympathy from peers may persuade them to refrain from participation in co-curricular activities. One student said, "I wouldn't make any friends, because to get friendly with somebody, to go places, I had to tell them that I didn't drive and all of that. So I never had many friends" (Hodges & Keller, 1999, p. 681). Anxiety about disclosure prevented this student from attempting to establish meaningful relationships with peers. Students with disabilities must first overcome their own internal attitudes before social connections can be established.

After students with disabilities have reconciled their own self-imposed attitudes, they must then battle the stereotypes and negative attitudes exhibited by their peers on campus. Students with physical disabilities often receive awkward looks and stares (Hodges & Keller, 1999). One student noted, "If you have got any type of disability being visual or mobile . . . people are a little standoffish. They really just don't know how to approach you and some won't even talk to you at all" (p. 682). To counteract people's tendency to distance themselves, this particular student took the onus upon herself to become more outgoing and pursue personal relationships. This approach worked for her; however, for students who feel uncomfortable being assertive, such an option is more difficult.

Attitudinal barriers are deeply ingrained and can be difficult to change. Internal attitudes can be transformed through positive confidence-building experiences and through activities such as counseling. External attitudes can be changed through educational measures, contact with people, and communication (Evans et al., 2005). Whether internal or external, attitudinal changes must occur in order for students with disabilities to feel comfortable engaging in college and university environments.

Theoretical Framework

In order to further understand the institutional, physical, and attitudinal barriers to engagement with which students with disabilities contend, we describe three relevant theories—social constructivism, universal design, and identity development. This theoretical framework forms the basis for the proposed interventions discussed in the final section of this chapter.

Social Constructivism

Learning and physical disabilities are typically defined as residing within the individual student who has a deficit that places her or him in contradistinction to the "normal" population. What this hegemonic discourse often ignores is the larger societal and political contexts in which students with disabilities are situated that attach specific meanings and labels to their disabilities (Simmons & Kameenui, 1996). From a social constructivist perspective, an individual does not have a disability on her or his own; rather, disabilities are constructed within a complex web of relationships and norms in the dominant culture (Jones, 1996).

In educational environments, students are diagnosed as displaying a learning disability in comparison to their peers, who are seen as exhibiting normal or above-average learning skills. Removed from the schooling environment, students who have learning disabilities will likely be seen as normal, as there is no comparison or standard against which to measure their perceived lack of abilities. Likewise, students who possess physical disabilities have them only in the context of relationships with their peers who do not. A physical impairment cannot occur in isolation from affiliations with others (Dudley-Marling, 2004); the relationships add meaning to the disability. The word "disability" is itself a socially constructed term; the meaning of disability is developed in contrast to "ability" and describes a limitation that a person possesses that situates her or him differently from "able-bodied" and supposedly "normal" persons.

Rather than perpetuate the individualism that pervades U.S. society (Dudley-Marling, 2004), a social constructivist view of disabilities critiques the larger societal culture and the relationships that contribute to deficit-oriented notions of disabilities (Jones, 1996). As Dudley-Marling (2004) suggests:

> What is important to understand is that LD [learning disabilities] is intelligible only in the context of schooling. It is in schools, where children are routinely sorted and evaluated in terms of certain learning behaviors, that LD comes to life. Individual students cannot have LD on their own (McDermott & Varenne, 1999). The performance of LD requires an institutional framework that assigns particular meanings to students' behaviors that, in other cultural contexts, do not carry the same significance. (p. 484)

Consequently, to view disability as a socially constructed idea demands that those without disabilities are also included in the analysis. In fact, people without physical and learning disabilities are often those who create the assumptions and beliefs about students with disabilities and the notion "disability" itself (Jones, 1996). Social constructivism places the responsibility for students' learning and development not solely on the individual student, but also on the larger educational community (e.g., teachers, parents, peers, and society at large) as a whole.

Universal Design

Akin to social constructivism, adherents of universal design argue for maximizing learning and access by students, not just those with disabilities, through placing emphasis on various factors (e.g., dominant cultural beliefs) outside of the individual student. Originating from architecture, the theory of universal design strives to create optimal conditions for accommodating the changing needs of multiple constituents. Within an educational environment, universal design provides flexibility in classroom instruction, assignments, activities, and collaborative ventures. Educators who practice universal design do not approach learning with a "one-size-fits-all" mentality, but instead tailor their pedagogical assumptions and approaches to students' differing learning styles and preferences (Meyer & Rose, 2000; Rose & Meyer, 2000). Furthermore, these educators design structures from the outset that take physical disabilities into consideration, rather than viewing these students' needs as an afterthought (Rose & Meyer, 2000).

Providing an appropriate balance of challenge and support is a common principle in student affairs research and practice to optimize students' learning and developmental outcomes. Too much challenge with insufficient support can hamper learning and development and vice versa. Yet, from the outset of their educational experiences, students with disabilities face myriad difficulties in culturally exclusive classrooms and physically inaccessible campus environments that reflect the expectation of assimilation to dominant norms and practices, rather than the environment accommodating to student needs. This expectation of adaptation to inflexible pedagogical, environmental, and curricular approaches places an unfair burden on students with disabilities (Junco & Salter, 2004). As Rose and Meyer (2000) underscore:

> For many learners, printed books provide access to the knowledge of our culture, but for students with physical, sensory, and cognitive disabilities, among others, books present insurmountable barriers. Print presents information one way for everyone, yet students' varied learning needs and styles call for alternative formats. (p. 2)

Universal design recognizes that students learn by different means. It works to include their diverse talents by using various curricular and teaching strategies. Additionally, universal design acknowledges that access to information does not signify that learning will occur; rather, learning also requires an awareness of students' divergent needs and an understanding of how to enable them to reach their potential. Facilitating learning requires that educators move beyond simply assisting students with disabilities (i.e., the problem resides within the student). Instead, educators must revise the curriculum, contextual factors, pedagogical strategies, and learning philosophies guiding their work (i.e., the focus is the overarching educational system) to improve learning and development among students with disabilities (Rose & Meyer, 2000). Universal design means thinking about curricular approaches from the outset that accommodate different learners (Rose & Meyer, 2000).

Identity Development

Students' development is improved when educators deem them capable learners (Baxter Magolda, 2001). However, there is a tendency to view students with learning and physical disabilities as inept in comparison to their counterparts (Kelly et al., 1994). Chickering (1969) proposed seven vectors of student development, which he later revised (Chickering & Reisser, 1993). The first vector, developing competence, is relevant to understanding the needs of students with disabilities. Students deem themselves competent when they achieve their own aims and the expectations of educators (Evans, Forney, & Guido-DiBrito, 1998). For instance, if the mark of success on an exam is 100 percent, students who score 90 will likely deem themselves more competent than those who earn a 50.

For students, particularly those who have difficulty in learning or with mobility, developing competence is a critical issue. As previously mentioned, the term "disability" has negative connotations that judge students with disabilities as incapable persons. Therefore, students subject to this label have to overcome challenges to their capabilities within conventional learning environments. Educational contexts socialize students to value achievement primarily as reflected in test scores. It is important that educators work to broaden narrow conceptions of merit in order for students to demonstrate their proficiencies in multiple ways. Doing so can enable students with disabilities to develop healthy identities in the company of their peers without disabilities.

Integrating the Theories

When educators view disabilities as socially constructed, they challenge excessive individualism and examine the social context in which students with disabilities are situated. The social constructivist theory of disabilities necessitates that educators shift from a deficit-minded orientation of students with disabilities to a view of students as capable, and requires them to provide optimal levels of challenge and support to enable students with disabilities to develop their competencies. Educators who operate from a social constructivist theory capitalize on universal design because they understand that in order to maximize the learning outcomes of students with disabilities, they must familiarize themselves with students' needs and recognize the larger social relationships embedded within students' learning environments.

Engagement Strategies

Having discussed the issues faced by students with disabilities and theories to better understand their engagement challenges, we shift to proposing strategies to improve these students' academic and social engagement on campus. These strategies address the institutional, physical, and attitudinal obstacles that students with disabilities must overcome to achieve within postsecondary institutions.

Social Justice Workshops for Students by Students

Implement peer-facilitated social justice workshops for students. Social justice allies, or members from dominant groups who actively do their part to end oppressive practices (Broido, 2000), are useful for improving the academic and social experiences of students with disabilities. For this strategy to be meaningful, students both with and without disabilities must be involved in the process. Peer-facilitated sessions, which expose students to how the campus environment can be improved to meet the needs of students with disabilities, are a mechanism for these workshops. Because the sessions are peer-led, students are more likely to attend, in contrast to the typical situation in which students are expected to gain information from authority figures.

Orientations, Bridge Programs, and First-Year Programs

Develop specific programs, similar to those designed for racial/ethnic minority students, devoted to supporting students with disabilities before and during their first year at an institution. Specialized orientations and summer bridge programs will allow these students to become acquainted with the campus, meet important administrators and faculty, and familiarize themselves with the available resources. Providing these opportunities to students with disabilities can develop confidence within them and provide them with tools necessary for success. In addition to orientations and summer bridge programs, institutions should develop first-year programs designed to aid in the retention of students with disabilities by facilitating their transition from high school to their new institution. These programs are useful avenues for assisting students with problems they may encounter throughout their first year and helping them establish constructive study skills, productive routines, and healthy relationships. All three types of programs can remove some of the attitudinal and institutional barriers that prohibit the academic and social engagement of students with disabilities.

Assessment of Institutional Practices and the Physical Environment

Hire consultants to assess institutional practices and the physical environment. They will be able to determine if physical barriers exist that may inhibit the social and academic engagement of students with disabilities. After checking the accessibility and location of, for example, ramps, curb cuts, handrails, bathrooms, laboratories, and elevators, consultants will be able to provide written reports to administrators indicating what additions are needed and what facilities need improvement. Additionally, consultants can also suggest ways to make institutional practices more inclusive for students with disabilities. They can also facilitate focus group interviews with students with disabilities to learn about their experiences at the institution and what they need to enhance their engagement.

Student Mentoring Programs

Establish formal student-to-student mentoring programs and provide avenues for students with disabilities to initiate their own informal mentoring relationships. Formal mentoring relationships are spawned by programs that match mentors with mentees. This type of mentoring, if established before students arrive on campus, can provide new students with an immediate support system. Mentors can offer advice, talk about their own academic and social experiences, and introduce their mentees to other students, staff, and faculty. In the case of formal mentoring, matches should be based upon commonalities. Pairing students with disabilities and/or interests in common will more likely lead to positive relationships. On the other hand, informal mentoring relationships are established through direct outreach from a potential mentor or mentee. These types of relationships typically develop because of common interests or connections outside of the obvious commonality (e.g., disability, academic major, or race/ethnicity). Since students typically establish informal mentoring relationships themselves, they tend to be more productive and enduring. Throughout the academic year, student affairs educators should sponsor events and create opportunities for students to meet and interact. In the proper environment and with ample encouragement, informal mentoring relationships between students can develop. Both types of mentoring, formal and informal, should assist students in making social connections with and acquiring academic insight from their peers.

Offices for Students with Disabilities

As previously noted, offices that serve students with disabilities are usually understaffed and underfunded (Measel, 1999). In order to support these students, colleges and universities must make a concerted effort and investment into meeting their needs. For these offices to be successful, more than one or two full-time staff members must be employed. Moreover, adequate budgets must be set aside for these offices to operate. Institutions should reserve certain percentages of tuition to support programs, staff, and services that benefit these students. When feasible, offices should also consider hiring qualified graduate students from related disciples (e.g., higher education/student affairs, occupational therapy, and social work) as interns or graduate assistants. With proper financial support and sufficient staffing, offices for students with disabilities will be able to combat some of the institutional barriers facing students.

Assessment of Campus Climate and Current Programs

Assess the campus climate for students with disabilities. Various researchers have explored the impact of institutional climate on students' academic and social development, particularly among racial/ethnic minority students (Cabrera, Nora, Terenzini, Pascarella, & Hagedorn, 1999; Hurtado, 1992; Hurtado, Milem, Clayton-Pedersen, & Allen, 1999). Likewise, evaluating how campus climate affects students with disabilities is a prerequisite for gaining knowledge about the distinctive barriers that preclude their achievement. A welcoming campus climate will enable educators to develop myriad approaches for facilitating the success of students with disabilities and generating focused attention to their specific needs.

Research on Retention Rates of Students with Disabilities

Employ research on the attrition rate of students with disabilities. There is a lack of empirical and reliable data on the graduation rates of students with disabilities; the few data that exist report varied degrees of graduation rates. Therefore, it is important for institutions to effectively track the completion rates of students who declare their disabilities as a means of understanding the conditions that facilitate and hamper their abilities to persist and have value-added educational experiences. Studying students' attrition can also clarify other issues and challenges that students with disabilities face and will demonstrate to these students that the institution genuinely cares about their needs and is interested in effectively responding to them.

Educational Sessions for Faculty and Student Affairs Educators

Provide educational sessions for faculty members and student affairs educators to underscore the needs of students with disabilities. As outlined earlier in this chapter, this population often remains hidden on campuses, as the number of students with physical impairments is small and those with learning disabilities typically remain hidden. Therefore, there is a lack of knowledge about who these students are and about their unique needs, interests, and skills. Periodic sessions throughout the academic year in which faculty and student affairs educators can converse about students with disabilities and hear their stories will be vital to awareness and understanding. These sessions can be led by students with disabilities, who can share their experiences at the college or university, or can be facilitated by speakers who are knowledgeable about the conditions that impede the success of students with disabilities. Either way, participants will have opportunities to engage with each other, ask questions, and educate themselves about this population to challenge misconceptions and stereotypes.

Universal Design among Faculty

Utilize universal design in course planning. As noted earlier, universal design is a means for optimizing the needs of multiple students through flexibility and removal of barriers. Universal design is often perceived as solely beneficial to students with disabilities. However, the unique aspect of universal design is that it assists multiple persons. For instance, employing pedagogical techniques aimed at diverse learning styles enables students to achieve better outcomes. When educators gain a deeper understanding of universal design and consciously practice it in educational efforts, the campus becomes more welcoming to students with disabilities.

Interaction between Students with and without Disabilities

Facilitate numerous, sustained opportunities for students with disabilities to engage with other similar students within and outside of the classroom. Students often associate with those who share common experiences and interests. Though educators should encourage students to interact with those with different backgrounds and experiences, for students with disabilities this has likely been the norm throughout their upbringing and educational experiences. It is important that they are able to form relationships with other students with disabilities as a means of gaining a support group through which they can express their frustrations and develop concrete mechanisms for academically and socially achieving at the institution. This exposure can occur in residence halls, student organizations, courses, or other venues where students regularly congregate.

In addition, encourage interaction between students with disabilities and their peers without disabilities. When students have ample opportunities to interact with their peers from diverse backgrounds and vantage points, learning across differences is facilitated (Zúñiga, 2003). As discussed earlier in this chapter, many students who do not have disabilities develop myths and assumptions about their peers with disabilities. Providing structured opportunities for them to engage in dialogue, rather than expecting this to happen by chance, is one useful way to ensure that meaningful learning occurs.

Hiring Disabilities Specialists

Hire more educators who have specialized and thorough knowledge of research pertaining to students with disabilities. Many students with disabilities note a lack of preparedness and knowledge among tutors and faculty members regarding their needs. Just as institutions seek to hire the most qualified and knowledgeable scholars in their fields, they must recruit and target those persons who have an understanding of students with disabilities and how to improve their educational experiences. Doing so demonstrates to students that they matter and that their unique situations are worthy of consideration.

Campus Organizations for Students with Disabilities

Encourage the development of organizations for students with disabilities dedicated to fostering academic and social development. These organizations will provide students with a safe and welcoming environment conducive to open expression, a forum in which to discuss issues relevant to their needs, and an opportunity to deal with their personal experiences. These organizations can also function as avenues for advocacy and activism. Furthermore, student groups can serve as social outlets that present students with opportunities to interact, network, and establish meaningful relationships. These rare opportunities for underrepresented students to interact with students who share common needs are invaluable. These types of activities can transform attitudinal perspectives and stimulate social engagement.

Conclusion

The proposed interventions concretely address the institutional (e.g., assessment of campus climate and current programs), attitudinal (e.g., interactions between students with and without disabilities), and physical (e.g., assessment of institutional practices and the physical environment) barriers that preclude students with disabilities from academically and socially engaging at postsecondary institutions. As the quotes presented throughout this chapter illustrate, living with disabilities impedes the academic and social engagement of students. It is important for educators to gain more knowledge about these students so that they are no longer a forgotten minority group within higher education (Junco & Salter, 2004).

Academic and social disengagement stem from institutional, physical, and attitudinal barriers that often remain ignored or insufficiently addressed. Living with a learning or physical disability should not make students deem themselves less competent than their peers. Purposeful partnerships between students, student affairs educators, and faculty members with the goal of developing a complex understanding of the needs of students with disabilities and a willingness to address them is one useful way to foster campus environments that are more welcoming and engaging for these students.

References

Aksamit, D., Morris, M., & Leuenberger, J. (1987). Preparation of student services professionals and faculty for serving learning-disabled college students. *Journal of College Student Personnel, 28*, 53–59.

Americans with Disabilities Act of 1990 (1991), PL No. 101-336, 42 U.S.C., 12101–12132.

Aune, B. P., & Kroeger, S. A. (1997). Career development of college students with disabilities: An interactional approach to defining the issues. *Journal of College Student Development, 38*(4), 344–356.

Babbitt, C. E., Burbach, H. J., & Iutcovich, M. (1979). Physically handicapped college students: An exploratory study of stigma. *Journal of College Student Personnel, 20*(5), 403–407.

Baggett, D. (1994). *A study of faculty awareness of students with disabilities.* Paper presented at the annual meeting of the National Association for Developmental Education, Kansas City, MO. (ERIC Document Reproduction Service No. ED369208)

Barga, N. K. (1996). Students with learning disabilities in education: Managing a disability. *Journal of Learning Disabilities, 29*(4), 413–421.

Baxter Magolda, M. B. (2001). *Making their own way: Narratives for transforming higher education to promote self-development.* Sterling, VA: Stylus.

Belgrave, F. Z. (1985). Reactions to a black stimulus person under disabling and non-disabling conditions. *Journal of Rehabilitation, 51*, 53–57.

Belgrave, F. Z., & Mills, J. (1981). Effect upon desire for social interaction with physically disabled person of mentioning the disability in different contexts. *Journal of Applied Social Psychology, 11*(1), 44–57.

Broido, E. M. (2000). The development of social justice allies during college: A phenomenological investigation. *Journal of College Student Development, 41*(1), 3–18.

Bursuck, W. D., Rose, E., Cowen, S., & Yahaya, M. A. (1989). Nationwide survey of postsecondary education services for students with learning disabilities. *Exceptional Children, 56*(3), 236–245.

Cabrera, A. F., Nora, A., Terenzini, P. T., Pascarella, E., & Hagedorn, L. S. (1999). Campus racial climate and the adjustment of students: A comparison between White students and African-American students. *Journal of Higher Education, 70*(2), 134–160.

Chickering, A. W. (1969). *Education and identity.* San Francisco: Jossey-Bass.

Chickering, A. W., & Reisser, L. (1993). *Education and identity* (2nd ed.). San Francisco: Jossey-Bass.

Dudley-Marling, C. (2004). The social construction of learning disabilities. *Journal of Learning Disabilities, 37*(6), 482–489.

Durlak, C. M., Rose, E., & Bursuck, W. D. (1994). Preparing high school students with learning disabilities for the transition to postsecondary education: Teaching the skills of self-determination. *Journal of Learning Disabilities, 27*(1), 51–59.

Elacqua, T. C. (1996). *Perceptions of classroom accommodations among college students with disabilities.* (ERIC Document Reproduction Service No. ED400640)

English, K. M. (1993). *The role of support services in the integration and retention of college students who are hearing-impaired.* Unpublished doctoral dissertation, Claremont Graduate School, Claremont, CA, and San Diego State University, San Diego, CA.

Evans, N. J., Assadi, J. L., & Herriott, T. K. (2005). Encouraging the development of disability allies. In R. D. Reason, E. M. Broido, T. L. Davis, & N. J. Evans (Eds.), *Developing social justice allies. New Directions for Student Services* (No. 110, pp. 67–79). San Francisco: Jossey-Bass.

Evans, N. J., Forney, D. S., & Guido-DiBrito, F. (1998). *Student development in college: Theory, research, and practice.* San Francisco: Jossey-Bass.

Fichten, C. S., & Amsel, R. (1986). Trait attributions about college students with a physical disability: Circumplex analyses and methodological issues. *Journal of Applied Social Psychology, 16*(5), 410–427.

Fichten, C. S., Robillard, K., Judd, D., & Amsel, R. (1989). College students with physical disabilities: Myths and realitites. *Rehabilitation Psychology, 34,* 243–257.

Fichten, C. S., Robillard, K., Tagalakis, V., & Amsel, R. (1991). Casual interaction between college students with various disabilities and their nondisabled peers: The internal dialogue. *Rehabilitation Psychology, 36*(1), 3–20.

Fine, M., & Asch, A. (1988). Disability beyond stigma: Social interaction, discrimination, and activism. *Journal of Social Issues, 44*(1), 3–21.

Gething, L., & Wheeler, B. (1992). The interaction with disabled persons scale: A new Australian instrument to measure attitudes towards people with disabilities. *Australian Journal of Psychology, 44*(2), 75–82.

Greenbaum, B., Graham, S., & Scales, W. (1995). Adults with learning disabilities: Educational and social experiences during college. *Exceptional Children, 61*(5), 460–471.

Hahn, H. (1988). The politics of physical difference: Disability and discrimination. *Journal of Social Issues, 44*(1), 39–47.

Henderson, C. (2001). *College freshmen with disabilities: A biennial statistical profile.* Washington, DC: American Council on Education, HEATH Resource Center.

Hodges, J. S., & Keller, M. J. (1999). Perceived influences on social integration by students with physical disabilities. *Journal of College Student Development, 40*(6), 678–686.

Houck, C. K., Asselin, S. B., Troutman, G. C., & Arrington, J. M. (1992). Students with learning disabilities in the university environment: A study of faculty and student perceptions. *Journal of Learning Disabilities, 25*(10), 678–684.

Hurtado, S. (1992). The campus racial climate: Contexts of conflict. *Journal of Higher Education, 63*(5), 539–569.

Hurtado, S., Milem, J., Clayton-Pedersen, A., & Allen, W. (1999). *Enacting diverse learning environments: improving the climate for racial/ethnic diversity in higher education.* ASHE-ERIC Higher Education

Report (Vol. 26, No. 8). Washington, DC: The George Washington University, Graduate School of Education and Human Development.

Jones, S. R. (1996). Toward inclusive theory: Disability as social construction. *NASPA Journal, 33*, 347–354.

Jorgensen, S., Fichten, C. S., Havel, A., Lamb, D., James, C., & Barile, M. (2003). *Students with disabilities at Dawson College: Success and outcomes.* Montreal: Adaptech Research Network, Dawson College. (ERIC Document Reproduction Service No. ED481553)

Junco, R. & Salter, D. W. (2004). Improving the campus climate for students with disabilities through the use of online training. *NASPA Journal, 41*(2), 263–276.

Katz, I., Huss, R. G., & Bailey, J. (1998). Attitudinal ambivalence and behavior toward people with disabilities. In H. E. Yuker (Ed.), *Attitudes toward persons with disabilities* (pp. 47–57). New York: Springer.

Kelly, A. E., Sedlacek, W. E., & Scales, W. R. (1994). How college students with and without disabilities perceive themselves and each other. *Journal of Counseling and Development, 73*(2), 178–182.

Kinney, W., & Coyle, C. (1989). Predicting life satisfaction among adults with physical disabilities. *Archives of Physical Medicine and Rehabilitation, 73*, 863–869.

Kriegsman, K. H., & Hershenson, D. B. (1987). A comparison of able-bodied and disabled college student on Erickson's ego stages and Maslow's needs levels. *Journal of College Student Personnel, 28*, 48–52.

Kuh, G. D., Schuh, J. H., Whitt, E. J., & Associates. (1991). *Involving colleges: Successful approaches to fostering student learning and development outside the classroom.* San Francisco: Jossey-Bass.

Livneh, H. (1988). A dimensional perspective on the origin of negative attitudes toward persons with disabilities. In H. E. Yuker (Ed.), *Attitudes toward persons with disabilities* (pp. 35–46). New York: Springer.

Matthew, P., Anderson, D., & Skolnick, B. (1987). Faculty attitude toward accommodations for college students with learning disabilities. *Learning Disabilities Focus, 3*(1), 46–52.

McCune, P. (2001). What do disabilities have to do with diversity? *About Campus, 6*(2), 5–12.

Measel, D. (1999). *Big Ten survey data 1998–99.* Session presented at the annual meeting of the Association of Higher Education and Disability, Atlanta, GA.

Merchant, D. J., & Gajar, A. (1997). A review of the literature on self advocacy components in transition programs for students with learning disabilities. *Journal of Vocational Rehabilitation, 8*, 223–231.

Meyer, A., & Rose, D. H. (2000). Universal design for individual differences. *Educational Leadership, 58*(3), 39–43.

National Center for Education Statistics (NCES) (1999). *An institutional perspective on students with disabilities in postsecondary education.* Washington, DC: U.S. Government Printing Office.

National Center for Education Statistics (NCES) (2003). *The condition of education, 2003.* Washington, DC: U.S. Government Printing Office.

National Center for Education Statistics (NCES) (2004). *Digest of education statistics, 2004.* Washington, DC: U.S. Government Printing Office.

Nelson, J. R., Dodd, J. M., & Smith, D. J. (1990). Faculty willingness to accommodate students with learning disabilities: A comparison among academic divisions. *Journal of Learning Disabilities, 23*(3), 185–189.

Neubert, D. A., Moon, M. S., & Grigal, M. (2004). Activities of students with significant disabilities receiving services in postsecondary settings. *Education and Training in Development Disabilities, 39*(1), 16–25.

Nutter, K. J., & Ringgenberg, L. H. (1993). Creating positive outcomes for students with disabilities. In. S. Kroeger & J. Schuck (Eds.), *Responding to disability issues in student affairs. New Directions for Student Services* (No. 64, pp. 45–58). San Francisco: Jossey-Bass.

Palombi, B. J. (2000). Recruitment and admission of students with disabilities. In H. A. Belch (Ed.), *Serving students with disabilities. New Directions for Student Services* (No. 91, pp. 41–53). San Francisco: Jossey-Bass.

Paul, S. (2000). Students with disabilities in higher education: A review of the literature. *College Student Journal, 34*(2), 200–211.

Robillard, K., & Fichten, C. S. (1983). Attributions about sexuality and romantic involvement of physically disabled college students: An empirical study. *Sexuality and Disability, 6*(3–4), 197–212.

Rose, D., & Meyer, A. (2000). Universal design for learning. *Journal of Special Education, 15*(1). Retrieved August 13, 2005, from http://jset.unlv.edu/15.1/asseds/rose.html.

Satcher, J. (1992). Community college faculty comfort with providing accommodations for students with learning disabilities. *College Student Journal, 26*, 518–524.

Schuh, J. H., & Laverty, M. (1983). The perceived long term influence of holding a significant student leadership position. *Journal of College Student Personnel, 24*(1), 28–32.

Senge, J. C., & Dote-Kwan, J. (1995). Information accessibility in alternative formats in postsecondary education. *Journal of Visual Impairment and Blindness, 89*(2), 120–128.

Simmons, D. C., & Kameenui, E. J. (1996). A focus on curriculum design: When children fail. *Focus on Exceptional Children, 28*(7), 1–16.

Stage, F. K., & Milne, N. V. (1996). Invisible scholars: Students with learning disabilities. *Journal of Higher Education, 67*(4), 426–445.

Strange, C. C. (2000). Creating environments of ability. In H. A. Belch (Ed.), *Serving students with disabilities. New Directions for Student Services* (No. 91, pp. 31–39). San Francisco: Jossey-Bass.

Strange, C. C., & Banning, J. H. (2001). *Educating by design: Creating campus environments that work*. San Francisco: Jossey-Bass.

Sweener, K., Kundert, D., May, D., & Quinn, K. (2002). Comfort with accommodations at the community college level. *Journal of Developmental Education, 25*(3), 12–18.

Tagalakis, V., Amsel, R., & Fichten, C. S. (1988). Job interview strategies for people with a visible disability. *Journal of Applied Social Psychology, 18*(6), 520–532.

Thomas, S. B. (2000). College students and disability law. *Journal of Special Education, 33*(4), 248–257.

Vogel, S. A., & Adelman, P. B. (1992). The success of college students with learning disabilities: Factors related to educational attainment. *Journal of Learning Disabilities, 25*(7), 430–441.

Weinberg-Asher, N. (1976). The effects of physical disability on self-perception. *Rehabilitation Counseling Bulletin, 23*, 15–20.

West, M., Kregel, J., Getzel, E. E., Zhu, M., Ipsen, S. M., & Martin, E. D. (1993). Beyond Section 504: Satisfaction and empowerment of students with disabilities in higher education. *Exceptional Children, 59*(5), 456–467.

Zadra, P. D. (1982). *Special college support services and mobility-impaired college freshmen*. Unpublished doctoral dissertation, Columbia University, New York.

Zúñiga, X. (2003). Bridging differences through dialogue. *About Campus, 7*(6), 8–16.

Chapter 4
Fostering Safe, Engaging Campuses for Lesbian, Gay, Bisexual, Transgender, and Questioning Students

Leah A. Schueler, Jeffrey A. Hoffman, and Elizabeth Peterson

Ramon is a Latino gay student who is majoring in Theater and Visual Arts with an emphasis on Film and Media. Sharing his sexual identity with others has been a gradual process. He first told his best friend while in high school and waited a year later to tell another friend. His coming-out process led him to tell most of his friends prior to high school graduation. Upon entering college, he was openly gay to those he met. However, he has not disclosed his sexual identity to his family. He is waiting to inform them once he is involved in a serious relationship. Ramon has few people with whom to converse about the struggles he faces as a gay student and finds it difficult to relate to his heterosexual friends. He finds that few people at his institution are concerned about the needs of lesbian, gay, bisexual, transgender, and questioning (LGBTQ) students.

Dharshini is an African American bisexual woman attending college. Her friends and family have known her bisexual identity for almost five years. She sees heterosexism as a problematic issue on campus that few people confront. In addition, she finds it demeaning that the LGBTQ group on campus does not have its own location to meet. Dharshini believes that an office designated as a home for LGBTQ students will facilitate their academic and social success and provide a safe and visible physical space for LGBTQ students to meet on campus.

Joshua, a Caucasian man majoring in Biology, is a third-year undergraduate student. He has been openly gay since he began college. Joshua is constantly reminded of heterosexism on campus and in society. For example, on the artwork that adorns residence halls and classrooms, there are no images or words that acknowledge LGBTQ students' existence on campus. He describes dating as a challenge because of the limited number of LGBTQ students. He recognizes that there needs to be proactive measures that will enable him and his LGBTQ peers to feel accepted and noticed within the campus community.

Shelly moved from her home state to be with her same-sex partner during college. She finds this new environment not only heterosexist but also anti-LGBTQ students. She would marry her partner if it were legally recognized in the state in which they are both attending college. She also has experienced discrimination in the classroom. During her first year, she had a computer science professor who discussed his personal disagreement with and disdain for homosexuality openly in class. He stated that homosexual relationships were "unnatural" and "disgusting." She did not want to hear these kinds of opinions in the classroom. She was outraged and confronted him during class, but her challenge only strengthened his objections. Shelly recognizes that there are faculty and student affairs educators who support and accept LGBTQ students; however, these supportive people are largely outnumbered by those who are openly or subtly hostile toward the LGBTQ community.

Jocelyn, a Korean American student who identifies as a lesbian, is majoring in Urban and Environmental Policy. She publicly disclosed her sexual identity during her sophomore year. She wants her institution to create an anti-discrimination policy that includes LGBTQ students. She does not feel personally threatened because of her lesbian identity, but knows other students who do. She stresses that her college needs to be committed to social programming about the needs of LGBTQ students. Since there is no LGBTQ resource center on campus, she is considering transferring to a different institution that is more committed to improving the engagement of LGBTQ students.

Jerry is a gay man attending a Christian college. He does not consider this environment safe enough for him to share his sexual identity; consequently, he keeps it secret. Jerry knows that if he told a faculty or staff member, they would be required to report his sexual orientation to the chaplain. Most of the faculty members rarely challenge offensive language used by fellow students; many of Jerry's professors also use insensitive language in reference to LGBTQ people. Jerry suspects that there are some gay and lesbian faculty members and student affairs educators on campus and desperately wants them to come out and openly support LGBTQ students. No organization on campus exists for LGBTQ students; additionally, there is no education for members of the campus community on responding to the needs of LGBTQ students. After his first year, Jerry transfers to another institution that is more welcoming and supportive.

Although these are the personal stories of only six college students, their experiences validate the documented issues faced by many within this population during their college years. Students who identify as LGBTQ are confronted with a range of challenges that require varied approaches to improving their postsecondary experiences. Although it may be limiting to examine this population in the aggregate, it is possible to identify some of the shared experiences, issues, and struggles that impact their identity formation, personal development, and academic engagement. In this chapter, we first synthesize the issues and needs with which many LGBTQ college students contend. Following this discussion, we provide a theoretical framework for understanding these issues in the context of student development. We conclude the chapter with a wide range of practical strategies to support the personal and academic success of LGBTQ college students.

Synthesis of Needs and Issues

In order to understand the needs of LGBTQ students, one must situate their identity development within a heterosexist culture and a homophobic collegiate environment that marginalize sexual minority students (Engelken, 1998; Turrell & de St. Aubin, 1995). In examining this population's multifaceted profile, it is evident that some of their greatest struggles involve (1) invisibility, (2) multiple social identities, (3) homophobia, and (4) a dominant heteronormative culture.

Invisibility

A major obstacle to LGBTQ students developing a positive self-concept is that they continue to remain invisible (Turrell & de St. Aubin, 1995). As Sanlo, Rankin, and Schoenberg (2002) note, the lack of a presence of LGBTQ centers for students demonstrates their invisibility on most college and university campuses. This invisibility works detrimentally in two ways, of which the students in the introduction are aware: a lack of positive, visible role models among faculty, staff, and administrators (Sanlo, 1998; Yescavage & Alexander, 1997) and a lack of resources on campus (Rankin, 2003). Literature has shown that when students do not have role models with whom to identify, their engagement and persistence are adversely affected (Gándara & Mejorado, 2005; Grossman & Johnson, 1999). When programs and activities sponsored by the institution seem to be advertised for heterosexual students only, it sends a message that LGBTQ students and their needs and issues do not matter (Bourassa & Shipton, 1991). Invisibility reinforces the beliefs of LGBTQ students that those within society and on their own campuses wish for their continued marginality (Rhoads, 1994).

Multiple Social Identities

The influence of multiple identity dimensions (e.g., sexual orientation, religion, and race/ethnicity) and socially contextual influences (e.g., family background and life experiences) has recently begun to be researched with regard to LGBTQ students (Abes & Jones, 2004; Jones & McEwen, 2000). However, being open about one's LGBTQ identity may not be tolerated within one's family, religion, or culture. Lesbian, gay, bisexual, transgender, and questioning students of color experiencing the weight of this double oppression often feel the pressure to choose one identity over another depending on the social context of the setting (Green, 1998; Palma & Stanley, 2002). For LGBTQ women of color, they must attend to three social identities that historically have been oppressed—their gender, race, and sexual orientation (Ferguson & Howard-Hamilton, 2000). LGBTQ students of color feel the need to decide which part of their identity is most important (Wall & Evans, 1991). Furthermore, students of color experience an

LGBTQ community that is largely defined by the privileged majority-White culture (Dumas, 1998; Ferguson & Howard-Hamilton, 2000; Rankin, 2003). This means that those students who wish to associate themselves with other LGBTQ students often find that they are discriminated against in this community on the grounds of their racial/ethnic background (Rankin, 2003).

Homophobia

College and university campuses continue to be chilly climates at best and places of violence at worst for LGBTQ students (Draughn, Elkins, & Roy, 2002; Engstrom & Sedlacek, 1997; Rankin, 2003; Renn, 2000; Rhoads, 1995). The hatred aimed at LGBTQ people continues to be an allowable prejudice within the culture (Draughn et al., 2002). Crimes committed in 2002 because of bias against the victim's perceived sexual orientation represented 16.7 percent of reported hate-crime incidents (Federal Bureau of Investigation [FBI], 2003)—the highest level in the 12 years since the FBI had begun collecting these statistics. In 2003, the percentage of hate crimes based on sexual orientation had gone down only slightly to 16.4 percent (FBI, 2004). Hate crimes based on sexual orientation constituted the third-largest category reported and made up 13.9 percent of all reported hate crimes (FBI, 2002). Only crimes based on racial and religious prejudice were more prevalent than hate crimes based on sexual orientation. Hate crimes committed on educational campuses made up almost 10 percent of all hate crimes in 1998 (FBI, 1999). Eliason (1997) found that 43 percent of heterosexual college students believed that gay men were unacceptable and 38 percent thought that lesbians were also unacceptable. Eliason's research also measured and captured attitudes toward bisexual persons: heterosexual students were evenly divided in their attitudes toward acceptability of bisexual women (50 percent), but more strongly rated bisexual men as unacceptable (61 percent).

More subtle forms of homophobia continue to exist throughout college campuses. However, limited research has been conducted on the experiences of LGBTQ students inside the classroom (Connolly, 2000). Professors teach more than just the subject matter when they express their personal negative beliefs about homosexuality or fail to address the issue when appropriate (Renn, 1998). Lopez and Chism's research (as cited in Engstrom & Sedlacek, 1997) assessed the classroom experiences of gay and lesbian students. They found that these students tended to be fearful of retaliation, ill treatment, and lowered grading should they disclose their sexual identity to faculty. Furthermore, they were discouraged by homophobic remarks made by peers that went unchallenged by faculty. LGBTQ students also perceived that they received less consideration and support from professors than their heterosexual peers on academic and career matters (Nauta, Saucier, & Woodard, 2001). Consequently, opportunities for the consideration of LGBTQ perspectives were often suppressed or unacknowledged. In this hostile and unwelcoming environment, many LGBTQ students chose to keep their sexual identities hidden from faculty and peers in the classroom (Engstrom & Sedlacek, 1997).

Homophobia is a common problem within postsecondary institutions, but it is most rampant in men's and women's intercollegiate athletics (Baird, 2002; Greendorfer & Rubinson, 1997; Salkever & Worthington, 1998). Lesbian, gay, bisexual, transgender, and questioning students rarely find role models in peers or coaches, from whom they keep their sexual orientation secret out of fear of being considered "less than" by those peers and coaches (Salkever & Worthington, 1998). Women's sports are particularly targeted, with the assumption that if a woman plays sports, she must be a lesbian; also, parents are cautioned about rival college and university coaches and athletes being lesbians as a reason to attend one school over another (Krane & Barber, 2005).

Unfortunately, homophobia is not only a fear found within heterosexual society (Wall & Evans, 1991). Homophobia can manifest itself within the LGBTQ community. Having been socialized in a homophobic culture, LGBTQ students may find that they, too, have inherited internalized homophobic ideologies and may even actively engage in homophobic persecution and mistreatment—of themselves, others, or often both (Obear, 1991; Palma & Stanley, 2002). This internalized oppression can lead to emotions ranging from low self-esteem to self-hatred and often involves questioning one's self-worth (Rhoads, 1995; Wall & Evans, 1991). LGBTQ students can become so beleaguered by homophobic sentiments that they find it difficult to make sense of their own sexuality (Engelken, 1998). Green (1998) found that internal and external homophobia may hinder questioning students' self-understanding and meaning making by prohibiting full exploration of their sexual identity. Thus, they may never understand, accept, and appreciate their gay, lesbian, bisexual, or transgender identity.

Heteronormative Culture

Throughout society, most persons receive the message that heterosexuality is the "right," normal, and preferred sexual identity and that this identity is always based on one's gender, which is confirmed at birth (Green, 1998; O'Brien, 1998; Palma & Stanley, 2002). This normative assumption creates a dichotomous "either/or" distinction between heterosexuality and homosexuality. These assumptions, however, do not reflect or value the experience of LGBTQ students, who are considered deviant by heterosexual normative standards. Moreover, heterosexuality is consistently affirmed in society and campuses throughout the United States, through laws, policies, practices, the media (e.g., campus newspapers and television stations), and the acceptance of public displays of affection between males and females (O'Brien, 1998; Palma & Stanley, 2002).

Left searching for acceptance and affirmation, lesbian and gay students often find solace and comfort away from mainstream culture by creating their own subculture (e.g., in the arts, literature, music, bars, and restaurants). However, for bisexual students, no such opportunities exist (O'Brien, 1998). For example, most bars, social clubs, and institutions are predominantly either heterosexual or same-sex. No such venues exist for people wanting to meet others of both genders who have a shared bisexual identity. This lack of acknowledgment sometimes forces bisexual people to choose one identity or the other, either gay/lesbian or heterosexual (again, a dichotomy), and thus to deny a part of themselves (O'Brien, 1998).

Transgender students face their own distinct set of challenges with regard to adaptation in a heterosexual dominant culture. College, especially if one lives away from home, often provides transgender students their first opportunity to defy the gender identity and role assigned to them at birth. However, transgender students are also oppressed by a heteronormative culture found on college campuses. For instance, first-year residence halls are sometimes designated as "all-female" or "all-male" floors, with single-sex community bathrooms. For the transgender student, this "either/or" dichotomy poses a real problem, as the transgender student is neither female nor male as defined by dominant societal standards (O'Brien, 1998). Moreover, applications and forms predominantly used by colleges and universities often ask students to identify themselves as either male or female, without providing the opportunity to declare both genders or neither, or to decline to state at all. In developing their identity during their college years, transgender students are faced with living in an environment that does not acknowledge their existence (Green, 1998; O'Brien, 1998).

Theoretical Framework

The needs and issues of LGBTQ students necessitate the development and application of models and theories to guide student affairs educators, faculty members, and staff in their policies and practices. Programmatic efforts and support systems should be based not only on the college or university's understanding of LGBTQ students' experiences and challenges, but also on current research focusing on college student identity development.

Model of Multiple Dimensions of Identity

Jones and McEwen's (2000) Model of Multiple Dimensions of Identity suggests that students define their own core sense of self in the midst of contextual influences, such as family background and life experiences, and according to dimensions of identity such as race/ethnicity, religion, and sexual orientation. The model highlights the complexity and uniqueness of students' identity development, demonstrating how difference and privilege impact the influence of personal identity formation. In addition, the model explains that the salience of individual identity dimensions to the student is fluid and non-linear.

Jones and McEwen emphasize that no two students have the same developmental experience. They further develop the idea that sexual orientation and self-identification cannot be understood without consideration of other identities and the intersection of these identities with external or environmental influences. The model does not define a developmental process. Rather, it provides a snapshot of the influence of the multiple dimensions of identity on the development of LGBTQ students. It can help bring meaning to and understanding of developmental growth patterns and experiences.

Jones and McEwen's model can be used for helping LGBTQ students through their identity development. It emphasizes the importance of authentically listening to students to find out what is most central to their identities. Student affairs educators and faculty members are reminded to see students and their development in totality and to view students in terms of how they want to be viewed and understood. Students of color have may grapple with multiple dimensions of identity and its consequences, such as various levels of oppression as a racial/ethnic minority student, an LGBTQ student, or both. Students might also struggle with religious beliefs that are unsupportive of LGBTQ persons, which can bring even more complications into the picture. When students question their own sexual identity because of religious beliefs about the wrongness or unacceptability of homosexuality or bisexuality, a difficult identity formation process can result (Jones & McEwen, 2000). Therefore, when striving to improve the engagement and development of this population, it is important to understand how the various dimensions of students' identity intersect and to understand the challenges that ensue from this process.

Inclusive Model of Lesbian, Gay, and Bisexual Identity Development

Fassinger's (1998) Inclusive Model of Lesbian, Gay, and Bisexual Identity Development represents sexual identity development as more inclusive of demographics and cultural influences, is not monolithic in its understanding LGBTQ identity development, and is less reliant on identity disclosure as an indication of developmental maturation. The theory behind this model posits dual "processes of personal development of same-sex sexual orientation and redefinition of group membership and group meaning" (McCarn & Fassinger, 1996, p. 521). The first internal process is awareness and identification of a same-sex sexual orientation; the second process is group membership that results in a changed identity (Fassinger, 1998). Both individual and group processes involve navigation through the four phases of awareness, exploration, deepening/commitment, and internalization/synthesis. Individuals may be going through more than one of Fassinger's processes at any one time. For example, a person may be active in promoting gay rights (phase 3, group deepening/commitment) while simultaneously coming to a consciousness about feelings for a same-sex friend (phase 1, individual awareness).

Fassinger's model has significant implications for those wanting to support LGBTQ students on campus. A student's publicly sharing his or her sexual orientation can be an important starting point of the lesbian, gay, bisexual identity process, but not necessarily the indication that a stable, clear, and positive identity has already been formed. Listening to the concerns and struggles of students to understand them as individuals as well as members of a group is an indicator that one comprehends both the personal and community dynamics potentially impacting LGBTQ students' development. Last, a public declaration may not be a reasonable expectation for some students given pressure from environmental, social, and cultural influences. In order for some LGBTQ students to maintain close ties to certain valued groups in which homophobia is particularly entrenched, the decision not to disclose their sexuality is understandable (Fassinger, 1998).

Identity Development and Sexual Orientation Model

D'Augelli's (1994) Identity Development and Sexual Orientation Model for lesbian, gay, and bisexual students, formulated within a human development framework, suggests that identity is an evolving process whereby an individual engages in many social interactions during a sociohistorical period. Pivotal to this model is the impact of cultural and sociopolitical circumstances on the individual's experiences. Lesbian, gay, and bisexual students live in a heterosexist society that necessitates conformity to prescribed personal, interpersonal, and social customs (Palma & Stanley, 2002). The process of developing one's self as a lesbian, gay, or bisexual person entails the dual progressions of separating from a societally prescribed heterosexual identity and forming a new lesbian, gay, or bisexual identity (D'Augelli, 1994).

D'Augelli's model incorporates the variables of personal subjectivities and actions, interactive intimacies, and sociohistorical connections. These variables interact, creating six processes of lesbian/gay/bisexual development:

1 Exiting heterosexual identity. Acknowledging that one does not have heterosexual feelings, or that one's sexual feelings are not solely heterosexual, and beginning the process of telling others of one's sexual identity.

2 Developing a personal lesbian/gay/bisexual identity status. During this process, the person challenges stereotypes and assumptions about lesbian, gay, and bisexual people and develops ideas about what it means to be a non-heterosexual person.

3 Developing a lesbian/gay/bisexual social identity. Once the person decides that she or he is lesbian, gay, or bisexual, she or he creates a network of supportive people who accept the person's sexual identity.

4 Becoming a lesbian/gay/bisexual offspring. At this status, the person discloses her or his sexual orientation to guardians and begins to redefine the guardian–child relationship thereafter. This process can be particularly challenging for students in college who are still particularly dependent upon guardians financially and emotionally (Evans, Forney, & Guido-DiBrito, 1998).

5 Developing a lesbian/gay/bisexual intimacy status. Given the lack of role models for healthy intimate relationships among lesbian, gay, and bisexual persons within society, it can be difficult for students to enter this status of establishing a close, intimate relationship with another person who identifies as lesbian, gay, or bisexual.

6 Entering a lesbian/gay/bisexual community. When the student decides to enter this community, she or he makes a personal commitment to participating in political and social action to improve the conditions for lesbian, gay, and bisexual people.

Characteristics of this model support the proposition that students are unique in their development and that they change and develop over the course of the lifespan. This theory propounds a belief in the plasticity of sexual identity, in that it is fluid during some periods and more static during others. Furthermore, the theory suggests that lesbian, gay, and bisexual persons must figure out how to develop their identities in the midst of a heterosexist culture with few examples of positive identity formation (D'Augelli, 1994).

There are several implications for the use of this theory in creating safe, academic environments in which LGBTQ students can thrive. Collegiate faculty and student affairs educators need to listen more closely to students, as students untangle their identity beliefs from their individual experiences and personal qualities. It is also important to understand that the creation of a lesbian/gay/bisexual identity is commonly a prolonged and difficult process for most LGBTQ students. Educators must be ready to support these students as they come to understand the unfortunate reality that the common view held by society is that heterosexual identity is natural, as opposed to socially constructed, whereas homosexual identity and behavior are deviant (D'Augelli, 1994). D'Augelli also reminds educators to acknowledge that heterosexist privilege and homophobia exist.

Strategies for Fostering Environmental Inclusiveness

Specific and well planned strategies are needed to combat the oppressive forces of LGBTQ community invisibility, homophobia, and the heteronormative culture prevalent on college campuses. What follows are innovative approaches tailored toward the larger college and university campus, student affairs educators and faculty, and individual students. We stress that the combination of multiple strategies will facilitate the engagement and development of LGBTQ students.

Assessment of the Campus Climate

Assessment of classroom learning environments is critical for creating a safe and comfortable campus community for LGBTQ students. As indicated earlier in this chapter, the problem of homophobia and intolerance by faculty members inside the classroom and in advising settings is widespread. The usual heterosexist environment hinders the academic and career growth of LGBTQ students. Therefore, all departments, especially academic departments, should be evaluated to determine their effectiveness in meeting the needs of LGBTQ students and in fostering a welcoming climate. One evaluation could be used for all academic departments, but evaluations may need to be tailored to the needs of each non-academic department. Once data have been collected, the information should be published as a report submitted to the college or university president and provost. The president should then assemble a task force to educate the campus on the findings and to develop an action plan to make the necessary changes to improve the climate for LGBTQ students.

Partnerships for Research with Peer Institutions

Partnering with peer institutions can be an effective move to develop ways to best serve and support LGBTQ students. Partner institutions can engage in research on the campus climate to come up with concrete methods for addressing the needs of this student population. Partner institutions should share similarities among key variables such as institutional size, mission, and demographics to maximize the applicability of the research findings. Presidents of the participating colleges and universities must communicate the importance of the study before and after the assessment is conducted. Departments should partner with institutional researchers to develop a survey with a solid theoretical foundation to provide data that are credible, convincing, and can be used to effectively improve the campus learning environment for LGBTQ students.

Development of Scholarships

Special efforts to encourage academic achievement among LGBTQ students will enhance engagement among and within this community. Scholarships designated for LGBTQ students can be developed with at least one dedicated to a student from every academic department within the institution. These customized, department-specific scholarships will best support the needs of students in different disciplines, encourage LGBTQ scholarship and achievement broadly across the institution, and publicize the fact that there are LGBTQ students in every department and major (thereby dispelling the myth that LGBTQ students only major in certain stereotypical fields). To respect the developmental level and needs of students, the scholarship can be anonymously awarded if a student chooses this option. Funding for these scholarships can be obtained through identifying alumni with a commitment to LGBTQ students. The fund-raising campaign can be guided by the support of student, faculty, and staff liaisons from the LGBTQ campus community. Additionally, LGBTQ student scholarship could be fostered further through the creation of an LGBTQ-specific academic honors program.

Lavender/Rainbow Graduation Ceremonies

Institutions can offer LGBTQ students opportunities to celebrate their accomplishments by holding Lavender/Rainbow graduations to honor and acknowledge LGBTQ students. Many institutions hold Latino/a or African American graduations, but extending this idea to LGBTQ students would enable them to have a sense of pride and a time of celebration for having obtained their ultimate goal of receiving their diploma. Special care should be taken not to overlap these different ceremonies in case students want to be able to celebrate the different aspects of their identities. Lesbian, gay, bisexual, transgender, and questioning alumni and campus career center staff can be invited to encourage and inspire current and future graduates. Doing so can connect students with others beyond graduation, since they will seek employment that will offer a safe environment after graduation.

Identification of LGBTQ Role Models and Mentors

Because of the "invisible" nature of LGBTQ persons and the fear of some students, faculty, and student affairs educators to publicly disclose their sexual identity in what they perceive as a hostile environment, students have a limited pool of role models and mentors who understand and empathize with the experiences and struggles of LGBTQ students. Students would receive the greatest benefit and support in their identity development by having other self-identified LGBTQ faculty members or student affairs educators with whom they can comfortably develop meaningful, supportive relationships. Students would also benefit from mentor programs that matched upper-division undergraduate or graduate students with entering students. This peer-to-peer mentoring model may be less threatening and feel safer to some students. In either case, students will gain more confidence and build self-esteem through the formation of relationships with LGBTQ role models and mentors who have successfully navigated challenges and feelings of marginality to become successful in their careers.

Respecting Multiple Social Identities

LGBTQ students are not a monolithic group. LGBTQ students of color as well as international students have multiple identities. In many cases, students struggle to balance these identities, especially when they conflict. Lesbian, gay, bisexual, transgender, and questioning students have needs that are unique to their own various races/ethnicities, religious backgrounds, and cultures and may find better support among others with similar identities and experiences. It is important for colleges and universities to develop racial/ethnic-, religious-, and/or culture-specific support groups and services. For institutions with cultural centers or organizations, developing and hosting support groups and programs could be the responsibility of these already established entities along with the leadership of an LGBTQ cultural center coordinator or director. For example, if there is a Black Student Alliance on campus, this group could create a support group for African American LGBTQ students on campus. Many international students face challenging cultural barriers as LGBTQ-identified people. International centers should also develop programs for this population. Similarly, the LGBTQ center should be a place that constantly monitors itself to ensure that it is inclusive and is meeting the diverse needs of students. Some students will identify strongly by race/ethnicity and find an LGBTQ support group in a race/ethnicity-based cultural center helpful, whereas other students who identify more strongly with their sexual orientation might find a mixed group at the LGBTQ center more beneficial in meeting their needs.

Student Clubs and Organizations

We have previously mentioned that students can have a profound impact on shaping the behavior, attitudes, and values of their peers. Nowhere is this more evident than in clubs and organizations. At mid- to large-sized institutions, it is not uncommon for several hundred student clubs or organizations to be officially recognized. Many clubs and organizations regularly plan and carry out programs for students. Many student affairs educators also develop programs as a result of their functional or teaching responsibilities. Staff within student affairs should work with key student leaders, both LGBTQ students and their allies, to form programming and communication guidelines for student clubs, organizations, and campus departments that help foster and support an inclusive, non-heterosexist environment. These guidelines can then be used to train student leaders and staff with programming responsibilities to avoid holding events and activities that perpetuate homophobia and heterosexism. The training would include how to create positive brochures and recruitment materials that use inclusive images and language. For example, lectures or programs that address dating would acknowledge same-sex relationships and encourage the use of inclusive terms like "partner" or "spouse." This training should take place at the start of each academic year through an organization orientation program and can be facilitated by a team of students and staff or on a peer-to-peer basis. These guidelines should be integrated into all college or university print and electronic communications and made available year-round by including them online. The training materials can also be made available on a student life website and a brochure or packet through the student life office.

Support and Advocacy Centers

One of the most significant steps that a campus can take in providing the support needed by LGBTQ students is establishing an LGBTQ support and advocacy center staffed by a full-time director or coordinator. Although there are some examples of campuses where such centers exist, few colleges and universities have them. A support and advocacy center provides the visibility necessary for LGBTQ students' needs and voices to be heard and sends the message to students that they matter. An LGBTQ center can also offer the resources necessary to create a positive campus climate for this population. The center's staff can take the lead in providing web resources that are accessible. Web resources are important because they provide anonymous and confidential access for students as well as enable faculty and staff to receive information that they may not be comfortable acquiring by visiting the center itself. Web resources should include information on support services that are available both on and off campus. The LGBTQ center should partner with the counseling center, cultural centers, residence life, and other campus entities to make sure that resources are shared between these different offices. It is also important for campuses to develop social programming opportunities for LGBTQ students if they are not already doing so. These may include an academic year opening mixer between LGBTQ faculty, staff, administrators, and allies. Although it should be the responsibility of all programming entities on campus to provide diverse and inclusive events and activities, the LGBTQ center must ensure that it is meeting the needs of this population.

Language on Applications and Forms

Gender identity is particularly critical for transgender students because they compose a population that is often overlooked. Transgender students can get their first impression of how open the campus will be when they complete a form to apply for admission to the college or university. In order to foster a more inclusive environment for transgender students, all applications and forms should present an opportunity to write one's gender rather than only providing check boxes for male and female.

Gender-Neutrality in Living Spaces

Gender-neutral bathrooms should also be established on various sectors of campus, especially community gathering spaces such as the student union. Once bathrooms are determined, create a campus map of where to find them. In addition, residence life departments could create gender-neutral floors or a living/learning (group-living) community for LGBTQ students to support their needs. Doing so may alleviate anxieties for some LGBTQ students who feel uncomfortable living with a roommate who may be homophobic. Support mechanisms should also be put in place through this living/learning community. For example, resident assistants who are placed in residence halls but assigned to support LGBTQ students in the living/learning community can plan specific programs for the population in the residence hall in concert with the LGBTQ center.

Guardian Sessions during Orientation

During orientation, there should be a break-out session on resources available for guardians of LGBTQ students. Since a good number of guardians have an LGBTQ child who may or may not have come out to them, it is important for the college to offer support, education, and care to guardians through sharing resources on where to get support and how to be supportive of their child. This information could also be included on the website of the LGBTQ center.

Training and Development of Student Leaders

Training and developing student leaders are critical functions of student affairs educators and faculty in creating a positive campus environment. Student leaders have a profound influence on the behaviors, values, and attitudes of their peers. Students who learn to be effective, ethical, and compassionate leaders can influence their peers positively by modeling behaviors that demonstrate acceptance and inclusion of LGBTQ students. Therefore, it is important that educators offer training or orientation sessions that teach student leaders how to create, support, and sustain a campus climate that is welcoming of students regardless of their sexual orientation or gender identity. These training workshops should incorporate inclusive language and could develop a non-discrimination policy for clubs and organizations (a template could be created for use by any group) while teaching aspects of LGBTQ student culture, ethical leadership, and how to create and promote non-heterosexist programs, identify and combat homophobia, be an effective ally, and challenge hate and intolerance among faculty and staff members.

Safe Zone Programs

Colleges and universities must develop, support, and sustain learning environments that are safe and inclusive. Following the lead of some proactive colleges and universities across the country, campuses should create Safe Zone programs that include education on being an effective and visible ally to LGBTQ students and creating inclusive physical environments. The Safe Zone program creates a visible support system for students by offering symbols in the form of stickers and posters that indicate spaces on campus dedicated to providing a safe and accepting place for students, especially the invisible LGBTQ student community. For this program to be successful and to maximize impact, effective efforts must be undertaken to involve members from all sectors of the campus. Institutions should form an organizing or steering committee that includes representatives from every division at the college or university—administrators, student affairs educators, faculty, staff, students, alumni, and other community stakeholders. Employ the services of the institution's marketing or public relations office to develop a campus-wide educational plan so that students see large-scale and broad-based commitment from the institution. This campaign will increase the number of allies, assist in building a culture that values the contributions and dignity of every student, and provide a safer learning environment for LGBTQ students. Ideally, this program should be offered to all students, faculty, staff, and administrators so that they can gain a shared understanding of inclusive language and the issues faced by LGBTQ students. Incentives may be offered to student groups who make concerted efforts to engage in this sort of campaign. For those who may be interested in training their colleagues or peers, train-the-trainer programs can be developed to utilize trained staff in facilitating sessions for other members of the campus community.

Strategic Planning

Institutions of higher education should engage in developing a college- or university-wide "Stop the Silence Strategic Plan." The strategic plan will recognize the importance of creating an environment where students feel safe coming out if they choose to and will receive support and acceptance from campus members. The purpose of this plan will be to change the campus climate in order for students to comfortably and publicly self-identify as an LGBTQ student. The plan should acknowledge practical objectives and strategies that will create immediate as well as lasting structural and institutional change. Plan outcomes should address the specific and unique needs of LGBTQ students such as the financial assistance necessary for some LGBTQ students, since some LGBTQ students who come out will no longer receive financial support from their guardians. When these students face this challenge, it is important that the financial aid office or other relevant departments on campus understand and accommodate wherever possible. The financial aid office can play a pivotal role in painlessly converting these students to independent status.

Speakers Panel

Since LGBTQ students' issues are often overlooked, colleges and universities should foster an open environment for the discussion of sexual orientation issues by developing and supporting a speakers panel that includes LGBTQ student affairs educators, faculty, staff, and students. High-level LGBTQ and ally administrators and respected faculty members should be recruited and invited to participate as panel members. The speakers panel will be promoted as a safe and honest way to discuss issues of sexual orientation. When LGBTQ students hear the experiences of their peers, faculty members, student affairs educators, and allies, they will have role models with whom to connect as they navigate the campus environment.

Hiring of Multiculturally Competent Student Staff Members

For student staff positions that require frequent contact with new students, guardians, visitors, and alumni, colleges and universities should hire students that demonstrate multicultural competence and a respect for diversity. Tour guides, resident assistants, and orientation leaders are examples of student positions that have substantial influence on communicating the values of the institution. By stressing institutional values of respect for and acceptance of difference, students in these positions can have an influential role in creating an inclusive environment.

Academic Advisor Training

Greater support should be offered for LGBTQ students at the college or academic department level by training academic advisors (faculty and non-faculty) on the issues and challenges that this population might experience. Academic advisors should be aware of the language they use and how this affects students. For example, when preparing an exercise for class, care should be given to ask about a "partner" rather than a "boyfriend" or "girlfriend." Similar to the case of student staff members, it is important that only people who understand the needs of LGBTQ students and are committed to creating safe environments for learning are hired.

Conclusion

"Despite their valiant efforts in the midst of educational neglect, LGB[TQ] students may struggle in their development of an authentic sense of identity and experience difficulty succeeding academically" (Connolly, 2000, p. 125). For those of us in higher education, it is our obligation and privilege to serve students, particularly those who are disengaged because of campus environments that are unresponsive to their needs. We must create and sustain safe and supportive campuses where LGBTQ students can be engaged and achieve academic and social success.

At the outset of this chapter, we presented vignettes of LGBTQ students who struggled to disclose their sexual identity to guardians, faculty members, and their peers, experienced hostile and antagonistic campus environments, and had virtually no mentors and role models with whom to connect on campus. Imagine what a campus might look like if some of the strategies proposed here were implemented. Michael is a gay high school senior trying to decide which college to attend. As he looks at the website for Ideal University, he notices that the mission statement and non-discrimination policies include sexual orientation and gender identity. He decides to apply, and when he completes the application materials, he can indicate his gender, rather than checking a box, and his sexual orientation. Given the demographic information provided on his application, upon being offered admission to Ideal University, Michael receives a phone call from a faculty member who identifies as a lesbian. She asks Michael questions about what he wants in a college and listens to his needs as an incoming student. She also tells Michael of the various programs that Ideal University makes available for LGBTQ students.

When deciding where to live on campus, he finds that there is a living/learning community in which students explore sexual orientation and gender identity issues. When Michael comes to campus for orientation, he learns about the LGBTQ center on campus. The center is offering many different activities; staff members from the center have come to his residence hall to share what they have to offer at the center. This is helpful for him since he was apprehensive of people seeing him walk into the LGBTQ center, out of fear that he might be targeted on campus. Michael gets involved with the mentoring project on campus and meets a junior student who is able to serve as a role model. She is especially helpful in enabling Michael to share his sexual identity with his peers and faculty members. He appreciates having someone that understands the issues he is experiencing. As a second-year student, Michael decides to help with the scholarship program for LGBTQ students who may need this support. Because of how his university supported his identity development, he is competent and confident to be a role model for other LGBTQ students.

Unfortunately, many LGBTQ students are not enrolled at institutions like Ideal University. Instead, they strive to succeed within homophobic environments that silence their voices and identities. As we have suggested throughout this chapter, it is important to challenge assumptions about heterosexuality as the standard to which other groups are subjected. The issues faced by LGBTQ students are complex and require approaches that do not treat these students as a monolithic group. Although they share common challenges, it is important to speak with students directly to understand how to address their individual and collective needs. Doing so will push us closer toward developing healthy campus environments in which LGBTQ students are visible and engaged.

References

Abes, E. S., & Jones, S. R. (2004). Meaning-making capacity and the dynamics of lesbian college students' multiple dimensions of identity. *Journal of College Student Development, 45*(6), 612–632.

Baird, J. A. (2002). Playing it straight: An analysis of current legal protections to combat homophobia and sexual orientation discrimination in intercollegiate athletics. *Berkeley Women's Law Journal, 17,* 31–67.

Bourassa, D., & Shipton, B. (1991). Addressing lesbian and gay issues in residence hall environments. In N. J. Evans & V. A. Wall (Eds.), *Beyond tolerance: Gays, lesbians, and bisexuals on campus* (pp. 79–96). Lanham, MD: University Press of America.

Connolly, M. (2000). Issues for lesbian, gay, and bisexual students in traditional college classrooms. In V. A. Wall & N. J. Evans (Eds.), *Toward acceptance: Sexual orientation issues on campus* (pp. 109–130). Lanham, MD: University Press of America.

D'Augelli, A. R. (1994). Identity development and sexual orientation: Toward a model of lesbian, gay, and bisexual development. In E. J. Trickett, R. Watts, & D. Birman (Eds.), *Human Diversity: Perspectives on people in context* (pp. 312–333). San Francisco: Jossey-Bass.

Draughn, T., Elkins, B., & Roy, R. (2002). Allies in the struggle: Eradicating homophobia and heterosexism on campus. *Journal of Lesbian Studies, 6*(3/4), 9–20.

Dumas, M. J. (1998). Coming out/coming home: Black gay men on campus. In R. L. Sanlo (Ed.), *Working with lesbian, gay, bisexual, and transgender college students: A handbook for faculty and administrators* (pp. 79–86). Westport, CT: Greenwood Press.

Eliason, M. J. (1997). The prevalence and nature of biphobia in heterosexual undergraduate students. *Archives of Sexual Behavior, 26*(3), 317–326.

Engelken, L. C. (1998). Making meaning: Providing tools for an integrated identity. In R. L. Sanlo (Ed.), *Working with lesbian, gay, bisexual, and transgender college students: A handbook for faculty and administrators* (pp. 23–30). Westport, CT: Greenwood Press.

Engstrom, C. M., & Sedlacek, W. (1997). Attitudes of heterosexual students toward their gay male and lesbian peers. *Journal of College Student Development, 38*(6), 565–576.

Evans, N. J., Forney, D. S., & Guido-DiBrito, F. (1998). *Student development in college: Theory, research, and practice.* San Francisco: Jossey-Bass.

Fassinger, R. E. (1998). Lesbian, gay, and bisexual identity and student development theory. In R. L. Sanlo (Ed.), *Working with lesbian, gay, bisexual, and transgender college students: A handbook for faculty and administrators* (pp. 13–22). Westport, CT: Greenwood Press.

Federal Bureau of Investigation (FBI) (1999). *Hate crime statistics 1998*. Washington, DC: Author.

Federal Bureau of Investigation (FBI) (2002). *Hate crime statistics 2001*. Washington, DC: Author.

Federal Bureau of Investigation (FBI) (2003). *Hate crime statistics 2002*. Washington, DC: Author.

Federal Bureau of Investigation (FBI) (2004). *Hate crime statistics 2003*. Washington, DC: Author.

Ferguson, A. D., & Howard-Hamilton, M. F. (2000). Addressing issues of multiple identities for women of color on college campuses. In V. A. Wall & N. J. Evans (Eds.), *Toward acceptance: Sexual orientation issues on campus* (pp. 283–298). Lanham, MD: University Press of America.

Gándara, P., & Mejorado, M. (2005). Putting your money where your mouth is: Mentoring as a strategy to increase access to higher education. In W. G. Tierney, Z. B. Corwin, & J. E. Colyar (Eds.), *Preparing for college: Nine elements of effective outreach* (pp. 89–110). Albany, NY: SUNY Press.

Green, B. C. (1998). Thinking about students who do not identify as gay, lesbian, or bisexual but . . . *Journal of American College Health, 47*(2), 89–91.

Greendorfer, S. L., & Rubinson, L. (1997). Homophobia and heterosexism in women's sport and physical education. *Women in Sport & Physical Activity Journal, 6*(2), 189–212.

Grossman, J. B., & Johnson, A. (1999). Assessing the effectiveness of mentoring programs. In J. B. Grossman (Ed.), *Contemporary issues in mentoring*. Philadelphia, PA: Public/Private Ventures.

Jones, S. R., & McEwen, M. K. (2000). A conceptual model of multiple dimensions of identity. *Journal of College Student Development, 41*(4), 405–414.

Krane, V., & Barber, H. (2005). Identity tensions in lesbian intercollegiate coaches. *Research Quarterly for Exercise and Sport, 76*(1), 67–81.

McCarn, S. R., & Fassinger, R. E. (1996). Revisioning sexual minority identity formation: A new model of lesbian identity and its implications for counseling and research. *Counseling Psychologist, 24*(3), 508–534.

Nauta, M. M., Saucier, A. M., & Woodard, L. E. (2001). Interpersonal influences on students' academic and career decisions: The impact of sexual orientation. *Career Development Quarterly, 49*(4), 352–373.

Obear, K. (1991). Homophobia. In N. J. Evans & V. A. Wall (Eds.), *Beyond tolerance: Gays, lesbians, and bisexuals on campus* (pp. 39–66). Lanham, MD: University Press of America.

O'Brien, K. M. (1998). The people in between: Understanding the needs of bisexual students. In R. L. Sanlo (Ed.), *Working with lesbian, gay, bisexual, and transgender college students: A handbook for faculty and administrators* (pp. 31–36). Westport, CT: Greenwood Press.

Palma, T. V., & Stanley, J. L. (2002). Effective counseling with lesbian, gay, and bisexual clients. *Journal of College Counseling, 5*(1), 74–89.

Rankin, S. R. (2003). *Campus climate for gay, lesbian, bisexual, and transgender people: A national perspective*. New York: National Gay and Lesbian Task Force Policy Institute.

Renn, K. A. (1998). Lesbian, gay, bisexual, and transgender students in the college classroom. In R. L. Sanlo (Ed.) *Working with lesbian, gay, bisexual, and transgender college students: A handbook for faculty and administrators* (pp. 231–238). Westport, CT: Greenwood Press.

Renn, K. A. (2000). Including all voices in the classroom: Teaching, lesbian, gay, and bisexual students. *College Teaching, 48*(4), 129–135.

Rhoads, R. A. (1994). *Coming out in college: The struggle for a queer identity*. Westport, CT: Greenwood Press.

Rhoads, R. A. (1995). Learning from the coming-out experience of college males. *Journal of College Student Development, 36*(1), 67–74.

Salkever, K., & Worthington, R. L. (1998). Creating safe space in college athletics. In R. L. Sanlo (Ed.), *Working with lesbian, gay, bisexual, and transgender college students: A handbook for faculty and administrators* (pp. 193–202). Westport, CT: Greenwood Press.

Sanlo, R. L. (Ed.) (1998). *Working with lesbian, gay, bisexual, and transgender college students: A handbook for faculty and administrators*. Westport, CT: Greenwood Press.

Sanlo, R. L., Rankin, S., & Schoenberg, R. (Eds.) (2002). *Our place on campus: Lesbian, gay, bisexual, transgender services and programs in higher education*. Westport, CT: Greenwood Press.

Turrell, S. C., & de St. Aubin, T. (1995). A relationship-focused group for lesbian college students. *Journal of Gay & Lesbian Psychotherapy, 2*(3), 67–84.

Wall, V. A., & Evans, N. J. (1991). Using psychosocial development theories to understand and work with gay and lesbian persons. In N. J. Evans & V. A. Wall (Eds.), *Beyond tolerance: Gays, lesbians, and bisexuals on campus* (pp. 25–38). Lanham, MD: University Press of America.

Yescavage, K., & Alexander, J. (1997). The pedagogy of marking: Addressing sexual orientation in the classroom. *Feminist Teacher, 11*(2), 113–122.

Chapter 5

Creating Welcoming Campus Environments for Students from Minority Religious Groups

Caitlin J. Mahaffey and Scott A. Smith

Esther and Vince are members of minority religious groups who experience college differently than their non-religious and Christian peers. They often feel unwanted and unwelcome, as the atmosphere of campus life comes into conflict with their religious identities. On several instances, they have pondered leaving their institution, but instead decided to seek opportunities to educate their peers about their religious practices. Despite their efforts, they continue to experience difficulties with which students from dominant religious groups (e.g., Christians) do not contend.

Esther and Vince regularly enter campus dining facilities and are unable to eat any of the food that their peers enjoy. Vince is Muslim and Esther is Jewish, and they find that their dining halls offer few halal or kosher meal options and that those options are often unappetizing. They routinely forgo eating with their peers in favor of preparing their own food, even though, as first-year students, they are required to purchase a campus meal plan. When they approach dining services staff to ask for accommodations, they are told that costs prohibit offering meals that cater to everyone's individual needs.

Given Vince's appearance, since the September 11, 2001, terrorist attacks, he reports that he has been the object of negative stereotyping on campus by his peers and professors. He has received suspicious glances and verbal threats, and experienced vandalism of his books, clothes, and the door of his residence hall room. Thoughtless comments and unchallenged stereotypes undermine Vince's sense of community and safety. He does not feel comfortable on campus and chooses to withdraw from social and academic activities in order to avoid conflict.

In their residence halls, Vince and Esther often report feeling marginalized by student-initiated norms that place an emphasis on alcohol consumption and themed parties on weekends. One of these parties, with the theme of "Fighting Terrorism in Iraq," included White students wearing turbans and holding toy machine guns. Not only do Esther and Vince deal with stereotypical portrayals, they also have difficulty finding alcohol-free social activities, even within their residence halls. Vince believes that it is a religious obligation to leave any room where alcohol is being consumed. He finds it difficult, however, to confront his peers when they are drinking in close proximity, and is often frustrated by poorly enforced alcohol policies.

In order to educate their peers about their religions, Esther and Vince invite them to reflect on the ways in which they are privileged. For instance, they ask their peers to consider being required to take an examination on Thanksgiving or Christmas, feeling embarrassed to ask for an alternative test date, and dealing with professors who do not understand the importance of the holiday. On many campuses, students from non-Christian religions, such as Vince and Esther, face a similar dilemma on significant religious holidays. Even when Vince and Esther are able to attend classes on Muslim and Jewish holidays, they participate in fasts, which makes it difficult to concentrate during long class periods. Some of their professors do offer accommodations such as rescheduling, but Esther and Vince fear the impact that these requests may have on their academic progress.

Given their underrepresentation on campus, Esther, Vince, and other students from various minority religious groups face struggles that their Christian and non-religious peers do not. Even some student affairs educators working in campus offices devoted to diversity issues do not consider the ways in which Esther and Vince are marginalized because of their participation in minority religious groups. This marginalization impacts their identity development, engagement, and willingness to participate in academic and social activities with their peers. In this chapter, we provide an overview of issues faced by students from minority religious groups. We explore the historical roots of present issues and the current climate for religious minority students on various campuses. We ground the chapter in relevant theories that further enable an understanding of the issues students face because of their minority religious status. Finally, we introduce concrete suggestions for creating a welcoming and supportive campus environment for these students. Before delving into the unique challenges with which students from religious minority groups contend, it is important to understand historical influences that have led to the marginalization of these students in higher education. We then use this history to describe the current campus climate for religious minority students and the needs of this particular population.

Historical Context

American higher education has roots in Christian religious institutions, though several historical factors have contributed to a strongly secular (and sometimes even anti-religious) atmosphere at many institutions of higher education. The Christian origins of some institutions, the secular origins of others, and the prevailing secular atmosphere in American higher education contribute to the challenges that students from minority religious groups face on American campuses (Geiger, 1999).

The first American colleges were founded largely for the purpose of educating clergy to serve Puritan colonists (Geiger, 1999). For example, the stated mission of Harvard University, the first institution of American higher education, was "to advance learning and perpetuate it to Posterity; dreading to leave an illiterate Ministry to the Churches, when our present Ministers shall lie in the Dust" (Kohlbrenner, 1961, p. 45). American institutions of higher education continued to have religious orientations until the mid-nineteenth century, and until this time, most institutions employed clergymen as presidents and professors and required Bible study and daily chapel attendance by students (Kohlbrenner, 1961; Rudolph, 1990).

The process of secularization differed across institutions, but several factors affected colleges and universities across the country. For example, the Morrill Land Grant Act of 1862 allowed for the founding of many state schools and made secular higher education widely available in America for the first time (Rudolph, 1990). The influx of German-trained professors encouraged secularization even in religiously founded institutions, as the ideal of *Lernfreiheit* (academic freedom) prompted students and professors alike to generate new knowledge rather than simply disseminate old values, many of which came out of religious traditions (Kohlbrenner, 1961). Also, many institutions removed their formal ties to the denominations that founded them after 1905, when the Carnegie Foundation established a pension plan for professors specifying that the pension was for the exclusive use of non-denominational schools (Kohlbrenner, 1961).

Most institutions of higher education continued to become increasingly secular throughout the twentieth century. This was owing in part to the strengthening influence that science had on the objectivism of academic culture (Eisenmann, 1999). Secularization was also influenced by a number of shifts away from organized religion in the culture at large, including the "modernist despair" of the post-World War I era, the anti-establishment movements of the 1960s and 1970s, and the materialism of the 1980s (Eisenmann, 1999; Jablonski, 2001). Many constituents at institutions also became uncomfortable with addressing religion on campus because they feared that they might alienate members of their increasingly diverse student bodies or violate students' Constitutional rights (R. T. Clark, 2003; Jablonski, 2001).

Contemporary Climate

Though religion is still a taboo subject on many campuses, student affairs educators have begun to reexamine the role of religion during the last decade (Jablonski, 2001). Beginning in the 1990s, many student affairs professionals began to see policies that ignored or isolated religious issues as inadequate in light of increased student interest in religion (Jablonski, 2001). Spirituality also became a subject of interest in the larger culture, and student affairs educators borrowed ideas from fields such as organizational theory to develop programs to meet the spiritual needs of students (Allen & Kellom, 2001; Manning, 2001).

Astin and Astin (2003) found that religion would continue to be an increasingly important issue for colleges and universities to address. Their survey of 112,242 students at 236 colleges and universities across the nation showed that 80 percent of participants had an interest in religion, 81 percent attended religious services occasionally or frequently, and 48 percent believed that it was "essential" or "very important" that colleges encourage personal expression of religion. With the increased attention to issues of religion on campus, the time is ripe for student affairs professionals to focus on the experiences of students from religious minority groups. Three factors in the climate of higher education and the nation at large make it imperative for these students' needs to be examined and addressed.

The first of these factors is increased religious diversity in American student populations. In the past, students were largely assumed to be either Christian or non-religious. However, Astin and Astin (2003) found that 8 percent of the surveyed students identified themselves as Jewish, Buddhist, Hindu, Islamic, or a member of another non-Christian religion. In a similar study, Schlosser and Sedlacek (2001) found that 20 percent of students enrolled at a large, public university identified as Buddhist, Hindu, Muslim, or Jewish. Student affairs educators may also work with students who identify as Bahá'í, Jain, Pagan, Wiccan, or members of other religious groups.

The high profile of religion in American politics and culture is another important factor for student affairs professionals to consider. The terrorist attacks of September 11, 2001, were a turning point for discussions of religion in the United States (Machacek, 2003; Peek, 2003). Media outlets and politicians on the national stage framed both the terrorist attacks and the U.S. military response in terms of religion. This helped fuel hostility toward Muslims, Sikhs, and other people portrayed or perceived as potential terrorists (Peek, 2003). Though some Muslim students reported that their colleges and universities were supportive of them in the wake of the terrorist attacks, they did experience intense scrutiny, negative comments, and even violence in the larger community (Peek, 2003). In some instances, community organizations and the media made a special effort to educate non-Muslims about Islam in an effort to combat this kind of discrimination, and these efforts initiated an ongoing national dialogue about religious differences (Machacek, 2003; Peek, 2003).

Last, student affairs educators have recognized that issues of privilege and oppression based on race/ethnicity, gender, and sexual orientation cannot be addressed apart from religion (R. T. Clark, 2003). Religious beliefs and religious identities often interact with racial/ethnic, gender, and sexual identities in complex ways, and ignoring religion is simply no longer an option for professionals who work to ensure that students are not oppressed or marginalized on campus based on their personal identities (R. T. Clark, 2003).

Issues Facing Students from Minority Religious Groups

Although some student affairs educators have begun to address religion on their campuses, most of the current work in the field still looks at religion as a whole, rather than at specific issues faced by students from minority religious groups. These students face a host of issues that their Christian (and non-religious) counterparts do not. In this section, we focus on five key challenges with which these students contend: (1) isolation, (2) dietary restrictions, (3) religious holidays, (4) campus spaces, and (5) identity development.

Isolation

In a qualitative study of Muslim women and veiling before September 11, 2001, Muslim women who chose to veil on a large, Midwestern university campus reported that students, faculty, and staff often reacted to them with fear and suspicion (Cole & Ahmadi, 2003). As a result, these women felt isolated and often chose not to participate in university-sponsored activities. As Astin (1993) and Kuh (1995) have shown, when students are engaged in educationally purposeful activities, they are more likely to persist toward degree attainment and gain more from college. Consequently, the feelings of isolation among Muslim women negatively impact their engagement and persistence (Cole & Ahmadi, 2003). The cultural climate and world events following the terrorist attacks of September 11, 2001, deepened the fear and isolation felt by some Muslim students (Peek, 2003). As Abu El-Haj (2002) found, shortly after the attacks, Muslim and Arab students found themselves targeted on college and university campuses and often felt alone and unsafe at their institutions.

Dietary Restrictions

At many higher education institutions, students with religious dietary restrictions must eat at home or limit themselves to unappetizing, prepackaged meals (Farmer, 2001; Rifkin, 2003). At the University of Pittsburgh and Carnegie Mellon University, for example, the options for kosher dining are so limited that some Jewish prospective students have chosen other universities based strictly on their inability to eat at the two Pittsburgh schools (Rifkin, 2003). College is a time when incoming students seek to find groups to join and develop mature relationships with their peers (Chickering & Reisser, 1993). For many students, this may mean building connections with peers who share similar beliefs and values. For students with religious dietary needs, feelings of isolation can be exacerbated by peers who do not understand why they cannot eat meat or must forgo dishes that are non-kosher and non-halal (Rifkin, 2003). Therefore, the campus environment is not welcoming to these students, as their dietary needs are not met.

Religious Holidays

Students often find that their religious holidays conflict with exams or required classes, even though religious allowances are provided for their Christian peers (Schlosser & Sedlacek, 2001). Policies permitting alternative schedules are often unclear and may require students to give faculty members advance notice of holidays or supply written notes from religious leaders excusing them from activities. Although these practices are meant to respect religious diversity, they can actually reinforce exclusion among students from minority religious groups, since the requirements do not take into account power imbalances between students and faculty that lead students to be hesitant in requesting different policies from their peers (Schlosser & Sedlacek, 2001). The onus is on students to educate their professors about their religious needs, and faculty members are often reluctant to accommodate students' religious practices for fear of unfairly advantaging certain students over others (Garcia & Smith, 1996; Schlosser & Sedlacek, 2001). Furthermore, campus religious policies largely overlook the possibility that some students may observe holy days apart from religious leaders; therefore, requiring students to obtain notes from these leaders is not always possible or entirely realistic (Schlosser & Sedlacek, 2001).

Campus Spaces

The issue of spaces on campus and their use can also be a barrier for students from religious minority groups. Requirements that students live in mixed-sex campus housing may conflict with religious principles of modesty between the sexes (Kahan, 2003). The design and allocation of space used for religious meetings and services may also be problematic. Chapels originally designed with crosses and stained glass windows depicting biblical scenes for Christian services, for example, may be inappropriate spaces for other students to use for worship, even if they are made available to all groups (Clark & Brimhall-Vargas, 2003; McMurtie, 1999). As Strange and Banning (2001) assert, the ways in which physical spaces are designed can welcome some students while creating an atmosphere that is hostile and antagonistic toward others.

Identity Development

Developing one's identity during college can be a challenging process for students, particularly those from religious minority groups. Recent studies have shown that students develop and define their religious identities during college, just as they might explore their racial/ethnic heritage or sexual orientation, and that these explorations are a key part of their college experience (Astin & Astin, 2003; Love, 2001; Love & Talbot, 1999; Nash, 2001). However, because religious minority students have few mentors and supportive peers on campus, they often must negotiate and resolve identity tensions and struggles on their own within campus environments that marginalize their identities and privilege those of their Christian and non-religious counterparts (Abu El-Haj, 2002). The result is that their engagement and identity development are adversely affected (Chickering & Reisser, 1993).

Theoretical Framework

Based on the examination of the issues affecting minority religious students, it is evident that their development and engagement are adversely affected by misunderstanding and stereotypical beliefs about their religious practices among their peers and faculty members, as well as campus environments that are not inclusive of their needs. In this section, we begin broadly by discussing social justice theories to further clarify the challenges facing these students and then utilize social justice ally development theory to demonstrate the roles of persons from privileged groups working to redress the differential treatment of minority religious students.

Theoretical Perspectives on Social Justice

For some students, college is a time when they work to build equitable campus environments that are nurturing of diverse students (McAdam, 1986). However, current events, such as the terrorist attacks of September 11, 2001, can also lead to prejudice, racism, and discrimination among students. Social justice theories describe the process of students struggling to develop attitudes and behaviors that are free from intolerance and discrimination and instead focused on equity for all persons (Reason, Roosa Millar, & Scales, 2005). Prior to discussing the development of social justice allies, it is important to distinguish among three forms of discrimination that are present in social justice theories: individual, institutional, and structural discrimination (Pincus, 2000).

Individual and Institutional Discrimination

In instances of individual discrimination, a person makes a conscious decision to act in order to deny someone rights or privileges based on any of several facets of that person's identity (e.g., race/ethnicity, gender, sexual orientation, religion, or socioeconomic status). These overt forms of discrimination are relatively easy to notice and are therefore often the targets of regulation, education, and intense dialogue designed to mitigate their effects (Pincus, 2000). Related to individual discrimination is institutional discrimination. Far too often, people assume that racism, sexism, homophobia, and the like are perpetuated by random, individual people and occur only in rare cases. However, institutional discrimination results when inequality and injustice are woven into the fabric of an institution (e.g., a church, government, workplace, or postsecondary education institution), which, in turn, affects policies, procedures, norms, and standards (Delgado & Stefancic, 2001). For example, women must worry about being sexually harassed or being treated differently than men because of their gender in classroom, out-of-class, and work settings, an experience that rarely troubles men. This is in part due to institutional structures in place that privilege men and disadvantage women (Kelley & Parsons, 2000). Likewise, the racial profiling of Arab and Muslim students serves as an example of the ways that police officers (i.e., individual discrimination) and campus policies (i.e., institutional discrimination) work in partnership to reproduce unfairness and injustice among certain groups of people (Abu El-Haj, 2002).

Structural Discrimination

Structural discrimination "involves behavior that is race/ethnic/gender [or other identity] neutral in intent" (Pincus, 2000, p. 33). Thus, it is classifiable as discrimination based on its negative effects rather than on its intent. For example, bankers might practice color-blind philosophies in issuing loans but deny a racial/ethnic minority person a loan based solely on her or his credit score. However, because racial/ethnic minority persons tend to have lower incomes than White people, they are less likely to receive loans. Pincus describes this systemic phenomenon as an example of structural discrimination since it has disproportionately negative effects on low-income racial/ethnic minority groups. Structural discrimination is more difficult to identify than other forms of discrimination, even for those who may be fostering it, because the individual practices that carry it out appear to be innocuous. However, as the example of lending practices shows, structural discrimination does reinforce the disadvantaged status of minority groups (Pincus, 2000).

Structural discrimination stems from privilege and oppression. Young (1990) defines oppression as "systematic constraints on groups . . . [that are] structural, rather than the result of a few people's choices or policies" (p. 41). According to Young, the causes of oppression "are embedded in unquestioned norms, habits, and symbols, in the assumptions underlying institutional rules and the collective consequences of following those rules" (p. 41). Privilege is the ability of the dominant group (e.g., White people, men, heterosexual persons, and Christians) to function in society without constraints and often without the knowledge that restrictions exist for others. Members of advantaged groups can exercise their privilege and oppress others without intending to do so. Therefore, privileged persons define and are rewarded by societal norms and values to which all other groups are subjected (Wildman & Davis, 2000). Social justice theorists illuminate the ways in which privilege and oppression tend to overlook issues of particularity. As Young noted, "an ideal of justice that defines liberation as the transcendence of group difference [is] an ideal of assimilation" (p. 157). In this view, justice requires equal participation and inclusion of all groups, even if this means the different application of policies for some groups (e.g., affirmative action).

Seen through the lens of social justice theories, people who practice non-dominant religions are an oppressed group. Privilege exists for Christians and non-religious persons. By having their needs consistently met and their religious beliefs embedded in institutional practices, Christians rarely have to confront their assumptions or question their belonging at higher education institutions (Schlosser & Sedlacek, 2001). However, students from religious minority groups are consistently expected to thrive in conditions that do not satisfy their needs or validate their religious values and beliefs. Student affairs professionals must be conscious of the ways in which privilege and discrimination subtly benefit dominant or non-religious groups to the detriment of students from minority religions. In the next section, we discuss the development of social justice allies.

Social Justice Ally Development Models

Even though privileged persons rarely acknowledge their advantages, there are cases when members of dominant groups can work to consider the ways in which their identities afford them privileges and build relationships with people who are oppressed to challenge inequitable practices. This describes social justice allies, as defined by Broido (2000): "members of dominant groups (e.g., men, Whites, heterosexuals) who are working to end the system of oppression that gives them greater privilege and power based on their social-group membership" (p. 3). By developing attitudes and behaviors emblematic of social justice, these allies strive to use their power in ways that are conducive to creating more equitable and welcoming campus environments (Reason et al., 2005).

According to psychosocial and moral development theories, higher levels of development in these areas and increased contact with like-minded peers enable students to exhibit attitudes associated with social justice allies (Blanchard, Crandall, Brigham, & Vaughn, 1994; Chickering & Reisser, 1993). And when Christian students witness their Christian peers engaging in dialogues with Muslim and Jewish students and working to understand their beliefs, they are likely to do so as well. The development of social justice attitudes, however, is a complex process. Broido (2000) found that three factors affected participants' abilities and willingness to become social justice allies: (1) information about social justice issues, (2) engagement in meaning-making processes, and (3) self-confidence.

Social Justice Information

As participants in Broido's (2000) study collected information on diversity-related initiatives and developed knowledge about members of minority groups, their social justice attitudes increased. This information often challenged participants' assumptions and biases and led them to revise their conceptualizations of their peers from different groups. As members of dominant groups learn more about students from minority religious groups, they can develop beliefs that are more consistent with their actual experiences of these students and refrain from believing inaccurate media or family representations of different religions. Additionally, through forming friendships with Muslim and Jewish students, like Vince and Esther, Christian and non-religious students can learn more about them and explore the beliefs and values they share as well as those that are different (Broido, 2000).

Meaning-Making Processes

Broido's (2000) theory revealed not only the importance of privileged persons having multiple sources of information about minority groups, but also that the ways in which they made sense of that information was critical to ally development. Students in her study described how they discussed information with their peers, reflected on their own and others' experiences, and used classroom and out-of-class dialogues to adopt the perspectives of their peers. By being exposed to experiences that were different from their own, they began to see campus life from the vantage point of their marginalized counterparts. Students commented that this prompted them to reflect on how their lives differed and how their identities granted them opportunities not equally afforded to others. Similarly, minority religious students need numerous, sustained opportunities to engage in dialogues with their Christian and non-religious peers. As Broido's research confirms, these chances to engage in open and honest interactions are necessary for ally development. Students from dominant groups can learn the challenges faced by students akin to Esther and Vince and work to collaborate with them to build welcoming campus environments.

Self-Confidence

Reason et al. (2005) and Broido (2000) found that ally development depended upon students' levels of confidence with their dominant identities. Acknowledging that one has privileges, which grant her or him special rewards not available to members of minority groups, can cause one's sense of self to feel diminished. Because students are led to believe erroneously that achievement within American society is based solely on individual merit, accepting that one has been successful thanks in part to her or his identity can be difficult (MacLeod, 1995). However, for ally development to occur, students need to acknowledge their advantages, refrain from apologizing or feeling guilty for their membership in dominant groups, and work to understand the needs and experiences of those not granted similar privileges.

Listening to how students from minority religious groups perceive the campus environment and how norms perpetuated by their Christian and non-religious peers influence their experiences can be a challenge to students. Consequently, social justice theories and social justice ally development theories remind us of the importance of looking at how discrimination—in its three forms—affects students and the role of privilege in giving advantage to certain students while marginalizing others. Social justice ally development theory demonstrates the significance of dominant group members working to challenge oppression in its multiple forms; doing so can establish campuses in which minority religious students are able to worship without reservation or fear.

Strategies for Inclusiveness

The issues affecting students from religious minority groups are complex and multifaceted. Therefore, various strategies must be used to improve their engagement and development within higher education institutions. In this section, we build on the discussion up to this point and offer ways to combat individual, institutional, and structural discrimination against students from religious minority groups.

Initiate Dialogues with Students

The first suggestion for improving the campus climate for students from religious minority groups is the simplest: Ask them about their experiences. Religion is a taboo subject on many campuses, but student affairs educators must be willing to break this silence and ask students to reflect on their experiences and identify what they need to be engaged on campus. Students often do not have a chance to discuss issues related to their religious identity with anyone other than their peers; they seldom receive the message from faculty or staff members that they have an interest in this aspect of students' lives.

The result of talking openly with students about their beliefs, needs, and religious identity will be twofold. First, by asking students about their experiences and what can be done to improve them, students will know that student affairs professionals care about them and are interested in their particular needs. Second, students can provide concrete suggestions for increasing their engagement on campus. The conversation about religion should be ongoing and begin as soon as students arrive on campus. By starting these discussions early and continually reinforcing them, students are provided with numerous, sustained opportunities to discuss their religious identities and practices with those in positions to respond to their needs.

Collaborate with Others on Campus

Collaborate with as many people and campus organizations as possible to provide services for students from religious minority groups. Student affairs educators and faculty members can begin with the college or university's office of religious life, which usually bears the responsibility for meeting the religion-based needs of students. Developing a line of communication with these offices may provide student affairs professionals with an idea of the issues students from religious minority groups face on campus. In turn, these partnerships can help persons who work within religious life feel a stronger sense of institutional support for their work with religious minority students.

Consider partnering with outside organizations that serve the needs of religious minority students. Many institutions have a Hillel and/or Chabad (a branch of Hasidic Judaism) organization, and others may have local temples, mosques, and gurdwaras (a Sikh place of worship) that host student groups, provide advisors, or simply serve as students' spiritual homes. Leaders within these organizations will likely have a good sense of the needs of the students they serve and may even be able to provide resources to help meet those needs.

In addition, collaborations can occur within student affairs and other administrative units on campus. Residential life, orientation, international student services, food services, recreational sports, and classroom scheduling are just a few examples of departments that may be able to provide services to support students from minority religious groups. People working in these offices, however, may not consider the needs of students from minority religious groups until approached. In other cases, these offices may already have encountered and addressed specific challenges associated with students from minority religious groups, but have perceived these as isolated incidents rather than the results of a pattern of structural discrimination. Inviting representatives from across campus to serve on a religious diversity task force or otherwise engaging them in a broad discussion of issues affecting religious minority students will help to raise awareness of these issues and help develop a campus-wide network of advocates.

Raise Awareness about Religious Holidays

Create a calendar of religious holidays that students observe and distribute it to students, faculty, student affairs educators, and staff at the beginning of each term. Be sure to note dates when students may be absent from class and days during which students may be fasting. Send reminder memos and/or emails before holidays that are likely to have an impact on students' abilities to attend class. Encourage professors to allow students to leave the classroom if instructional times coincide with religious observances and to make these offers known to the entire class.

Advocate policies that take students' religious obligations into account when scheduling classes, labs, and examinations. Allow students to reschedule tests that conflict with religious observances. Department heads should work with faculty members to encourage them to place statements regarding academic accommodations for religious reasons in their syllabi so that students are aware of them. Even if such policies exist, students may be unaware of them, or may be reluctant to approach professors about them unless they are specifically encouraged to do so.

These suggestions foster a campus culture in which accommodations are offered in an open, supportive manner, rather than classified as exceptions to the "normal" order. Simply avoiding the use of the word "exception" to describe policies that accommodate the needs of religious minority students can enable these students to feel welcome and included.

Help New Students Find Religious Groups

During orientation, student affairs professionals should work to help first-year and transfer students discover the religious resources available to them on campus. A brochure with contact information for student religious groups, locations for different types of religious services and gatherings, and other similar information can be helpful. Allowing new students to decide if they want to be contacted by specific student groups can also help them connect with students from similar religious backgrounds.

Guest speakers at orientation and welcome events can help new students network with people from the groups they may be interested in joining. Student leaders, faculty advisors, staff members, and religious advisors would all be appropriate guests and could inform students about the various religious groups on campus available to them. Not only would these efforts help students from minority religious groups feel at home on campus, they could also help those students interested in exploring different religious pursuits understand their options for participation on campus.

Support Small Groups

Student religious groups are an important resource for religious exploration and growth and are often the primary source of students' religious development during their college years. They can provide support for students as well as a sense of safety and community to members of minority religions on campus. As with other types of student groups, though, small groups may struggle to survive if they do not have the active support of staff members or advisors. Particularly on smaller campuses, some religious groups may have few, if any, student members in a given year, and groups may dissolve when an important student leader graduates.

It is important to offer advisors to smaller student religious groups who can help bridge the knowledge gap from one group of students to the next, particularly in cases where student groups need to re-form. Including leaders from student religious groups in general leadership training seminars and retreats (often offered to the leaders of other groups on campus, such as those in student government) can also be an important step in sustaining the vitality of these groups. In addition, small student religious groups may benefit from participation in a forum, such as an interfaith council, that allows them to meet members of other religious groups, learn from their experiences, and collaborate on campus activities.

Encourage Mentoring

Identify faculty and staff members who are willing and able to assist students from religious minority groups in meaningful ways. These might be fellow members of the students' religion, or people simply interested in encouraging student development and ensuring that students feel at home on campus. Alumni from a particular religious group may also be able to return to campus to serve as advisors and mentors for current students. Training should be provided to these mentors so that they are familiar with theoretical and practical approaches for maximizing student growth and learning. These training sessions will equip mentors with the knowledge and skills to serve as facilitators of the learning process without taking ownership of the religious organization.

Offer Alcohol-Free Environments

Provide substance-free housing, support alcohol-free social events, and nurture a campus culture that does not depend on alcohol. Students from various religious (and sometimes secular) backgrounds may feel alienated from campus life if they sense that most social events feature alcohol as a primary form of entertainment. For example, Muslims and Bahá'ís, as well as students from a variety of Christian backgrounds, may withdraw from campus activities if alcohol is involved.

Strive to enforce existing alcohol policies and stress to residential life staff and others responsible for enforcing them that alcohol policies are in place not only for students' health and safety, but also to ensure that members of the campus community are able to live in accordance with their religious beliefs.

Sponsor Theme Housing

Consider creating theme housing that serves specific religious groups. This may provide a space that meets the modesty, dietary, and prayer requirements of students. It may also offer an opportunity for students from minority religious groups to create a community, even if not all of the students from that group actually live in the designated space. In some cases, students from differing religious backgrounds may have similar needs that could be met by theme housing; as such, these residence halls could also serve as an opportunity for students from different religious groups to interact with and learn about one another's practices and beliefs.

Be Conscious of Religious Diversity

Consider religious identity when crafting office documents, surveys, applications, and other forms that gather information about students. If students see their religious group listed on documents, such as an admissions application or a housing information form, it can help them feel that they belong to an understanding and accepting community that values their faith.

Campus ceremonies should also be a welcoming and inclusive experience for people of diverse religious backgrounds. Inviting representatives (especially student representatives) from different campus religious groups to participate in key ceremonies such as convocation helps emphasize that religious diversity is present on campus and is celebrated by the college or university community. In addition, including an opportunity for personal reflection during important campus gatherings is also a way to express support for a diversity of religious groups without featuring any one particular faith. Inviting a moment of silent reflection can be powerful, broadly inclusive, and respectful of those who practice different religions.

Be Cognizant of Intersecting Identities

Students from religious minority groups should not be seen as a monolithic group. It is important that faculty members, staff, and student affairs educators learn about the various parts of students' identities and how they intersect with their religious beliefs and practices. Students should be encouraged to reflect on their identities and engage in dialogues with their peers from different backgrounds and experiences. Programming should include opportunities for students to learn more about their religions, racial/ethnic identity, gender, and sexual orientation, among other backgrounds. Moreover, it is vital to provide training for those who work with students on how to enable students to question, reflect on, and embrace the various parts of their selves, particularly when they face a conflict between different parts of their identities. For instance, students who identify as lesbian, gay, bisexual, or transgender might struggle with religious beliefs that condemn homosexuality.

Develop Multifaith Programming

Create multifaith programming on campus, such as religious diversity awareness events or multifaith celebrations. These programs can help increase knowledge of religious diversity on campus and enable students to learn about a range of beliefs and practices in a non-threatening environment. Zúñiga (2003) advocates an inter-group dialogue approach in which two students from different backgrounds (e.g., a Muslim student and a Christian student) co-facilitate discussions about differences with their peers. The purpose of these intergroup dialogues is to promote an atmosphere that is conducive to open dialogue, self-reflection, questioning, and safety among students. Combining multifaith programming with intergroup dialogues can support students in learning not only about the differences in their beliefs and practices, but also possible similarities across various religions. Relationships can be built based on shared values and norms as well as differences. Multifaith programming can help to illuminate the diversity of religions on campus for those who are non-religious or who adhere to the dominant religion on campus.

Provide Campus Spaces

Providing appropriate spaces on campus to meet religious needs is essential for welcoming and supporting students from the various religious backgrounds that exist. Not only is space necessary to ensure that students from religious minority groups can congregate and worship, the design and allocation of space is also a subtle yet meaningful way of conveying to students that those in positions of power at the institution recognize their needs and care about them. In allocating these spaces for student groups, it is important to issue spaces for minority religious groups that are comparable in appearance, location, and amenities.

Although dedicated spaces are ideal, the first step is to examine the unique needs of various religious minority groups and make an effort to meet those needs. For example, Muslim students must pray at five specific times during the day. Simply designating and making empty classroom spaces around campus available during times for prayer will allow Muslim students to pray with some privacy without needing to make a special trip to a mosque, residence hall room, or other location between classes.

Consider Layout and Scheduling Options at Fitness Facilities

Many religions have requirements for physical modesty, making it essential to examine privacy and space allocation in campus facilities, such as athletic centers, where religion is often not a consideration. For example, Muslim men must cover themselves at all times from their knees to their navel, even when only around other men, meaning that they can neither shower nor change clothes in most open locker room facilities. Muslims are also not permitted to see other people—of either sex—disrobed, making it impossible to use a locker room even to store personal items.

Further, the layout of some facilities require students to pass through a locker room simply to enter weight rooms or swimming pools, thereby making these places unavailable to students whose religious beliefs prohibit them from seeing others disrobed. Muslims and other students whose religious requirements for modesty cannot be met in available athletic facilities are forced to make a choice between attending the event and being uncomfortable or forgoing athletic participation entirely. Providing individual shower areas and private changing spaces is an important step toward making these students feel welcome on all parts of campus.

Conclusion

Students who identify as members of minority religious groups can face a variety of barriers to their full participation in the campus culture and are at risk of feeling isolated or marginalized. Because the obstacles these students face are the result not only of individual and institutional discrimination, but also of structural discrimination, they can be further exacerbated and overlooked. Support for these students can be strengthened and improved, however, through advocacy and intentional changes to policies and campus spaces.

Recent trends in higher education and the larger culture have brought issues of religion to the forefront. This has created a climate in which it is essential for student affairs professionals to reach out to students, faculty, and campus administrators to increase understanding, support, and accommodation for students from minority religious groups. Religion is a critical aspect of identity for many students and should be prioritized and supported in the same way as race/ethnicity, gender, sexual orientation, and other aspects of identity. The proposed strategies have the potential to improve the campus climate for students from diverse religious backgrounds, and most of these interventions may be employed without placing great demands on the limited resources of institutions. For the sake of students like Vince and Esther, it is important that the needs of students from religious minority groups are given attention and that innovative strategies are implemented to improve their engagement and development in higher education.

References

Abu El-Haj, T. R. (2002). Contesting the politics of culture, rewriting the boundaries of inclusion: Working for social justice with Muslim and Arab communities. *Anthropology and Education Quarterly, 33*(3), 308–316.

Allen, K. E., & Kellom, G. E. (2001). The role of spirituality in student affairs and staff development. In M. A. Jablonski (Ed.), *The implications of student spirituality for student affairs practice. New Directions for Student Services* (No. 95, pp. 47–55). San Francisco: Jossey-Bass.

Astin, A. W. (1993). *What matters in college? Four critical years revisited.* San Francisco: Jossey-Bass.

Astin, A. W., & Astin H. S. (2003). *The spiritual life of college students: A national study of college students' search for meaning and purpose.* Retrieved June 25, 2007, from the University of California, Los Angeles, Higher Education Research Institute website: www.spirituality.ucla.edu/spirituality/reports/FINAL%20REPORT.pdf.

Blanchard, F. A., Crandall, C. S., Brigham, J. C., & Vaughn, L. A. (1994). Condemning and condoning racism: A social context approach to interracial settings. *Journal of Applied Psychology, 79*(6), 993–997.

Broido, E. M. (2000). The development of social justice allies during college: A phenomenological investigation. *Journal of College Student Development, 41*(1), 3–18.

Chickering, A. W., & Reisser, L. (1993). *Education and identity* (2nd ed.). San Francisco: Jossey-Bass.

Clark, C., & Brimhall-Vargas, M. (2003). Diversity initiatives in higher education: Secular aspects and international implications of Christian privilege. *Multicultural Education 11*(1), 55–57.

Clark, R. T. (2003). The law and spirituality: How the law supports and limits expression of spirituality on the college campus. In M. A. Jablonski (Ed.), *The implications of student spirituality for student affairs practice. New Directions for Student Services* (No. 95, pp. 37–46). San Francisco: Jossey-Bass.

Cole, D., & Ahmadi, S. (2003). Perspectives and experiences of Muslim women who veil on college campuses. *Journal of College Student Development, 44*(1), 47–66.

Delgado, R., & Stefancic, J. (2001). *Critical race theory: An introduction.* New York: New York University Press.

Eisenmann, L. (1999). Reclaiming religion: New historiographic challenges in the relationship of religion and American higher education. *History of Education Quarterly, 39*(3), 295–306.

Farmer, S. (2001, April 25). Good-faith gesture: Bruin offensive lineman Efseaff has shown an appetite for school while strictly adhering to religious tenets as Russian Molokan. *Los Angeles Times,* pp. D1, D9.

Garcia, M., & Smith, D. G. (1996). Reflecting inclusiveness in the college curriculum. In L. I. Rendón & R. O. Hope (Eds.), *Educating a new majority: Transforming America's educational system for diversity* (pp. 265–288). San Francisco: Jossey-Bass.

Geiger, R. (1999). The ten generations of American higher education. In P. G. Altbach, R. O. Berdahl, & P. J. Gumport (Eds.), *American higher education in the twenty-first century: Social, political, and economic challenges* (pp. 38–69). Baltimore, MD: The Johns Hopkins University Press.

Jablonski, M. A. (2001). Editor's notes. In M. A. Jablonski (Ed.), *The implications of student spirituality for student affairs practice. New Directions for Student Services* (No. 95, pp. 1–5). San Francisco: Jossey-Bass.

Kahan, D. (2003). Islam and physical activity: Implications for American sport and physical educators. *Journal of Physical Education, Recreation, and Dance, 74*(3), 48–54.

Kelley, M. L., & Parsons, B. (2000). Sexual harassment in the 1990s: A university-wide survey of female faculty, administrators, staff, and students. *Journal of Higher Education, 71*(5), 548–568.

Kohlbrenner, B. J. (1961). Religion and higher education: An historical perspective. *History of Education Quarterly, 1*(2), 45–56.

Kuh, G. D. (1995). The other curriculum: Out-of-class experiences associated with student learning and personal development. *The Journal of Higher Education, 66*(2), 123–155.

Love, P. G. (2001). Spirituality and student development: Theoretical connections. In M. A. Jablonski (Ed.), *The implications of student spirituality for student affairs practice. New Directions for Student Services* (No. 95, pp. 7–16). San Francisco: Jossey-Bass.

Love, P., & Talbot, D. (1999). Defining spiritual development: A missing consideration for student affairs. *NASPA Journal, 37*(1), 361–375.

Machacek, D. W. (2003). The problem of pluralism. *Sociology of Religion, 64*(2), 145–161.

MacLeod, J. (1995). *Ain't no makin' it: Aspirations & attainment in a low-income neighborhood.* Boulder, CO: Westview Press.

Manning, K. (2001). Infusing soul into student affairs: Organizational theory and models. In M. A. Jablonski (Ed.), *The implications of student spirituality for student affairs practice. New Directions for Student Services* (No. 95, pp. 27–35). San Francisco: Jossey-Bass.

McAdam, D. (1986). Recruitment to high-risk activism: The case of Freedom Summer. *American Journal of Sociology, 92,* 64–90.

McMurtie, B. (1999, December 3). Pluralism and prayer under one roof. *Chronicle of Higher Education, 46*(15), pp. A48–A50.

Nash, R. J. (2001). *Religious pluralism in the academy: Opening the dialogue.* New York: Peter Lang Publishing.

Peek, L. A. (2003). Receptions and response: Muslim students' experiences on New York City campuses post 9/11. *Journal of Muslim Minority Affairs, 23*(2), 271–283.

Pincus, F. L. (2000). Discrimination comes in many forms: Individual, institutional, and structural. In M. Adams, W. J. Blumenfeld, R. Castañeda, H. W. Hackman, M. L. Peters, & X. Zúñiga (Eds.), *Readings for diversity and social justice: An anthology on racism, antisemitism, sexism, heterosexism, ableism, and classism* (pp. 31–35). New York: Routledge.

Reason, R. D., Roosa Millar, E. A., & Scales, T. C. (2005). Toward a model of racial justice ally development. *Journal of College Student Development, 46*(5), 530–546.

Rifkin, J. M. (2003). Lack of Kosher choices at Pitt, CMU is driving students away. *Jewish Chronicle, 43*(20), p. 1.

Rudolph, F. (1990). *The American college and university.* Athens, GA: University of Georgia Press.

Schlosser, L. Z., & Sedlacek, W. E. (2001). *Religious holidays on campus: Policies, problems, and recommendations.* College Park, MD: Office of the Vice President for Student Affairs, University of Maryland. (ERIC Document Reproduction Service No. ED456681)

Strange, C. C., & Banning, J. H. (2001). *Educating by design: Creating campus learning environments that work.* San Francisco: Jossey-Bass.

Wildman, S. M., & Davis, A. D. (2000). Language and silence: Making systems of privilege visible. In M. Adams, W. J. Blumenfeld, R. Castañeda, H. W. Hackman, M. L. Peters, & X. Zúñiga (Eds.), *Readings for diversity and social justice: An anthology on racism, antisemitism, sexism, heterosexism, ableism, and classism* (pp. 50–60). New York: Routledge.

Young, I. M. (1990). *Justice and the politics of difference.* Princeton, NJ: Princeton University Press.

Zúñiga, X. (2003). Bridging differences through dialogue. *About Campus, 7*(6), 8–16.

Chapter 6

Gender-Specific Approaches to Enhancing Identity Development among Undergraduate Women and Men

Frank Harris III and Jaime Lester

A requirement for any volume is a wide range of research that spans many decades. Identity development theory generally and college student identity development specifically fits this category with at least 60 collective years of research spanning multiple disciplines including psychology, sociology, and education. Gender, however, did not garner attention until a few individuals began to question the gender neutrality of identity development theories (Belenky, Clinchy, Goldberger, & Tarule, 1986; Connell, 1987; Gilligan, 1982; Josselson, 1987; Kimmel, 1987; Pleck, 1981). Yet attention to the complexities of identity development is still lacking. Other populations such as gay and lesbian students, students of different socioeconomic statuses, and underrepresented racial/ethnic minorities have received even less attention. Each of these identities (race/ethnicity, gender, sexuality, religion, and class) is integral to identity development among college students.

For the purposes of this chapter, we define identity as "the interface between the individual and the world, defining as it does what the individual will stand for and be recognized as" (Josselson, 1987, p. 8). Identity is a principle central to the college student population as traditional-age students enter college at a time when they are beginning the adult development process. Institutions of higher education continue to place insufficient emphasis on the importance of gender and identity development. Take for example a recent advertisement for a director of a university women's center:

Director

University Women's Center

The Director is the chief academic, fiscal, and administrative officer of the University Women's Center and reports to the Vice President for Curriculum and Instruction and Dean, University College. In consultation with the heads of other departments, the Director is responsible for developing, coordinating, implementing, and maintaining the center's programs and facilities. In addition to the above, the Director is responsible for hiring, training, and supervising the staff. The Director oversees the daily operation of the Women's Center by maintaining records; evaluating programs through assessment measures; allocating, tracking, and forecasting budget; and investigating internal and external sources of funds. Additionally, the Director is responsible for the center's collaboration with the Women's Studies program and the other multicultural centers and programs. The Director is also responsible for planning and giving presentations about the center's services and other related topics to various groups across campus; overseeing the development and maintenance of women center publications, including the web page, instructional materials, and publicity efforts. The Director also engages in ongoing professional development through conference presentations, workshop participation, and university committee service.

This advertisement details the administrative duties and responsibilities of the director, but it fails to ask for qualifications related to facilitating student development among women. In fact, the word "student" is not mentioned in this job posting. The job description describes the director's position as collaborator, a campus resource for issues related to gender, but fails to indicate that the position is student-centered. (Despite this shortcoming in this advertisement, this particular institution does deem it important to a have a women's resource center.)

To begin the discussion of gender and identity development, we first outline the issues of identity development among men and women in colleges and universities across the United States. Intricate pictures of gender in universities illustrate the complexities of the experiences of male and female students. Next, to provide a foundation for how researchers have conceptualized identity development generally and gender more specifically, we review the literature. Two alternative paradigms—feminist poststructuralism and the social constructionist model—and their implications for practice follow. Finally, we provide an extensive discussion of strategies for applying these perspectives to a college or university setting.

Female Student Identity Development Issues

In reviewing student outcomes, female college students do not appear to suffer academically while exploring identity development during early adulthood. In fact, since the mid-1970s, the enrollment of women in college and universities across the nation has exceeded that of men. In 2000, 56 percent of the enrolled undergraduates were women (National Center for Education Statistics [NCES], 2003). Women also earned the majority (58 percent) of college degrees in the academic year 2002–2003 (NCES, 2005). Graduate enrollment and degree attainment have also been skewed towards women. Since 1984, the number of women in graduate schools has exceeded the number of men (NCES, 2003) and women were conferred 59 percent of all master's degrees in 2002 (NCES, 2005). Enrollment and degree attainment statistics, however, only provide a small picture of the overall status and experience of women in higher education. Women may enter and complete college at greater rates than men, but the pressure to maintain femininity causes identity conflicts that are not evident in student outcome statistics. Several of the issues that result from gender identity conflicts include eating disorders and segregation into traditionally female majors and occupations.

Female college students take on multiple identities while in college that are oftentimes related to their involvement in campus activities and student organizations. Sports, sororities, social clubs, and academic organizations are a few groups that influence college student identity. When conflicts arise and these identities are threatened, female students are found to exhibit psychological stress and physical symptoms (Rozin, Bauer & Catanese, 2003). Women are more likely than men to suffer from eating disorders (Smolak & Murnen, 2001) due to media images that portray beauty alongside thinness (Levine & Smolak, 1996) and to the intense relationship between body image and athletics. For women whose identity is closely related to a sport, particularly a sport that focuses on their bodies, eating disorders have emerged as a significant issue. In a meta-analysis of eating disorders and female athletes, researchers found that female athletes are more at risk for eating problems than non-athletes (Smolak, Murnen, & Ruble, 2000). Sports that emphasize thinness, such as dancing, were found to report larger numbers of students with eating disorders. Another group that has been found to be at risk for eating disorders is sorority members, who were more likely to strive for thinness and exhibit eating disorders than non-sorority women (Allison & Park, 2004). The pressure to adhere to the ideals of femininity by maintaining a thin physique or succumbing to the norms of groups such as some sororities has negative effects on female students.

Another outcome of student identity conflicts among female college students is academic segregation. Despite the large numbers of female college students overall, many are segregated into traditionally feminine academic disciplines. In fact, women account for only 18.4 percent of undergraduate engineers (National Science Foundation, 2003). Research has noted that increasing the numbers of women in science or engineering is dependent on developing a science identity from adolescence (Brickhouse, Lowery, & Schultz, 2000). However, women in science and engineering classrooms in higher education find an overwhelmingly male-dominated environment and are expected to conform to masculine ways of learning (Tonso, 1996a, 1996b). Unfortunately, the underrepresentation of women in these fields has long-term effects. Women who graduate from college are likely to earn incomes that are lower than their male peers with the same level of credentials. In 2000, the average woman with a bachelor's degree made $40,415 per year compared with $56,334 for men (NCES, 2003). The discrepancy between average salaries for men and women is attributed to the types of jobs that men and women populate after college graduation. Science and engineering graduates earn significantly higher incomes upon graduation than those with degrees in the social sciences. Tying academic identity for men and women students to particular disciplines leads to unfair long-term financial disadvantages for women. Identity conflicts are not unique to female students; as we describe in the next section, male students also experience gender-related challenges that impact their development and outcomes.

Male Student Identity Development Issues

At the heart of the issues concerning college men and identity development is the pressure men face to conform to narrowly constructed and stereotypically masculine behavioral norms. For example, men are expected to suppress their emotions, excel at sports, and pursue sexual relationships with women. Individuals serving as significant others in the lives of boys, such as parents and male peers, often discourage behaviors that lie outside of the rigid boundaries of masculinity. As noted by Harper (2004), "no father wants his son to grow up being a 'pussy,' 'sissy,' 'punk,' or 'softy'—terms commonly associated with boys who fail to live up to the traditional standards of masculinity in America" (p. 92). The concept of *male gender role conflict* describes the negative consequences that accrue from men's inability to conform to rigid and restricted male gendered norms (O'Neil, 1981). O'Neil, Helms, Gable, David, and Wrightsman (1986) identified six behavioral patterns associated with male gender role conflict: (1) restrictive emotionality, (2) homophobia, (3) socialized control, power, and competition, (4) restrictive sexual and affectional behavior, (5) obsession with achievement and success, and (6) health care problems.

The consequences of male gender role conflict are well documented as findings from multiple empirical studies link these behavioral patterns in college men to alcohol and substance abuse (Capraro, 2000; Courtenay, 1998), poor help-seeking and coping strategies (Good & Wood, 1995; O'Neil, et al., 1986), depression (Good & Mintz, 1990), violence and aggression (O'Neil, 1981), homophobia and fear of femininity (Davis, 2002; O'Neil, 1981), and misbehavior (Harper, Harris, & Mmeje, 2005). To further illustrate the nexus between male gender role conflict and issues concerning the gender identity of college men, we highlight several male behavioral trends occurring on college campuses. Specifically, we discuss disengagement, alcohol abuse, and the perpetration of sexual assault among college men.

Gender disparities in the level and intensity of campus engagement are of increasing concern for postsecondary educators. Several published reports indicate that college males are not as engaged in educationally purposeful activities as their female peers. For example, in an annual assessment of campus-based community engagement, 35 percent of the surveyed male students reported participating in service activities (Salgado, 2003, as cited in Kellom, 2004). According to Astin and Sax (1998), women are more likely than men to pursue community service opportunities while in college. Though specific to African American students, Cuyjet's (1997) examination of College Student Experience Questionnaire (CSEQ) data collected from nearly 7,000 students (2,431 men and 4,308 women) revealed low levels of male student involvement on important indicators of campus engagement. Specifically, when compared with the women in the sample, the men in his study reported lower levels of involvement in campus activities; searching the campus newspaper for notices about campus events and student organizations; attending a meeting, program, or event sponsored by a campus group; and serving on campus committees.

Sax and Harper's (2007) examination of gender differences in college outcomes revealed that women have a greater orientation towards social activism (described as "helping others, influencing social values, and working in the community," p. 680) whereas college men have a "status striving orientation" and express greater concern for earning money, gaining recognition, and having authority over others. Given the empirical evidence that connects purposeful campus engagement to a host of positive outcomes for all students (Astin, 1984; Kuh, 1995; Pascarella & Terenzini, 2005), disengagement among college men warrants attention and concern.

Alcohol abuse has also been widely discussed as a critical issue in the current published literature on college men. Reportedly, college men overconsume alcohol for various reasons—conforming to peer pressure, taking risks, and coping with stress, to name a few (Capraro, 2000). Men's overconsumption has also been linked to their tendencies to embrace stereotypical expectations of masculine expression (Capraro, 2000; Courtenay, 2004; McCreary, Newcomb, & Sadave, 1999; O'Neil, 1990; Sabo, 2005). Capraro (2000) argues that the heavy drinking that characterizes college male cultures is a strategy for coping with the "paradox of masculinity." He writes: "My interpretation of a variety of evidence suggests that men may be drinking not only to enact male privilege but also to help them negotiate the emotional hazards of being a man in the contemporary American college" (p. 307). The privilege that comes with being a male is a source of power for men. Yet the physical and emotional vulnerability that result from alcohol-induced conformity to traditional masculine expression render men powerless—hence the inherent paradox of masculinity suggested by Capraro.

A host of negative outcomes accrue from college men's abuse of alcohol. For example, a key finding from Wechsler, Davenport, Dowdell, Moeykens, and Castillo's (1994) national survey of 17,600 students at 140 colleges was that among the male participants who reported regularly binge-drinking, 60 percent admitted to driving a vehicle after doing so. Furthermore, disproportionate male involvement in acts of violence, sexual assault, risky and irresponsible sex, and accidental injuries have also been linked to alcohol abuse (Burda, Tushup, & Hackman, 1992; Capraro, 2000; Courtenay, 1998, 2004). Empirical studies also confirm that environments that characterize male-dominated subcultures, such as fraternities and sports teams, often encourage irresponsible drinking behavior among men (Capraro, 2000; Hill, Burch-Ragan, & Yates, 2001; Kuh & Arnold, 1993; Rhoads, 1995).

The alarming rate of sexual assaults perpetrated by male students on college campuses is another critical issue concerning college men. One in four college women report being victims of a sexual assault (Choate, 2003; Earle, 1996; Foubert & Cowell, 2004; O'Donohue, Yeater, & Fanetti, 2003). Approximately 60–80 percent of the assaults are perpetrated by men with whom the victims are acquainted (Boswell & Spade, 1996). Researchers attribute a variety of reasons and factors to why college men commit sexual assaults, such as the use and abuse of alcohol and drugs; men's tendencies to view sexually forceful behavior as acceptable; cultural norms that promote male dominance and aggression towards women; and men's lack of understanding of how a victim is affected by a sexual assault (Boswell & Spade, 1996; Choate, 2003). Sax and Harper (2007) found that college men, more so than women, embraced views of sexual entitlement, particularly when they believe a woman has "led them on" (p. 682). They correlated this view with values of status and power, which are associated with masculinity.

Our comparison and acknowledgement of the gender-related conflicts and issues that challenge college men does not aim to devalue the realities of gender inequities in higher education. We agree that there is a system of patriarchy in higher educational institutions that has historically oppressed women. However, men are also constricted by the same system that privileges patriarchy and stereotypical notions of masculinity. To address the identity development among college men and women, this chapter seeks to apply new ways of considering gender identity development.

Feminist Poststructuralism: An Alternative Approach to Female Student Identity Development

Decades of research on female student identity development discuss the profound effect that social relationships have in forming and framing identity. Gilligan (1982), for example, found that women define themselves in relations to others and within the context of intimate relationships. Similarly, Belenky et al. (1986) noted five epistemological perspectives—silence, received knowledge, subjective knowledge, procedural knowledge, and constructed knowledge—that are created in direct connection to patterns of family interaction during childhood. Josselson (1987) used the models of Erickson (1968) and Marcia (1960) to argue that the primary site for identity development among women occurred in relationships with family and during contact with others. This finding was dramatically different from that relating to men, who have been found to develop individual identity through separation, individuation, and autonomy. The focus on relationships as the site of female student identity development presupposes a fixed and universal development for all women. The diversity of experience as well as the intersections of class, race, and sexuality and the fluidity of identity development have been largely ignored. In order to provide an alternative perspective of female identity development, we present a feminist poststructural approach to identity, which claims that identity is fluid, subjective, and contextually bound.

Feminist poststructuralism begins from the assumption that gender is socially constructed in a society that systematically places women in oppressive positions. The development of a gender identity is rooted in the fluid nature of social construction, but is also connected to societal notions of gender. Women, for example, have multiple identities associated with race, socioeconomic class, religion, and sexuality that affect their gender development. Regardless of the differences among women, the societal norms of femininity still apply. Feminist poststructuralism explains that these social norms regarding gender are expressed in language, which, in turn, constructs women's identities (Weedon, 1997). The ways in which women come to know the social norms regarding gender is through language. Furthermore, language is contextually bound. Specific contexts alter the messages of gender thus affecting identity development. For example, male students are twice as likely as female students to speak in the classroom environment (Sadker & Sadker, 1994) and teachers are often more likely to interrupt female students (Hall & Sandler, 1982). By silencing women in the classroom, their identities as college students are constructed alongside silence.

According to feminist poststructuralism, identity is not singular. A female college student can have multiple identities, relating to her race, gender, sexuality, and class. The multiplicity of identities does not infer that they are separate. Rather, identities, such as race, socioeconomic class, and sexuality, tend to intersect. A female student may simultaneously represent her ethnicity and sexuality. For example, a female student may be a member of an organization for gay, lesbian, bisexual, and transgendered students of color. In this context, she will likely foreground her race and sexual orientation simultaneously.

Not only does a feminist poststructural perspective reconceptualize the formation and permanence of identities, the perspective also assists in connecting individual experience and social structures in new ways. According to Tisdell (2000), one of the basic tenets of feminist poststructuralism includes shifting identities within different social structures. Social settings convey meaning and place value on particular identities through both implicit and explicit messages. The college classroom is a social setting that conveys many implicit and explicit messages about gender. For example, consider a traditional, male-dominated course. The desk will be organized in a row configuration, the course content will focus on so-called objective and observable facts. The passive acceptance, memorization, and subsequent regurgitation of course content on exams will be the primary mechanisms for learning. Course content will be delivered exclusively by way of lectures. Thus, students will not be co-constructors of learning as their experiences and voices will not be heard. The polar opposite of this social setting is a diverse, gender-balanced course in which the desks are configured in a circle, individuals' experiences are valued and emphasized through class discussions, and multiple strategies for learning and demonstrating mastery of course content will be used. Although the traditional classroom setting may value the identity of students, the non-traditional setting places meaning on a student's gender, race, and other social identities that emerge during discussions.

There are a few studies that have adopted feminist poststructural ideas regarding identity. Anderson and Hayes (1996) found that "life-ties," which are "a set of related experiences and the perceptions these experiences evoke within the lives of adults," have a meaningful impact on individual identities (p. xiii). These same researchers also found that an individual's position in the social structure (often termed "positionality") also affects identity development. By evoking positionality as an important concept within identity development, ideas of the multiplicity and intersection of identities are brought forth. For example, a female college student from a high social class may not experience the financial difficulties of paying high tuition whereas another female college student from a lower social class may have to consider financial aid or finding a job to pay for college. By virtue of the identity related to social class, an individual's identity and experience positions her differently within higher education. Other researchers have applied feminist poststructuralism to women as learners (Flannery & Hayes, 2000). Although this is not directly related to identity development among women, Flannery and Hayes note that to examine women as learners through the lens of feminist poststructuralism "gives legitimacy to the particularity of each women's experience, helping us recognize the complexity of our identities and our differences as well as our similarities" (p. 14).

A feminist poststructural model provides an alternative paradigm to identity development. Starting from the premise that identities are fluid, contextual, and multiple, identity is not a fixed category, but one that is constantly constructed. In this sense, each individual has multiple identities that are available based on the particular context. A female undergraduate student, for example, may emphasize her socioeconomic class in a sorority setting, but her academic interests in the classroom. Importantly, poststructuralist assumptions about gender debunk the ways in which identity development among women have been previously conceived. This model refutes singular and monolithic definitions of identity as they relate to gender; identity does not develop through a single process or at one exact time. To focus on the complexities of identity development as presented by feminist poststructuralism, studies examine individual experiences and refute the possibility of constructing universal theories. Tisdell (2000) explains that by looking at identity as complex and often intersecting, researchers can address identity development in new ways and possibly facilitate social change.

The Social Constructionist Model: An Alternative Approach to Male Student Identity Development

The early research on men and masculinity focused primarily on examining male "sex roles" and sought to link empirically what were believed to be essential characteristics of masculinity to men's biological and cognitive compositions (Connell, 1995; Kimmel & Messner, 2007). Researchers who subscribed to the sex role paradigm argued that acts of violence, sexual aggression, athleticism, competitiveness, and other characteristics that are culturally associated with masculinity were, in fact, "natural" male behavioral traits that were inherent to their biology, psychology, or other physiological factors (Connell, 1995; Kimmel & Messner, 2007). A major shortcoming of the sex role paradigm is that it fails to acknowledge the "complex social meanings" that are associated with masculinity and the interrelated social processes by which these meanings are produced and reinforced (Kimmel & Messner, 2007, p. xvi). Consequently this approach was effectively challenged by feminist scholars (e.g., Chodorow, 1978; Gilligan, 1982), and afterwards by men's studies scholars (e.g., Connell, 1987; Kimmel, 1987; Pleck, 1981) who maintained that gender was not an objective, predetermined phenomenon, but rather a performance of socially prescribed roles and behaviors that are assigned to men and women. They also made transparent the ways in which socially prescribed gender roles privileged some groups (notably White, heterosexual, middle- and upper-class men) while oppressing and marginalizing others (women, people of color, poor, gay, and disabled individuals). Their work serves as the foundation of the social constructionist model, a theoretical perspective that is advocated by Kimmel and Messner (2007) for understanding masculinity. This perspective is underpinned by the notion that masculine behavior is learned and reinforced in social institutions and through human interactions. It is this perspective that we propose as an alternative model for understanding male student identity development.

Like feminist poststructuralism, the social constructionist model is grounded in the assumption that gender is not a fixed characteristic, but rather one that is produced, negotiated, and reinforced within social structures. Another key assumption of the model is that masculinity is not experienced and expressed uniformly by all groups of men. The performance of masculinity is influenced by multiple factors, including one's gender (since both men and women can express masculinity). On this point, Kimmel and Messner (2007) acknowledge that there are "varieties of men" and write: "In the contemporary United States, masculinity is constructed differently by class culture, by race and ethnicity, and by age" (p. xxii). An important implication follows from this assumption: that a single, universal, or normative masculinity does not actually exist. Instead, masculinity is a collection of rules and norms that govern gendered behavior for men in particular contexts. Thus, it is not uncommon for men's studies scholars to refer to masculinity in the plural as "masculinities." Doing so acknowledges the range of behaviors and conceptualizations that can be associated with masculinity.

Research that considers the social construction of masculinity focuses on the ways in which male gender identities develop by way of socializing practices. Socializing practices are the primary means by which boys develop during the early stages of gender identity (Adams & Coltrane, 2005; Connell, 1987; Kimmel & Messner, 2007; Mac an Ghaill, 1994; Pollack, 2001; Swain, 2005; Whitson, 1990). Socializing practices take place within normative social structures, such as school settings, sports culture, popular culture, and families. Within these structures, boys learn at an early age that they are expected to be physically and mentally tough, sexually aggressive, homophobic, and athletically superior to women (Whitson, 1990).

To further articulate the ways in which male gender identity is socially constructed, we consider some typical social processes by which this phenomenon occurs. Specifically, we highlight the influences of male peer groups, sports culture, popular culture, and homophobia in informing appropriate gendered behavior for men. Although this discussion focuses primarily on White heterosexual social constructions of male gender identity, scholars have also recognized non-normative constructions, particularly among African American and Latino men (Abreau, Goodyear, Campos, & Newcomb, 2000; Harper, 2004; Majors & Billson, 1992; Mirande, 2004). In some ways, non-mainstream social constructions and performances of masculinity differ from those that are reserved for White heterosexual males.

Kimmel (1996) argues that male gender identity is constructed through peer interactions, which are distinguished by fellowship, camaraderie, validation, homophobia, and hegemonic masculine expressions. Consistent with Kimmel's assertion, Connell (1993) claims that men are often forced to "negotiate" their gender identities in order to gain the approval and validation of their same-sex peers. Thus, it is not uncommon for males to conform by exhibiting behaviors and expressing attitudes that are consistent with perceived social norms (Swain, 2005).

Sports also play a central role in reinforcing societal expectations of male behavior (Messner & Sabo, 1990). Critical functions of sports participation for boys include allowing for meaningful interaction between fathers and sons; providing an exclusive space for boys and men to socialize in the absence of women; introducing boys to customary male language; acculturating boys to male traditions such as homophobia and the sexual objectification of women; and confining men to the rigid boundaries of male gendered behavior (Fine, 1987; Griffin, 1998; Oriard, 1984; Whitson, 1990).

Representations of men in media and popular culture also contribute to the construction of male gender identity. Male gender identity, as depicted in popular culture, serves both comparative and aspirational purposes for everyday men. In other words, men use these images to measure and place themselves on the spectrum of masculinity. In addition, most male images appearing in the media and through popular culture strive to differentiate men from women (McKay, Mikosza, & Hutchins, 2005). Thus, men are commonly portrayed as authoritative, powerful, tough, defiant, and sexually aggressive (McKay et al.). Images of high-profile male athletes are often constructed in this regard (Messner & Sabo, 1990).

Homophobia and its behavioral manifestations go hand-in-hand with socially constructed male gender identity (Herek, 1987; Kimmel, 2001; Kimmel & Messner, 2007; Messner, 2007; Plummer, 1999). Homophobia relates directly to men's fear of being viewed as gay or feminine, and their perceived need to separate their gender identities from those of women. "Gay men symbolize parts of the self that do not measure up to cultural standards [of masculinity]; directing hostility at [gay men] is a way to externalizing the conflict" (Herek, 1987, p. 77). In learning to become men, boys are taught to avoid traits and behaviors that are typically associated with girls and women (Herek, 1987). They also discover at an early age that homophobia is one of the most accessible and socially acceptable ways to assert themselves as men (Plummer, 1999). Thus, homophobia allows boys and men to affirm their heterosexual identities while also differentiating themselves from women and their gay male peers. Heterosexual expression via homophobia is also an example of what Messner describes as "doing heterosexuality," an ongoing practice through which men avoid being stigmatized as gay or feminine, by portraying themselves as "real men." Accordingly, real men are those "who are able to compete successfully with other males in sport, work, and sexual relations with women" (Messner, 2007, p. 365).

The social constructionist model is a much needed alternative to the sex role paradigm and other frameworks that rely upon biological differences between men and women to make sense of gendered behavior. This model provides insight into the extent to which the conceptions of masculinity that are shared among male undergraduates are both consistent with and divergent from the conceptions that are salient within mainstream, non-collegiate male populations.

Programmatic Strategies

Feminist poststructuralism and the social constructionist model are two frameworks with which to examine gender identity development among the college student population. These two paradigms are far from separate. In fact, both feminist poststructuralism and the social constructionist model rely on beliefs in the socially constructed nature of gender and the importance of social structures in communicating gender norms. Each framework also presents the specificity of identity development as it relates to gender rather than singular monolithic categories. Both also reframe the discussion of the importance of social contexts in the creation of gender identity and place significance on social institutions. Postsecondary educators are responsible for understanding how institutional practices and programmatic decisions may impact the development of students. Below is a set of alternatives for student affairs professionals and faculty who are committed to assisting students in developing healthy gender identities and responding productively to gender-related challenges.

Gender-Specific Recommendations for Male and Female Student Identity Development

Provide Reflection Opportunities
A basic principle of feminist poststructuralism is the multiplicity of identities. Students have multiple and sometimes conflicting identities that may make identity development difficult or complicated. One suggestion is to provide structured and facilitated reflection opportunities for students. Reflection gives students a chance to recognize identity intersections and make sense of identity conflicts. Published literature on male gender identity unequivocally suggests that men are traditionally socialized to believe in hegemonic conceptions of masculinity and to adopt sexist, homophobic, and unhealthy attitudes. Thus, providing opportunities for male students to recognize the effects of traditional male socialization is necessary, and may encourage some to seek more productive ways to express their gender identities. Facilitated discussions with peers and professionals with an expertise in gender identity are obvious first steps in this regard.

Offer Group Reflection Opportunities
Similar to the first recommendation, higher education institutions and student affairs programs should consider group reflection opportunities. Encouraging students to talk and collaborate with others with different identities and facilitating dialogue across differences encourages reflection and self-understanding (Tierney, 1993). An exploration of the experiences of others also connects individual experiences to social structures (i.e., the college or university).

Develop Student Support Groups
Student support groups that address issues relating to gender identity development, particularly among male students, have proven effective. Intentional collaboration with men's and women's centers, faculty with expertise in gender identity and student development, counseling services, and the student health center will enhance the effectiveness of these groups. In some cases, these groups may need to be homogeneous on the basis of gender, given the unique needs and challenges that characterize the identity development process for men and women. In addition, faculty and administrators who advise and facilitate these groups should create strategies for reaching out to racial/ethnic minority students, student-athletes, and gay, lesbian, and bisexual students as they are typically underrepresented in student support groups.

Train Student Affairs Educators
Student paraprofessionals, specifically residential life staff and others serving in peer-supervisory roles, must be adequately trained to support and appropriately

refer students who may need or seek assistance with gender-related issues and identity development. To this end, periodic follow-up trainings with fully credentialed college or university personnel are necessary.

Policy Change and Interventions

Restructure Programs to Focus on Identity Development

With a look back to the advertisement for the women's center director above, we suggest that higher educational institutions consider altering existing programs to create a more explicit focus on identity development. These programs can also be enhanced by a stated initiative to support both male and female students. The inclusion of men in the mission of these centers creates a more diverse environment where male and female students have an opportunity to reflect and support one another.

Offer Transition Programs

Programmatic efforts sponsored by offices of orientation, residential life, campus life, and first-year programs focus primarily on assisting students in successful transitions and adjusting to college. However, rarely do these programs focus intentionally on issues directly related to gender identity. Transition programs provide timely opportunities to engage students in discussions involving their gender identities.

Examine Campus Cultural Symbols

In addition to the aforementioned programmatic recommendations, colleges and universities need to consider cultural symbols and discourses that diffuse throughout the institution. Messages that promote idealized notions of gender place students in a paradigm of dichotomy. For example, male students receive messages that in order to be masculine, they must idolize and emulate athletes. These idealized images may not be comfortable identities for all students. Being more intentional about the messages that are being sent to students will have a profound and positive effect on their gender identity development.

Devote Attention to Judicial Affairs Offices

Scholars have discussed the overrepresentation of male students as campus judicial offenders (Harper, Harris & Mmeje, 2005; Ludeman, 2004). Male students are also a group most frequently cited on multiple occasions for violating campus policies. Therefore, campus judicial officers are uniquely positioned to encourage men to explore and consider appropriate and healthy ways to express their gender identities. To the extent possible, books, films, magazines, and male peers should be incorporated into the sanctioning process in order to engage students effectively.

Recommendations for Curricular or Classroom-Based Support

Integrate Gender Identity Development across Curricula

Conversations about identity development are important in the context of peer groups as described above. These conversations need to also occur in the college classroom as an integrated component of curricula. We suggest that higher education institutions infuse the curricula of all courses with opportunities for students to discuss how gender impacts their lives and experiences as college students.

Offer Service-Learning Opportunities

Service-learning projects have been very effective in enhancing student learning, primarily by connecting course content outside of the classroom (Markus, Howard, & King, 1993). Thus, faculty should develop projects that allow students to examine gender-related issues within and beyond the campus context. Ideally, students will gain some insight into the ways in which gender plays a part in common, real-world social issues. Partnerships with local middle and high schools, family shelters, and sexual assault treatment centers correspond logically with this strategy.

We recognize that most of the strategies we offer will require institutions to reinvest or shift resources. Although we understand that this may not be possible on some campuses, all institutions are capable at the very least of providing opportunities for students to confidently and proactively address gender-related issues. One strategy to begin understanding the specific issues within one's college population is to ask students directly about their experiences. This will assist in understanding how a particular campus context both hinders and facilitates gender identity development. Campus faculty and administrators who have an interest in gender-related trends and issues can be invited to participate in the inquiry as interviewers, as group facilitators, and in other important roles. Campuses have options. With thoughtful and purposeful action on the part of campus leaders, students can receive the support they need to manage the challenging, but necessary, process of gender identity development.

Conclusion

The challenges and issues that male and female students face during their undergraduate years are noticeably different. Many women are academically successful yet often exhibit eating disorders or other unhealthy habits in order to "fit in" and maintain the idealized norm of beauty. Female students also succumb to the pressure of traditional occupations and are deterred from math, science, and engineering fields. Men often attempt to maintain and live up to the idealized images of masculinity. As a result, some male students exhibit poor help-seeking behaviors, abuse drugs and alcohol, and perform poorly academically.

In this chapter, we presented two alternative theories to consider when addressing gender identity development among college men and women. Each theory extends previous conceptualizations of gender and identity development by focusing on the fluidity of identity and the contextual meaning associated with identities. Feminist poststructuralism maintains that cultural norms regarding the appropriate behavior and identities for women are communicated within the context of higher education. These idealized norms for women and men may lead to unhealthy behaviors and work against personal and academic success. Similarly, the social constructionist model addresses hegemonic masculinity and its detrimental impact on male identity development. We suggest that postsecondary leaders consider how their institutional cultures may contribute to gender identity conflicts and that they design and implement innovative strategies to support students as they develop their gender identity. With a few important programmatic efforts, student affairs educators and faculty can help students successfully manage identity development conflicts.

References

Abreau, J. M., Goodyear, R. K., Campos, A., & Newcomb, M. D. (2000). Ethnic belonging and traditional masculinity ideology among African Americans, European Americans, and Latinos. *Psychology of Men and Masculinity, 1*, 75–86.

Adams, M., & Coltrane, S. (2005). Boys and men in families. In M. Kimmel, J. Hearn & R. W. Connell (Eds.), *Handbook of studies on men & masculinities* (pp. 230–248). Thousand Oaks, CA: Sage.

Allison, K. C., & Park, C. L. (2004). A prospective study of disordered eating among sorority and nonsorority women. *International Journal of Eating Disorders, 35*(3), 354–358.

Anderson, D. A., & Hayes, C. L. (1996). *Gender, identity, and self-esteem.* New York: Springer.

Astin, A. W. (1984). Student involvement: A developmental theory for higher education. *Journal of College Student Personnel, 25,* 297–308.

Astin, A. W. & Sax, L. J. (1998). How undergraduates are affected by service participation. *Journal of College Student Development, 39*(3), 251–263.

Belenky, M. F., Clinchy, B. M., Goldberger, N. R., & Tarule, J. M. (1986). *Women's ways of knowing: The development of self, voice, and mind.* New York: Basic Books.

Boswell, A. A., & Spade, J. Z. (1996). Fraternities and collegiate rape culture: Why are some fraternities more dangerous places for women? *Gender & Society, 10*(2), 133–147.

Brickhouse, N. W., Lowery, P., & Schultz, K. (2000). What kind of a girl does science? The construction of school science identities. *Journal of Research in Science Teaching, 37*(5), 441–458.

Burda, P. C., Tushup, R. J., & Hackman, P. S. (1992). Masculinity and social support in alcoholic men. *Journal of Men's Studies, 1*(2), 187–193.

Capraro, R. L. (2000). Why college men drink: Alcohol, adventure, and the paradox of masculinity. *Journal of American College Health, 48,* 307–315.

Choate, L. H. (2003). Sexual assault prevention programs for college men: An exploratory evaluation of the men against violence model. *Journal of College Counseling, 6,* 166–176.

Chodorow, N. (1978). *The reproduction of mothering.* Berkeley: University of California.

Clayton, O., Hewitt, C. L., & Gaffney, E. D. (2004). Reflecting on reconnecting males to higher education. In G. E. Kellom (Ed.), *Developing effective programs and services for college men. New Directions for Student Services.* (No. 107, pp. 9–22). San Francisco: Jossey-Bass.

Connell, R. W. (1987). *Gender and power: Society, the person and sexual politics.* Palo Alto, CA: Stanford University Press.

Connell, R. W. (1993). Disruptions: Improper masculinities and school. In L. Weis & M. Fine (Eds.), *Beyond silenced voices: Class, race, and gender in United States schools* (pp. 169–182). New York: State University of New York Press.

Connell, R. W. (1995). *Masculinities*. Berkeley, CA: University of California Press.

Courtenay, W. H. (1998). College men's health: An overview and call to action. *Journal of American College Health, 46*(6), 279–290.

Courtenay, W. H. (2004). Best practices for improving college men's health. In G. E. Kellom (Ed.), *Developing effective programs and services for college men. New Directions for Student Services* (No. 107, pp. 59–74). San Francisco: Jossey-Bass.

Cuyjet, M. J. (1997). African American men on college campuses: Their needs and their perceptions. In M. J. Cuyjet (Ed.), *Helping African American men succeed in college. New Directions for Student Services* (No. 80, pp. 79–91). San Francisco: Jossey-Bass.

Davis, T. (2002). Voices of gender role conflict: The social construction of college men's identity. *Journal of College Student Development, 43*(4), 508–521.

Earle, J. P. (1996). Acquaintance rape workshops: Their effectiveness in changing the attitudes of first year college men. *NASPA Journal, 34*(1), 2–18.

Erickson, E. (1968). *Identity, youth, and crisis*. New York: Norton.

Flannery, D. D., & Hayes, E. (2000). Women's learning: A kaleidoscope. In E. Hayes & D. D. Flannery (Eds.), *Women as learners: The significance of gender in adult learning* (pp. 1–22). San Francisco: Jossey-Bass.

Fine, G. A. (1987). *With the boys: Little League baseball and preadolescent culture*. Chicago: University of Chicago Press.

Foubert, J. D., & Cowell, E. A. (2004). Perceptions of a rape prevention program by fraternity men and male student-athletes: Powerful effects and implications for changing behavior. *NASPA Journal, 42*(1), 1–20.

Gilligan, C. (1982). *In a different voice: Psychological theory and women's development*. Cambridge, MA: Harvard University Press.

Good, G. E., & Mintz, L. B. (1990). Gender role conflict and depression among college men: Evidence of compounded risk. *Journal of Counseling and Development, 69*(1), 17–21.

Good, G. E., & Wood, P. K. (1995). Male gender role conflict, depression, and help seeking: Do college men face double jeopardy? *Journal of Counseling & Development, 74*, 70–75.

Griffin, P. (1998). *Strong women, deep closets: Lesbians and homophobia in sports*. Champaign, IL: Human Kinetics.

Hall, R. M., & B. R. Sandler. (1982). *The classroom climate: A chilly one for women?* Washington, DC: Association of American Colleges.

Harper, S. R. (2004). The measure of a man: Conceptualizations of masculinity among high-achieving African American male college students. *Berkeley Journal of Sociology, 48*(1), 89–107.

Harper, S. R., Harris, F., III & Mmeje, K. (2005). A theoretical model to explain the overrepresentation of college men among campus judicial offenders: Implications for campus administrators. *NASPA Journal, 42*(4), 565–587.

Herek, G. M. (1987). On heterosexual masculinity: Some psychical consequences of the social construction of gender and sexuality. In M. Kimmel (Ed.), *Changing men: New directions in research on men and masculinity* (pp. 68–82). Newbury Park, CA: Sage.

Hill, K., Burch-Ragan, M., & Yates, D. Y. (2001). Current and future issues and trends facing student-athletes and athletic programs. In M. F. Howard-Hamilton and S.K. Watt (Eds.), *Student services for athletes. New Directions for Student Services* (No. 93, pp. 65–80). San Francisco: Jossey-Bass.

Josselson, R. (1987). *Finding herself: Pathways to identity development in women*. San Francisco: Jossey-Bass.

Kellom, G. E. (2004). Editor's notes. In G. E. Kellom (Ed.). *Developing effective programs and services for college men. New Directions for Student Services* (No. 107, pp. 1–7). San Francisco: Jossey-Bass.

Kimmel, M. (Ed.) (1987). *Changing men: New directions in research on men and masculinity*. Newbury Park, CA: Sage.

Kimmel, M. (1996). *Manhood in America: A cultural history.* New York: Free Press.

Kimmel, M. S. (2001). Masculinity as homophobia: Fear, shame, and silence in the construction of gender identity. In S. M. Whitehead & F. J. Barrett (Eds.) *The masculinities reader* (pp. 266–287). Cambridge, UK: Polity.

Kimmel, M. S., & Messner, M. A. (Eds.). (2007). *Men's lives* (7th ed.). Boston: Allyn & Bacon.

Kuh, G. D. (1995). The other curriculum: Out-of-class experiences associated with student learning and personal development. *Journal of Higher Education, 66* (2), 123–155.

Kuh, G. D., & Arnold, J. C. (1993). Liquid bonding: A cultural analysis of the role of alcohol in fraternity pledgeship. *Journal of College Student Development, 34,* 327–334.

Levine, M. P., & Smolak, L. (1996). Media as a context for the development of disordered eating. In L. Smolak, M. P. Levin, & R. Striegel-Moore (Eds.), *The developmental psychopathology of eating disorders* (pp. 235–257). Mahwah, NJ: Erlbaum.

Ludeman, R. B. (2004). Arrested emotional development: Connecting college men, emotions, and misconduct. In G. E. Kellom (Ed.), *Developing effective programs and services for college men. New Directions for Student Services* (No. 107, pp. 75–86). San Francisco: Jossey-Bass.

Mac an Ghaill, M. (1994). *The making of men: Masculinities, sexualities, and schooling.* Philadelphia: Open University Press.

Majors, R. G., & Billson, J. M. (1992). *Cool pose: The dilemmas of Black manhood in America.* New York: Lexington Books.

Marcia, J. (1960). Development and validation of ego-identity status. *Journal of Personality and Social Psychology, 3*(5), 55–558.

Markus, G., Howard, J., & King, D. (1993). Integrating community service and classroom instruction enhances learning: Results from an experiment. *Educational Evaluation and Policy Analysis, 15,* 410–419.

McCreary, D. R., Newcomb, M. D., & Sadave, S. (1999). The male role, alcohol use, and alcohol problems. *Journal of Counseling Psychology, 46*(1), 109–124.

McKay, J., Mikosza, J., & Hutchins, B. (2005). Gentlemen, the lunchbox has landed?: Representations of masculinities in popular media. In M. Kimmel, J. Hearn, & R. W. Connell (Eds.), *Handbook of studies on men & masculinities* (pp. 270–288). Thousand Oaks, CA: Sage.

Messner, M. A. (2007). Becoming 100 percent straight. In M. Kimmel & M. A. Messner (Eds.), *Men's lives* (7th ed., pp. 361–366). Boston: Allyn & Bacon.

Messner, M. A., & Sabo, D. F. (Eds.) (1990). *Sport, men, and the gender order: Critical feminist perspectives.* Champaign, IL: Human Kinetics.

Mirande, A. (2004). "Macho": Contemporary conceptions. In M. Kimmel & M. Messner (Eds.), *Men's lives* (6th ed., pp. 28–38). Boston: Allyn & Bacon.

National Center for Education Statistics (2003). *Digest of education statistics, 2003* (NCES 2005-025). Washington, DC: U.S. Government Printing Office.

National Center for Education Statistics (2005). *The condition of education, 2005* (NCES 2005-094). Washington, DC: U.S. Government Printing Office.

National Science Foundation (2003). *Engineering workforce commission, engineering & technology enrollments: Fall 2002.* Washington, DC: U.S. Government Printing Office.

O'Donohue, W., Yeater, E. A., & Fanetti, M. (2003). Rape prevention with college males: The roles of rape myth acceptance, victim empathy, and outcome expectancies. *Journal of Interpersonal Violence, 18*(5), 513–531.

O'Neil, J. M. (1981). Patterns of gender role conflict and strain: Sexism and fear of femininity in men's lives. *Personnel and Guidance Journal, 60,* 203–210.

O'Neil, J. M. (1990). Assessing men's gender role conflict. In D. Moore & F. Leafgren (Eds.), *Men in conflict: Problem solving strategies and interventions* (pp. 23–38). Alexandria, VA: American Counseling Association.

O'Neil, J. M., Helms, B. J., Gable, R. K., David, L., & Wrightsman, L. S. (1986). Gender role conflict scale: College men's fear of femininity. *Sex Roles, 14*(5/6), 335–350.

Oriard, M. (1984). *The end of autumn.* Garden City, NJ: Doubleday.

Pascarella, E. T., & Terenzini, P. (2005). *How college affects students: A third decade of research*. San Francisco: Jossey-Bass.

Pleck, J. H. (1981). *The myth of masculinity*. Cambridge, MA: MIT Press.

Plummer, D. (1999). *One of the boys: Masculinity, homophobia, and modern manhood*. Binghamton, NY: Harrington Park Press.

Pollack, W. S. (2001). *Real boys' voices*. New York: Random House.

Rhoads, R. A. (1995). Whales tales, dog piles, and beer goggles: An ethnographic case study of fraternity life. *Anthropology & Education Quarterly, 26*(3), 306–323.

Rozin, P., Bauer, R. & Catanese, D. (2003). Food and life, pleasure and worry, among American college students: Gender differences and regional similarities. *Journal of Personality and Social Psychology, 85*, 132–141.

Sabo, D. (2005). The study of masculinities and men's health: An overview. In M. Kimmel, J. Hearn, & R. W. Connell (Eds.), *Handbook of studies on men & masculinities* (pp. 326–352). Thousand Oaks, CA: Sage.

Sadker, M., & Sadker, D. (1994). *Failing at fairness*. New York: Charles Scribner's Sons.

Salgado, D. M. (2003). *Campus compact annual membership survey*. Accessed April 6, 2006 at http://www.compact.org/newscc/stats2003/.

Sax, L. J., & Harper, C. E. (2007). Origins of the gender gap: Pre-college and college influences on differences between men and women. *Research in Higher Education, 48*(6), 669–694.

Smolak, L., Murnen, S. K., & Ruble, A. E. (2000). Female athletes and eating problems: A meta-analysis. *International Journal of Eating Disorders, 27*(4), 371–380.

Smolak, L., & Murnen, S. K. (2001). Gender and eating problems. In R. H. Striegel-Moore & L. Smolak (Eds.), *Eating disorders: Innovative directions in research and practice* (pp. 91–110). Washington, DC: American Psychological Association.

Swain, J. (2005). Masculinities in education. In M. Kimmel, J. Hearn, & R. W. Connell (Eds.), *Handbook of studies on men & masculinities* (pp. 213–229). Thousand Oaks, CA: Sage.

Tierney, W. G. (1993). An anthropological analysis of student participation in college. *Journal of Higher Education, 63*(6), 603–618.

Tisdell, E. J. (2000). Feminist pedagogies. In E. Hayes & D. D. Flannery (Eds.), *Women as learners: The significance of gender in adult learning* (pp. 155–184). San Francisco, CA: Jossey-Bass.

Tonso, K. L. (1996a). Student learning and gender. *Journal of Engineering Education, 85*(2), 143–150.

Tonso, K. L. (1996b). The impact of cultural norms on women. *Journal of Engineering Education, 85*(3), 217–225.

Weedon, C. (1997). *Feminist practice and poststructuralist theory*. Malden, MA: Blackwell Publishers.

Wechsler, H., Davenport, A., Dowdell, G., Moeykens, B., & Castillo, S. (1994). Health and behavioral consequences of binge drinking in college: A national survey of students at 140 campuses. *Journal of the American Medical Association, 272*(21), 1672–1677.

Whitson, D. (1990). Sport in the social construction of masculinity. In M. Messner & D. Sabo (Eds.), *Sport, men, and the gender order: Critical feminist perspectives* (pp. 19–29). Champaign, IL: Human Kinetics.

Chapter 7

Environmental and Developmental Approaches to Supporting Women's Success in STEM Fields

Candace Rypisi, Lindsey E. Malcom, and Helen S. Kim

In January 2005, Harvard University President Lawrence Summers' remarks regarding gender equity in science and engineering sparked a national furor. In explaining possible reasons for the gender gap among tenure track faculty, Summers (2005a) offered three hypotheses: (1) women are less willing to work the hours it requires to be successful; (2) women and men have different aptitudes for science and engineering; and (3) to a lesser extent, gender-role socialization and discrimination. Summers added his views to an already complex dialogue on issues of equitable representation, educational outcomes, and campus experiences for women in science, technology, engineering, and mathematics (STEM) fields. For many, his comments demonstrate the pervasive inequity that plagues women in higher education. In the weeks that followed Summers' comments, scientists, academics, college and university administrators, lawmakers, professional organizations, and students were quick to respond loudly.

In February of that same year, Summers spoke to the Faculty of Arts and Sciences at Harvard to respond to his critics and publicly apologize. He commented:

> All of the many stories that I have heard from members of this faculty and many others in the last few weeks have an underlying and obvious, if some-times hidden, fact: that universities like ours were originally designed by men and for men. And that reality shapes everything from the way career paths

in academic life are conceived, to assumptions about effectiveness in teaching and mentoring, to concepts of excellence. We can make our university a better place for both women and men by rethinking our assumptions in these areas and many more. (2005b, p. 3)

Despite Summers' retreat from his initial statements, his comments serve as the catalyst for this chapter's focus on the developmental needs of and issues faced by women in STEM fields.

The purpose of this chapter is to provide a foundation upon which administrators and faculty can base their understanding of the issues facing female undergraduate students in STEM fields and the factors that support or inhibit their academic advancement and professional success. The developmental and environmental issues that female students in STEM fields face are highlighted in the first section of this chapter. Next, we explore psychosocial and cognitive theories in order to better understand the undercurrents of these experiences. Finally, strategies are offered to both address the needs of female students in STEM disciplines and initiate institutional transformation.

Women in STEM: An Overview of Needs and Issues

Gender inequity continues to be one of the most significant challenges that face many institutions of higher education. This issue is most prevalent in the STEM disciplines. Nationally, whereas women earn 57 percent of all bachelor's degrees, they constitute only 39 percent of those awarded in STEM fields (National Science Foundation [NSF], 2004). As women continue to be underrepresented in STEM fields, female students pursuing these disciplines need to negotiate a male-dominated culture that can pose challenges to both their academic and personal development. In this section, the literature on gender gaps in enrollment, retention and persistence, on the academic experience, and on campus climate issues for women in STEM is reviewed.

Enrollment, Retention, and Persistence

Research indicates that women at all levels of STEM fields are underrepresented (Clewell & Campbell, 2002; NSF, 2004; Rosser, 2004). Additionally, the STEM disciplines remain severely stratified, with large gender disparities in specific subfields. For example, although women have reached parity with men at the undergraduate level in the biological and agricultural sciences, they remain severely underrepresented in the physical sciences and engineering (NSF, 2004). In 2001, whereas women earned 60 percent of undergraduate degrees in biology, only 22 percent of physics degrees, 28 percent of computer science degrees, and 20 percent of engineering degrees were awarded to women (NSF, 2004).

Retention and persistence rates for women in STEM fields continue to lag behind those of their male counterparts. In a six-year longitudinal study, Brainard and Carlin (1998) studied retention trends and factors affecting undergraduate women pursuing degrees in science and engineering at the University of Washington. They noted that although the enrollment of female students in engineering programs had risen consistently in the last 30 years, retention rates for female students had decreased by nearly 30 percent. In addition, fewer women graduate in STEM fields than those who initially declare STEM majors. Chang's (2002) meta-analysis of the literature on factors that affect the under-representation of women in science and engineering indicates that STEM fields have the lowest retention rates among all academic disciplines. Research from the Center for Institutional Data Exchange and Analysis (as cited by Chang, 2002) confirms that nearly 50 percent of students entering college with an intention to major in STEM disciplines change majors within the first two years. In engineering alone, national retention rates for female students are less than 60 percent (Brainard & Carlin, 1998).

Retention of female students in STEM disciplines is most fragile during the first year. It is precisely during the early years that students encounter "gateway" courses that are designed to weed out "unsuitable" students. Similarly, the first year often brings students' first exposure to the academic culture of science. Research shows that many of the women who leave science or engineering fields begin to do so at end of the first year (Brainard & Carlin, 1998; Civian, Rayman, & Brett, 1997; Seymour & Hewitt, 1997; Thom, 2001). Female students in Brainard and Carlin's (1998) study demonstrate a significant drop in academic self-confidence during their first year despite being "highly-filtered achievers who start off with high levels of self-confidence in their academic abilities in math and science" (p. 374). Brainard and Carlin (1998) further write: "not surprisingly, the reasons for leaving are also the most frequently reported concerns, or 'barriers to progress' reported by women students who persist: lack of self-confidence, poor advising, and not being accepted in their department" (p. 374). Although much of the research findings regarding women in STEM majors stands in agreement with national data, an analysis of National Survey of Student Engagement (NSSE) responses conducted by Zhao, Carini, and Kuh (2005) found that female students in STEM majors are as engaged as male students in these fields; are at least as, if not more, satisfied with their college experience compared with males; and report a more positive campus environment than their male counterparts. Furthermore, the analysis conducted by Zhao and colleagues was not able to isolate these female students' perceptions of the climate in their STEM discipline from their perceptions of the wider campus environment and experience.

National trend data also indicate high attrition rates for women in STEM fields at other transition points in higher education (Thom, 2001). Sax (2001) conducted a nine-year longitudinal study of 12,000 students to examine predictors of graduate school enrollment and to determine if those factors are influenced by gender. Her findings indicate that of all STEM undergraduates, 25.9 percent of women and 32.6 percent of men enroll in STEM graduate programs. Interestingly, the data show no difference in the percentage of women and men in biology and engineering who go on to graduate programs. However, men in the physical sciences (48.0 percent, compared with 28.6 percent of women), math, and computer sciences are more likely to go on to graduate school. Sax determined that predictors for both women and men include a passion for scientific inquiry, an undergraduate environment that values science, and high levels of academic involvement (i.e., research) as an undergraduate. Sax also concludes that gender differences do come into play in understanding students' motives for entering graduate school; many men are driven by desire for "status and authority," whereas many women tend to be motivated by a desire to create social change and contribute to society. Sax continues to discuss various policy implications to support gender equity, such as increased mentoring and fellowship opportunities, "stop the clock" tenure policies, and flexible hours. However, Sax (2001) cautions that "while we must continue to strive toward equity and an improved climate for women in the sciences, we must also remember to caution prospective scientists about the realities of these fields" (p. 169).

As the data above show, enrollment, retention, and persistence rates of women vary widely depending on the STEM discipline. Women in STEM majors tend to be clustered in biology and other life sciences, and are grossly underrepresented in the physical sciences and engineering (NSF, 2004). While there is no definitive explanation for these skewed patterns of enrollment and degree attainment along the lines of gender, it is important to question whether there may be specific characteristics of the natural and life sciences that attract women to these fields and ultimately foster their success. These factors may be related to the traditions and foundations of the discipline, institutional or departmental attributes, or characteristics of the faculty members. Similarly, there may be specific characteristics of the physical sciences and engineering disciplines that contribute to the underrepresentation of women in these fields and their low levels of retention and persistence. Alternatively, there could be a connection between historical gender-role stereotypes of women as nurturer and mother and gender-role socialization that increases women's propensity to study biology and life sciences.

Not only do disparities in enrollment, retention, and persistence rates exist along gender lines, but it also appears that race- and ethnicity-based disparities exist among women in STEM fields. African American, Native American, and Latina women participate in the sciences at rates lower than White and Asian women (NSF, 2004). It is important to note, however, that African American, Native American, and Latina women earn science and engineering bachelor's degrees at significantly higher rates than their same-race male counterparts (NSF, 2004). The gender disparities among these traditionally underrepresented groups, combined with their very small numbers, may cause women of color to experience the STEM disciplines differently than White and Asian women. The intersection of race, ethnicity, and gender in the identities of women of color often means that they must contend with the dual problems of racism and sexism (Hanson, 2004; Malcom, Hall, & Brown, 1976). Therefore, although women in STEM majors may share some common experiences across populations, the group should not be treated as a monolithic one. Hanson (2004) reminds readers that "[n]ot all women have the same experiences in science education and occupations and that our understanding of the unique talents, interests, and experiences of subgroups of women is heightened when we consider their experiences through a multicultural lens" (p. 96).

The Academic Experience

Isolation, lack of mentors, and the shortage of role models can adversely affect the academic experience for female students in STEM fields. Given that in 2001 only 18 percent of faculty members in the STEM disciplines were women (NSF, 2004), it is likely that a female student may go her entire undergraduate career without working closely with a female faculty member, either in the classroom or in a research setting. A study conducted by Evans (as cited in Blaisdell, 1995) found that undergraduate women believe that the lack of female role models contributes to the underrepresentation of women in STEM fields, and many of those surveyed conveyed that the lack of contact with female faculty was problematic.

The small number of women in faculty positions in the STEM fields may also negatively affect the self-efficacy levels of female undergraduates by further perpetuating societal stereotypes that women are not capable of doing science (Blaisdell, 1995). Self-efficacy plays a large role in women's career choices, particularly with respect to those women who choose to enter traditionally male-dominated fields, such as the STEM disciplines (Blaisdell, 1995). Women's confidence in their abilities as scientists may also play a role in their persistence in STEM fields. In addition, the negative perceptions held by many undergraduate women in STEM fields (e.g., of gender-based discrimination and "stereotype threat"; see below) may also affect these students' levels of self-efficacy (Steele, James, & Barnett, 2002).

Campus Climate

Although the academic and campus climate for women in higher education has been a topic of interest and controversy for over twenty years, women in STEM fields continue to report climates that range from "chilly" to downright hostile (Chesler & Chesler, 2002; Hall & Sandler, 1982). Female students in STEM disciplines often struggle to persist and succeed in "a man's world." Anne Wilson Schaef (1992) argues that women live in a foreign culture in a world that is dominated by a "White Male System" (p. 8). The effects of living under this system are so pervasive that most people are unaware or unconscious of its existence. It can be characterized by the following tenets: it is the only system that exists; it is innately superior; it knows and understands everything; and it is possible to be "totally logical, rational and objective" (p. 16). Under this system, women must struggle to exist in an "alien" culture that does not recognize their unique identities and talents. Instead, women in the White Male System must conform to narrowly prescribed roles (Schaef, 1992). One can think of the STEM disciplines as a microcosm of the larger White Male System in which women are often not valued as individuals who can make worthy contributions to the professions.

Similarly, academic institutions can hinder the development of women by rendering them silent and reinforcing the hierarchy of gender. In their interviews with students, Belenky, Clinchy, Goldberger, and Tarule (1986) found that female students were told by male science professors that women were "incapable of making [it in] science" (p. 44).

Hall and Sandler (1982) found that, in contrast, male students in the classroom were more likely to "have taken and held the floor for presenting their views and to have received a greater amount and more effusive public praise for their achievements than were the women" (p. 3). This preferential treatment creates a "chilly classroom climate [that] puts women at a significant disadvantage" (p. 3). Hall and Sandler conclude that this climate discourages female students from participating in class, dampens career aspirations, undermines their self-confidence, prevents them from seeking help outside the classroom, and causes them to avoid or drop certain courses taught in a sexist manner. This gender-biased treatment is further exacerbated by the underrepresentation of female faculty or senior administrators in STEM fields (Belenky et al., 1986).

Peggy Mcintosh (1995) further debunks the myth of meritocracy and argues that men reap undeserved rewards in society. Mcintosh claims that the centrality of men in the inner sanctums of society's most powerful institutions cannot be attributed to a merit-based system, but instead to the fact that males receive "overreward[s]" (p. 77). She argues that a "systemic tendency in disciplinary frameworks or epistemology [exists] to overpower men as a group" (p. 77). Mcintosh cautions against thinking that sexism is only carried on through "intentional, individual acts of discrimination, meanness, or cruelty" (p. 86). Instead individuals should think of sexism as an "invisible system conferring unsought dominance on certain groups" (p. 86).

Women in STEM majors are also affected by a negative campus climate outside of the classroom. Researchers estimate that 20–40 percent of female undergraduate and graduate students experience some form of sexual or gender harassment during their college experience (Kelley & Parsons, 2000). Women in the male-dominated arena of science and engineering report higher levels of discrimination than women in other academic areas (Steele, James, & Barnett, 2002). These experiences of both overt and subtle forms of discrimination undoubtedly affect the personal and academic development of women in STEM disciplines as they navigate these male-dominated fields.

Theoretical Framework

It is critical that administrators and faculty understand how gender affects the psychosocial and cognitive development of female students. For women in STEM fields, it is perhaps even more necessary that educators and administrators examine the complexity of their experiences, since they are affected by an array of developmental and environmental factors. In examining the developmental needs and issues that face women in STEM fields, three theoretical models guide our analysis.

Women's Identity and Feminist Identity Development

Many of the classic studies of identity development were conducted exclusively with male subjects (Chickering, 1969; Erickson, 1968; Perry 1968). As a result, universal theories of identity development emerged that rendered women invisible in the process. Women's development was analyzed in a framework that often left them marginalized and viewed as inferior. In her longitudinal study, Josselson (1987, 1996) examined the process of identity development in women. Over the course of her study, she questioned women on issues related to occupation, religion, politics, and sexual mores in order to better understand their identity development process. She conceptualized women's identity development in terms of competence and connection. Josselson (as cited by Evans, Forney, & Guido-DiBrito, 1998) found that women's notion of competence was more likely to focus on the "kind of person [they want] to be" (p. 64), whereas men's identity formation was based on such factors as ambition, occupation, and ideological beliefs. Josselson also noted that connection, especially interpersonal relationships, was more important to women, and they were able to elicit "autonomous satisfaction" (p. 64) from these relationships. Essentially, women's identity often developed in relation to their connection with others.

Much like the early literature on psychosocial development theories, cognitive development theories also focused on men's experience. In their seminal work, *Women's Ways of Knowing*, Belenky and colleagues (1986) examined how women experienced the learning process. Through their study of a group of women from "diverse ages, circumstances, and outlooks," they argued that there are five "epistemological perspectives from which women know and view the world: silence, received knowledge, subjective knowledge, procedural knowledge, and constructed knowledge" (p. 15).

With regard to the population of women in STEM fields, the perspective of procedural knowledge is the most illuminating. Procedural knowledge comprises two approaches to learning: separate knowing and connected knowing. Separate knowing is characterized by critical thinking and listening to reason, and in separate knowing the "procedures for meaning making are strictly impersonal" (Belenky et al., 1986, p. 109). This way of knowing has been traditionally identified as masculine, and this type of knowing is validated and recognized in scientific culture. In contrast, connected knowing is rooted in the notion that relationships of trust, empathy, and care are also important components of the process of learning. Connected knowing also validates the knowledge that can be discovered firsthand through personal experience. Belenky and colleagues advocated that women need models of "connected teaching" that can help them develop and nurture their own voices. "Connected teaching" emphasizes connection, respects and supports personal experience as a source of knowledge, and encourages student-induced work patterns.

Although identity development theories tend to examine common experiences among groups of individuals, it is important that women are not viewed as a monolithic group and that the multiple dimensions that compose women's identities are considered. Based on her interviews with female students, Jones (1997) found that they conceived of identity as a fluid entity "evolving in an ongoing negotiation between the outside and inside worlds" (p. 381). The participants were clear that their identities would not be constrained by rigid, externally imposed definitions from society. Jones found that these processes of negotiation between their inside and outside worlds became increasingly complex based on the number of dimensions that students said constituted their identities (e.g., race, gender, religion). One can see how these fluid conceptions of identity can clash with the values of a positivist and rationalist scientific culture. The field of science demands that the identity of scientist supersede all other aspects of one's identity. This might cause women in STEM fields to feel compelled to suppress other aspects of their identities in order to be scientists.

Cultural Capital

The academic culture of STEM disciplines may also be inhospitable to women because it disregards their unique needs and experiences and forces them to conform to a previously established culture. Cultural capital theory, first conceptualized by Pierre Bourdieu (1986), refers to a set of evaluative, institutionalized standards imposed upon a non-dominant group by a dominant group. Bourdieu's cultural capital theory aimed to explain the inability of members of lower social classes to gain membership in the aristocracy. According to the theory, members of the non-dominant group must conform to institutionalized standards—a process known as acquiring "cultural capital"—in order to advance their social standing. However, the norms and standards are constructed in a way that disadvantages the non-dominant group and makes compliance to these standards difficult, if not impossible (Lareau & Weininger, 2003). In other words, cultural capital theory describes the means through which a dominant group maintains its hegemonic authority and reproduces societal norms (Bourdieu, 1986; Lareau & Weininger, 2003).

Although much of the educational research that employs cultural capital theory focuses on the social status of particular student populations such as women and racial and ethnic minorities (Dumais, 2002; Lareau, & Weininger, 2003; Monkman, Ronald & Théramène, 2005), the theory can also be applied when examining the culture of educational institutions and academic disciplines. In the case of the STEM fields, the dominant culture is composed of the prevailing values, beliefs, practices, and norms established or maintained by men (Gerholm, 1990; Herzig, 2004). Although an in-depth discussion of the philosophy of science is beyond the scope of this work, scientific culture tends to be based on empiricism, positivism, and a strong belief in objectivism (Schick, 2000). In the academy, the culture of the STEM disciplines encompasses standards or rules regarding behaviors that students are expected to follow. These standards may include tacit understandings about the number of hours students should spend in the lab per week, the manner in which students should interact with faculty, or the way in which students should learn. Many aspects of scientific culture are largely unspoken and are seemingly transmitted to the new generation of scientists and engineers through osmosis. The extent to which an individual in a STEM discipline complies with these behavioral standards determines the value of her or his cultural capital.

The problem, however, is that the standards of behavior in scientific culture were created largely by White men, and disadvantage women and racial minorities. Women may find it very difficult, or simply undesirable, to comply with the cultural practices of the STEM disciplines. For example, despite a passion and talent for science, women may feel conflicted about the balance they must strike between long hours in the laboratory and family obligations (Herzig, 2004). Cultural capital in the STEM disciplines has thus been constructed in a way that limits the participation and success of women.

Women in STEM fields most likely experience their first exposure to scientific culture as undergraduates. Higher education institutions should be cognizant of the needs of women students in the STEM disciplines as they navigate an inhospitable culture and struggle to determine their place in these disciplines. We do not advocate that women adapt to this exclusionary culture (Harding, 1991); instead, we hold the position that the scientific establishment must modify its culture to incorporate the unique experiences and needs of women. In the meantime, however, faculty members, administrators, and student affairs professionals should be aware of the complicated issues that undergraduate female students face as they negotiate scientific culture and determine their place in the STEM disciplines.

Stereotype Threat and the Imposter Phenomenon

Administrators and faculty members must also consider the sociocognitive and motivational factors that contribute to the low levels of persistence, retention, and inequitable educational outcomes of women in STEM majors (Berg & Ferber, 1983; Blaisdell, 1995; Clance & Imes, 1978; Hackett & Betz, 1989; Herzig, 2004; Steele, 1997). Two notable theories that can have a profound effect on the academic and social development of women in STEM majors are stereotype threat (Steele, 1997) and the imposter phenomenon (Clance & Imes, 1978).

Stereotype threat, introduced by Claude Steele (1997), describes how "societal stereotypes about groups can influence the intellectual functioning and identity development of individual group members" (p. 613). According to the theory, negative stereotypes can act as "achievement barriers" to educational performance (p. 613). In particular, African American and female students who aim to succeed in school may fear being associated with negative societal stereotypes regarding their academic ability. This "threat" posed by negative societal perceptions of the intellectual and educational capabilities of women and minorities acts to increase cognitive load, thereby depressing their academic performance. Stereotype threat theory was validated through Steele's research involving African American and female students at Stanford University. Steele administered portions of the quantitative section of the Graduate Record Examination (GRE) to two groups of students. Prior to taking the test, the first group of students was told that the test produced significant differences in scores based on gender. Female students in this first group significantly underperformed compared to their male counterparts. A second group of students were given the same test; however, they were not told that the GRE produced a gap along gender lines. This second group of women performed at levels comparable to that of their male counterparts. Steele concludes that negative stereotypes can have a significant effect on the academic performance of students, even those who are highly capable.

Unfortunately, many negative stereotypes regarding women in STEM exist at all levels of the educational system and in society at large. Research demonstrates that gender stereotypes held by parents correspond with more positive perceptions of sons' performance in math and science compared with that of daughters (Jacobs, 1992; Jacobs & Eccles, 1992). As with other values and beliefs, parents can transmit these stereotypes regarding gender and science ability to their children, thereby socializing girls to show less interest in STEM fields (Jacobs, 1992; Jacobs & Eccles, 1992). These stereotypes can continue to be reinforced if parents respond to girls' resulting lower levels of interest in science by purchasing dolls for daughters and chemistry sets for sons. Jacobs and Eccles (1992) found that mothers as well as fathers perpetuate this gender-role socialization process.

By college, many societal gender stereotypes regarding women in science have taken root in the minds of both female and male students. On the college campus, gender stereotypes regarding women in STEM fields can manifest themselves in many settings, including the laboratory and the classroom. For example, a male student may make a derogatory remark about his female colleague, or intentionally exclude women from his study group. Alternatively, a female student may be hesitant to answer questions in lecture owing to her gender stereotypes, or she may feel obligated to act as a "lab mom," completing "domestic" tasks in the laboratory such as washing equipment, cleaning, or ordering food. At the college level, both female and male students subscribe to the negative stereotypes regarding women in STEM fields. Brownlow, Smith, and Ellis (2002) found that among students of both sexes, perceptions of a female chemist were more negative than those of a male chemist or a female studying the humanities. Because both women and men have been shown to have negative perceptions of women in STEM disciplines, it should be noted that an undergraduate woman studying science may be discouraged by her female peers as well as her male peers.

An additional factor that can affect women's self-perceptions of their intellectual and academic abilities is the imposter phenomenon. Clance and Imes (1978) coined this term to describe women who "maintain a strong belief that they are not intelligent" and are "convinced that they have fooled anyone who thinks otherwise" (p. 241). Women who hold these beliefs regarding their own "intellectual phoniness" often attribute their success to luck and downplay external validation such as degrees, awards, or promotions, claiming that these accolades do not reflect their true abilities. Clance and Imes found that the imposter phenomenon occurs with a much higher frequency among women than men, and is especially prevalent among high-achieving women.

The imposter phenomenon can cause women students in all majors, including those in STEM, to display behaviors that may hinder their academic and personal development. Clance and Imes (1978) note that once a woman has assumed the "posture of an intellectual phony" (p. 244), she tends to work overly hard, engage in intellectual inauthenticity, rely on charm and perceptiveness to gain the approval of superiors, and display high levels of anxiety related to gaining societal acceptance. The imposter phenomenon is difficult to overcome, and many of the behaviors resulting from internal beliefs of "phoniness" work to maintain the phenomenon. As a result, the imposter phenomenon should be a primary concern for educators who work with women in STEM majors.

Lawrence Summers' (2005a, 2005b) comments demonstrate that negative stereotypes regarding women in the sciences abound inside the academy and in society at large (Steinke, 1997). Stereotype threat and the imposter phenomenon are potential barriers to the development, persistence, and academic performance of women students in STEM majors. Thus, faculty, administrators and student affairs educators should aim to help these students develop a healthy sense of self in order to increase their likelihood of success.

Strategies for Meeting the Needs of Women in STEM

In this section we use the theoretical framework outlined above to develop a set of innovative approaches to address the developmental and environmental needs of and issues faced by female students in STEM disciplines. It is important to acknowledge that there are many "best practices" employed by colleges and universities across the country. The goal of these strategies is to provide a foundation to guide transformational change that will improve the personal, academic, and professional lives for women in STEM fields. The following strategies focus on four main areas: the classroom and curriculum; living-learning spaces; creating community; and assessment and evaluation.

The Classroom and Curriculum

Course Clustering

Engage in "course clustering" to ensure that no one female student is in a class with only male students and, where there are sufficient numbers of female students, to intentionally create cohorts of women undergraduates. A cohort structure will provide women in STEM majors with a ready-made academic and personal support structure. The relationships formed with other female students in the classroom will facilitate collaboration on class assignments and the formation of study groups—structures that may better address the needs of women and their ways of knowing. Course clustering can reduce the feelings of isolation that may cause female students to leave the STEM disciplines. In fact, clustering may attract more women to the STEM fields because of the increased sense of community among female students in these disciplines. This cohort structure, also known as a learning community, has been shown to positively impact student persistence, educational outcomes, and the quality of experience for undergraduate students (Tinto, 1998). In order to enact course clustering, an institution's academic departments will have to work with the registrar to schedule courses in such a way that allows for the formation of learning communities.

Summative Capstone Project

Create a summative capstone project for all STEM students in which they need to synthesize their undergraduate experience. Types of capstone projects include senior theses and projects. A capstone project is recommended for women in STEM fields because of the cumulative nature of the knowledge and expertise that is acquired in these disciplines. Upper-class students will be able to utilize and build upon concepts and theories learned in previous coursework. These projects will reinforce what students have learned throughout their undergraduate years and help to ameliorate the effects of imposter syndrome. This can boost the self-efficacy of students and correspondingly increase the number of women who choose to attend graduate school in STEM fields.

Curricular Opportunities

Provide curricular opportunities for students to engage with research and scholarship on areas of gender, race, and ethnicity by offering regularly scheduled women's/gender studies and race/ethnicity studies courses. These courses provide students—women and men—an opportunity to think critically about the role of gender and the intersections of race and gender and their impacts on the contemporary lives of women. Additionally, such courses provide women students an opportunity to place themselves at the center of the production of knowledge, thereby strengthening their views on their own roles as scientists and learners. Faculty should integrate the history of women in science, the philosophy of science, and feminist science studies into course materials. By doing so, students will be able to develop critical thinking skills in order to understand the culture of science and its role in supporting or inhibiting women's success.

Center for Teaching and Learning

Create a center for teaching and learning to address issues of pedagogical strategies, women's ways of learning, classroom equity, and curriculum development. If budgetary concerns do not make it feasible for a center to be created solely for this purpose, new faculty members should be required to attend workshops on the these issues as part of new faculty orientation. Tenured faculty members should also be required to attend workshops on a yearly basis.

Service-Learning

Integrate service-learning components into the academic curriculum. Participating in community projects, such as partnerships with local K–12 schools or Engineers Without Borders, will provide women students a chance to apply classroom concepts to social justice efforts. Organizations such as Engineers Without Borders partner with underserved communities to improve their quality of life through implementation of environmentally and economically sustainable engineering projects, while developing internationally responsible engineering students. Such programs exemplify what Belenky et al. (1986) describe as a "connected teaching" environment. Women students tend to thrive in "connected teaching" environments that emphasize connection, rather than separation, understanding, and collaboration.

Living-Learning Spaces

Common Areas and Themed Floors

Create living-learning spaces for female students within both academic units and residence halls. Create a common area for women STEM majors with a computer lab, study space, and kitchenette in a main STEM building. This environment will help foster the idea that women in STEM literally have a home in their discipline. This space will be open to all, but celebrates the accomplishments and achievements of women in STEM. In addition, create a women in STEM–themed floor in residence halls. These living-learning environments will provide opportunities for women to integrate their personal and academic development.

Scholar-in-Residence Program

Develop a scholar-in-residence program that targets bringing junior and senior female scholars to campus for 3- to 12-month periods. Although scholars should represent the full array of STEM disciplines, special effort should be made to recruit women from those fields with less representation (i.e., physics, math, and computer science). A multidisciplinary committee of faculty, postdoctoral scholars, and students should meet at least twice annually to determine scholars to invite. While on campus, visiting scholars should teach a first-year seminar, give a minimum of two science seminars, and participate in programs focused on women in STEM. Visiting scholars should live in the residence halls in order to maximize student–scholar interaction. This strategy serves as a way to increase the number of female faculty, role models, and mentors, as well as a recruitment tool to diversify the professoriate.

Multidisciplinary Seminar Series

Develop a multidisciplinary seminar series that brings to campus prominent female alumnae, faculty, and industry leaders in STEM fields. In addition to conducting a science seminar or public talk, speakers should meet with women students to discuss their personal and professional paths. The environment for this discussion should be intimate and allow female students to ask questions, voice concerns or fears about their own journeys, and ask for strategies on dealing with their academic and professional journeys. Speakers should also meet with campus constituencies (e.g., president, provost, deans or department chairs, women faculty, scholars, and students) during their visit to share their ideas on how their current employers work toward meeting the needs of women in STEM fields.

Offices for Women in STEM

Ensure that there are professionally staffed offices for women in STEM and campus-wide women's centers. It appears that some campuses have either a women's center or a women in science and engineering office or neither. Ironically, some women in STEM fields who attempt to use the services of the women's center leave feeling that their needs are not understood or met by women's center staff. This results in an approach to student development that leaves many students feeling further isolated and marginalized. In order to effectively meet the needs of all students, women's center staff and STEM office staff must develop collaborative programs and services to meet both the academic and personal developmental needs of students.

New Student Orientation Fishbowl Exercise

Conduct a "fishbowl" exercise during new student orientation for both female and male first-year students. In this type of exercise, a panel of upper-class women students in STEM majors relate their experiences while the audience listens quietly. Ideally these exercises should take place in smaller, intimate group settings such as residence halls. The fishbowl provides an opportunity for women students in STEM fields to give voice to their experiences as a minority group on campus, and thus ameliorates their situation of being silenced or not heard. It also informs first-year students about the issues that women in STEM face: for example, as first-year students being told by male or upper-class students that they are not as good as the men who were admitted, or having it suggested that their SAT scores are lower than that of their male counterparts. Comments such as these can decrease feelings of self-efficacy and exacerbate feelings women students may have about being impostors. The fishbowl exercise will encourage students of both sexes to be mindful about how their individual actions can affect the campus climate and learning environment for all students.

Creating Community

Funding for Women in STEM

Provide opportunities and funding for female students to engage with organizations for women in STEM at both the regional and national level. Female students should be encouraged and given financial support to attend conferences that specifically focus on women in STEM (e.g., the Grace Hoper Conference and the Women in Astronomy Conference of the American Astronomical Society). Students should also be supported in developing campus-based student organizations linked to national professional societies (e.g., the Society of Women in Engineering, the Association of Women in Science). Opportunities for this type of engagement will help students to learn personal and professional strategies for persistence as well as advancement.

Mentoring Program

Develop a comprehensive, multipronged mentoring program that allows female students to become both protégés and mentors in different settings. The program should include opportunities for peer-to-peer mentoring, faculty-to-student mentoring, graduate student-to-undergraduate mentoring; and undergraduate-to-K–12 student mentoring. Giving female STEM undergraduates a chance to connect with more senior women provides them with role modeling, support networks, and a community of women scientists. These connections encourage undergraduate women to envision themselves persisting up the "pipeline" and provide them with opportunities for their experiences to be heard and validated. Having a chance to mentor younger women and girls will help foster new generations of women in STEM and help the undergraduate mentors to continually rediscover the excitement of science, which will also facilitate their persistence.

Symposia on Women in STEM

Sponsor annual symposia on women in science and engineering in which female undergraduates, graduate students, postdoctoral scholars, and faculty members present their research, attend academic and professional development workshops, and network with each other. It is critical that women in STEM disciplines have an opportunity to discuss their research and personal experiences in welcoming and nurturing environments. This symposium should strive to create an environment where the research of undergraduate women is celebrated and given high visibility. Additionally, it is important that undergraduates are exposed to role models of female graduate students and faculty. Included in this symposium should be an opportunity for a panel composed of the president, provost, and academic deans to present on the status of women on campus and the findings of the annual review of indicators of success (see next section). All students, scholars, faculty, and alumni/ae—female and male—should be invited to attend. The event should be organized by a committee of students, scholars, and faculty from across STEM disciplines, the women in STEM office, the alumni association, and corporate development.

Assessment and Evaluation

Analysis of Data

Systematically conduct an annual analysis of pre- and postenrollment data and its impact on indicators of success (i.e., year-to-year retention, performance in gateway courses, cumulative GPA, major GPA, graduation rates, and postgraduation plans). It is vital that these data be disaggregated by gender, race, and ethnicity so that institutional actors can identify gaps in educational outcomes and determine the state of academic equity on the campus. Each year, a team comprising core faculty, academic deans/division chairs, student affairs educators, institutional researchers, and undergraduate students should actively review the data in order to analyze trends and determine an appropriate course of action for meeting the needs of students and eliminating academic inequities. This ongoing, in-depth data analysis will allow institutions to determine if women are underparticipating in STEM disciplines and to identify the specific problem areas that cause this underparticipation. For example, if the data show that women drop the first-year mathematics course at a higher rate than men, faculty members who teach the course can further inquire into why this is so through focus groups, interviews, or other assessment instruments. Armed with this knowledge, faculty can take the necessary steps to alleviate the causes of attrition identified. This may involve offering academic and personal support earlier in the semester, making changes in teaching style, or paying more attention to improving classroom climate.

Environmental Climate Assessments

Conduct annual environmental climate assessments to examine the experiences of women in STEM disciplines. First, each STEM school, division, or department should administer an annual survey and hold focus groups to determine how female students perceive the academic setting and to identify the issues they encounter in their majors. It is important that the survey and focus group methodologies maintain a level of safety, anonymity, and confidentiality to ensure full participation and disclosure. Survey results should be disaggregated by discipline to determine where problem areas exist and should also be reviewed in their entirety to determine if systemic, cross-discipline issues exist. In addition, every three years academic divisions should conduct gender equity peer review by hosting a site visit. Site visits can be carried out in conjunction with a national professional society or teams composed of valued colleagues from peer institutions. The site team should meet with students, faculty, staff, and administrators. It should then produce a report of its findings and make recommendations for improvement efforts.

Exit Surveys

Conduct exit surveys with students who leave prematurely or who are graduating. These surveys can be used to help assess the extent of the impact of gender bias on students' experiences and future plans. The exit surveys should be designed to expand upon the annual climate assessments, with questions added to determine how students' campus experiences have affected their plans to leave or their postgraduation plans and persistence in STEM fields. For example, a sophomore may say she is leaving because she has always felt marginalized and isolated on campus; she has decided to leave science altogether and pursue a career in music. Or a graduating senior may talk about how summer research made all the difference to how she felt about school; as a result, she has made the decision to attend graduate school in astrophysics. In order to maximize survey results, exit interviews should be mandatory and tied to other mandatory exit structures that may already exist (e.g., financial aid exit meeting, withdrawal procedures, and graduation processes).

Conclusion

As more women enter science, technology, engineering and mathematics fields, the landscape of these fields will continue to be questioned, challenged, and stretched in order to best meet the needs of female students. Fortunately, at this moment in time the dialogue and professional debate about women in STEM disciplines is strong. The national conversation in the aftermath of Lawrence Summers' remarks serves to highlight the importance of administrators and faculty understanding the issues facing female undergraduate students in STEM fields and the factors that support or inhibit their academic advancement and professional success. The literature on gender gaps in enrollment, retention, and persistence, on the academic experience, and on campus climate indicates that more needs to be done to improve the experiences of female students in STEM fields. The strategies offered in this chapter provide a foundation to help guide transformational change in the areas of classroom and curriculum, living-learning spaces, creating community, and assessment and evaluation.

References

Belenky, M. F., Clinchy, B. M., Goldberger, N. R., & Tarule, J. M. (1986). *Women's ways of knowing: The development of self, voice, and mind*. New York: HarperCollins.

Berg, H. M., & Ferber, M. A. (1983). Men and women graduate students: Who succeeds and why? *Journal of Higher Education, 54*, 629–648.

Blaisdell, S. (1995). *Factors in the underrepresentation of women in science and engineering: A review of the literature* (Working Paper 95-1). West Lafayette, IN: Women in Engineering Program Advocates Network, Purdue University Center.

Bourdieu, P. (1986). The forms of capital. In J. G. Richardson (Ed.), *Handbook of theory and research for the sociology of education* (pp. 241–258). New York: Greenwood Press.

Brainard, S. G., & Carlin, L. (1998). A six-year longitudinal study of undergraduate women in engineering and science. *Journal of Engineering Education, 87*(4), 369–375.

Brownlow, S., Smith, T. J., & Ellis, B. R. (2002). How interest in science negatively influences perceptions of women. *Journal of Science Education and Technology, 11*(2), 135–144.

Chang, J. C. (2002). *Women and minorities in the science, mathematics and engineering pipeline* (Report No. EDO-JC-02-06). Los Angeles: ERIC Clearinghouse for Community Colleges. (ERIC Document Reproduction Service No. ED467855)

Chesler N., & Chesler M. (2002). Gender-informed mentoring strategies for women engineering scholars: On establishing a caring community. *Journal of Engineering Education, 91*(1), 49–55.

Chickering, A. W. (1969). *Education and identity*. San Francisco: Jossey-Bass.

Civian, J. T., Rayman, P., Brett, B. (1997). *Pathways for women in the sciences. The Wellesley report, Part II*. Wellesley, MA: Wellesley College.

Clance, P. R. & Imes, S.A. (1978). The impostor phenomenon in high achieving women: Dynamics and therapeutic intervention. *Psychotherapy: Theory, Research and Practice, 15*(3), 241–247.

Clewell, B. C., & Campbell, P. B. (2002). Taking stock: Where we've been, where we are, where we're going. *Journal of Women and Minorities in Science and Engineering, 8*, 255–284.

Dumais, S. A. (2002). Cultural capital, gender, and school success: The role of habitus. *Sociology of Education, 75*(1), 44–68.

Erikson, E. H. (1968). *Youth and crisis.* New York: Norton.

Evans, N. J., Forney, D. S., & Guido-DiBrito, F. (1998). *Student development in college: Theory, research, and practice.* San Francisco: Jossey-Bass.

Gerholm, T. (1990). On tacit knowledge in academia. *European Journal of Education, 25*, 263–271.

Hackett, G., & Betz, N. E. (1989). An exploration of the mathematics self-efficacy/mathematics performance correspondence. *Journal for Research in Mathematics Education, 20*(3), 261–273.

Hall, R. R., & Sandler, B. R. (1982). *The classroom climate: A chilly one for women.* Project on the Status and Education of Women. Washington, DC: Association of American Colleges.

Hanson, S. L. (2004). African American women in science: Experiences from high school through the post-secondary years and beyond. *NWSA Journal, 16*(1), 96–115.

Harding, S.G. (1991). *Whose science? Whose knowledge?: Thinking from women's lives.* Ithaca, NY: Cornell University Press.

Herzig, A. H. (2004). Becoming mathematicians: Women and students of color choosing and leaving doctoral mathematics. *Review of Educational Research, 74*(2), 171–214.

Jacobs, J. E. (1992). The influence of gender stereotypes on parent and child math attitudes. *Journal of Educational Psychology, 83*, 518–527.

Jacobs, J. E., & Eccles, J. S. (1992). The impact of mothers' gender-role stereotypic beliefs on mothers' and childrens' ability perceptions. *Journal of Personality and Social Psychology 63*(6), 932–944.

Jones, S. (1997). Voices of identity and difference: A qualitative exploration of the multiple dimensions of identity development in women college students. *Journal of College Development, 38*(4), 376–386.

Josselson, R. (1987). *Finding herself: Pathways to identity development in women.* San Francisco: Jossey-Bass.

Josselson, R. (1996). *Revising herself: The story of women's identity from college to midlife.* New York: Oxford University Press.

Kelley, M. L., & Parsons, B. (2000). Sexual harassment in the 1990s: A university-wide survey of female faculty, administrators, staff, and students. *Journal of Higher Education, 71*(5), 548–568.

Lareau, A., & Weininger, E.B. (2003). Cultural capital in educational research: A critical assessment. *Theory and Society, 32*, 567–606.

Malcom, S. M., Hall, P. Q., & Brown, J. W. (1976). *The double bind: The price of being a minority woman in science* (AAAS Report No. 76-R-3). Washington, DC: American Association for the Advancement of Science.

Mcintosh, P. (1995). White privilege and male privilege: A personal account of coming to see correspondence through work in women's studies. In M. Anderson & P. Collins (Eds.), *Race, class, and gender: An anthology* (pp. 76–87). Belmont, CA: Wadsworth Publishing.

Monkman, K., Ronald, M., & Thérámène, F. (2005). Social and cultural capital in an urban Latino school community. *Urban Education, 40*(1), 4–33.

National Science Foundation (2004). *Women, minorities, and persons with disabilities in science and engineering: 1998.* Arlington, VA: Author.

Perry, W. G., Jr. (1968). *Forms of intellectual and ethical development in the college years: A scheme.* New York: Holt, Rinehart & Winston.

Rosser, S. V. (2004). *The science glass ceiling: Academic women scientists.* New York: Routledge.

Sax, L. J. (2001). Undergraduate science majors: Gender differences in who goes to graduate school. *Review of Higher Education, 24*(2), 153–172.

Schaef, A. W. (1992). *Women's reality: An emerging female system in a White Male society.* New York: HarperCollins.

Schick, T., Jr. (Ed.) (2000). *Readings in the philosophy of science: From positivism to postmodernism.* Mountain View, CA: Mayfield.

Seymour, E., & Hewitt, N. (1997). *Talking about leaving: Why undergraduate women leave the sciences.* Boulder, CO: Westview Press.

Steele, C. M. (1997). A threat in the air: How stereotypes shape intellectual identity and performance. *American Psychologist, 52*(6), 613–629.

Steele, J., James, J. B., & Barnett, R. C. (2002). Learning in a man's world: Examining the perceptions of undergraduate women in male-dominated academic areas. *Psychology of Women Quarterly, 26,* 46–50.

Steinke, J. (1997). A portrait of woman as scientist: Breaking down barriers created by gender-role stereotypes. *Public Understanding of Science, 6*(4), 409–428.

Summers, L. (2005a, January 14). *Faculty Diversity: Research Agenda.* Remarks at the 2005 NBER Conference on Diversifying the Science & Engineering Workforce, Cambridge, MA. Retrieved April 23, 2005 from www.president.harvard.edu/speeches/2005/nber.html.

Summers, L. (2005b, February 15). *Opening remarks at the February 15 FAS faculty meeting.* Cambridge, MA. Retrieved June 19, 2005 from www.president.harvard.edu/speeches/2005/meeting.html.

Thom, M. (2001). *Balancing the equation: Where are women and girls in science, engineering and technology?* New York: National Council for Research on Women.

Tinto, V. (1998). Colleges as communities: Taking research on student persistence seriously. *Review of Higher Education, 21*(2), 167–177.

Zhao, C., Carini, R. M., & Kuh, G. D. (2005). Searching for the peach blossom Shangri-la: Student engagement of men and women SMET majors. *Review of Higher Education, 28*(4), 503–525.

Chapter 8

Institutional Seriousness Concerning Black Male Student Engagement

Necessary Conditions and Collaborative Partnerships

Shaun R. Harper

A recent experience compels me to question the seriousness with which educators and administrators are willing to accept personal responsibility for Black male student success. I was invited to give a presentation for the annual staff development day at a college. Because data revealed several racialized and gendered disparities in student outcomes, the president and other administrators decided to frame the event around minority males. In advance of my visit, the organizers described to me some of the problems plaguing these students and asked that I unapologetically direct considerable attention to Black male undergraduates, the population for whom engagement and outcomes were especially troublesome. I recall being initially impressed that institutional leaders relied on data to inform the thematic focus of the half-day set of activities in which all faculty and staff were required to participate—unfortunately, my enthusiasm dwindled once the professional development day began.

Ironically, the event was held in the gymnasium on this particular campus. Perhaps this was the most appropriate venue in which to talk about Black male students, being that they composed the overwhelming majority on the basketball team there. From the center of the gym floor, I presented to what appeared to be a 95 percent White audience (as an aside, most of the persons of color were dressed in blue service uniforms). Given that I have taught and written extensively on engagement, I easily recognize disengagement when I see it. Despite my enthusiastic presentation style, the majority appeared, at best, marginally interested in the topic about which I had been invited to speak. Never have I seen a crowd respond so chillingly to a Black guy on a basketball court—perhaps their response would have been different had I been dribbling a ball instead of giving practical recommendations for improving outcomes among Black men and other male students of color. In some ways, I felt booing might have been better than the obvious disengagement their faces and body language communicated; verbal disapproval would have at least signified the faculty and staff were seriously paying attention.

After the presentation, a Black professor approached me with praise and gratitude for raising issues that were widely known and longstanding, but had gone unaddressed at the college. I left the gym feeling reasonably confident that few who attended would actually do something purposeful to improve the conditions for and outcomes among Black males. There were other indicators throughout the day that suggested collaborative efforts were unlikely to ensue in ways that would help this college close achievement gaps. Despite its devoting three hours to the topic, requiring all faculty and staff to attend, compensating me for sharing my expertise, and espousing a commitment to diversity on its website and in other materials, at the end of my visit I concluded (perhaps erroneously) that this institution was not serious in an actionable way about engaging, retaining, and improving outcomes for minority males.

In this chapter, I review recent research and highlight findings from national survey data that justify the need for institutional seriousness concerning Black male student engagement. Although some literature I review seemingly attributes problems to the expenditure of student time and effort, I firmly believe that much of what I describe is a byproduct of institutional negligence in fostering conditions and environments that compel Black males to take advantage of resources and engagement opportunities. These issues are placed in a multidimensional theoretical framework, which informs the necessary conditions and collaborative partnership ideas I present at the end of the chapter.

A Compelling Case for Engaging Black Males

Consistent with other parts of this book, what I call for in this chapter is a shifting of the onus from students to faculty, staff, and administrators. Because there are other chapters related to engaging women, men, and racial/ethnic minority students, some might ask, "Why the special emphasis on Black male undergraduates?" Below are four points to justify this population-specific call for institutional effort.

The Shamefulness of Student Attrition

The commission appointed by U.S. Secretary of Education Margaret Spellings to examine the future of American higher education emphasized the need to drastically improve the rates at which students graduate from colleges and universities. In their 2006 report, *A Test of Leadership: Charting the Future of U.S. Higher Education*, commission members argued the following:

Among high school graduates who do make it on to postsecondary education, a troubling number waste time and taxpayer dollars . . . some never complete their degrees at all, at least in part because most colleges and universities don't accept responsibility for making sure that those they admit actually succeed. (p. vii)

Although retention is lousy for students in general (as noted in Chapter 1, only 56 percent graduate within six years), it continues to be most problematic among Black male undergraduates.

Fewer than one-third (32.4 percent) of Black men who start college graduate within six years (National Center for Education Statistics [NCES], 2005), which is the worst college completion rate among both sexes and all racial/ethnic groups (Harper, 2006a). As indicated throughout this book, engagement and persistence through baccalaureate degree attainment are inextricably bound. Thus, any effort to improve the rate with which Black male students graduate must include an aggressive focus on eradicating the disengagement trends I later describe in this chapter. Put another way, graduation rates will remain ridiculously low as long as Black men are continually disengaged.

Engagement Now = Socioeconomic Progression Later

Placing greater emphasis on engaging and retaining Black male undergraduates now would ultimately increase the proportion of Black men with bachelor's degrees in the U.S. population. This is essential for narrowing socioeconomic gaps between them and their White counterparts. Over 20 years ago, Perry and Locke found "Black men have lower median incomes, higher unemployment, and employment in less prestigious occupations than do White men" (1985, p. 107). The most recent *Report on the American Workforce* indicates that 49 percent of White men served in professional and leadership roles, compared with 37.3 percent of Black men (U.S. Department of Labor, 2001). Conversely, 62.7 percent of Black men worked labor-intensive and service jobs, compared to 51 percent of White male employees.

Furthermore, Mickelson and Smith (1992) as well as Shapiro (2004) found that White men earn on average significantly more than do Black males with comparable educational credentials. In 2000, the median annual salary for White males with bachelor's degrees was $51,099, compared with $40,360 for Black male bachelor's degree recipients (NCES, 2003). These findings validate Gordon, Gordon, and Nembhard's assertions that "Black male professionals continue to be excluded from positions of authority, are often deemed incapable of management or technical work, and continue to earn less than their White male counterparts" (1994, p. 518). Thus, it is important to expose Black male undergraduates to engagement opportunities that will strengthen their likelihood of attaining bachelor's degrees and competing successfully for financially rewarding jobs after college.

Thousands of students participate in internships each year that enable them to acquire the skills necessary for effectiveness in the workplace after college (Harper, 2006b; Kuh,

1993, 1995). Given this, internships are part of the Enriching Educational Experiences benchmark in the National Survey of Student Engagement (NSSE, 2007). The relationship between internship acquisition, engagement, and post-college economic outcomes for Black men is clear: Those who are actively engaged are more likely to compete successfully for internships that will later render them competitive for better jobs with higher salaries and leadership responsibilities. The title of Thomas Shapiro's (2004) book, *The Hidden Cost of Being African American: How Wealth Perpetuates Inequality*, perhaps best captures the point I am attempting to make here. That is, active engagement in college offers wealth to students by way of outcomes for future advancement—Black males are continually shortchanged in this regard.

Empty-Handed Applicants Need Not Apply

Similar to the insufficient readiness for career competition I just described, those who were disengaged as undergraduates are less likely to be deemed attractive for admission to highly selective graduate and professional schools. This is especially true at institutions that do a holistic evaluation of applicants and place some value on prior engagement in campus activities. Having evaluated more than 3,500 applications in past roles as a graduate admissions officer for the MBA program at Indiana University and Executive Director of the Doctor of Education Program at the University of Southern California, I know firsthand the difference that engagement makes. Those with solid grade point averages, good test scores, and undergraduate leadership experiences consistently rose to the top of applicant pools. On a related note, despite its being a weak indicator of performance in graduate school, most universities still rely on the Graduate Record Exam (GRE) to conveniently sift through applications and limit access to post-baccalaureate degree programs (Nettles & Millett, 2006). A recent report from the producers of the exam indicated that only 2 percent of all GRE takers in 2005–2006 were Black males (Educational Testing Service, 2007). This could signify that Black men are not engaged in experiences that compel them to even think about preparing themselves for educational opportunities beyond the baccalaureate. As a case in point: In 2005, only 28.6 percent of Black students enrolled in master's degree programs were male, and Black males constituted only 3.1 percent of all master's students in the United States (NCES, 2007).

Better Off Ball'n? Not Really

"Perhaps nowhere in higher education is the disenfranchisement of Black male students more insidious than in college athletics at major universities" (Harper, 2006a, p. 6). This assertion is substantiated by the following data points offered in a report I authored for the Joint Center for Political and Economic Studies in Washington, D.C.

- In 2004, Black males represented 30.5% of student-athletes in Division I men's sports, the National Collegiate Athletic Association's highest level of competition. They comprised 54.6% of football teams and 60.8% of men's basketball teams.

- Across four cohorts of college student-athletes, 47% of Black men graduated within six years, compared to 60% of White males and 62% of
  student-athletes overall. The averages across four cohorts of basketball
  players were 39% and 52% for Black men and White men, respectively.
  Forty-seven percent of Black male football players graduated within six
  years, compared to 63% of their White teammates. (Harper, 2006a, p. vii)

These data have led me to two conclusions that admittedly come across as editorial, but
in my view are indisputable.

First, if colleges and universities expended even half as much effort engaging and
retaining Black male students as they do recruiting them to play football and basketball,
the problems described in this chapter would not be nearly as enormous. In the Joint
Center Report I note that in 2002 Black men composed only 4.3 percent of all students
enrolled at institutions of higher education, the exact same percentage as in 1976. Stagnation in Black male college participation rates over a 26-year period is both surprising
and absurd, given that institutions seem to have no trouble at all finding suitable students to play on revenue-generating athletic teams. The same is true with engagement.
That is, if educators and administrators undertook the task of fostering the conditions
that enable engagement for Black males with the same deliberation and intensity as
coaches and athletics departments approach recruitment activities, it would very likely
end up being the case that this would suddenly become the most engaged population
among all that are written about in this book.

My second point is related to racialized outcomes disparities among male student-athletes. Although athletics departments offer specialized resources and support services,
their effects obviously differ by race. Much about aggressively targeting Black men to
make up more than half of certain sports teams, but having their White teammates
graduate at significantly higher rates, is wrong. Although Black male student-athletes
graduate at higher rates than do their same-race male peers who are not on intercollegiate sports teams (47 percent vs. 32.4 percent), racial disparities for both groups make
clear the need to engage them more purposefully. Moreover, as Brandon Martin notes
in Chapter 15 of this book, only 1.8 percent of college football players are drafted in the
National Football League (NFL), and 1.2 percent of men's basketball players are drafted
in the National Basketball Association (NBA). Thus, it is essential to ensure that student-athletes are exposed to value-added engagement experiences that will equip them
with the credentials needed to compete for jobs and admission to graduate schools, as
the overwhelming majority will not go on to play professional sports. Just because they
graduate at 14.6 percentage points higher does not necessarily mean Black male student-
athletes will have accrued the outcomes requisite for success after college.

Most Useful: Engagement and Race/Gender-Specific Outcomes

As noted in Chapter 1 and in the Afterword to this book, a plethora of gains, outcomes, and benefits are associated with educationally purposeful engagement for all
students, regardless of race or gender. But I have documented elsewhere the ways in

which active engagement specifically enables Black men to resolve masculine identity conflicts (Harper, 2004); acquire social capital and access to resources, politically well positioned persons (e.g., college presidents and provosts), and exclusive information networks (Harper, 2008); negotiate support for achievement among their same-race peers (Harper 2006c); craft productive responses to racist stereotypes encountered inside and outside the classroom (Harper, 2005); develop political acumen for survival in professional settings and environments in which they are racially underrepresented (Harper, 2006b); overcome previous educational deficiencies and socioeconomic disadvantage (Harper, 2007); and develop strong Black identities that incite productive activism on predominantly White campuses (Harper & Quaye, 2007). Indeed, the general engagement-related outcomes for all students and specific gains for Black males are too rich and plentiful to handle haphazardly. However, despite all that is known about the associated outcomes, several data sources shed light on the alarming rates at which Black men remain disengaged.

Black Male Disengagement Trends

In 2001, a special edition of the publication formerly known as *Black Issues in Higher Education* (now *Diverse Issues in Higher Education*) called attention to troublesome educational outcomes among Black male undergraduates. In one article, reporter Ronald Roach (2001) noted that college and university administrators often say male students are increasingly withdrawing from campus leadership positions as enrollment gaps widen between Black men and women. It should be noted that engagement-related gender disparities among Black collegians is not a new phenomenon, but the trend has reversed. Researchers in the 1970s and 1980s (Allen, 1986; Fleming, 1984; Gurin & Epps, 1975) found that Black men were considerably more engaged than were Black women. Reportedly, Black men gained more, were more actively engaged in the classroom, interacted more frequently with faculty, and developed more positive identities and educational and career aspirations during that era.

More recent evidence confirms the engagement pendulum has swung in the other direction, as Black women now report significantly higher levels of engagement. In their study of gender differences in engagement, Harper, Carini, Bridges, and Hayek found, "women no longer lag behind men in their academic and social engagement experiences. Overall, the engagement picture for women appears to be considerably less grim . . . women have overcome the engagement odds and social passivity of years past" (2004, pp. 277, 279). This claim is substantiated by other empirical research studies published in recent years. Gender shifts in engagement have occurred across a range of institutional types, including two-year and community colleges. In comparison with their same-race male peers, Black female respondents to the Community College Survey of Student Engagement (2005) were more likely to:

- *Discuss ideas from readings or classes* with others outside of class "often" or "very often" (57% women vs. 45% men).
- *Use the Internet* to work on an assignment "often" or "very often" (60% women vs. 52% men).
- Report that their college encouraged them *to spend significant time studying* (80% of women vs. 73% of men reported "quite a bit" or "very much").
- *Have plans to continue their studies* (31% of men vs. 24% of women had no plan or were uncertain about their intent to continue college). (pp. 7–8)

Cuyjet's (1997) analysis of data from the College Student Experiences Questionnaire also captured many alarming gender disparities, but at four-year institutions. His study was based on data from 6,765 Black student respondents to the national survey who attended a wide range of colleges and universities across the country. Cuyjet found that Black men devoted less time to studying, took notes in class less often, spent significantly less time writing and revising papers, and participated less often in class-related collaborative experiences than did Black female respondents to the survey. Furthermore, Black women in comparison with their same-race male peers were more engaged in campus activities, looked more frequently in their campus newspapers for notices about upcoming events and engagement opportunities, attended more meetings and programs, served on more campus committees, and held more leadership positions at their institutions. Playing recreational sports and exercising in campus fitness facilities were the only areas on the survey where Black men reported higher levels of engagement.

Black male student leaders in Harper's (2006b) study indicated that while Black women were reaping the benefits of leadership and engagement, the overwhelming majority of their male counterparts were spending their time doing nothing, pursuing romantic endeavors with female students, playing basketball and working out in the campus fitness center, video gaming, and working jobs to earn money for familial responsibilities and material possessions (clothes, shoes, cars, etc.). Participants overwhelmingly indicated their Black male peers invested minimal out-of-class time to academic endeavors. These claims are supported by findings in Harper et al.'s (2004) study. In their analysis of data collected from 1,167 Black undergraduates at 12 historically Black colleges and universities (HBCUs) that participated in the National Survey of Student Engagement, the researchers found significant differences between men and women on the Level of Academic Challenge benchmark of the survey. As mentioned in Chapter 1, activities in this area include studying, reading, rehearsing, preparing for class, writing long papers, applying theories and course concepts to practical situations, and working hard to meet professors' expectations. Black male HBCU students were less engaged than were their female counterparts in this domain.

Also regarding out-of-class engagement trends at HBCUs, the general consensus among the Black male student leaders in Kimbrough and Harper's (2006) qualitative study is that Black men are grossly disengaged. Data were collected from Student Government Association presidents, fraternity chapter leaders, and resident assistants (RAs) at nine different HBCUs. Among the numerous engagement-related gender disparities cited, Kimbrough and Harper note that only 7 of 49 student government members at two different HBCUs were men. In sum, the student leaders confirmed that purposeful engagement, especially outside the classroom, is extremely unpopular among Black men at HBCUs (as is the case throughout most of higher education). At HBCUs and predominantly White institutions (PWIs) alike, Sutton and Kimbrough (2001) report sororities and fraternities are among the most popular venues for out-of-class engagement among Black undergraduates. However, Harper and Harris (2006) contend these groups have declined in popularity among men, as chapters on many campuses have fewer than 10 members.

Participants in Kimbrough and Harper's (2006) study offered five explanations for these Black male disengagement trends: (1) Men deem sports, physical activity, and athleticism more socially acceptable and "cooler" than campus leadership and purposeful engagement; (2) male students typically encounter difficulty working together, which is often required in student organizations; (3) many Black men come to college having already been socialized to devalue purposeful engagement; (4) there is a shortage of Black male role models and mentors on campus who actively and strategically promote purposeful engagement; and (5) many Black men are unable to meet the minimum 2.5 grade point average requirement for membership in one of the five historically Black fraternities. Harper (2006b) contends that gender disparities in Black student enrollments have contributed to a decline in male leadership on most campuses. Since they do not see many others who are highly engaged on campus, many Black men conclude that engagement is socially inexpedient and perhaps even feminine—definitely not normative (Harper, 2004).

Although all are most likely true and some have been empirically proven, the problem with these explanatory factors is that they almost exclusively attribute disengagement to students' attitudes and behaviors, not the institutions they attend. Educators and administrators are in many ways complicit in the cyclical reproduction of these trends. Negligence in fostering the necessary conditions for engagement and the infrequency of collective efforts to study and craft strategic responses to factors that compel Black men's detachment from the educational experience have been inadequately considered. Perhaps institutions, especially predominantly White colleges and universities, just have not recognized the value in engaging, retaining, and graduating Black male students. Furthermore, deficit views of Black men usually compel institutional fascination with the undercurrents of disengagement instead of learning from highly engaged and successful students within this population.

Theoretical Framework

As mentioned earlier, I am approaching the treatment of Black male disengagement differently by shifting the responsibility from students to educators and administrators. To this end, I have decided against placing Black male engagement issues in an explanatory framework comprising developmental, psychosocial, and student-centered theories. Instead, I have chosen a framework that helps make sense of college and university campuses as organizations for learning and environments that can be changed. Moreover, I make use of theories pertaining to the racial implications of engendering care for this population at predominantly White institutions (PWIs) and possibilities associated with anti-deficit views of Black male college achievement.

Organizational Learning Theory

According to Argyris and Schön (1996), learning occurs when organizations "adapt to changing environments, draw lessons from past successes and failures, and detect and correct errors of the past, anticipate and respond to impending threats, engage in continuous innovation, and build and realize images of a desirable future" (p. xvii). Organizational learning extends beyond individuals, and is instead collective (Kezar, 2005). In the case of Black male student engagement, educators and administrators on the campus could tap available data sources and engage in dialogues that help illuminate the undercurrents of inequities, make clear what is needed to foster an environment for success, and come to understand the complexity of factors that require mediation for the actualization of institutional goals. Theories suggest that organizational stakeholders would share this knowledge and make sense of it collectively.

Despite the focus on collaboration, individuals play an important role in the learning process. For example, Bensimon (2005) describes three key concepts related to individuals in organizational learning:

(1) Learning is done by individuals who are members of an organizational entity such as a college or university, an administrative division, an academic department, or a research team; (2) individuals inquire into a problem collectively, on behalf of an organizational entity; and (3) organizational culture and structures can promote or inhibit individual learning. (p. 101)

Moreover, Kezar (2005) contends that trust between individual collaborators, the establishment of new information systems, rewards and incentives, knowledge sharing and open communication, collaborative inquiry teams, and staff development are all necessary features of organizational learning.

Argyris and Schön (1996) describe two types of learning in organizations: single-loop and double-loop. The former places emphasis on external factors for problems in organizations (e.g., "these Black males do so poorly because they are insufficiently prepared for college"). This version of learning leads to incremental change, as organization members fail to recognize their own role in the stifling of desired outcomes (Kezar, 2005). In short, problems are narrowly examined; attribution is almost always external; and organizational toxins often remain unexamined. Bensimon (2005) posits that equity requires double-loop learning, which "focuses attention on the root causes of a problem and the changes that need to be made in the attitudes, values, beliefs, and practices of individuals" (p. 104). This version of organizational learning would require, for example, an inward examination of why a Black male student sits passively and performs poorly in courses where he is constantly stereotyped by the professor and classmates, exposed to culturally irrelevant perspectives in assigned readings, and expected to be engaged only when an opportunity arises for him to be the token spokesperson for all Black persons. Double-loop learning would also oblige teams of educators to gather qualitative insights into how Black males view the campus as a normative space for engagement—what they learn should guide future efforts to make necessary environmental adjustments.

Theoretical Perspectives on Environmental Press

Environmental press refers to the norms of a campus environment that can be described as distinctive to the institution by students, faculty, and staff, as well as visitors (Pace & Stern, 1958; Stern, 1970; Strange, 2003). Presses are characteristic of what is generally acceptable and normative within the campus environment (Pace, 1969). As such, they shape the behaviors students display and the degrees to which they buy into perceived consensus on a campus. If the majority of Black males are disengaged, then most will conclude that engagement is not the "thing to do." Strange and Banning (2001) explained that certain environmental presses can inhibit student growth, particularly when there is significant distance between what the student needs and the prevailing press of the campus. For example, Black male students need to be engaged to acquire the political acumen required for the cultivation of meaningful relationships with administrators, but if the normative press of the campus is disengagement among this particular population, then few are likely to act in ways counter to it.

Baird (1988) noted the following: "Presses are of two types, first as they exist in reality or an objective inquiry discloses them to be (alpha press), and second as they are perceived or interpreted by the individual (beta press)" (p. 3). Baird also presents two versions of beta presses, *private* and *consensual*. The first is related to the unique view a student has about her or his experience, whereas the latter pertains to estimations of commonalities in experiences and outcomes. At the end of a three-day visit that included observations and several focus groups, a consultant could conclude that Black males are disengaged and it is primarily the institution's fault. The real indicators of disengagement would be the alpha press. An individual Black male sophomore could attribute his disengagement to the insufficient provision of clubs and activities that appeal to his unique cultural interests (private beta press), but might also believe most of his same-race male peers are disengaged on account of the overwhelming Whiteness of social offerings on the campus (consensual beta press).

Were the current problems concerning Black male achievement strategically addressed, then the consensual beta press could become that most within this population are actively engaged—it would be seen as normal. Likewise, the alpha press that a Black male prospective student would encounter might lead him to the following conclusion: "Wow, should I choose to enroll at this university, there is going to be a serious expectation that I become as actively engaged as all the other Black dudes here." It is my view that presses can be changed, but only if educators willingly accept responsibility for undertaking the complex work of cultural change.

Critical Race Theory and Interest-Convergence

Based on scholarly perspectives from law, sociology, history, ethnic studies, and women's studies, critical race theory (CRT) illuminates the inequitable distribution of power and privilege as well as racism and racial disadvantages within organizations (Bell, 1987; Delgado & Stefancic, 2001). CRT also challenges misconceptions regarding color-blindness, merit, and racial equity; critiques claims of liberalism; and ignites consciousness that leads to social justice and advances for people of color (Crenshaw, Gotanda, Peller, & Thomas, 1995). One of the tenets of CRT is interest-convergence, which, according to Delgado (1995), "encourage racial advances for Blacks only when they also promote white self-interests" (p. xiv). It is used in this theoretical framework to help answer a question like, "why would an institution whose faculty and staff are almost exclusively White engage in double-loop learning and take on the challenge of creating a normative culture of engagement for Black male students?"

Interest-convergence helps explain the motivating factors that might compel majority advocacy on minority issues—essentially, there has to be something in it for Whites and they must see value in their efforts. Critical race theorists argue that White persons rarely act on behalf of minority groups "out of the goodness of their hearts." Delgado and Stefancic (2001) contend that consequently efforts to eradicate racism have produced minimal results owing to the insufficient convergence of interests. That is, Black Americans have hoped for racial justice, equity, and fairness, but those interests have not converged effectively with the goals of the powerful persons from whom those things have been sought. Black students could want more Black faculty, but in most instances it is not until protests ensue, media attention is garnered, and the institution is embarrassed by the public exposure of its structural problems with race that administrators move in any serious way to hire cohorts of minority faculty.

"We cannot ignore and should learn from and try to recognize situations when there is a convergence of interests" (Bell, 2000, p. 9). Making clear how retaining Black men will ultimately increase the overall retention rates for a predominantly White college is one way to do this. Another is pointing out the outcomes that will accrue for White student leaders via their interactions with Black men (e.g., developing cross-cultural communication skills that will be employable in future settings, which will make the institution look like it graduates progressive people who are not ignorant racists). And a third is arguing that changing the environmental press of the campus could garner for the institution a better reputation that will ultimately stimulate increased financial contributions from Black alumni. Donnor (2005) offers an example of when interests do not converge effectively between Black male student-athletes and universities with major sports programs:

Critical race theory offers a means to better recognize and more fully understand the forces that have constructed a system in which African American athletes are cheered on the field by wealthy alumni and powerful fans while at the same time denied opportunities to earn the degree that could lead to wealth and power of their own (p. 63).

A college president is quite powerful and could steer most agendas she or he deems worthwhile. But agenda movement often comes at a cost; hence White presidents and other senior administrators must see the value of expending their political capital in support of equity and engagement for Black male students. Surely there will be resistance from faculty and others if the ways in which the White majority will benefit are not made clear.

Anti-Deficit Achievement Theory

I have described elsewhere the anti-deficit achievement theory that emerged from my National Black Male College Achievement Study, the largest-known empirical research project on Black male undergraduates (see Harper, 2007). Essentially, it is an informative view of how Black males navigate social settings, such as schools and colleges, despite all we know to be stacked against them. It counters the *orientation* (focus on stereotypical characteristics associated with the culture of disadvantage and poverty), *discourse* (lack of preparation, motivation, study skills, blaming students and/or their backgrounds), and *strategies* (compensatory educational programs, remedial courses, special programs, all focused on fixing the student) associated with the "deficit cognitive frame" that Bensimon (2005, p. 103) describes.

Instead of always striving to "fix them," I argue that institutions can learn much from Black male achievers about what worked well, which could guide institutional efforts to engage more Black men. Although considerable attention has already been devoted to examining the problems with Black men in education and society (Cuyjet, 1997, 2006; Ferguson, 2000; Gordon et al., 1994; Harper, 2006a; Polite & Davis, 1999; White & Cones, 1999), it remains important to continually expend institutional energies on investigating the undercurrents of outcome disparities and social disadvantage. Never have I argued to altogether abandon this approach. However, it is my belief that at this point much is known about the problems, but too little about those who achieve despite them.

My approach is a theoretical perspective on institutional change that relies on learning from Black males who have chosen to make the most of college, inside and outside the classroom—active learners and doers who have high GPAs, impressive records of leadership and engagement in enriching educational experiences, large networks of institutional agents and supporters, and more social capital at the end of college than at the beginning. I argue that institutions can learn more about the conditions required for success by collecting qualitative insights from successful students. Instead of asking why so few Black men take advantage of counseling, career development, and academic support resources on a college campus (which remains an important question worthy of pursuing), perhaps more could be learned from those who actually utilize programs and services. Discovering the impetus for their engagement could be most instructive to those who endeavor to attract more of their same-race disengaged peers. This lens rejects deficit-minded treatments of Black male students, while simultaneously recognizing the continued need to better understand the factors that stifle achievement.

Indicators of Institutional Seriousness

Before presenting a set of strategies, I first describe some conditions I believe are necessary before an institution can claim to be serious about improving Black male student engagement. First, campus leaders must make this a high institutional priority. Recognizing there are countless issues that merit the attention of senior administrators, the decision to focus on this particular population should be data-driven. At many colleges and universities, analyses of engagement and retention data could easily justify the need to devote immediate attention to this particular population. These findings should stimulate a cross-campus campaign that is aggressive and conveyed with urgency. Institutional leaders also must have goals for the gains, outcomes, and levels of engagement they hope to see among Black male undergraduates; resources must be invested toward these efforts in order to confirm that creating a culture of engagement is indeed a priority. These goals should be documented, widely disseminated, and frequently discussed across the campus. An assistant professor in the English department, for example, should not accidentally discover the university has goals for addressing many of the same engagement issues that plague Black males in her courses—it would be better if she and others across the campus received communiqués articulating the institution's objectives for improving engagement and outcomes for this specific student population.

Institutional leaders must also have high expectations for Black male students and those who are positioned to engage them, both inside and outside the classroom. Clarity in the articulation of these expectations is critical. Strategic planning by administrators and other stakeholders is also essential. Strategy must permeate the campus at large as well as specific aspects of the institution (the student affairs division, the mathematics department, classes that emphasize writing, etc.). Given that Black males are retained least often on most college and university campuses (Harper, 2006a), it seems appropriate to suggest that presidents hire an outside strategist to advise senior administrators on how to best reverse this trend. Accountability is another necessary condition. Faculty, staff, and administrators should be held accountable for advancing the institution's agenda for Black male student success. For example, if improving Black male student-athlete retention rates and increasing student-athlete engagement in activities outside the athletics department have been identified as institutional goals, the athletic director must be willing to hold coaches and others within the department accountable for implementing new approaches, documenting efforts, and demonstrating effectiveness in this regard. Also, the person to whom the athletic director reports (usually the president) must hold her or him accountable for contributing to the institution's goals by making engagement a proven priority in the athletics department.

Lastly, collaboration among various institutional stakeholders—from food service workers to the director of residence life to the dean of engineering and students themselves—is also a requisite indicator of seriousness. Stakeholders from across the campus must be brought together to help actualize the institution's goals and develop ways to reinforce expectations for Black male achievement and engagement. Simply convening faculty and staff once in a gymnasium to listen to a speaker and expecting them to be compelled to partner is the exact opposite of what I am recommending here. Instead, specific approaches to fostering collaborative partnerships must be written into the aforementioned strategic plans. In sum, high priority, goals, high expectations, strategy, accountability, and collaboration are all necessary indicators of institutional seriousness. To be clear, I am asserting that institutional stagnation will ensue and disengagement will remain normative among Black male undergraduates in the absence of these important conditions. Notice that everything I have written in this section requires leadership, specifically presidential action. Having now worked at four postsecondary institutions, I have not yet seen something become a serious campus-wide priority without the president being involved.

Engagement Strategies

As indicated in the previous section, evidence of collaborative effort across the campus is one way to determine if an institution is serious about improving Black male student engagement. In this section I present possible ways that faculty, staff, and administrators can partner to reverse problematic trends and outcomes. This is not to diminish the worth of individual action and one-on-one work with students. But no lone academic advisor, faculty member, or Black administrator in multicultural affairs (or anywhere else) can single-handedly create a campus-wide culture of engagement. Caring and committed individuals are important, but it is usually the case that a small cohort of such persons is treated as the default source of advocacy for minority students (and this group is often primarily composed of staff of color). Student engagement must be everyone's responsibility at the institution, especially if the status of Black males is ever to be improved. To this end, below are five ideas for collaborative partnerships.

◇ The Equity Scorecard process developed by Professor Estela Mara Bensimon and a team of researchers in the Center for Urban Education (CUE) at the University of Southern California is perhaps the best available model of collaboration and organizational learning (see Bauman, 2005; Bauman, Bustillos, Bensimon, Brown, & Bartee, 2005; Bensimon, 2004; Harris & Bensimon, 2007; Peña, Bensimon, & Colyar, 2006). It is one I highly recommend for institutions that are serious about closing racialized and gendered gaps that disadvantage Black male students. This process brings together faculty, staff, administrators, and institutional researchers who work in teams to examine unique data sources that could provide some insights into inequities that would otherwise remain hidden. Ideally, there should be alignment between a group's representation in the student body and its members' engagement in various experiences or acquisition of certain outcomes. For example, an analysis of students listed on the dean's list might reveal that Black males make up 4.3 percent of the student population on campus but 0.3 percent of achievers on the dean's list. The team not only makes this discovery, but also partners to investigate the origins of and explanatory factors for this gap. In the process, team members are engaged in thinking about how their own practices contribute to the inequities they have uncovered, and they learn much about the organization in which these disparities are continually reproduced. This enables them to approach planning and institutional transformation efforts with greater enthusiasm, purpose, and focus. What I have offered here is a simplified summary of the process; thus, readers are encouraged to retrieve the published work I cited above. Any institution looking to take on the enormous task of engaging Black males should consider consulting CUE to help facilitate the Equity Scorecard process. The ways in which it can guide institutional action and facilitate organizational learning have not been overstated here.

◇ A second collaborative strategy is the formation of *engagement teams* for Black male students. These teams can comprise academic advisors, faculty, and professionals in athletics, student activities, residence life, ethnic culture centers, and first-year student program offices. Members of this team can work to create with students individual engagement plans that guide the expenditure of their time outside of class and provide a set of strategies for managing engagement in different types of classroom environments (being engaged in an Introduction to African American History class may be more challenging for some than a physics course). The team can work together to establish protocols and common approaches to engagement planning; meet at least twice per semester or quarter with each of the Black men whose engagement plans they supervise; and meet with each other periodically to assess effectiveness, share approaches that have worked for them individually, and learn from each other strategies for reaching resistant students whose engagement plans have not quite taken shape.

◇ A committee on improving the academic status of Black males is a third collaborative partnership idea. Deans and department chairs, administrators from student affairs and multicultural affairs, basketball and football coaches, faculty, and students can work together to envision, implement, and assess a systematic set of initiatives to improve grades, transfer trends (at community colleges), and retention and graduation rates specifically among Black male undergraduates. An equally important function of this committee should be ensuring that Black males are introduced to the rich harvest of learning opportunities that are available on and external to the campus (e.g., study abroad programs, internships, and summer research programs with faculty). The team should rely on data from the Equity Scorecard team, as well as qualitative interviews with Black men who have persisted, performed well, and benefited from participation in enriching educational experiences. The committee should coordinate an initiative that is data-driven and imaginative. Its work will not prosper if committee members hold low expectations for their work or deficit views of Black men on campus.

◇ Staff from the counseling office, Black male graduate students, faculty, and student affairs educators, to name a few, can partner to offer advisory support to Black male student organizations. Harper and Quaye (2007) as well as several contributors to Cuyjet's (2006) edited volume amplify the important role such groups play on predominantly White and historically Black campuses alike. Accordingly, they provide an outlet for Black men to gather and be themselves; learn from the diversity within the group and challenge stereotypes they have about each other; discuss ideas and problems that pertain directly to them without fear of judgment from White onlookers and Black women; and share resources and navigational insights that could help improve their individual and collective existence on campus. Although these groups are enormously powerful, they would benefit greatly from a strong web of supporters who collaboratively offer advisement. These advisors should work with student leaders in these groups to create an agenda that addresses many of the strengths and weaknesses Black men bring to the college setting; having a counselor (preferably a Black male) on the team would be especially helpful.

◇ Given some of the problems noted earlier with Black male readiness for graduate school and careers after college, a *futures team* composed of athletic administrators, staff from the career development center, faculty, and Black male alumni could be created. The futures team could collaborate to offer events and resources that are targeted directly at Black males. For instance, a panel made up of former student-athletes who thought they were going to play professional sports, but were denied such opportunities after college and found themselves insufficiently prepared to compete for desirable jobs, could be instructive to current students who may have constructed similarly narrow pathways. Furthermore, there could be tremendous synergy between this futures team and the aforementioned engagement teams, as they could work together to ensure that individual students' engagement plans include experiences that will render them competitive for post-college roles they desire for themselves. Moreover, student leaders and advisors for Black male student organizations can also rely on the futures team to bring in guest speakers for programs and introduce the group's members to influential Black male professionals who can leverage connections on their behalf.

These partnership ideas are not meant to be prescriptive—meaning, it was not my aim to offer five ideas that will solve every engagement problem plaguing Black males on all college and university campuses. Instead, it is the essence, seriousness, and coordinated nature of these ideas that I am hoping will inspire readers. Again, all efforts should be data-driven and context-specific—the problems with and possibilities for Black male student engagement at the University of Pennsylvania are surely different from those at the Community College of Philadelphia. Thus, thoughtful and well informed implementation by collaborators is essential.

Conclusion

I hope I have made plain in this chapter that the formation of active collaborative teams that involve stakeholders from across the campus who start with assessment and then act in aggressive and strategic ways is the ultimate demonstration of institutional seriousness concerning Black male student success. But an institution must be ready to take on this challenge—presidents and other senior leaders must convey with enthusiasm the high priority, goals, and expectations the institution has for reversing troublesome engagement trends; they must be actively involved in the formation of strategy; and they must hold themselves and everyone else employed by the institution accountable. To make this work, the ways in which White faculty, staff, and students at PWIs will ultimately benefit must be made clear.

The problems and possibilities of Black male student engagement are too critical to leave at bringing in a speaker for a three-hour professional development workshop. Such an approach is neither enduring nor likely to compel audience members to immediately act in the collaborative ways described in this chapter. Serious issues (e.g., Black men dropping out of college more than any other group) require serious partnerships and planning. Institutional leaders must be involved, and efforts cannot be isolated to a certain segment of the campus (e.g., student affairs or multicultural affairs). Resources should not be wasted flying in speakers for professional development workshops if the institution does not mean what it says about equity and diversity in its mission statement, on its website, and in public speeches made by its president. Prior to talking about these issues in a gymnasium filled with disengaged faculty and staff, I had tremendous hope for the college I visited. That experience notwithstanding, I remain optimistic that readers of this chapter will be inspired to treat Black male achievement with greater seriousness.

References

Allen, W. R. (1986). *Gender and campus differences in Black student academic performance, racial attitudes, and college satisfaction*. Atlanta, GA: Southern Education Foundation.

Argyris, C., & Schön, D. A. (1996). *Organizational learning II: Theory, method, and practice*. Reading, MA: Addison-Wesley.

Baird, L. L. (1988). The college environment revisited: A review of research and theory. In J. C. Smart (Ed.), *Higher education: Handbook of theory and research* (Vol. 4, pp. 1–52). New York: Agathon.

Bauman, G. L. (2005). Promoting organizational learning in higher education to achieve equity in educational outcomes. In A. J. Kezar (Ed.), *Organizational learning in higher education. New Directions for Higher Education* (No. 131, pp. 23–35). San Francisco: Jossey-Bass.

Bauman, G. L., Bustillos, L. T., Bensimon, E. M., Brown, M. C., & Bartee, R. D. (2005). *Achieving equitable educational outcomes with all students: The institution's roles and responsibilities*. Washington, DC: Association for American Colleges and Universities.

Bell, D. A. (1987). *And we are not saved: The elusive quest for racial justice*. New York: Basic Books.

Bell, D. A. (2000). Brown vs. Board of Education: Forty-five years after the fact. *Ohio Northern Law Review, 26*, 1–171.

Bensimon, E. M. (2004). The diversity scorecard: A learning approach to institutional change. *Change, 36*(1), 45–52.

Bensimon, E. M. (2005). Closing the achievement gap in higher education: An organizational learning perspective. In A. J. Kezar (Ed.), *Organizational learning in higher education. New Directions for Higher Education* (No. 131, pp. 99–111). San Francisco: Jossey-Bass.

Community College Survey of Student Engagement. (2005). *Engaging students, challenging the odds: 2005 findings*. Austin, TX: University of Texas.

Crenshaw, K., Gotanda, N., Peller, G., & Thomas, K. (Eds.) (1995). *Critical race theory: The key writings that formed the movement*. New York: New Press.

Cuyjet, M. J. (1997). African American men on college campuses: Their needs and their perceptions. In M. J. Cuyjet (Ed.), *Helping African American men succeed in college. New Directions for Student Services* (No. 80, pp. 5–16). San Francisco: Jossey-Bass.

Cuyjet, M. J. (2006). *African American men in college*. San Francisco: Jossey-Bass.

Delgado, R. (1995). *Critical race theory: The cutting edge*. Philadelphia, PA: Temple University Press.

Delgado, R., & Stefancic, J. (2001). *Critical race theory: An introduction*. New York: New York University Press.

Donnor, J. K. (2005). Towards an interest-convergence in the education of African American football student-athletes in major college sports. *Race, Ethnicity and Education, 8*(1), 45–67.

Educational Testing Service (2007). *Factors that can influence performance on the GRE general test, 2005–2006*. Princeton, NJ: Author.

Ferguson, A. A. (2000). *Bad boys: Public schools in the making of Black masculinity*. Ann Arbor: University of Michigan Press.

Fleming, J. (1984). *Blacks in college: A comparative study of students' success in Black and in White institutions*. San Francisco: Jossey-Bass.

Gordon, E. T., Gordon, E. W., & Nembhard, J. G. G. (1994). Social science literature concerning African American men. *Journal of Negro Education, 63*(4), 508–531.

Gurin, P., & Epps, E. G. (1975). *Black consciousness, identity and achievement: A study of students in historically Black colleges*. New York: Wiley.

Harper, S. R. (2004). The measure of a man: Conceptualizations of masculinity among high-achieving African American male college students. *Berkeley Journal of Sociology, 48*(1), 89–107.

Harper, S. R. (2005, November). *High-achieving African American men's behavioral responses to stereotypes at predominantly White universities*. Paper presented at the annual meeting of the Association for the Study of Higher Education, Philadelphia, PA.

Harper, S. R. (2006a). *Black male students at public universities in the U.S.: Status, trends and implications for policy and practice*. Washington, DC: Joint Center for Political and Economic Studies.

Harper, S. R. (2006b). Enhancing African American male student outcomes through leadership and active involvement. In M. J. Cuyjet (Ed.), *African American men in college* (pp. 68–94). San Francisco: Jossey-Bass.

Harper, S. R. (2006c). Peer support for African American male college achievement: Beyond internalized racism and the burden of "acting White." *Journal of Men's Studies, 14*(3), 337–358.

Harper, S. R. (2007). Using qualitative methods to access student trajectories and college impact. In S. R. Harper & S. D. Museus (Eds.), *Using qualitative methods in institutional assessment. New Directions for Institutional Research* (No. 136, pp. 55–68). San Francisco: Jossey-Bass.

Harper, S. R. (2008). Realizing the intended outcomes of Brown: High-achieving African American male undergraduates and social capital. *American Behavioral Scientist, 51*(7), 1029–1052.

Harper, S. R., Carini, R. M, Bridges, B. K., & Hayek, J. (2004). Gender differences in student engagement among African American undergraduates at historically Black colleges and universities. *Journal of College Student Development, 45*(3), 271–284.

Harper, S. R., & Harris, F., III (2006). The impact of fraternity membership on African American college men. In M. J. Cuyjet (Ed.), *African American men in college* (pp. 128–153). San Francisco: Jossey-Bass.

Harper, S. R., & Quaye, S. J. (2007). Student organizations as venues for Black identity expression and development among African American male student leaders. *Journal of College Student Development, 48*(2), 133–159.

Harris, F., III, & Bensimon, E. M. (2007). The Equity Scorecard: A collaborative approach to assess and respond to racial/ethnic disparities in student outcomes. In S. R. Harper & L. D. Patton (Eds.), *Responding to the realities of race on campus. New Directions for Student Services* (No. 120, pp. 77–84). San Francisco: Jossey-Bass.

Kezar, A. J. (2005). What campuses need to know about organizational learning and the learning organization. In A. J. Kezar (Ed.), *Organizational learning in higher education. New Directions for Higher Education* (No. 131, pp. 7–22). San Francisco: Jossey-Bass.

Kimbrough, W. M., & Harper, S. R. (2006). African American men at historically Black colleges and universities: Different environments, similar challenges. In M. J. Cuyjet (Ed.), *African American men in college* (pp. 189–209). San Francisco: Jossey-Bass.

Kuh, G. D. (1993). In their own words: What students learn outside the classroom. *American Educational Research Journal, 30,* 277–304.

Kuh, G. D. (1995). The other curriculum: Out-of-class experiences associated with student learning and personal development. *Journal of Higher Education, 66*(2), 123–155.

Mickelson, R. A., & Smith, S. S. (1992). Education and the struggle against race, class, and gender inequity. In M. L. Andersen & P. H. Collins (Eds.), *Race, class, and gender—an anthology* (pp. 359–376). Belmont, CA: Wadsworth.

National Center for Education Statistics (2003). *Status and trends in the education of Blacks.* Washington, DC: U.S. Department of Education, Institute of Education Sciences.

National Center for Education Statistics (2005). *Integrated Postsecondary Education Data System.* Washington, DC: U.S. Department of Education, Institute of Education Sciences.

National Center for Education Statistics (2007). *Digest of education statistics, 2006.* Washington, DC: U.S. Department of Education, Institute of Education Sciences.

National Survey of Student Engagement (2007). *Experiences that matter: Enhancing student learning and success, annual report 2007.* Bloomington, IN: Indiana University Center for Postsecondary Research.

Nettles, M. T., & Millett, C. M. (2006). *Three magic letters: Getting to Ph.D.* Baltimore, MD: Johns Hopkins University Press.

Pace, C. R. (1969). *College and university environment scales.* Princeton, NJ: Institutional Research Program for Higher Education, Educational Testing Service.

Pace, C. R., & Stern, G. G. (1958). An approach to the measurement of psychological characteristics of college environments. *Journal of Educational Psychology, 49,* 269–277.

Peña, E. V., Bensimon, E. M., & Colyar, J. C. (2006). Contextual problem defining: Learning to think and act from the standpoint of equity. *Liberal Education, 92*(2), 48–55.

Perry, J. L., & Locke, D. C. (1985). Career development of Black men: Implications for school guidance services. *Journal of Multicultural Counseling and Development, 13,* 106–111.

Polite, V. C., & Davis, J. E. (Eds.) (2003). *African American males in school and society: Practices and policies for effective education.* New York: Teachers College Press.

Roach, R. (2001). Where are the Black men on campus? *Black Issues in Higher Education, 18*(6), 18–24.

Shapiro, T. M. (2004). *The hidden cost of being African American: How wealth perpetuates inequality.* New York: Oxford University Press.

Stern, R. A. (1970). *People in context: Measuring person–environment congruence in education and industry.* New York: John Wiley & Sons.

Strange, C. C. (2003). Dynamics of campus environments. In S. R. Komives & D. B. Woodard (Eds.), *Student services: A Handbook for the profession* (4th ed., pp. 297–316). San Francisco: Jossey-Bass.

Strange, C. C., & Banning, J. H. (2001). *Educating by design: Creating campus learning environments that work.* San Francisco: Jossey-Bass.

Sutton, E. M., & Kimbrough, W. M. (2001). Trends in Black student involvement. *NASPA Journal, 39*(1), 30–40.

U.S. Department of Education (2006). *A test of leadership: Charting the future of U.S. higher education.* A report of the commission appointed by Secretary of Education Margaret Spellings. Washington, DC: Author.

U.S. Department of Labor (2001). *Report on the American workforce, 2001.* Washington, DC: Bureau of Labor Statistics.

White, J. L., & Cones, J. H., III (1999). *Black man emerging: Facing the past and seizing a future in America.* New York: Routledge.

Chapter 9

Engaging Racial/ Ethnic Minority Students in Predominantly White Classroom Environments

Stephen John Quaye, Tracy Poon Tambascia, and Rameen Ahmadi Talesh

There's a sense of isolation that's worse in predominantly White environments. When I look at a book or [enter the] classroom, the isolation is what kills you.
—Rob, Occidental College alumnus

The life of a racial/ethnic minority student in a predominantly White classroom is an often frustrating and lonely experience, as underscored above by Rob, a graduate (May 2005) of Occidental College in Los Angeles, California. A self-proclaimed radical, Rob describes his ethnic background as African, viewing African as a "political affiliation" and an "ideological base." While a student at Occidental, Rob spent some time in Ghana in order to learn more about his heritage and gain deeper insight into his major, international relations. As Rob articulated: "I never was really taught anything [positive] about Africa in any of my education; rather, [what my teachers taught me] was all negative and lies." Rob's description of the lies he discovered about his ethnic background upon his visit to Africa is similar to the experiences of many racial/ethnic minority students who progress through educational institutions without sufficiently learning about America's bleak history of racial oppression.

Similar to the students in Fries-Britt's (2000) and Harper's (2005) studies, Rob was a high-achieving Black student with lofty aspirations—one being his desire to build various community centers nationwide to support the needs of low-income youth. He achieved academically at Occidental; yet he struggled to find and maintain a sense of belongingness and confidence. "Sometimes, I don't feel like going to class," Rob verbalized, "because I'm always under the microscope. I'm always thinking: Where do I sit? How am I going to position myself? What does this professor think of me? A consciousness of who's in the class is always there." Given the underrepresentation of racial/ethnic minority students in predominantly White classroom contexts, it comes as no surprise that these students are acutely aware of their peers' races/ethnicities in their courses. As Rob shared, the low numbers of racial/ethnic minority students led him to question his fit in the classroom. "No matter how much I like the subject, or how confident I am, there's always an aspect of me that feels on edge."

In hooks's (1994) *Teaching to Transgress* she writes:

Often, if there is a lone person of color in the classroom she or he is objectified by others and forced to assume the role of "native informant." For example, a novel is read by a Korean American author. White students turn to the one student from a Korean background to explain what they do not understand. This places an unfair responsibility onto that student. (p. 43)

Rob understood this role of "native informant" given his experiences at Occidental. Though Rob found discussing his unique experiences with his classmates and professors stimulating, he resented having to represent his entire racial/ethnic group and continually ponders his ideas prior to voicing them. Additionally, he was cognizant of his behaviors so as to not perpetuate the negative stereotypes of racial/ethnic minority persons. In his own words: "I think more about how I answer things. When the subject matter is personal for me, it makes [my] participation different. My [White] peers tend to intellectualize issues dealing with people of color; [whereas] the issues are more personal for me." To resolve this "native informant" role, Rob placed responsibility on faculty. "Once professors engage the literature [on racial/ethnic minority groups], they don't have to ask students of color to teach the rest of the class. It [engaging diverse literature] lets students of color know that you [the professor] are aware of those issues and think they're central."

Rob offered sage advice on engaging racial/ethnic minority students in predominantly White classrooms. "Taking a look at who is doing the engagement is critical. [Researchers should be] looking at what the professor is doing, not so much what students are doing. If folks are going to be teaching and engaging racial/ethnic minority students, a better understanding of Whiteness is important." Given this, focusing on educators' responsibility to meeting the needs of racial/ethnic minority students is the premise of this chapter. Far too often, the onus is put on racial/ethnic minority students to assimilate to predominantly White classroom norms and divorce their cultures and identities from the learning process. In this chapter, we advocate placing the responsibility on educators by shifting their pedagogical practices to match the needs of racial/ethnic minority students, like Rob.

The remainder of this chapter is organized as follows. We begin by making a case for why racial/ethnic minority students in predominantly White classrooms warrant attention and customized services by describing the issues these students face. We then apply three theories—critical race, stereotype threat, and identity development—to further clarify the unique needs and concerns faced by racial/ethnic minority students in mostly White classroom spaces. Finally, we conclude with several concrete interventions that faculty and student affairs educators can employ to improve the educational experiences and outcomes of these students. Throughout this chapter, we return to Rob's story to provide additional evidence and a personal perspective to the claims made.

Issues Faced in Predominantly White Classrooms

As a high-achieving minority student, Rob still faced moments of doubt and questioned his academic fit in various courses while at Occidental. If those students who are the most capable still struggle in predominantly White classrooms, then the myth that racial/ethnic minority students are underachievers and unmotivated must be challenged and dispelled. To illustrate why engaging these students is of utmost importance, we illuminate five obstacles with which racial/ethnic minority students contend: (1) racial identity development; (2) being one of few racial/ethnic minority students; (3) lack of same-race/ethnicity faculty; (4) curricular content; and (5) culturally responsive pedagogy.

Racial Identity Development

Racial/ethnic minority students in predominantly White classrooms represent varying levels of racial identity development (Evans, Forney, & Guido-DiBrito, 1998). Faculty who lack the understanding of this process can misinterpret or fail to understand these students' behaviors in the classroom. Torres, Howard-Hamilton, and Cooper (2003) note that recognizing the role of racial identity development is essential to assisting students in understanding their own and others' views of knowledge. How will students at various stages of racial identity development respond to the material and to each other during classroom discussions? For instance, an African American student in the Immersion/Emersion phase might resist hegemonic readings that mainly reflect the experiences and contributions of White people (a more complete discussion of the racial identity development stages is provided in the Theoretical Framework section later in this chapter). An educator who is unaware of this might blame students for not wanting to engage material presented during class, rather than taking into account students' developmental levels, readiness, and interest in certain literature (Helms, 1994; Howard-Hamilton, 2000; Tatum, 1997).

The concept of academic identification is explored by Steele (1997) in his study of stereotype threat (described in the Theoretical Framework section later in this chapter). Steele posits that students' views of self reflect their abilities to establish an achievement-oriented belief in academic success, but that the threat of a negative stereotype can impede a student's ability to perform to the best of her or his ability. Therefore, students who are at later stages of racial identity development can respond to stereotypes in more productive ways. Baxter Magolda (2003) highlighted the importance of understanding student learning as a process of self-definition and the ability to construct knowledge for one's self. Faculty in predominantly White classrooms who accept the premise that students create knowledge must also understand that other factors, including students' racial identity development, are present in the learning environment and should be acknowledged.

Although it can be difficult for faculty to have the skills to determine students' racial identity development levels, the failure to recognize this element can lead to learning environments that are racially hostile, discriminatory, and psychologically damaging (Cokley, 1999). Tatum (1992) explored racial identity development for racial/ethnic minority and White students in her courses, drawing on racial identity development theories and literature related to oppression and privilege. She found that various levels of cognitive dissonance were essential to the learning process; deliberate structuring of opportunities for students to understand and reflect on their discomfort and struggles were instrumental for students to achieve intended learning outcomes. Tatum's work is just one illustration of why it is important for faculty members to have an awareness of racial identity development and expose students to a wide array of perspectives from the discipline(s) under study.

Being One of Few

The "proving process" is a phrase introduced by Fries-Britt and Turner (2001) that calls attention to the struggles of racial/ethnic minority students in predominantly White classrooms. These students tend to have a profound sense of loneliness, and often feel the need to prove their intellectual abilities. Negative stereotypes and deficit-minded approaches to understanding student achievement also pose barriers to racial/ethnic minority students, who often encounter questions about their academic capabilities and the right to enroll in higher education through being labeled an "affirmative action" admit (Chang, 1999). Even high-achieving students contend with issues of self-doubt and questions of belonging in higher education (Fries-Britt & Turner, 2001). Continually having to represent their entire race/ethnicity in discussions of diversity and feeling that one's actions as a racial/ethnic minority person will be generalized to the entire group are two other significant challenges faced by racial/ethnic minority students in predominantly White classrooms (Tatum, 1992). Rob's comment at the outset of this chapter pertaining to the isolation he felt reflects this experience of being one of few.

The campus racial climate at predominantly White colleges and universities also influences the climate in classrooms (Hurtado & Carter, 1997). In several studies, racial/ethnic minority students perceived far more discrimination on their campuses than White students perceived (Ancis, Sedlacek, & Mohr, 2000; Cabrera & Nora, 1994; Cabrera, Nora, Terenzini, Pascarella, & Hagedorn, 1999; Harper & Hurtado, 2007; Hurtado, 1992; Smedley, Meyers, & Harrell, 1993). Racial/ethnic minority students who perceived less racial tension were more likely to succeed academically (Hurtado, Milem, Clayton-Pedersen, & Allen, 1999). The discrimination racial/ethnic minority students experienced in comparison with their White counterparts illustrates the dire need for classroom environments to be spaces of comfort and inclusion where students are not questioned on the basis of their racial/ethnic backgrounds.

Lack of Same-Race/Ethnicity Faculty

In 1997, rates of tenure for racial/ethnic minority faculty (64 percent) continued to lag behind those of White faculty (75 percent) and disparities in faculty rank persist, with racial/ethnic minority faculty representing only 12 percent of full professorships (Harvey, 2001). This same study found that, in 1997, African American faculty represented only 5 percent of full-time faculty in higher education, Latino faculty less than 2 percent, and Asian Americans 5.7 percent. These data reveal the difficulties for racial/ethnic minority students who wish to find same-race/ethnicity faculty to serve as mentors and advisors. Additionally, racial/ethnic minority students interested in a career in academia might conclude such a feat is unattainable given the underrepresentation of racial/ethnic minority faculty across academe as a whole.

Smith (1989) summarizes the influence of racial/ethnic minority faculty on students' success in her case for diversifying campuses. Her five arguments for having racial/ethnic minority faculty members include their ability to serve as mentors to racial/ethnic minority students; their commitment to a more diverse campus climate; their role in creating comfortable and inclusive environments for faculty and staff; their ability to offer diverse perspectives on teaching and learning; and their commitment to a pluralistic view of higher education. For classroom environments to be more inclusive and welcoming for racial/ethnic minority students, attention needs to be given to ensuring that faculty members represent a wide array of backgrounds, perspectives, and experiences (Lundberg & Schreiner, 2004; Smith, 1989).

Curricular Content

Issues pertaining to the cultures of racial/ethnic minority students are often missing in classroom readings and discussions given the predominant exposure to monocultural literature (Banks, 1996, 2001). The choices made about instructional content represent a form of power (Delpit, 1988); curricula focused on Western or dominant cultures send the message to racial/ethnic minority students that Whiteness is normal and that other practices or beliefs from different cultures are not valued (Delpit, 1988; Schmitz, 1992). Weissman, Bulakowski, and Jumisko (1998) found that stereotypic content in courses created a negative environment for African American students at one community college in Chicago and deepened the racial divide in the classroom.

Curricular content can also invalidate the knowledge and experiences of racial/ethnic minority students, which are rarely present in any form in the higher educational setting (Terenzini, Cabrera, Colbeck, Bjorklund, & Parente, 2001). For these students, the curricula determined by the dominant culture begin in the K–12 setting, where little, if any, course content reflects the experiences and voices of racial/ethnic minority cultures (Au, 1998; Gallimore & Goldenberg, 2001).

Culturally Unresponsive Pedagogy

Culturally unresponsive pedagogy is an additional issue relevant to racial/ethnic minority students in White classroom contexts. A key question is the following: How does the content of the course enable students to develop and learn more about themselves if the material does not reflect topics, issues, or models that are meaningful to the student? Students' learning is maximized when educators capitalize on pedagogies that respond to their diverse needs (Bartolome, 1994; Baxter Magolda, 2001; Delpit, 1988; hooks, 1994; Ladson-Billings, 1995; Torres et al., 2003). Au (1998) argues that consideration of the language spoken at home, connections to the community, culturally responsive content, and classroom management are necessary components for creating learning environments that reflect the experiences of racial/ethnic minority students.

Not only do racial/ethnic minority students have differing cultural needs, they also exhibit diverse learning styles. Therefore, it is important that educators are cognizant of the varied ways that students learn and employ multiple strategies to engage students (Gardner, 1993). Other researchers, such as Bartolome (1994), advocate for developing pedagogy that not only addresses techniques and methods, but also incorporates a sociocultural perspective that recognizes the role of teacher bias, minority student experience, and the history of racial tension in education. The issue of pedagogy as a tool for power and control in the classroom was also studied by Gutierrez, Rymes, and Larson (1995), who identified the need for a more neutral third space for dialogue that allows students and educators a place to exchange knowledge. Adelman (1997) points to potential inequities in this arena, with wealthier institutions better equipped to support diverse learning styles and backgrounds through investments in technology. Regardless of the resources available, predominantly White colleges and universities must ensure that culturally responsive pedagogy is utilized in learning settings to minimize disparities in educational outcomes.

Theoretical Framework

Appropriately addressing the distinctive concerns of racial/ethnic minority students demands a theoretical framework that responds to their racial/ethnic backgrounds and identities. Three theories—critical race theory, stereotype threat theory, and identity development theory—frame our argument and are discussed respectively.

Critical Race Theory

Although we focus on engaging racial/ethnic minority students in predominantly White classroom environments, we cannot treat the classroom as an isolated space that is void of dominant cultural norms, values, and beliefs. Critical race theory (CRT) addresses this point and highlights the historical context in which racial/ethnic minority students are situated that limits their potential in predominantly White spaces (Delgado Bernal, 2002; Delgado & Stefancic, 2001; Solórzano & Villalpando, 1998; Solórzano, Ceja, & Yosso, 2000; Solórzano & Delgado Bernal, 2001; Villalpando, 2004). Three central elements form the basis for CRT: (1) challenge to dominant ideologies; (2) recognition of knowledge possessed by racial/ethnic minority groups; and (3) transformative practices.

Challenge to Dominant Ideologies

Hegemony is a key concept in CRT. Hegemony describes a situation created and sustained by a dominant culture in which it develops norms, values, and beliefs that become normalized and seen as natural (Hebdige, 1979). These norms become commonsensical, and subordinate groups (e.g., racial/ethnic minority students) rarely question them. Avoiding issues of race/ethnicity and difference in the classroom is one way to perpetuate the hegemony. Critical race theorists challenge conventional forms of schooling that deny students' racial/ethnic experiences in the classroom. The hegemonic environment is reinforced outside of the classroom as well, creating a climate on campuses that invalidates the unique experiences and needs of racial/ethnic minority students (Delgado & Stefancic, 2001).

Hegemony mirrors the racial climate of predominantly White institutions. Since racist practices in contemporary society are more covert, they are harder to detect, but still detrimental to racial/ethnic minority students' academic success (Delgado & Stefancic, 2001). Solórzano et al. (2000) refer to these seemingly innocuous forms of racism as microaggressions. Microaggressions are subtle verbal and nonverbal racist assaults targeted at racial/ethnic minority persons (Davis, 1989; Solórzano, 1998). They result in a "chilly climate" for racial/ethnic minority students, as they lead these students to question their belonging, worth, and academic abilities. As the discussion of stereotype threat (Steele, 1997; Steele & Aronson, 1995) will illuminate, one does not necessarily have to believe in what the microaggressions imply in order to be negatively impacted by them. The mere presence of microaggressions creates an unwelcoming environment for those targeted by them.

Solórzano et al. (2000) contend:

> When a collegiate racial climate is positive, it includes at least four elements: (a) the inclusion of students, faculty, and administrators of color; (b) a curriculum that reflects the historical and contemporary experiences of people of color; (c) programs to support the recruitment, retention and graduation of students of color; and (d) a college/university mission that reinforces the institution's commitment of pluralism. (p. 62)

Though all four dimensions are critical to an affirming campus climate, the culturally reflective curriculum is most relevant to engaging racial/ethnic minority students in predominantly White classrooms. When faculty utilize curricula that respect the contributions of diverse populations, they subvert hegemony and challenge the dominant ideology that deems Whiteness the norm and standard against which other cultural groups are measured. Many racial/ethnic minority students speak of feeling invisible in predominantly White classroom environments (Delgado & Stefancic, 2001; Matsuda,

Lawrence, Delgado, & Crenshaw, 1993). This invisibility is one of the many ways dominant ideologies ignore and omit the experiences of racial/ethnic minority groups in mostly White classrooms (Solórzano et al., 2000).

Recognition of Racial/Ethnic Minority Students' Knowledge

Critical race theorists validate and encourage the experiential knowledge of racial/ethnic minority students in academe (Delgado Bernal, 2002). Racial/ethnic minority students possess unique and varied insights pertaining to their experiences of oppression, discrimination, and microaggressions that warrant faculty members' attention (Tate, 1997). When racial/ethnic minority students speak from their vantage points, deeper understanding about their particular experiences is facilitated. The important point here is to not essentialize these students' experiences; that is, to conclude that simply because a student is from a particular racial/ethnic group, she or he shares knowledge particular to all people from that racial group. Such essentialist notions view racial/ethnic groups in monolithic ways, which is the antithesis of CRT (Villalpando, 2004).

Critical race theory enables people to understand the intersections among different social identities, such as race/ethnicity, gender, sexual orientation, and socioeconomic status, and promotes a discourse in which racial/ethnic minority students focus on the connections between different oppressed groups. According to Solórzano et al. (2000):

> When the ideology of racism is examined and racist injuries are named, victims of racism can find their voice. Further, those injured by racism discover that they are not alone in their marginality. They become empowered participants, hearing their own stories and the stories of others, listening to how the arguments are framed, and learning to make the arguments themselves. (p. 64)

Learning to make the argument themselves, racial/ethnic minority students come to believe in the importance of their insights and experiences and use those perspectives in the process of knowledge construction and dissemination.

Transformative Practices

Liberation and change are the ultimate agenda of CRT. As Tatum (1992) expresses, without action, discussions are insufficient. As Freire (1970) advocates, reflection (i.e., naming oppressive practices) must be combined with action (i.e., working to change oppressive structures) in order for liberation to occur. The goal of CRT is to provide students and educators with ways of transforming oppressive classroom practices (Solórzano et al., 2000).

Critical race theory's primary aim is critical consciousness, meaning that employers of the theory strive to foment dialogue about long-established classroom practices that silence students' unique perspectives and reinforce the primary authority of the professor. By developing narratives and perspectives that challenge dominant ways of thinking, racial/ethnic minority students learn ways to become actively engaged in predominantly White classroom environments and maintain their racial/ethnic identities in the process (Delgado & Stefancic, 2001; Solórzano, 1998; Solórzano & Villalpando, 1998; Solórzano et al., 2000; Villalpando, 2004).

Stereotype Threat Theory

The self-efficacy of racial/ethnic minority students affects their social and academic engagement (Bandura, 1986; Dembo & Seli, 2007; Schunk, 2004; Zimbardo & Gerrig, 1996). The historical context of oppression coupled with students' situatedness in predominantly White environments negatively affects these students' beliefs about success and academic achievement (Freire, 1970; Hardiman & Jackson, 1997). Typically, students with higher self-efficacy set higher goals and exhibit greater feelings of satisfaction and competence (Zimbardo & Gerrig, 1996). However, given oppressive classroom practices that deny racial/ethnic minority students' cultures and identities, some students display lower self-efficacy (Steele, 1997).

Steele (1997) and Steele and Aronson's (1995) research on stereotype threat demonstrates the influence of stereotypes on one's self-concept. Steele's study begins with an important premise: Students must identify with the postsecondary institution of which they are a part and possess an achievement-oriented mentality in order to achieve academic success. Students who do so have a higher sense of self, or self-efficacy. Additionally, self-efficacy is dependent upon one's belonging at the institution, a factor mentioned in the previous discussion of racial climate.

To demonstrate the effect of stereotypes, Steele (1997) selected groups of students who had high self-efficacy and were academically motivated. Steele demonstrated that even students who were academically successful throughout their educational experiences were impacted by stereotype threat. Steele defines stereotype threat as:

> A situational threat—a threat in the air—that, in general form, can affect the members of any group about whom a negative stereotype exists (e.g., skateboarders, older adults, White men, gang members). Where bad stereotypes about these groups apply, members of these groups can fear being reduced to that stereotype. And for those who identify with the domain to which the stereotype is relevant, this predicament can be self-threatening. (p. 614)

Steele stresses that stereotype threat is damaging because it affects the most academically motivated and successful students even when they do not believe in the accuracy of the stereotype (Fries-Britt & Turner, 2001).

Racial/ethnic minority students face a quandary in predominantly White classrooms as they struggle to prove themselves in the face of continual challenges about their academic potential (Fries-Britt, 2000; Fries-Britt & Turner, 2001; Solórzano et al., 2000). Common internal questions posed by students include:

> Do I have the requisite skills, talents, and interests? Have others like me succeeded in the domain? Will I be seen as belonging in the domain? Will I be prejudiced against in the domain? Can I envision wanting what this domain has to offer? (Steele, 1997, p. 616)

These questions affect the self-efficacy of racial/ethnic minority students and are issues that faculty must recognize in their work with students (Bandura, 1986). Students at various identity development phases respond to these questions and stereotype threat in differing ways, which is the topic explored next.

Identity Development Theories

Racial Identity Development

Racial identity development theories explore racial/ethnic minority students' progression through phases, the first of which is a lack of awareness of their race/ethnicity and an adoption of the dominant culture's standards for worth, beauty, and significance. They then experience a conflict, or dissonance, which prompts them to examine their racial identity and question the values of the dominant culture. During this period, students likely associate with members of their own racial/ethnic group and strive to learn more about their own culture. As they continue to explore their race/ethnicity, they begin to internalize what being a racial/ethnic minority person means, and are then able to successfully bridge cultural differences while holding on to a strong sense of self (Atkinson, Morten, & Sue, 1989; Cross, 1995; Cross & Vandiver, 2001; Helms, 1994; Helms & Cook, 1999; Keefe & Padilla, 1987; Kim, 2001; Ortiz & Rhoads, 2000; Phinney, 1992; Thompson & Carter, 1997; Vandiver, 2001).

Understanding where different students are in their racial identity development is critical to the use of effective pedagogy that is culturally relevant to students' needs. For instance, students who have experienced dissonance might resist literature that pertains to the dominant culture, and instead desire solely content that is specific to their racial/ethnic group. Educators working with students in this phase should recognize the possibility that those students will withdraw from the course and work to engage them with readings and experiences about their racial/ethnic group.

Cognitive Identity Development

Because it is difficult for faculty members to ascertain students' developmental places, a more appropriate method involves the utilization of diverse pedagogical strategies that meet the needs of racial/ethnic minority students at different developmental statuses. Baxter Magolda's (2004) Learning Partnerships Model (LPM)[1] is one approach for doing so. This model emerged from a 20-year longitudinal study of young adults' development. Framed around three assumptions about knowledge construction and three principles to promote complex knowledge development, the LPM is a useful mechanism for engaging racial/ethnic minority students in predominantly White classroom environments, as it acknowledges the unique backgrounds and identities of these students, which are often overlooked in predominantly White classrooms.

The LPM assumptions are the following: (1) knowledge is complex and socially constructed; (2) one's identity is central to knowledge construction; and (3) knowledge is mutually shared and constructed. Educators whose teaching is based on these three premises make use of three interrelated LPM principles: (1) validate students as knowers; (2) encourage students to use their experiences in learning; and (3) mutually construct knowledge with students (Baxter Magolda, 2001; Baxter Magolda, 2004; Baxter Magolda & King, 2004; Rogers, Magolda, Baxter Magolda, & Knight Abowitz, 2004). The assumptions and principles complement and build upon each other and are maximized when used in combination.

The LPM is a useful complement to critical race theory and stereotype threat theory. As previously detailed, the unique dimension of CRT is its emphasis on the knowledge of racial/ethnic minority groups, and its acknowledgement that students who exhibit high self-efficacy are more academically successful and display higher competence. When educators validate that students are able to develop knowledge, they deem the knowledge and experiences of racial/ethnic minority students as important to their academic success. Moreover, educators who validate students as knowers invite students to share their experiences and relate them to the material presented during the learning process. When racial/ethnic minority students do so, they challenge dominant ideologies as a means of transforming conventional classroom practices.

Faculty who mutually participate in developing knowledge with students relinquish their role as all-knowing authority figures (hooks, 1994). Given that predominantly White classrooms contain mainly White faculty members, it is even more important for faculty to mutually generate knowledge with racial/ethnic minority students. This practice dispels the myth that racial/ethnic minority students have no place in predominantly White classrooms and enables educators to address the stereotype threat present in these classrooms. Faculty who partner with racial/ethnic minority students do not deem these students as incompetent and underachieving, but instead validate their abilities and expect them to achieve and develop healthy identities.

Theoretical Integration: An Example

Returning to Rob's story will help crystallize the theoretical framework. When asked what faculty members can do to enrich his experience in the classroom, Rob spoke about the significance of educators engaging the experiences of racial/ethnic groups in the same way that they engage their disciplines: "Make issues related to racial/ethnic minority groups a central part of the curriculum. Engage this type of material as they [professors] would engage physics." Rob acknowledged that it is unreasonable for him to expect a physics professor to spend the majority of class time on, for example, literature related to Africans' experiences. Yet, he still stressed that physics professors should not overlook the contributions of African people.

For instance, the Learning Partnerships Model expects that educators validate students' experiences. Rob was an avid connoisseur of spoken word, a combination of poetry and hip hop that represents a form of activism. Rob's use of spoken word portrays a unique type of knowledge he possessed. Validating this as an important source of knowledge in the classroom is one way to challenge dominant ideologies in academic settings. By working with students like Rob to understand what motivates them to learn, educators inspire students to engage in transformative practices, which heighten their self-efficacy and challenge the negative stereotypes about racial/ethnic minority groups. These practices also enabled Rob to believe that members of his racial/ethnic group possess worthy insights.

Strategies for Engagement

A multipronged method is necessary to engage racial/ethnic minority students in predominantly White classroom environments, meaning that multiple strategies used in conjunction are more effective than one used in isolation. We divide our proposed interventions into four categories: assessment, student success, faculty success, and culturally responsive curricular strategies. We discuss assessment first because assessment informs the remaining three categories, since it is important to continually assess the ways in which institutions work with racial/ethnic minority students, to develop faculty members' multicultural competence, and to improve the curricular content to be more reflective of diverse students' contributions.

Assessment Strategies

Assessment of Engagement

Assess racial/ethnic minority students' engagement in predominantly White classrooms through collecting and interpreting data. Before one can assess engagement, an understanding of what engagement entails is necessary. For instance, does actively contributing to classroom discussions by speaking exemplify engagement? Does engagement mean students demonstrate knowledge of course content through synthesizing their own ideas with those of authors through papers and presentations? Various practices portray engagement, and student affairs educators and faculty should not limit engagement to narrow definitions. Students from different racial/ethnic groups likely define engagement in varied ways, and assessment practices should welcome these divergent insights. Conducting focus groups with racial/ethnic minority students and asking them to define engagement and provide illustrative examples of the activities in which they are engaged in class yield compelling insights about their engagement.

Assessment of Campus and Classroom Climate

Assess campus and classroom climate. Continuing with the previous strategy, assessing differing aspects of the classroom and campus climate becomes crucial for any institution attempting to respond to the needs of racial/ethnic minority students in classroom settings. Without assessment, administrators and faculty will not realize the extent to which these students are marginalized. Additionally, assessment enables educators to understand how harmful experiences, such as stereotype threat, are perpetuated (Steele, 1997; Steele & Aronson, 1995). "Campus assessments should include a review of existing, representative documents to determine whether only one culture is being advocated" (Torres et al., 2003, p. 81). Assessment of the racial climate in the classroom should include focus groups with racial/ethnic minority students and adding questions about campus climate to evaluations in courses.

Sharing Assessment Data

Share critical assessment data. Simply having data is not enough, as faculty and student affairs educators must utilize the information. Using instruments such as the Diversity Scorecard (Bensimon, 2004), educators should share data from the assessments with each other in order to clarify deficiencies and develop institutional strategies that address them. Data can be distributed annually to academic departments and shared with faculty and institutional research departments. Yearly reviews of the data will allow colleges and universities to examine how they can promote successful learning environments for racial/ethnic minority students.

Utilization of Consultants

Utilize external consultants and assessment teams to assist in ensuring a careful examination of classroom climate issues. These consultants and teams can gather information to understand the campus population and issues while providing vital feedback. They can make recommendations that have not been considered previously and share constructive feedback concerning classroom interactions and climate. Assessment would include interviews, document analysis of course syllabi, and classroom observations to gain a better understanding of challenges and limitations. Based on the conclusions gleaned from interviews and observations, the consultants and assessment teams will recommend strategies for the institution to pursue.

Attention to Specific Disciplines

Focus attention on disciplines where engagement of racial/ethnic minority students is a particular challenge. An example of this is monitoring the progress of racial/ethnic minority students in math or science or any department at an institution where the underrepresentation of racial/ethnic minority students is more pronounced. Though many departments may face challenges, initial efforts can be directed toward improving the climate for racial/ethnic minority students by reviewing the racial/ethnic composition of select departments and taking deliberate steps to make the academic environment engaging and welcoming. To remedy disparities, departments can bring in guest speakers, either alumni or professionals working in the field, who represent different racial/ethnic groups. This practice serves as a reminder that racial/ethnic minority people are present, visible, and successful in the field, even if they are not seen in that particular classroom or institution.

Student Success Strategies

Validation of Race/Ethnicity

Validate the concept of race/ethnicity as applicable to students, particularly White students. Faculty should not expect racial/ethnic minority students to discuss their experiences whenever the perspective of the "other" is needed to educate White students. By expecting White students to recognize their racial/ethnic background, it lessens the need for racial/ethnic minority students to feel overwhelmingly pressured to speak for their group. In addition, educators should not assume that racial/ethnic minority students speak from that particular perspective at all times. Workshops on White privilege should be conducted so that White students are provided with opportunities to reflect on and ask questions about their Whiteness.

Peer Networks

Provide opportunities for racial/ethnic minority students to formulate peer networks with other racial/ethnic minority students. To combat the detrimental desire to expect the sole racial/ethnic minority student in the class to speak on behalf of her or his entire cultural group, it is important for faculty to connect these students with their racial/ethnic minority peers. For instance, periodic forums composed of racial/ethnic minority students provide a space for students to develop and sustain relationships with students across multiple disciplines, where they can candidly discuss the challenges associated with being racial/ethnic minority students at predominantly White classrooms. Additionally, these forums enable students to share their frustrations, positive experiences, and strategies for achieving academically. Third- and fourth-year students can serve as peer mentors for incoming students and provide them with the social networks necessary to succeed during their collegiate tenures. From these forums, faculty and student affairs educators can learn additional ways to improve the engagement of racial/ethnic minority students. Providing spaces in which racial/ethnic minority students can connect with other students enables them to reenergize in the company of others who share similar experiences.

Summer Bridge Programs

Develop summer bridge programs. These programs enable racial/ethnic minority students to develop peer networks and engage in classroom settings prior to the start of the academic year. Students in these programs gain support and confidence from peers involved at the institution while also gathering knowledge and skills that will prepare them for their upcoming academic experience. Summer bridge programs enable students to navigate the campus environment in the company of their peers who are also striving to do the same. Additionally, upper-level students who have participated in the program before should be invited to mentor students during this experience. By involving students who have been actively engaged at the institution, racial/ethnic minority students see that they can also achieve in their courses despite their underrepresentation.

Collaborative Learning

Support collaborative learning experiences. Collaborative learning can signify to racial/ethnic minority students that the environment is an inclusive one. Examples of this include projects geared toward working in smaller groups, which create supportive environments as opposed to competitive learning spaces. Hurtado et al. (1999) note: "When students work cooperatively on course content, they learn more about one another as well as about the specific content areas" (p. 10). Peer editing, group presentations, and group study enable students to exchange ideas in a non-threatening environment. Cross-cultural learning and opportunities for intercultural competence are activated through processes like these. "Experiences such as intentionally directed study groups, course-related experiential learning, topical discussion, and reflections can play important roles in enabling students to build connections between in-class and out-of-class experiences" (Meyer & Schuh, 2001, p. 49). Living-learning communities, in which students live in the same building with students from their courses, is one way to ensure that students are connecting in smaller forums. Students work together to peer-edit papers, reflect on their experiences, and share their insights with classmates. By exchanging knowledge, students begin to develop an appreciation for others, which can translate into an acceptance of differences as they progress throughout their collegiate tenures.

Connection of Personal Experiences to Academic Content

Invite students to connect their personal experiences with academic content as a starting point for knowledge construction. As previously mentioned, racial/ethnic minority students possess unique and varied insights about their experiences in predominantly White classrooms that can offer their peers alternative perspectives. By encouraging students to share their personal insights, they can make sense of literature that otherwise seems abstract and unrelated to their cultures and identities. When faculty value racial/ethnic minority students' experiences, they validate different forms of knowledge that challenge and transform the status quo. Furthermore, doing so enables racial/ethnic minority students to ground academic content in culturally relevant and meaningful ways.

Student Advisory Committees

Develop student advisory committees in academic departments. These committees can comprise a variety of student who provide feedback to the academic dean or department chair about deficiencies in academic content, department offerings, and multicultural awareness among faculty members. The advisory committee can suggest readings reflective of students' cultural groups and recommend additional syllabus revisions or feedback that faculty can incorporate into their courses. Since students are in the best positions to evaluate whether their educational needs are being met, these advisory committees provide students with opportunities to be heard by those who have the power to make changes. Consequently, the dean can filter information to faculty to improve the climate for racial/ethnic minority students.

Faculty Success Strategies

Faculty Training and Development

Support faculty training and development. In order to address pedagogical limitations, postsecondary institutions should provide faculty training and development. Institutional support for multicultural awareness training should be in place for faculty members. This professional development will include readings, writing reflections, and sharing culturally relevant learning material and pedagogies, which the faculty can then incorporate in their courses. Each campus will be unique in identifying faculty leaders to model positive teaching practices. In-services or faculty conferences provide forums for modeling to occur through sharing diverse approaches and syllabi from faculty that utilize varied methods of teaching racial/ethnic minority students. Faculty who need additional training or are not able to revise their material can receive feedback and help from their colleagues. Institutions should offer support in assisting faculty in reviewing their pedagogy. Faculty who are knowledgeable about inclusive classroom settings can be asked to observe, evaluate, and give feedback to professors who are working toward changing their teaching practices.

Grants for Faculty Development

Secure grants to fund faculty development. This strategy enables faculty to attend workshops and conferences to improve curricula and pedagogy. Grant monies can also be used to hire teaching assistants or other staff to identify innovative and diverse academic material. Faculty members should be required to attend professional conferences that focus on ways to engage racial/ethnic minority students in predominantly White classrooms and share what they learn with their colleagues upon their return. This information can be used by campus centers for teaching excellence to further develop and support faculty members in revising curricula and pedagogical approaches.

Incentives and Rewards

Provide incentives and rewards for faculty members who use culturally relevant teaching methods. One way to change faculty culture is to reward those who create an enriching and supportive learning environment for racial/ethnic minority students. Upper-level administrators should provide incentives and rewards to those who continuously embrace diverse learning practices and are recognized by students as providing inclusive and culturally relevant learning environments. By giving recognition to faculty who connect with students, positive norms that recognize the needs of students are established at the faculty level. Other faculty will be more willing to change and incorporate alternative learning approaches into their classroom settings in order to improve their performance and receive recognition.

Expectations of Classroom Respect

Set clear expectations of conduct in the classroom that allows for healthy debate but does not tolerate a hurtful or unsafe climate for racial/ethnic minority students. Training should be made available to educators that provide them with the tools to confront discriminatory behaviors in classroom settings (Cabrera et al., 1999). When students share perspectives that are harmful to others, faculty members should address these comments immediately. However, it is equally important for faculty to not silence those who share controversial ideas. This tricky balance can be managed through creating classroom settings that respect differences. For example, White students should be invited to understand their privilege and be able to work through their own anxieties in classroom settings.

Recruitment and Hiring of Faculty

Aggressively recruit and hire racial/ethnic minority faculty. This obvious strategy is not necessarily innovative, yet it remains a vital, unmet objective of most colleges and universities. Racial/ethnic minority faculty are grossly underrepresented across postsecondary institutions as a whole. Like most White students, racial/ethnic minority students actively pursue fields in which they deem themselves competent and comfortable. For racial/ethnic minority students to consider the professoriate, for example, they must identify with same-race/ethnicity faculty who can serve as encouraging mentors and role models. Racial/ethnic minority faculty can also support students who may feel disconnected and isolated on predominantly White campuses. Exposure to racial/ethnic minority faculty in multiple disciplines enables students to see that they can also be successful in various careers, and in turn, positively influence the lives of other racial/ethnic minority students with whom they work.

Culturally Responsive Curricular Strategies

Diverse Academic Content

Utilize a diverse array of academic content to demonstrate the contributions of racial/ethnic minority persons in various disciplines. Many faculty who were not socialized to the use of culturally broad literature during their own graduate tenures still teach in culturally exclusive ways (Harper & Quaye, 2004). When racial/ethnic minority students are exposed to mainly White, mainstream perspectives, they come to believe that the contributions of their cultural group are trivial or nonexistent. Furthermore, when racial/ethnic minority students peruse the syllabi on the first day of class, they immediately receive a subtle message concerning the importance of their racial/ethnic group (or lack thereof). Faculty who wish to engage racial/ethnic minority students in predominantly White classrooms must intentionally incorporate readings that pertain to the experiences of these students. This practice recognizes that students are more likely to be engaged when their professors intentionally integrate culturally diverse perspectives into curricula.

Collaborative Peer Review of Syllabi

Employ collaborative peer review of course syllabi as a means of determining whether readings reflect diverse viewpoints. Faculty who are unaccustomed to academic content that pertains to racial/ethnic minority groups can benefit from collaborating with their colleagues in a review of syllabi. For instance, faculty in English and writing programs can work together to gather readings from racial/ethnic minority poets and authors in different writing genres. Collaborative peer review serves as a way for faculty to receive feedback and recognize limitations in course offerings before distributing syllabi to students.

Varied Assessment of Classwork

Assess classwork in varied ways. The use of multiple assessment criteria enables students to demonstrate proficiency in coursework in different ways. High-stakes testing, heavily weighted papers, and other singular forms of grading penalize students with weaker skills in one area, such as writing or test taking. In particular, weighing class discussion and participation heavily in a student's grade can disadvantage racial/ethnic minority students in predominantly White classrooms, who might refuse to speak because they do not want to be seen as representing their entire racial/ethnic group. Using portfolios, journals, group activities, presentations, and other projects offer alternative ways to assess student learning.

Conclusion

Rob's academic engagement was due in large part to the relationships he formed with his racial/ethnic minority peers. He developed many close relationships through the

Multicultural Summer Institute that took place the summer before his first year at Occidental College. Rob indicated that this experience enabled him to critically analyze readings and different perspectives and develop his critical eye. "I began to expect certain behaviors from students in the classroom. I began to look at the curriculum and see what was not offered and asked: Who were we reading?" This vital question became especially relevant in Rob's philosophy course. "I took a philosophy class my junior year, and my professors never mentioned where the philosophers got their thoughts from; Black, African philosophers were left out. People's experiences reflect the way they come at philosophy. Most tend to be White males."

The earlier excerpts from Rob shed light on how three of our proposed interventions—peer support, summer bridge programs, and literature—can inform and shape the experiences of racial/ethnic minority students. Merely continuing with the status quo is insufficient; educators can no longer expect racial/ethnic minority students to assimilate White classroom norms and practices. Fortunately, Rob was academically successful at Occidental because he purposefully formed peer and faculty relationships and found multiple, sustained opportunities to learn about his racial/ethnic identity. However, faculty and student affairs educators cannot expect racial/ethnic minority students to become engaged in predominantly White classrooms on their own. Rather, as our strategies suggest, educators must intentionally plan educational experiences that are enriching and place students' racial/ethnic identities at the forefront of the learning process.

Note

1 Since Baxter Magolda's (2004) Learning Partnerships Model developed from a mostly White sample, educators should exercise caution in applying it directly to other racial/ethnic groups. More research is needed to examine the utility of the LPM to diverse cultural groups. Despite this shortcoming, we regard the LPM here for its attention to students' holistic selves.

References

Adelman, C. (1997). Diversity: Walk the walk, and drop the talk. *Change, 29*(4), 34–45.

Ancis, J., Sedlacek, W., & Mohr, J. (2000). Student perceptions of campus cultural climate by race. *Journal of Counseling Development, 78*(2), 180–185.

Atkinson, D. R., Morten, G., & Sue, D. W. (1989). *Counseling American minorities* (3rd ed.). Dubuque, IA: William C. Brown.

Au, K. (1998). Social constructivism and the school literacy learning of students of diverse backgrounds. *Journal of Literacy Research, 30*(2), 297–319.

Bandura, A. (1986). *Social foundations of action: A social-cognitive theory.* Englewood Cliffs, NJ: Prentice Hall.

Banks, J. A. (1996). *Multicultural education, transformative knowledge, and action: Historical and contemporary perspectives.* New York: Teachers College Press.

Banks, J. A. (2001). Multicultural education: Goals, possibilities, and challenges. In C. F. Diaz (Ed.), *Multicultural education in the 21st century* (pp. 11–22). New York: Longman.

Bartolome, L. I. (1994). Beyond the methods fetish: Toward a humanizing pedagogy. *Harvard Educational Review, 64*(2), 173–194.

Baxter Magolda, M. B. (2001). *Making their own way: Narratives for transforming higher education to promote self-development.* Sterling, VA: Stylus.

Baxter Magolda, M. B. (2003). Identity and learning: Student affairs' role in transforming higher education. *Journal of College Student Development, 44*(2), 231–247.

Baxter Magolda, M. B. (2004). Learning partnerships model: A framework for promoting self-authorship. In M. B. Baxter Magolda & P. M. King (Eds.), *Learning partnerships: Theory and models of practice to educate for self-authorship* (pp. 37–62). Sterling, VA: Stylus.

Baxter Magolda, M. B., & King, P. M. (Eds.). (2004). *Learning partnerships: Theory and models of practice to educate for self-authorship.* Sterling, VA: Stylus.

Bensimon, E. M. (2004). The Diversity Scorecard: A learning approach to institutional change. *Change, 36*(1), 44–52.

Cabrera, A. F., & Nora, A. (1994). College students' perceptions of prejudice and discrimination and their feelings of alienation: A construct validation approach. *Review of Education, Pedagogy, and Cultural Studies, 16*(3–4), 387–409.

Cabrera, A. F., Nora, A., Terenzini, P. T., Pascarella, E., & Hagedorn, L. S. (1999). Campus racial climate and the adjustment of students: A comparison between White students and African-American students. *Journal of Higher Education, 70*(2), 134–160.

Chang, M. J. (1999). Does racial diversity matter?: The educational impact of a racially diverse undergraduate population. *Journal of College Student Development, 40*(4), 377–395.

Cokley, K. (1999). Reconceptualizing the impact of college racial composition on African American students' racial identity. *Journal of College Student Development, 40*(3), 235–246.

Cross., W. E., Jr. (1995). The psychology of nigrescence: Revising the Cross model. In J. G. Ponterotto, J. M. Casas, L. A. Suzuki, & C. M. Alexander (Eds.), *Handbook of multicultural counseling* (pp. 93–122). Thousand Oaks, CA: Sage.

Cross, W. E., Jr., & Vandiver, B. J. (2001) Nigrescence theory and measurement: Introducing the Cross Racial Identity Scale (CRIS). In J. G. Ponterotto, J. M. Casas, L. M. Suzuki, & C. M. Alexander (Eds.), *Handbook of multicultural counseling* (2nd ed., pp. 371–393). Thousand Oaks, CA: Sage.

Davis, P. (1989). Law as microaggression. *Yale Law Journal, 98*, 1559–1577.

Delgado, R., & Stefancic, J. (2001). *Critical race theory: An introduction.* New York: New York University Press.

Delgado Bernal, D. (2002). Critical race theory, Latino critical theory, and critical raced-gendered epistemologies: Recognizing students of color as holders and creators of knowledge. *Qualitative Inquiry, 8*(1), 105–126.

Delpit, L. D. (1988). The silenced dialogue: Power and pedagogy in educating other people's children. *Harvard Educational Review, 58*(3), 280–298.

Dembo, M. H., & Seli, H. (2007). *Motivation and learning strategies for college success: A self management approach* (2nd ed.). New York: Routledge.

Evans, N. J., Forney, D. S., & Guido-DiBrito, F. (1998). *Student development in college: Theory, research, and practice.* San Francisco: Jossey-Bass.

Freire, P. (1970). *Pedagogy of the oppressed.* New York: Continuum International Publishing Group.

Fries-Britt, S. (2000). Identity development of high-ability Black collegians. In M. B. Baxter Magolda (Ed.), *Teaching to promote intellectual and personal maturity: Incorporating students' worldviews and identities into the learning process. New Directions for Teaching and Learning* (No. 82, pp. 55–65). San Francisco: Jossey-Bass.

Fries-Britt, S. L., & Turner, B. (2001). Facing stereotypes: A case study of Black students on a White campus. *Journal of College Student Development, 42*(5), 420–429.

Gallimore, R., & Goldenberg, C. (2001). Analyzing cultural models and settings to connect minority achievement and school improvement research. *Educational Psychologist, 36*(1), 45–46.

Gardner, H. (1993). *Multiple intelligences: The theory in practice.* New York: Basic Books.

Gutierrez, K., Rymes, B., & Larson, J. (1995). Script, counterscript, and underlife in the classroom: James Brown versus Brown v. Board of Education. *Harvard Educational Review, 65*(3), 445–471.

Hardiman, R., & Jackson, B. W. (1997). Conceptual foundation for social justice courses. In M. Adams, L. A. Bell, & P. Griffin (Eds.), *Teaching for diversity and social justice: A sourcebook* (pp. 16–29). New York: Routledge.

Harper, S. R. (2005). Leading the way: Inside the experiences of high-achieving African American male students. *About Campus, 10*(1), 8–15.

Harper, S. R., & Hurtado, S. (2007). Nine themes in campus racial climates and implications for institutional transformation. In S. R. Harper & L. D. Patton (Eds.), *Responding to the realities of race on campus. New Directions for Institutional Research* (No. 120, pp. 7–24). San Francisco: Jossey-Bass.

Harper, S. R., & Quaye, S. J. (2004). Taking seriously the evidence regarding the effects of diversity on student learning in the college classroom: A call for faculty accountability. *UrbanEd, 2*(2), 43–47.

Harvey, W. (2001). *Minorities in Higher Education, 2000–01*. Washington, DC: American Council on Education.

Hebdige, D. (1979). *Subculture: The meaning of style*. London: Routledge.

Helms, J. E. (1994). The conceptualization of racial identity and other racial constructs. In E. J. Trickett, R. J. Watts, & D. Birman (Eds.), *Human diversity: Perspectives on people in context* (pp. 285–311). San Francisco: Jossey-Bass.

Helms, J. E., & Cook, D. A. (1999). *Using race and culture in counseling in psychotherapy: Theory and process*. Needham Heights, MA: Allyn & Bacon.

hooks, b. (1994). *Teaching to transgress: Education as the practice of freedom*. New York: Routledge.

Howard-Hamilton, M. F. (2000). Creating a culturally responsive learning environment for African American students. In M. B. Baxter Magolda (Ed.), *Teaching to promote intellectual and personal maturity incorporating students' worldviews and identities into the learning process. New Directions for Teaching and Learning* (No. 82, pp. 45–53). San Francisco: Jossey-Bass.

Hurtado, S. (1992). The campus racial climate: Contexts of conflict. *Journal of Higher Education, 63*(5), 539–569.

Hurtado, S., & Carter, D. (1997). Effects of college transition and perceptions of the campus racial climate on Latino college students' sense of belonging. *Sociology of Education, 70*(4), 324–345.

Hurtado, S., Milem, J., Clayton-Pedersen, A., & Allen, W. (1999). *Enacting diverse learning environments: improving the climate for racial/ethnic diversity in higher education*. ASHE-ERIC Higher Education Report Volume (Vol. 26, No. 8). Washington, DC: The George Washington University, Graduate School of Education and Human Development.

Keefe, S. E., & Padilla, A. M. (1987). *Chicano ethnicity*. Albuquerque: University of New Mexico Press.

Kim, J. (2001). Asian American identity development theory. In C. L. Wijeyesinghe & B. W. Jackson III (Eds.), *New perspectives on racial identity development: A theoretical and practical anthology* (pp. 67–90). New York: New York University Press.

Ladson-Billings, G. (1995). Toward a theory of culturally relevant pedagogy. *American Educational Research Journal, 32*(3), 465–491.

Lundberg, C. A., & Schreiner, L. A. (2004). Quality and frequency of faculty–student interaction as predictors of learning: An analysis by student race/ethnicity. *Journal of College Student Development, 45*(5), 549–565.

Matsuda, M., Lawrence, C., Delgado, R., & Crenshaw, K. (Eds.). (1993). *Words that wound: Critical race theory, assaultive speech, and the first amendment*. Boulder, CO: Westview Press.

Meyer, L. D., & Schuh, J. H. (2001). Evaluating a learning community. *Journal of College and University Student Housing, 29*(2), 45–51.

Ortiz, A., & Rhoads, R. A. (2000). Deconstructing Whiteness as part of a multicultural educational framework: From theory to practice. *Journal of College Student Development, 41*(1), 81–93.

Phinney, J. S. (1992). The multigroup ethnic identity measure: A new scale for use with diverse groups. *Journal of Adolescent Research, 7*, 156–176.

Rogers, J. L., Magolda, P. M., Baxter Magolda, M. B., & Knight Abowitz, K. (2004). A community of scholars: Enacting the learning partnerships model in graduate education. In M. B. Baxter Magolda & P. M. King (Eds.), *Learning partnerships: Theory and models of practice to educate for self-authorship* (pp. 213–244). Sterling, VA: Stylus.

Schmitz, B. (1992). *Core curriculum and cultural pluralism: A guide for campus planners.* Washington, D.C.: Association of American Colleges.

Schunk, D. (2004). *Learning theories: An educational perspective* (4th ed.). New Jersey: Pearson Education.

Smedley, B., Meyers, H., & Harrell, S. (1993). Minority-status stresses and the college adjustment of ethnic minority freshmen. *Journal of Higher Education, 64*(4), 434–452.

Smith, D. (1989). *The challenge of diversity: Involvement or alienation in the academy?* ASHE-ERIC Higher Education Report (No. 5). Washington, DC: The George Washington University, Graduate School of Education and Human Development.

Solórzano, D. G. (1998). Critical race theory, racial and gender microaggressions, and the experiences of Chicana and Chicano scholars. *International Journal of Qualitative Studies in Education, 11*, 121–136.

Solórzano, D. G., Ceja, M., & Yosso, T. (2000). Critical race theory, racial microaggressions, and campus racial climate: The experiences of African American college students. *Journal of Negro Education, 69*(1–2), 60–73.

Solórzano, D. G., & Delgado Bernal, D. (2001). Examining transformational resistance through a critical race and LatCrit theory framework: Chicana and Chicano students in an urban context. *Urban Education, 36*(3), 308–342.

Solórzano, D. G., & Villalpando, O. (1998). Critical race theory, marginality, and the experiences of students of color in higher education. In C. A. Torres & T. A. Mitchell (Eds.), *Sociology of education: Emerging perspectives* (pp. 211–224). New York: State University of New York Press.

Steele, C. M. (1997). A threat in the air: How stereotypes shape intellectual identity and performance. *American Psychologist, 52*(6), 613–629.

Steele, C. M., & Aronson, J. (1995). Stereotype threat and the intellectual test performance of African Americans. *Journal of Personality and Social Psychology, 69*, 797–811.

Tate, W. F., IV. (1997). Critical race theory and education: History, theory, and implications. *Review of Research in Education, 22*, 195–247.

Tatum, B. D. (1992). Talking about race, learning about racism: The application of racial identity development theory in the classroom. *Harvard Educational Review, 62*(1), 1–24.

Tatum, B. D. (1997). *"Why are all the Black kids sitting together in the cafeteria?": And other conversations about race.* New York: Basic Books.

Terenzini, P. T., Cabrera, A. F., Colbeck, C. L., Bjorklund, S. A., & Parente, J. M. (2001). Racial and ethnic diversity in the classroom: Does it promote student learning? *Journal of Higher Education, 72*(5), 509–531.

Thompson, C. E., & Carter, R. T. (1997). An overview and elaboration of Helms' racial identity development theory. In C. E. Thompson & R. T. Carter (Eds.), *Racial identity theory: Applications to individual, group, and organizational interventions* (pp. 15–32). Mahwah, NJ: Erlbaum.

Torres, V., Howard-Hamilton, M. F., & Cooper, D. L. (2003). *Identity development of diverse populations: Implications for teaching and administration in higher education.* ASHE-ERIC Higher Education Report (Vol. 29, No. 6). San Francisco: Jossey-Bass.

Vandiver, B. J. (2001). Psychological nigrescence revisited: Introduction and overview. *Multicultural Counseling and Development, 29*, 165–173.

Villalpando, O. (2004). Practical considerations of critical race theory and Latino critical theory for Latino college students. In A. M. Ortiz (Ed.), *Addressing the unique needs of Latino students. New Directions for Student Services* (No. 105, pp. 41–50). San Francisco: Jossey-Bass.

Weissman, J., Bulakowski, C., & Jumisko, M. (1998). A study of White, Black and Hispanic students' transition to a community college. *Community College Review, 26*, 19–38.

Zimbardo, P. G., & Gerrig, R. J. (1996). *Psychology and life* (14th ed.). New York: HarperCollins.

Chapter 10

Engaging Racial/Ethnic Minority Students in Out-of-Class Activities on Predominantly White Campuses

Viannda M. Hawkins and Heather J. Larabee

My first month was like being submerged in a sea of Whiteness. Every so often I would see a chocolate island of African American students congregating together looking as lost as I. It was like being lost in a neighborhood with no visible or recognizable signs to direct me to a desired destination. I was all alone on my own island. A turning point for me occurred when Jahi, an African American upperclassman, introduced himself and invited me to an Afrikan Student Union meeting. From that point on my network of friends grew.

— Bret, African American male student

Moving into the residential halls was crazy. It was like moving into a hotel and resort for White kids. It literally served as a personal playground for them to blast their music, drink alcohol, and hang out. I remember my mother telling me not to get involved with drugs or drinking. For the most part the wild parties were a strange type of entertainment for me. My biggest issue was living with students who advanced stereotypes behind my back, like I can't drive or I only eat with chop sticks. Many of my classmates assume that I am an "A" student. It really bothers me that they say these things and then come to me asking me to study with them. I can't help them because I need help with calculus too!

— Huong, Asian American female student

I grew up in East L.A. in a predominantly Latino community. Now I feel like I am the only Latino wherever I go. I hate it here! Somebody on campus is always staring at me or clinching their purses as I walk by. One time I walked onto an elevator with two White students and they walked off to wait for another elevator. For some reason the elevator would not move, so I walked off to wait for another elevator as well. They quickly boarded another elevator and I swooped in before the doors closed. In a sad way it was kinda' funny watching them squirm a bit. That is how uncomfortable I feel every day on this campus. If I could afford it, I would fly home every week. I have learned to tolerate it, but I still hate being here.

— Javier, Latino male student

These direct quotes represent, at least in part, the perceptions and realities of first-year racial/ethnic minority students who attend predominantly White institutions (PWIs) across the country. Such experiences complicate the college adjustment process and negatively affect student engagement, both inside and outside of the classroom. Active engagement in out-of-class activities is essential to student development, satisfaction, and success (Kuh, 1995). In fact, those who participate in learning communities, become actively involved in clubs and organizations on campus, and participate in purposeful campus activities are more likely than their disengaged peers to persist through the first year of college (Astin, 1984; Kuh, Palmer, & Kish, 2003; Tinto, 1993). Unfortunately, in comparison with their White peers, the first-year experience is often more complex and tumultuous for racial/ethnic minority students at PWIs. In addition to managing the normal academic rigors of college, these students must also adjust to an environment that is often foreign, socially exclusive, culturally irresponsive, and wrought with contradictions (Harper, Byars, & Jelke, 2005; Hurtado, Milem, Clayton-Pedersen, & Allen, 1998; Terenzini et al., 1994; Tinto, 1993).

In this chapter, we summarize the developmental needs of and challenges faced by first-year racial/ethnic minority students at PWIs, with a focus on barriers to engagement in out-of-class activities. Specifically, we describe these students' experiences in five areas and then consider these issues through appropriate theoretical lenses. We conclude by offering several innovative approaches to actively engaging first-year racial/ethnic minority students in clubs, organizations, and activities on predominantly White campuses.

Needs, Experiences, and Challenges

Starting college is a major adjustment for most first-year students. The first six to eight weeks of the first semester are the most crucial to this adjustment (Upcraft & Gardner, 1989; Upcraft, Mullendore, Barefoot, & Fidler, 1993). For most first-year students, it is during this time that enduring decisions are made regarding the ways they will spend their time outside of class. According to Cheng (2004), first-year students need to feel that they fit in on campus. Similarly, Eimers (2001) posits that first-year students need to feel that they made the right college selection in order to properly adjust and persist toward degree completion. To do this, first-year students need to feel welcomed on campus and believe that their needs matter. These needs can be fulfilled through campus involvement. Ultimately, for proper adjustment, first-year students need a positive environment where they feel comfortable and are a valued part of the campus community (Eimers, 2001).

For first-year racial/ethnic minority students at PWIs the adjustment experience is especially critical and usually more difficult than it is for White students (Harper et al.,

2005; Heard Hinderlie & Kenny, 2002; Kenny & Stryker, 1996). These students are faced with an additional set of unique challenges that include (1) campus climate, (2) culturally exclusive environmental norms, (3) overwhelming Whiteness, (4) racial/ethnic organizations, (5) academic preparation, and (6) utilization of campus support services. In this section, we explore how these challenges impact the engagement of first-year racial/ethnic minority students in out-of-class activities at PWIs.

Campus Climate

The "feel" of a campus can have a major influence on a student's involvement in campus activities, both academic and social (Cabrera, Nora, Terenzini, Pascarella, & Hagedorn, 1999; Sutton & Kimbrough, 2001). An environment that is perceived as prejudicial discourages student involvement and can lead to disconnection with the institution (Cabrera et al., 1999; Eimers, 2001; Harper et al., 2005). According to Sutton and Kimbrough (2001), campus climate plays a major role in engaging racial/ethnic minority students. A negative perception of campus climate can cause students to become detached from the college experience, resulting in dissatisfaction and disengagement (Cabrera et al. 1999). Many researchers have found that racial/ethnic minority students who attend PWIs experience alienation as well as social and cultural isolation on these campuses (Ancis, Sedlacek, & Mohr, 2000; D'Augelli & Hershberger, 1993; Feagin, Vera, & Imani, 1996; Harper & Hurtado, 2007; Nettles, 1991; Sedlacek, 1999; Smedley, Myers, & Harrell, 1993). Predominantly White institutions with actual and perceivably higher levels of prejudice not only diminish the sense of fit among these students, but also affect the frequency and quality of their engagement in out-of-class activities (Eimers, 2001; Harper et al., 2005). Owing to these negative environmental factors, first-year racial/ethnic minority students have reported more difficulty in making friends and finding social options that appeal to their cultural interests (Furr & Elling, 2002).

First-year racial/ethnic minority students typically feel pressured to blend their cultures with the majority culture of the institution, which leads to either conforming to White mainstream campus norms or being socially isolated (Ancis et al., 2000; Smedley et al., 1993). These students are often expected to undergo a one-way cultural assimilation (Feagin et al., 1996; Sedlacek, 1999). These feelings of social and cultural marginalization make it more difficult for first-year racial/ethnic minority students to find comfort within most PWIs, which negatively affects their engagement, persistence, and development (Cabrera et al., 1999; Harper et al., 2005; Hurtado et al., 1998; Sutton & Kimbrough, 2001).

Social alienation is not the only factor that impacts the campus environment at PWIs; physical spaces and campus administrators also affect the "feel" of these campuses. First-year racial/ethnic minority students often report feeling like outsiders in certain areas of these campuses (Feagin et al., 1996). These students quickly discover which areas of campus are unwelcoming and socially exclusive. It is not uncommon for first-year racial/ethnic minority students to be looked at strangely and to experience extreme hostility from White students when they are considered to be "intruding" on a certain space (Feagin et al., 1996). There have been reports of embedded benefits for White students at most PWIs, such as physical spaces (Hurtado et al., 1998). For example, almost all of the traditionally White Greek-letter organizations have houses on or nearby predominantly White campuses, which are spaces that members can call their own. However, this is rarely the case for the Black Greek-letter organizations, and students often encounter barriers to finding places on campus to meet and hold events. This added struggle of finding a comfortable physical space on campus contributes to the feeling of unwelcomeness that many racial/ethnic minority students at PWIs experience (Feagin et al., 1996).

Feagin et al. (1996) also report that university staff and administrators, whether consciously or not, help create and maintain racial barriers at PWIs. The Black students in their study reported institutional unresponsiveness to various cultural needs and issues. For example, many participants offered reports of being harassed or treated unfairly by campus police at PWIs. These students also described ways in which the enforcement of university rules are exaggerated for racial/ethnic minority students in comparison with their White counterparts. For example, many reported that they had been randomly stopped by campus police and asked to show their student identification cards. Organizations for racial/ethnic minority students also receive unjust treatment on PWI campuses. For example, these organizations are commonly required to have extra security because their events are thought to be more risky and prone to violence than are those sponsored by mainstream student organizations (Feagin et al., 1996). Ultimately, these events cost the racial/ethnic minority student organizations more money, which often results in fewer events (Feagin et al., 1996). Students also complained about unfair and negative representation of their events in campus newspapers. This constant misrepresentation of Black student organizations, in particular, in local media also resulted in differential treatment by campus police and university administrators (Feagin et al., 1996). These feelings of alienation and stories of hostility, along with the adjustment issues all first-year students face, represent only a fraction of the obstacles that first-year racial/ethnic minority students must overcome at PWIs.

Culturally Exclusive Environmental Norms

DeSousa and King (1992) assert that institutional characteristics and culture can affect levels of out-of-class engagement, especially for racial/ethnic minority students. More often than not, the campus culture at PWIs does not reflect the cultural backgrounds of racial/ethnic minority students (Hernandez, 2002). Many first-year racial/ethnic minority students find that an institution's diversity claims are exaggerated and its goals for multiculturalism are unreasonably high (Hurtado et al., 1998). This sense of false representation can be extremely discouraging for those who come to campus with different expectations. In addition, these students must deal with cultural biases and stereotypes (Sedlacek, 1999). Such unexpected realities can create additional adjustment challenges for first-year racial/ethnic minority students.

Research has shown that predominantly White institutions typically overlook the cultural interests and needs of racial/ethnic minority students, especially when it comes to campus activities (Cheng, 2004; Harper et al., 2005; Hernandez, 2002; Smedley et al., 1993). This lack of cultural fit results in feelings of marginality and incongruence (Gloria, Robinson Kurpius, Hamilton, & Willson, 1999; Sedlacek, 1999). Examples of this can be seen in residence halls, where nearly 70 percent of the college experience occurs (Johnson, 2003), and in residential learning communities (Knight, 2003). Many racial/ethnic minority students have reported that on-campus residential facilities do not support their cultural needs and interests, as demonstrated by the residence hall programming and dining options (Johnson, 2003). As discussed by Johnson (2003), racial/ethnic minority students tend to complain that residence hall staff, including resident assistants, do not embrace cultural differences. In fact, many students perceive racism and discrimination in the practices and attitudes of residence hall staff and student leaders.

Similar to the programming of residence hall events and campus activities are the focus and themes of learning communities. Residential learning communities are designed with the intent of linking students to academics, faculty, campus activities, and in some cases, residence halls (Knight, 2003). Learning communities also tend to produce positive outcomes for first-year students, which include retention, higher grade point averages, smoother student adjustment, increased levels of engagement in campus activities, and an overall satisfaction with the college experience (Tinto, 1996, 1998; Tinto & Goodsell, 1994). Despite these known benefits, most first-year racial/ethnic minority students choose not to become involved in learning communities because they often lack culturally appealing activities. Instead, these students create their own enclaves and social communities, such as race-specific student organizations (Guifridda, 2003; Harper & Quaye, 2007; Person & Christensen, 1996).

Another unexpected aspect of campus culture for first-year racial/ethnic minority students is the racial/ethnic composition of student organizations and leadership positions at PWIs. Racial/ethnic minority students often find that leadership in mainstream organizations can sometimes mean abandonment of one's cultural identity through being forced to assimilate to the White norms by which these groups are governed (Arminio et al., 2000). As a result, racial/ethnic minority students simply do not consider involvement in mainstream student organizations as being important to their lives outside of class (Kezar & Moriarty, 2000; Sutton & Kimbrough, 2001). Consequently, campus student leadership tends to be White. For first-year racial/ethnic minority students, the lack of representation in the campus student leadership can be discouraging and make the adjustment to college much more difficult.

Overwhelming Whiteness
Probably one of the biggest hurdles for racial/ethnic minority students at PWIs, and closely related to campus climate and culture, is the overwhelming Whiteness that

engulfs these students when they first come to campus. Prior to and during the initial weeks of beginning their first year of college, students participate in many traditional college "kickoff" activities including orientation, residence hall move-in activities, official university welcome/convocation, and Welcome Week festivities. For racial/ethnic minority first-year students, these events (and many others) can be their first real taste of campus life at PWIs, as well as the point where disengagement with out-of-class activities can begin (DeSousa & King, 1992; Harper et al., 2005; Sutton & Kimbrough, 2001).

Many of the activities mentioned above are dominated by rituals, historic symbols, wealth, and prestige, all of which are usually traditionally White (Feagin et al., 1996). Culturally insensitive comedians, the exclusive selection of White entertainers, student discussion panels with only White students, and parties with only rock and pop music are all examples of well intentioned programs that racial/ethnic minority students find unappealing. This constant "glorification of mainstream culture" contributes to the presumption that first-year racial/ethnic minority students must assimilate and to the feelings of exclusion that these students experience (Feagin et al., 1996).

As mentioned earlier, there is incongruence between the values that most institutions espouse and what they actually enact regarding diversity and multiculturalism (Harper & Hurtado, 2007; Hurtado et al., 1998). At most PWIs, racial/ethnic minority students feel that fostering cultural/racial diversity is simply not a high priority (Hurtado, 1992). For example, Hurtado and colleagues (1998) note that there are embedded benefits for White students, such as physical and social spaces, that racial/ethnic minority students do not receive. These experiences and others lead first-year racial/ethnic minority students to feel as though they are socially invisible and that their interests and needs will be largely ignored by the university administration (Feagin et al., 1996; Harper & Hurtado, 2007; Hurtado, 1992).

Ethnic Clubs and Organizations

Another key issue in engaging racial/ethnic minority first-year students centers on the need for ethnic clubs and organizations. According to Kezar and Moriarty (2000), the absence of social support and networks can have a negative effect on the adjustment of first-year students. As mentioned previously, first-year racial/ethnic minority students feel pressured to blend into mainstream organizations and tend to view traditionally White clubs and organizations as socially exclusive (Ancis et al., 2000; Sutton & Kimbrough, 2001). These students report the difficulty of identifying and interacting with peers who are not members of a racial/ethnic minority (Eimers, 2001). As a result, Eimers (2001) posits that these feelings have contributed to the isolation and alienation that many first-year racial/ethnic minority students experience. At PWIs, first-year racial/ethnic minority students need organizations that will provide a community of support and warmth, and a social niche, that traditional campus organizations do not provide (DeSousa & King, 1992; Guiffrida, 2003; Harper et al., 2005; Kenny & Stryker, 1996; Sutton & Kimbrough, 2001). This sense of comfort helps first-year racial/ethnic minority students to feel connected to their institution, thus improving their educational outcomes and overall satisfaction with the institution.

Developed primarily out of the dissatisfaction with the lack of cultural activities at PWIs, ethnic clubs and organizations provide comfort and cultural support in an otherwise hostile and unwelcoming environment. These clubs also provide networks for racial/ethnic minority students that are not found elsewhere on the campus. Ultimately, these organizations are beneficial in orienting first-year racial/ethnic minority students to the campus environment (Guiffrida, 2003; Harper & Quaye, 2007; Kenny & Stryker, 1996). Furthermore, Hurtado et al. (1998) state that participation in these organizations encourages involvement in other aspects of campus life.

Active out-of-class engagement is essential to the development of leadership skills in students (Kezar & Moriarty, 2000). Participation in student organizations, residence hall groups, and other campus activities enables students to "learn through action, contemplation, reflection and emotional engagement" (National Association of Student Personnel Administrators & American College Personnel Association, 2004, p. 11). These out-of-class activities are also vital to student development, as "every student club or organization provides learning opportunities for its participants to develop and practice such skills as leadership, time management, collaboration, and goal setting" (p. 11). For first-year racial/ethnic minority students, the option for ethnic integration through cultural organizations or activities provides a sense of mattering and belonging, thus reducing the feelings of alienation (Cheng, 2004; Gloria et al., 1999; Harper & Quaye, 2007; Kezar & Moriarty, 2000; Sutton & Kimbrough, 2001).

Academic Preparation

Research reveals that some first-year racial/ethnic minority students at PWIs feel that they are ill-prepared for the academic challenges they face in college (Roe Clark, 2005; Smedley et al., 1993). With academic underpreparedness being a potential issue, these students often opt out of being involved in out-of-class activities, and instead decide to devote their entire attention to academic endeavors (Eimers, 2001; Hernandez, 2002; Smedley et al., 1993). This decision is often misconstrued as disengagement, when in fact it can be effectively addressed through proper workshops and programs that demonstrate the possibility of performing well academically and also being actively involved in campus life. Making the choice between studying and participating in campus activities is yet another challenge that many first-year racial/ethnic minority students at PWIs must face.

Utilization of Student Services

The final key issue in engaging first-year racial/ethnic minority students in out-of-class activities is their use of existing student support services at PWIs. Designed to help retain racial/ethnic minority students, many of these services provide support and avenues for campus involvement (Gloria et al., 1999; Hefner, 2002; Kenny & Stryker, 1996). According to Person and Christensen (1996), student support services such as cultural centers help first-year racial/ethnic minority students create their own social and cultural networks in an otherwise unwelcoming environment. Supportive environments and specialized, culturally appealing programs and activities can greatly aid in engaging first-year racial/ethnic minority students (DeSousa & King, 1992; Gloria et al., 1999; Kenny & Stryker, 1996).

Despite these intended efforts, many first-year racial/ethnic minority students do not utilize support services. Research shows that various reasons lie behind this. Helm, Sedlacek, and Prieto (1998) found that not all of these programs address the various needs and interests of first-year racial/ethnic minority students. For example, depending on the stage of identity development at which a student is, some support services may not seem beneficial. Moreover, many first-year racial/ethnic minority students are simply unaware that certain resources and support sources exist on a campus (Kenny & Stryker, 1996; Roe Clark, 2005). If these students are immediately disengaged in campus activities because of the campus climate, culture, and overwhelming Whiteness, then they are unlikely to seek out any campus services or to learn that such services exist.

Theoretical Framework

Astin's Theory of Student Involvement, Phinney's Model of Ethnic Identity Development, and social identity development theory provide the theoretical foundation for our discussion. These theories were intentionally selected because of their ability to interrelate and support each other in a purposeful manner. No discussion centered on student engagement would be complete without exploring Astin's work, as it is necessary for understanding student development both in and outside the classroom. Phinney's work is appealing for its inclusion of all racial/ethnic minority students; choosing a theory focused on one specific racial/ethnic minority group could represent a distortion of information and result in misguided strategies. Finally, social identity development theory is relevant since it describes the stages of identity development for both oppressed and majority-culture students and details their "emotional and cognitive struggles with oppression" (Torres, Howard-Hamilton, & Cooper, 2003, p. 23). We also felt it was important to mention Schlossberg's concept of mattering and marginality because of its description of the experiences many racial/ethnic minority students face at predominantly White institutions.

Astin's Theory of Student Involvement

Astin (1984) defines involvement as "the quantity and quality of physical and psychological energy that students invest in the college experience" (p. 307). Astin's Theory of Student Involvement is "qualitatively different" from other types of developmental theory commonly used in the study of college students (e.g., psychosocial, cognitive-structural, moral, ethical) in that it does not suggest that development occurs in hierarchically arranged stages. Also, involvement refers to behaviors and what students actually do, instead of what they think, how they feel, and the meanings they make of their experiences. The theory is principally concerned with how college students spend their time and how various institutional processes and opportunities facilitate student development. "The extent to which students can achieve particular developmental goals is a direct function of the time and effort they devote to activities designed to produce these gains" (Astin, 1984, p. 301).

Emerging from a longitudinal study of college students, Astin (1984) offered five basic postulates in his theory: (1) involvement entails the investment of physical and psychological energy in different "objects" that range in the degree of their specificity; (2) involvement occurs along a continuum, with different students investing varying degrees of energy in various objects at different times; (3) involvement includes qualitative and quantitative components; (4) the amount of student learning and development is directly proportional to the quality and quantity of involvement; and (5) "the effectiveness of any educational policy or practice is directly related to the capacity of that policy or practice to increase student involvement" (p. 298).

It is important to note that Astin's theory is based on a broad definition of involvement that extends far beyond memberships in clubs and student organizations. Spending time on campus, living and participating in residence hall communities, interacting with faculty in class and out of class, and socializing with peers about academic and non-academic matters are all included in Astin's definition. The theory suggests that student time is the most precious resource during the college years and how students spend that time affects what they gain from college. This theory is a useful tool for designing programs and strategies to combat racial/ethnic minority students' adjustment problems and engage them in out-of-class activities.

Phinney's Model of Ethnic Identity Development

Racial/ethnic minority students at PWIs are inundated by the majority White culture. Phinney's Model of Ethnic Identity Development is especially relevant to these students since they are "resolving conflict between the level of prejudice and stereotyping perceived as prevalent from the majority culture and dissonance of values between minority and majority culture" (Torres et al., 2003, p. 36). Although this theory is more generic in terms of the broad range of ethnicities to which it applies, it is salient as it is most representative of all racial/ethnic students and their identity development journeys. As previously stated, it would be erroneous to choose an ethnic-specific theory that could potentially lead to misguided generalizations and insufficient engagement strategies. During progression through the model's three stages, students move from exhibiting little interest or awareness of their ethnic cultures, through a "heightened consciousness" of their ethnicity and the views of the majority culture regarding their ethnic group, to the final stage in which the student is accepting of his or her own ethnicity and ethnic minority group. This developmental journey combines conflict, challenge, pain, confusion, self-reflection, and growth, all of which can be made more manageable with purposeful programming and appropriate resources readily available to students.

Social Identity Development Theory

Roe Clark (2005) maintains "the importance of social identity in understanding college students" (p. 299) and emphasizes the relevance of social identities for first-year racial/ethnic minority students, as these students' college experiences will be influenced by their social encounters as members of a minority group. For this reason, Hardiman and Jackson's social identity development theory is included in our framework. Torres et al. (2003) describe the theory as "helpful in understanding the perspectives of students and developing training or teaching modules" (p. 23). This theory details simultaneously the development of majority and minority cultures, a point that is beneficial when working with racial/ethnic minority students at PWIs. This understanding of the social identity development process experienced by all students equips educators with the knowledge needed to design effective programs for the campus as well as programs and workshops tailored to those students who are "coping with different emotional and cognitive struggles with oppression" (Torres et al., 2003, p. 23).

Mattering and Marginality

It is important to recognize the role of "mattering" and marginality when discussing the college experiences of racial/ethnic minority students. Mattering is "the receipt of consistently positive messages from peers, faculty, and staff" and it "confirms for an undergraduate that she or he belongs in college and has the capacity to do well" (Harper et al., 2005, p. 395). Such messages can be conveyed via the provision of culturally relevant programs, services, and venues for racial/ethnic minority student engagement. In contrast, marginality is defined as "not fitting in and can lead to self-consciousness, irritability, and depression" (Evans, Forney, & Guido-DiBrito, 1998, p. 27). Feelings of marginality can be long lasting for racial/ethnic minority students (Evans et al., 1998). Moreover, Evans et al. (1998) suggest that mattering is a prerequisite to involvement. If so, student affairs educators must diligently work to let students know, through programs, activities, recognition and interactions, that they genuinely matter.

Engagement Strategies

The First-Year 15

To this point, we have discussed the developmental issues facing racial/ethnic minority students at PWIs and reviewed the theoretical framework. Now we combine the issues with theories to develop the First-Year 15. These are strategies that combat disengagement by creatively involving racial/ethnic minority students in out-of-class activities. This First-Year 15 is not to be confused with the infamous "Freshman 15" (pounds gained during the first year of college). Instead of gaining unwanted weight, racial/ethnic minority students will gain confidence, knowledge, and, best of all, become engaged in out-of-class activities. Ultimately, these students will develop a connection with their institutions. Here are our First-Year 15:

1 Provide a mentoring program specifically designed to meet the needs of first-year racial/ethnic minority students. Upon accepting admission, students should receive information about this program asking for their participation and completion of a form that enables students to detail their particular interests. As soon as the information forms are received, students are paired with a junior- or senior-level student with interests that most closely match those of the new student. Even before classes begin, the mentors will begin communicating with their mentees. The mentors are present to assist their mentees in moving in to their residence halls and, during Welcome Week, a special reception can be held to formally introduce the students to the program and the specific requirements of the first semester.

2 Represent racial/ethnic minority students in all campus publications. This includes admission viewbooks, websites, campus newspapers, general catalogs, and yearbooks. These publications provide both a written and pictorial account of campus life, but often they fail to adequately include pictures and articles of racial/ethnic minority students engaged in campus activities. Ample representation of racial/ethnic minority students engaged in out-of-class activities will help to provide these students with a sense of comfort and belonging. First-year racial/ethnic minority students who open a campus publication, such as a newspaper, and read culturally appealing articles and see pictures of culturally appealing events and activities will feel encouraged to become involved in out-of-class activities. This representation also helps to reduce the impression of "overwhelming Whiteness" that first-year racial/ethnic minority students encounter when they first arrive on predominantly White campuses. It is the responsibility of the staff that puts together campus publications to ensure that there are fair representations of all racial/ethnic minority groups in them. As the saying goes, "a picture is worth a thousand words."

3 Develop a campus involvement and incentive program that rewards racial/ethnic minority students who attend and participate in university programs with prizes or discounted campus services. Students join the program for free and receive a member number. For each program attended, they receive credit that can be use at the end of the semester/ quarter auction (e.g., $10 in credit for educational programs or $5 in credit for social programs). Students can be required to attend, for example,

at least 75 percent of a program to earn credit. The auction prizes can be purchased using allocated funds or donations from local or national businesses, and can include departmental services that cost money (for example, a $25 meal credit at the food court or $20 copy cards). Incentive programs work best if they are centralized in a department responsible for campus-wide programming. Participation can be tracked via the member numbers in a user-friendly database. Through a collaborative partnership between other programming departments (housing, student government, etc.), student service departments (career services, writing center, etc.), and academic support services (required first-year student courses, mentor programs, etc.) students will become engaged with many of the services they would otherwise overlook until needed in a crisis. This innovative initiative would provide first-year racial/ethnic minority students with a fun incentive to become engaged with the institution.

4 Develop a comprehensive racial/ethnic minority leadership program focused on the needs of racial/ethnic minority students. This program will not only engage racial/ethnic minority students and foster their leadership development, but will also encourage them to get involved in student organizations and campus leadership opportunities. The leadership program will not be based on traditional leadership development models, which are primarily centered on conventional White, male, middle-class values. Rather, the program will be created with an emphasis on non-positional leadership, community service, and cultural development activities with a focus on connecting the students to peers, helpful faculty and staff members, and support services. Racial/ethnic minority faculty and staff will be recruited to facilitate the program with upper-level, racial/ethnic minority student leaders serving as program coordinators. This program should only be offered to first-year racial/ethnic minority students during their second semester. Additionally, through continued assessment and evaluation, the students could provide valuable information regarding improvements to the program, thereby developing a leadership program that truly meets the needs of this population.

5 Create culture-specific resource guides for first-year racial/ethnic subpopulations. Mailed to their local or campus addresses or permanent addresses (for those who live with parents or other relatives), these resource guides will include details on the following: racial/ethnic organizations on campus and their contact information; campus activities planned for the fall and spring semesters; various campus resources and support services; related scholarship opportunities; and racial/ethnic minority faculty and staff. Resource guides can also include the location and contact

information of the particular campus cultural center that provided the guidebook, as well as photos of racial/ethnic minority students involved in various activities. The major benefit of culture-specific resource guides is that they inform racial/ethnic minority students about the culturally appealing involvement opportunities that exist on campus. When they are informed early on (within the first week or two of the fall semester), it is more than likely that first-year racial/ethnic minority students will become more engaged in out-of-class activities, thus forming a connection with the institution. It is important to note that this strategy is taken from the University of Southern California's Center for Black Cultural and Student Affairs (CBCSA). CBCSA currently produces the yearly African American Resource Handbook, which is distributed to all African American students.

6 During orientation, provide incoming racial/ethnic minority students with an information card so they can identify student services or student organizations about which they would like to know more. A first-year student task force could be charged with tabulating the first-year student results and delivering this information to the appropriate student service department or student organization during the first week of school. The second charge of the task force would be to reach out to the responding student pool via telephone or in person within four weeks of the beginning of school year to find out if they have connected with their interest selections.

7 Engage students through culturally based service-learning opportunities by creating an institutionally funded Special Interest Service Board. Consisting of faculty, staff, and students, the board would hear student proposals for culturally relevant service projects. The projects can range from tutoring children from a student's past school or neighborhood, to teaching English to members of a student's community, to working to raise money to purchase medicine and supplies to help educate Africans about HIV and AIDS prevention. The purpose of these projects is for students to create a program that is relevant to them, work through all the details, solicit help from peers, and see it through to completion. The board will select projects to be accomplished each semester or year and determine which projects will receive financial support. All the service-learning projects must include clear learning outcomes and include meaningful opportunities for reflection and group processing. These projects will enable racial/ethnic minority students to engage with peers, their community, and the institution, while gaining valuable leadership and organizational skills.

8   Develop professional development diversity training workshops for all staff and graduate assistants within student affairs. These workshops will be held monthly to ensure that racial/ethnic minority students are always on the minds of those professionals who work with the student community. The workshops can include guest speakers and panels of racial/ethnic minority students reviewing the latest literature on diversity and engaging students, and site visits to other institutions to share ideas. In addition, at the end of each semester, students can evaluate programs sponsored by student affairs and make suggestions for improvement. This is a critical evaluative move that makes the students aware of the genuine concern the staff has for student programming and allows students to give valuable input into the effectiveness of the programming.

9   Offer racial/ethnic-themed residential buildings or floors as housing options for first-year racial/ethnic minority students. Many predominantly White institutions offer themed residential floors based on gender, health and fitness, or academic interest, but they tend to exclude racial/ethnic minority-themed residential floors or buildings. By providing a warm and comforting environment, racial/ethnic-themed residential buildings or floors can foster personal growth and identity development, provide support and culturally appealing programs, and result in a better adjustment to college. These racial/ethnic-themed floors can help to fill the social and cultural void often felt by first-year racial/ethnic minority students. For example, Stanford University offers several racial/ethnic-themed residential floors, including African American, Chicano/Mexican American, and Native American/Alaska Native themed houses. The students who live on these floors and buildings tend to be very engaged in out-of-class activities and serve as leaders in many racial/ethnic clubs and organizations.

10 Create a student board of trustees that reflects the diversity of the student body. Students are selected by their peers through a democratic process, and some positions are designated for first-year students. Membership on such boards is prestigious and is often considered as one of the highest achievements a student may attain. The diverse composition of a board means that other students are likely to see their same-race peers in leadership positions, which will make the position seem more attainable. Student trustees, in conjunction with the undergraduate student government, can advocate for the needs of all students with particular emphasis on those who are traditionally underrepresented. The student board of trustees will be responsible for conducting an institutional audit each year through the use of evaluative surveys and focus groups. The findings produced can help drive the advocacy efforts of the board. Further, the board will meet

with the institution's own board of trustees, in which the students will have both a voice and voting privileges.

11 Encourage student leaders not only to recruit first-year racial/ethnic minority students for membership in their organizations, but also to encourage first-year student involvement in the executive boards of these organizations. To aid in recruitment efforts, racial/ethnic minority student organizations should hold a certain percentage of their events in first-year residence halls. This will bring culturally appealing programming to where the intended audience lives, thus making them more likely to attend. Another way to accomplish this is for the advisors to require that members from the racial/ethnic student organizations be involved in events such as move-in day and Welcome Week activities. To help encourage first-year involvement in the executive boards of these organizations, advisors should require that two positions in the executive board be allotted to first-year students. This will not only help get first-year students involved in the decision-making process of these organizations, it will also foster their future leadership in campus activities. Seeing other racial/ethnic minority first-year students, sophomores, juniors, and seniors involved in the planning of campus activities will more than likely result in the increased involvement of other first-year racial/ethnic minority students in campus activities.

12 Offer an open series of culture-specific self-empowerment sessions that focus on racial/ethnic minority students and enable them to engage in open dialogue about what they need to keep them motivated and empowered when they arrive on campus. This dialogue should be led by an active student leader, staff, or faculty member who represents the racial/ethnic group. A panel of peers should represent a cross-section of majors, genders, and affiliations. In these empowerment sessions, students should be provided a benchmark checklist of key activities, services, and behaviors in which every successful student should engage as a first-year, sophomore, junior, and senior student.

13 Forge a collaborative programming partnership between the academic, campus activities, service, and housing and residential life departments to set goals and expectations for involvement levels for first-year racial/ethnic student populations. After receiving current statistical information and information on the specific developmental needs on a targeted racial/ethnic subpopulation on campus, a programming team develops a timeline addressing the most pressing issues facing each population. In addition, the team can set outreach and attendance goals to engage first-year racial/ethnic minority students. By combining resources, departments

can design, promote, and present a specific program that overlaps their respective areas.

14 Ensure that learning community themes and activities are culturally appealing to first-year racial/ethnic minority students. The themes should incorporate relevant cultural and historical themes to grab the interest of these students. To ensure they do so, learning community coordinators should conduct a series of focus groups. The first series of focus groups should consist of racial/ethnic minority students who have participated in learning communities as first-year students. Such topics as what they liked, disliked, and wanted to see different about these learning communities should be discussed. Another series of focus groups should consist of randomly selected racial/ethnic minority students, who are sophomores, juniors, and seniors, who did not participate in learning communities as first-year students. These groups should explore what themes would have met their cultural interests and encouraged them to participate as first-year students. Learning community coordinators should also recruit former racial/ethnic minority participants not only to serve as the peer advisors to these communities, but also to help in the planning of activities and events. It is important to note here that not all learning communities are residential, but this strategy can be beneficial whether or not a residential component exists.

15 Systematically collect data for engaged and seemingly disengaged racial/ethnic minority students. It is important to have a comprehensive assessment plan to determine what compelled a student to take part in activities, join various organizations, and pursue leadership positions. Understanding these factors could be instructive for engaging others. Likewise, data collected from disengaged students could reveal toxins in the campus environment (for example, racism and perceptions of overwhelming whiteness in organizations) that warrant institutional action. Attempts to engage more racial/ethnic minority students in educationally purposeful activities will be incomplete and likely ineffective if educators do not engage in ongoing assessment of engagement trends and students' reactions to various environmental norms on campus.

Conclusion

In this chapter, we have identified issues that shape the social engagement of first-year racial/ethnic minority students. Research has documented that the out-of-class experiences of first-year racial/ethnic minority students heavily influence their social engagement, and thus their success (Upcraft & Gardner, 1989). The first-year experience for racial/ethnic minority undergraduates has been investigated; yet engaging these students in campus activities remains problematic. Framed by student development theories, this chapter provides readers with the current developmental issues facing first-year racial/ethnic minority students at predominantly White institutions. Most importantly, we have provided innovative, yet certainly not exhaustive, strategies that can be implemented at PWIs. However, there is still much work to be done. More research on racial/ethnic minority students' involvement preferences and the reasons behind these choices would be quite beneficial. Student affairs educators need to constantly evaluate their programs to ensure inclusion of all students and students' healthy development. Through departmental collaborations, networking, and pooling of financial resources, increased engagement of first-year racial/ethnic students can be accomplished. This chapter has provided tools, suggestions, and ideas.

References

Ancis, J. R., Sedlacek, W. E., & Mohr, J. J. (2000). Student perceptions of campus cultural climate by race. *Journal of Counseling and Development, 78*(2), 180–185.

Arminio, J., Carter, S., Jones, S., Kruger, K., Lucas, N., Washington, J., Young, N., & Scott, A. (2000). Leadership experiences of students of color. *NASPA Journal, 37*(3), 496–510.

Astin, A. (1984). Student involvement: A developmental theory for higher education. *Journal of College Student Development, 40*(5), 518–529.

Cabrera, A., Nora, A., Terenzini, P., Pascarella, E., & Hagedorn, L. (1999). Campus racial climate and the adjustment of students to college: A comparison between white students and African American students. *Journal of Higher Education, 70*(2), 134–160.

Cheng, D. (2004). Students' sense of campus community: What it means, and what to do about it. *NASPA Journal, 41*(2), 216–234.

D'Augelli, A. R., & Hershberger, S. L. (1993). African American undergraduates on a predominantly White campus: Academic factors, social networks, and campus climate. *Journal of Negro Education, 62*, 67–81.

DeSousa, D. J., & King, P. M. (1992). Are White students really more involved in collegiate experience than Black students? *Journal of College Student Development, 33*(4), 363–369.

Eimers, M. (2001). The impact of student experiences on progress in college: An examination of minority and nonminority differences. *NASPA Journal, 38*(3), 386–409.

Evans, N. J., Forney, D., & Guido-DiBrito, F. (1998). *Student development in college: Theory, research, and practice.* San Francisco: Jossey-Bass.

Feagin, J. R., Vera, H., & Imani, N. (1996), *The agony of education: Black students at White colleges and universities.* New York: Routledge.

Furr, S., & Elling, T. (2002). African American students in a predominantly White university: Factors associated with retention. *College Student Journal, 36*(2), 188–202.

Gloria, A. M., Robinson Kurpius, S. E., Hamilton, K. D., & Willson, M. S. (1999). African American students' persistence at a predominantly White university: Influences of social support, university comfort, and self-beliefs. *Journal of College Student Development, 40*(3), 257–268.

Guiffrida, D. A. (2003). African American student organizations as agents of social integration. *Journal of College Student Development, 44*(3), 304–319.

Harper, S. R., Byars, L. F., & Jelke, T. B. (2005). How membership affects college adjustment and African American undergraduates student outcomes. In T. L. Brown, G. S. Parks, & C. M. Phillips (Eds.), *African American fraternities and sororities: The legacy and the vision* (pp. 393–416). Lexington: University Press of Kentucky.

Harper, S. R., & Hurtado, S. (2007). Nine themes in campus racial climates and implications for institutional transformation. In S. R. Harper and L. D. Patton (Eds.), *Responding to the realities of race on campus. New Directions for Student Services* (No. 120, pp. 7–24). San Francisco: Jossey-Bass.

Harper, S. R., & Quaye, S. J. (2007). Student organizations as venues for Black identity expression and development among African American male student leaders. *Journal of College Student Development, 48*(2), 127–144.

Hefner, D. (2002, February). Black cultural centers: Standing on shaky ground? *Black Issues in Higher Education, 18*(26), 22–29.

Helm, E. G., Sedlacek, W. E., Prieto, D. O. (1998). The relationship between attitudes toward diversity and overall satisfaction of university students by race. *Journal of College Counseling, 1*(2), 111–120.

Hernandez, J. C. (2002). A qualitative exploration of the first-year experience of Latino college students. *NASPA Journal, 40*(1), 69–84.

Heard Hinderlie, H., & Kenny, M. E. (2002). Attachment, social support, and college adjustment among Black students at predominantly White universities. *Journal of College Student Development, 43*(3), 327–340.

Hurtado, S. (1992). The campus racial climate: Contexts of conflict. *Journal of Higher Education, 63*(5), 539–569.

Hurtado, S., Milem, J. F., Clayton-Pedersen, A. R., & Allen, W. R. (1998). Enhancing campus climates for racial/ethnic diversity: Educational policy and practice. *Review of Higher Education, 21*(3), 279–302.

Johnson, V. D. (2003). Cultural group perceptions of racial climates in residence halls. *NASPA Journal, 41*(1), 114–134.

Kenny, M. E., & Stryker, S. (1996). Social network characteristics and college adjustment among racially and ethnically diverse first-year students. *Journal of College Student Development, 37*(6), 649–658.

Kezar, A., & Moriarty, D. (2000). Expanding our understanding of student leadership development: A study exploring gender and ethnic identity. *Journal of College Student Development, 41*(1), 55–69.

Knight, W. E. (2003). Learning communities and first-year programs: Lessons for planners. *Planning for Higher Education, 31*(4), 5–12.

Kuh, G. (1995). The other curriculum: Out-of-class experiences associated with student learning and personal development. *Journal of Higher Education, 66*(2), 123–155.

Kuh, G. D., Palmer, M., & Kish, K. (2003). The value of educationally purposeful out-of-class experiences. In T. L. Skipper & R. Argo (Eds.), *Involvement in campus activities and the retention of first-year college students.* The First-Year Experience Monograph Series (No. 36, pp. 19–34). Columbia: University of South Carolina, National Resource Center for the Freshman Year Experience.

National Association of Student Personnel Administrators and American College Personnel Association. (2004). *Learning reconsidered: A campus-wide focus on the student experience.* Washington, DC: Authors.

Nettles, M. T. (1991). Racial similarities and differences in the predictors of college student achievement. In W. R. Allen, E. Epps, & N. Z. Haniff (Eds.), *College in Black and White: African-American students in predominantly White and in historically Black public universities* (pp. 75–91). Albany: State University of New York Press.

Person, D. R. & Christensen, M. C. (1996). Understanding Black student culture and Black student retention. *NASPA Journal, 34*(1), 47–56.

Roe Clark, M. R. (2005). Negotiating the freshman year: Challenges and strategies among first-year college students. *Journal of College Student Development, 46*(3), 296–316.

Sedlacek, W. E. (1999). Black students on White campuses: 20 years of research. *Journal of College Student Development, 40*(5), 538–550.

Smedley, B. D., Myers, H. F., & Harrell, S. P. (1993). Minority-status stresses and the college adjustment of ethnic minority freshmen. *Journal of Higher Education, 64*(4), 434–452.

Sutton, E. M., & Kimbrough, W. (2001, Fall). Trends in Black student involvement. *NASPA Journal, 39*(1), 30–40.

Terenzini, P. T., Rendón, R. I., Upcraft, M. L., Miller, S. B., Allison, K. W., Gregg, P. L., & Jalomo, R. (1994). The transition to college: Diverse students, diverse stories. *Research in Higher Education, 35*(1), 57–74.

Tinto, V. (1993) *Leaving college: Rethinking the causes and cures of student attrition.* Chicago: University of Chicago Press.

Tinto, V. (1996). Learning communities and the reconstruction of the first year of college. *Planning for Higher Education, 25*(1), 1–7.

Tinto, V. (1998). Colleges as communities: Taking research on student persistence seriously. *Review of Higher Education, 21*(2), 167–178.

Tinto, V., & Goodsell, A. (1994). Freshman interest groups and the first-year experience: Constructing student communities in a large university. *Journal of the Freshman Year Experience, 6*(1), 7–28.

Torres, V., Howard-Hamilton, M. F., & Cooper, D. L. (2003). *Identity development of diverse populations: Implications for teaching and administrations in higher educations.* ASHE-ERIC Higher Education Report (Vol. 29, No. 6). San Francisco: Jossey Bass.

Upcraft, M. L., & Gardner, J. N. (1989). A comprehensive approach to enhancing freshman success. In M. L. Upcraft, J. N. Gardner, & Associates (Eds.), *The freshman year experience: Helping students survive and succeed in college* (pp. 48–69). San Francisco: Jossey-Bass.

Upcraft, M. L., Mullendore, R. H., Barefoot, B. O., & Fidler, D. S. (Eds.) (1993). *Designing successful transitions: A guide to orienting students to college.* Columbia: University of South Carolina, National Resource Center for the Freshman Year Experience.

Chapter 11

Engaging White Students on a Multicultural Campus

Developmental Needs and Institutional Challenges

Margaret W. Sallee, Moreen E. Logan,
Susan Sims, and W. Paul Harrington

It is residence hall move-in day at Center University, a small religiously affiliated liberal arts college located in the Midwest. The campus is abuzz with excitement as first-year students meet their new roommates and returning students reunite with old friends. Stacy is a White first-year student from a small town a few hours away. All summer, she has been looking forward to starting college. She wonders if her classes will be different from high school and if her professors will be as nice as her teachers were. She is most excited about making new friends. Since she comes from a town with a predominantly White population, she is especially interested in meeting students of other races/ethnicities, though she is a little unsure about how to go about finding such friends. She does not spend too much time worrying about this, however, and figures that friendships will form naturally.

A few months pass and, aside from adjusting to food in the dining hall, Stacy is happy at Center University. She has made some nice friends through her involvement in choir and the campus church group. All of Stacy's friends look like her. In fact, most of the students at Center University look like her. Ninety percent of the 2,000 students on campus are White and only 8 percent of faculty members are of color. Stacy still wants to meet students of other races/ethnicities, but does not know how. Since she sees African American students interacting in the Multicultural Student Center, she desires to go there to meet some new people. However, she has not been able to gather the courage to enter, telling herself that she does not belong there.

One day while reading the campus newspaper, Stacy comes across the following letter to the editor:

> I am writing to complain about the existence of the Multicultural Student Center. Why do Black, Asian, and Hispanic students have somewhere to go, but there is nothing for White students? Why does our campus offer programs designed specifically for these students but there is nothing for us? If they have special programs, White people

should have them too. The Multicultural Student Center needs to offer a Western European club. Failing to do so is reverse discrimination!

Signed, Ross Johnson

Stacy does not know what to think. She understands the author's point, but something about it does not feel quite right. Though Stacy has not formed any conclusions, the rest of the campus certainly has. Several of the racial/ethnic minority students are angry. They start a letter writing campaign to the newspaper, decrying Ross's comments as racist. Some White students respond and challenge the racial/ethnic minority students; others write letters of support for the Multicultural Student Center. Tensions on campus begin to rise.

Doug, the African American director of the Multicultural Student Center, and Vanessa, the White dean of student affairs, decide to call a forum in the campus lounge to address the mounting racial tensions. They hope to provide an opportunity for structured dialogue between the racial/ethnic minority students who disagree with Ross' comments and the White students who support Ross. They know that this forum has the potential to help calm the situation, but, if it goes poorly, tensions may escalate. As the start time nears, the lounge is jammed to capacity. Among the many students in attendance is Stacy, who has come to try to understand what is happening on campus. Knowing that they should not keep the audience waiting, Doug looks at Vanessa before stepping forward to address the crowd.

Many similar incidents occur each year on campuses across the nation. Sometimes, actions arise from hatred; other times they are due to ignorance. These incidents make the campus an uncomfortable place for students, faculty, and staff. Educators are often tempted to avoid the discomfort, ignore the necessary dialogue, and return to the status quo. Educators must learn to resist that temptation, and instead strive to create an environment that encourages students of all races/ethnicities to work together to build a multicultural campus.

For White students to become invested in the creation of a multicultural campus, they must recognize that they have as much to contribute as racial/ethnic minority students. However, at the same time, they must acknowledge the ways in which the White majority has historically dominated most colleges and universities, thereby excluding racial/ethnic minority students. To engage authentically in a multicultural campus, White students must consider how their race/ethnicity influences their experiences as well as the experiences of those around them. In this chapter, we describe the challenges that educators face in trying to engage White students in multicultural programming. We then turn to a discussion of several theories that help clarify specific individual and institutional challenges before offering strategies to engage students in multicultural programming, on both an individual and an institutional level.

Challenges to Engaging White Students in Multicultural Programming

At most colleges and universities, students are involved in a range of co-curricular activities, from student clubs to sports teams to fraternities and sororities. Whereas some racial/ethnic minority students are active in multicultural activities, White students often do not gravitate toward such activities. In this section, we review the reasons behind White students' hesitations to engage in multicultural programming. Since many White students lack exposure to different cultures, they may not understand the benefits that they can accrue through involvement in multicultural activities. However, attending multicultural campus events is not enough. Institutions should work to provide students with opportunities to confront racism and challenge White privilege before they can benefit from participation in multicultural programming.

Lack of Exposure to Different Racial/Ethnic Groups

Like Stacy in the opening vignette, college may be the first time many White undergraduates interact with people of different races/ethnicities. Some students come to college with little knowledge of other races/ethnicities and may be hesitant to form cross-racial or cross-cultural friendships, often waiting for racial/ethnic minority students to initiate such interactions (Tatum, 2003). Although states such as California, Texas, Florida, and New York are often exceptions to the rule, the majority of the United States remains overwhelmingly segregated and mostly White (Hu & Kuh, 2003). However, demographics are changing. White students account for only 60 percent of all children in public schools nationwide; nearly one quarter of students live in states where the majority is no longer White (Orfield & Lee, 2004). Despite this increase in diverse populations, most White students have little contact with students of other races/ethnicities.

Many White students come from small towns that have few, if any, families of color. Others come from larger cities that, despite increased levels of structural diversity, remain segregated (Orfield & Lee, 2004); often White students attend K–12 schools where there are few racial/ethnic minority students while their African American and Latina/o peers are clustered in low-resource schools across town (Orfield & Lee, 2004). Despite the desegregation mandated over 50 years ago by the decision in *Brown* v. *Board of Education*, the United States remains a society divided. There is still "massive segregation, a court system that has dismantled critically important policy tools, and a public that supports desegregation, but has no consensus about how to get it" (Orfield & Lee, 2004, p. 39). Given the peculiar nature of U.S. society that allows for such continued segregation, many White undergraduates have minimal contact with their racial/ethnic minority counterparts in college (Chang, Astin, & Kim, 2004).

According to data from the U.S. Department of Education, 67 percent of undergraduates enrolled in postsecondary institutions in 1999–2000 were non-Hispanic Whites. Of the remaining 33 percent, African Americans accounted for 12 percent, Latina/os for 11 percent, and Asian Americans for 5 percent of all undergraduates (National Center for Education Statistics, 2002). Since most postsecondary institutions across the U.S. are predominantly White, there are not many opportunities for cross-racial interactions to occur (Chang et al., 2004). Educators cannot expect cross-racial discussions to occur solely in social situations on campus; these interactions must be a formal part of the curriculum, programming in residence halls, and co-curricular activities.

Researchers have found that White undergraduates who are exposed to students of other races/ethnicities accrue a variety of cognitive and social outcomes (Chang, 1999;

Gurin, Dey, Hurtado, & Gurin, 2002). As Hu and Kuh (2003) posited, owing to their limited exposure to peers of other races/ethnicities, White students may experience greater gains in learning and personal development from interactional diversity experiences than do their peers of other races/ethnicities. In a study of first-year undergraduates, Pascarella and his colleagues (1996) found that living on campus and participating in a racial/ethnic and cultural awareness workshop had significant positive effects on White students' openness to diversity and challenge. However, the authors found a significant negative effect on openness to diversity for White students who had joined a fraternity or sorority in their first year. Since many fraternities and sororities are predominantly White and members often associate exclusively with others in the organization, they have few opportunities to interact with students of other races/ethnicities. In a longitudinal study of 25,000 undergraduates attending 217 four-year institutions, Astin (1993) claimed that the frequency with which students socialized with people from different racial/ethnic groups or engaged in discussions of racial/ethnic issues was associated with an increase in cultural awareness and a commitment to promoting racial/ethnic understanding. Given the potential benefits of cross-racial interaction, institutions need to enable White students to interact with students of other races/ethnicities by creating deliberate opportunities for their involvement in multicultural programming. However, before White students can successfully engage with racial/ethnic minority students, they must learn to confront the racism and White privilege that pervade U.S. society.

Confronting Racism

For White students to explore and develop their racial/ethnic identities, they must be willing to confront racism. Racism is not limited to acts of prejudice. Building on the work of Wellman (1993), Tatum (2003) defines racism as "a system of advantage based on race" (p. 7). White students have a difficult time confronting racism as it means they must also acknowledge the privilege and benefits they have enjoyed as a result of racism. In the subsequent section, we explore the notion of White privilege and its applications to college students in greater depth. Most people would hesitate to call themselves racists. However, as Tatum argues, unless individuals actively work to combat racism, they are all complicit in its reproduction:

> I sometimes visualize the ongoing cycle of racism as a moving walkway at the airport. Active racist behavior is equivalent to walking fast on the conveyor belt. The person engaged in active racist behavior has identified with the ideology of White supremacy and is moving with it. Passive racist behavior is equivalent to standing still on the walkway. No overt effort is being made, but the conveyor belt moves the bystanders along to the same destination as those who are actively walking. Some of the bystanders may feel the motion of the conveyer belt, see the active racists ahead of them, and choose to turn around, unwilling to go to the same destination as the White supremacists. But unless they are walking actively in the opposite direction at a speed

faster than the conveyer belt—unless they are actively antiracist—they will find themselves carried along with the others. (pp. 11–12)

Educators need to help White college students walk backwards on the moving walkway. To do so, White students must be willing to confront racism, acknowledge their privilege, and use it in ways that actively resist racist assumptions and practices.

College students will have a range of reactions when challenged with the notions of racism and privilege. Some, like Stacy, may want to confront racism, but might not know how to begin. Other students, acting out of the same confusion, may display overtly racist behavior. Educators can take steps to encourage students to challenge their racial stereotypes and explore their racial/ethnic identities. As Engberg (2004) found, enrollment in a diversity course challenged White students to question their racist assumptions and simultaneously provided them with a network of support, from both their professors and classmates. In his study of the impact of diversity course requirements, Chang (2002) concluded that enrollment in a diversity-related course reduced students' racial prejudice, especially toward African Americans. However, Hogan and Mallott (2005) noted that the effects of completing a college-level course on race or gender issues had only limited effects on reducing racial prejudice. Despite the conflicting findings, both studies concluded that reducing students' prejudice required more than one diversity course. Colleges and universities should develop and implement a variety of methods, ranging from courses on diversity or race relations to co-curricular activities, to help students combat their racist assumptions.

White students who confront racism are inevitably faced with complicated moral and ethical dilemmas as they seek to develop their own identities. Milem (2003) found that completing an academic course that addressed issues of diversity is correlated with a decrease in racial bias. Similarly, Rankin and Reason (2005) argued that participating in diversity workshops or other comparable out-of-class experiences provided students with a creative outlet for discussing racism and cultural awareness. In another study of over 2,800 White students at 17 institutions, attending a racial or cultural awareness workshop was the strongest predictor of students' attitudes toward race after their sophomore year (Springer, Palmer, Terenzini, Pascarella, & Nora, 1996). However, simply learning more about racism does not provide students with adequate tools to build a healthy White identity. To do so, they must also learn about White privilege.

Exploring White Privilege

It is difficult for White students to understand and accept how they benefit from White privilege. Goodman (2001) defines privileged groups as those who have determined a society's dominant ideology and mainstream culture. Whereas racism consists of acts specifically perpetuated to hurt people of other races, White privilege is a system of advantages that benefits the dominant group and, as a result, penalizes minority groups. Tatum (2003) argues that racism "is not only a personal ideology based on racial prejudice, but a *system* involving cultural messages and institutional policies and practices as well as the beliefs and actions of individuals" (p. 7). Although persons may not practice racism in their lives, White people benefit from privilege while other groups are disadvantaged by it.

It is important for White students to understand the notion of White privilege in order to participate in multicultural programming. Some educators engage students in a discussion of privilege by drawing upon the often-cited work of McIntosh (2004), who describes White privilege as "an invisible package of unearned assets which I can count on cashing in each day, but about which I was 'meant' to remain oblivious" (p. 104). McIntosh provides a list of privileges that she received on account of her skin color, including the freedom to rent or purchase a home in an area she can afford, the ability to see people of her race positively represented in the media, and the ability to buy beauty products and bandages that match her skin tone. For many students, these privileges can serve as a revelation, leading them to begin to generate their own list of privileges.

However, as Ancis and Szymanski (2001) discovered, not all students were ready to recognize White privilege. The researchers asked 34 White students (31 female and 3 male) enrolled in a master's-level counseling program to read and respond to two items on McIntosh's list of White privilege. They found that students' answers could be divided into three categories: those who had no understanding or engaged in denial of White privilege; those who understood White privilege, but were unwilling to take action; and those who understood White privilege and expressed a commitment to action. Although the authors acknowledged the potential for response bias from students, this preliminary study demonstrated that even when exposed to the idea of privilege, some White students do not acknowledge its existence or, worse, find no compelling reason to work for its eradication.

Many White students have a difficult time coming to terms with the reality of White privilege. For some, this is the first time that they are asked to consider themselves as members of a group, rather than as individuals, shattering their belief in the American myth of meritocracy (McIntosh, 2004; Tatum, 2003). Many students in grade school read Horatio Alger stories, the classic example featuring a protagonist who "pulls himself up by his bootstraps." Others learned about the Old West, where cowboys and settlers forged new lives for themselves. Accepting White privilege is to acknowledge that some of an individual's accomplishments might not be due to her or his effort, but attributable to the color of one's skin (MacLeod, 1995). For many White students, coming to such a realization destroys the foundations of their belief systems.

Though acknowledging White privilege is difficult for many students to accept, postsecondary educators must not avoid engaging students in discussions of privilege. Reason, Scales, and Roosa Millar (2005) encourage student affairs educators and faculty members to help White students become racial justice allies. They suggest that educators support students in developing a new understanding of what it means to be White by encouraging them to reflect on their racial/ethnic backgrounds and how power and privilege influence their lives. Ultimately, as Reason and his colleagues contend, students should come to embrace their Whiteness, but actively reject its accompanying power and privilege. This is one important step toward participating actively in multi-cultural programming.

Institutional Barriers to White Student Engagement

If educators are interested in facilitating White racial identity development, individual intervention is not enough. As Scheurich and Young (2002) discuss, many different levels of racism pervade U.S. society, affecting the way people think, how they act, and how they evaluate those around them. In an educational environment, faculty members must be particularly aware of both the biases they hold as well as the ingrained racism that is embedded in the curriculum. Scheurich and Young (2002) argue that faculty members and researchers must pay particular attention to epistemological racism, which promotes a Western perspective of research and the accompanying potential for marginalizing people of color and suppressing alternative methods of research and practice. If faculty members only celebrate a Western orientation, White students will see few incentives for exploring different cultures.

To ensure the inclusion of multiple perspectives, educators can make use of the Cultural Environment Transitions Model by Manning and Coleman-Boatwright (1991), which offers indicators and initiatives that characterize the five different stages that institutions face as they progress from being monocultural to multicultural. The authors posit that their model does not provide a way for institutions to control the environment, but rather offers a map for institutions to follow as they attempt to become multicultural. Institutions in the monocultural stage are characterized by a climate that is unwelcoming for anyone outside of the dominant culture; all campus programming is based on the needs of one culture. To move toward multiculturalism, the institution will face a series of crises, often led by dissatisfied racial/ethnic minority students on campus. The letter to the editor at Center University could provide the impetus to move the institution toward multiculturalism. The multicultural campus embraces multiple cultures and perspectives. All races/ethnicities and cultures are represented in campus art and architecture, diverse leadership styles are honored, and power is equitably shared between groups.

Student affairs educators and faculty who want White students to question their privileges need to have institutional structures in place that support the creation of diverse campus environments. Hurtado and her colleagues (1999) present four factors that influence the climate for racial/ethnic diversity on a college or university campus: (1) the historical legacy of inclusion or exclusion; (2) structural diversity; (3) the psychological climate; and (4) behavioral elements. Although Hurtado et al. focus on creating an environment that is welcoming for racial/ethnic minority students, we maintain that such an environment is equally important to promote the development of White racial identity and to facilitate White students' involvement in multicultural activities.

Institutional climate cannot be altered overnight. Even the best-intentioned educators often face decades, sometimes centuries, of history that impedes efforts for change. Hurtado et al. (1999) argue that an institution's past of excluding racial/ethnic minority persons influences how these students are welcomed within the present campus. Although segregation and intolerance create an unwelcoming climate for racial/ethnic minority students, these practices are also harmful for White students. The authors found that adults who attended desegregated schools as children held reduced racial stereotypes and were less fearful in interracial settings than their counterparts from segregated neighborhoods. Although these findings provide a catalyst for institutional change, history is difficult to overcome.

Structural diversity—or the numerical representation of students, faculty, and staff—also plays a critical role in promoting multiculturalism. "An institution's proactive stance in increasing the representation of various racial/ethnic groups conveys the message that the campus maintains a multicultural environment as a high institutional priority" (Hurtado et al., 1999, p. 19). As the number of racial/ethnic minority students increases, both the opportunities for cross-racial interaction increase as does the likelihood that racial/ethnic minority students will find same-race peer groups to serve as sources of support. However, simply because opportunities for cross-racial interaction exist does not mean that students will take advantage of them. Stacy, the first-year student in the opening vignette, passed the Multicultural Student Center many times, but never went inside. Faculty and administrators of color also provide an important source of support for students of various races/ethnicities. For racial/ethnic minority students, faculty of color serve as role models, and White students can benefit by increased interaction with those of different races/ethnicities (Garcia & Van Soest, 2000).

Although a campus needs to have a critical mass of racial/ethnic diversity to ensure a positive climate, simply increasing the number of students on campus is not enough. The psychological climate can still be oppressive, regardless of the number of racial/ethnic minority students. Often, racial/ethnic minority students and White students have different conceptions of the racial climate (Cabrera, Nora, Terenzini, Pascarella, & Hagedorn, 1999; Harper & Hurtado, 2007). Whereas White students may perceive race/ethnic relations as positive, racial/ethnic minority students may have differing experiences. In their study of over 7,000 undergraduates, Rankin and Reason (2005) found that White students tended to characterize the campus climate as more accepting and less racist than racial/ethnic minority students. Whereas only 18.3 percent of White students characterized their institutions as racist, 32.3 percent of racial/ethnic minority students described their institutional campus climate as racist.

At Center University, Ross Johnson's letter to the editor and students' responses to it caused racial tensions to escalate. For White students, this incident may have been the first time they considered race relations; for racial/ethnic minority students, the letter may have been just another addition to a long list of discriminatory actions. Any intervention to decrease racial tensions needs to consider the importance of peer groups for undergraduates (Hurtado et al., 1999). White students who socialize exclusively with peers of their same race/ethnicity are likely to have a difficult time engaging in cross-racial interactions. Although increasing structural diversity increases opportunities for cross-racial interaction, casual contact is rarely beneficial (Allport, 1954; Gurin et al.,

2002). Rather, structured interactions need to be implemented to facilitate cross-racial dialogue and understanding.

The behavioral dimension of Hurtado and her colleagues' (1999) model addresses cross-racial interactions as well as the impact of diversity on campus and classroom involvement. Of particular relevance to this chapter, institutions need to celebrate diversity across campus in the classroom and through co-curricular activities. Faculty can play an important role by infusing their curricula with diversity-related content and also employing pedagogical techniques that create structured opportunities for cross-racial discussions. Faculty cannot recoil from discussing racism and privilege in the classroom; there needs to be sustained dialogue, both to have an impact on students as well as to demonstrate to the campus community that multiculturalism is an integral element of the institution's identity (Zúñiga, 2003).

While institutions should be concerned with encouraging White students to explore their racial/ethnic identities, they must also encourage faculty and staff to engage in similar journeys (Bensimon & Tierney, 1992/1993). In their study of over 500 student affairs educators across the country, Mueller and Pope (2001) found that White racial consciousness may be related to multicultural competence, suggesting that institutions interested in encouraging White students to engage in diversity initiatives must support these efforts for all campus populations, including faculty, staff, and administrators. To engage White undergraduates in multicultural programming and diversity initiatives, institutions must focus on helping students recognize their own race/ethnicity while simultaneously creating an environment that promotes engagement for students of all backgrounds.

Theoretical Framework

We continue our discussion of White student engagement with three theories that frame the research and support our issues and strategies: (1) White racial identity development; (2) psychosocial development; and (3) deconstructing Whiteness. The combination of these theories can facilitate White students' abilities and willingness to confront racism, explore their White privilege, and participate actively in dialogues focused on racial/ethnic issues.

Theory of White Racial Identity Development

Helms' (1993, 1995) research on White racial identity development helps explain the varying ways that White students think about diversity and racism. To develop a healthy White racial identity, students must work through a process to abandon racism before developing a non-racist White identity. Helms' original model, based on interactions between White and African American people, consisted of six stages through which persons progress in the process of developing a healthy White racial identity. The six stages are: Contact, Disintegration, Reintegration, Pseudo-Independence, Immersion/

Emersion, and Autonomy. In her later work, Helms (1995) renamed the stages "statuses" to reflect the fluidity of development.

A person enters the Contact status as soon as she or he first encounters someone of another race/ethnicity. For many, this contact occurs not through direct experience, but rather through exposure through the media. When Stacy first arrived at Center University, she was in the Contact status; she wanted to make friends with racial/ethnic minority students, but did not know how. People in this stage tend to have no understanding of their identities as White people or of the ingrained racism pervasive in society. However, Helms (1993) argues that with repeated direct or indirect contact, the person eventually is compelled to recognize inequities in the ways in which African American and White people are treated. Such a realization pushes the student into the second status, Disintegration.

For most people, Disintegration is the most uncomfortable of all the statuses. For the first time, White persons are forced to grapple with the fact that skin color affects life experiences. Feelings of guilt and anxiety characterize this status as White people begin to feel responsible for their privilege. Students experience conflict between what they have been taught in the classroom (e.g., "with liberty and justice for all") and the realities that they observe. Since no one can lead a healthy existence in a constant state of conflict, the person will seek ways to resolve this status. Resolution often occurs through avoiding interaction with people of color or by developing a set of beliefs that affirms the superiority of the White race, which leads the student into the most volatile of statuses, Reintegration.

Ross Johnson, the person who wrote the letter in the opening vignette, is a prime example of an individual in Reintegration. Whereas those in Disintegration generally experience feelings of guilt or anxiety, in Reintegration these feelings have been transformed into hatred, anger, and fear toward African American people. As Helms (1993) argues, much of an person's behavior in this status is motivated by these feelings, perhaps leading her or him to engage in blatantly racist behavior in order to protect White privilege. Ross lashes out at the racial/ethnic minority students because he feels that they are gaining too much power on campus. In this status, people withdraw almost completely from contact with students of other races/ethnicities. Any discussion of racial matters is "most likely to occur among same-race peers who share or are believed to share a similar view of the world" (Helms, 1993, p. 60). Whereas leaving students in Reintegration to discuss racial/ethnic issues among themselves may be counterproductive, institutions that utilize structured activities can help White students consider their own racial/ethnic identities. Often, the only way for students to move out of Reintegration and begin to develop a non-racist White identity is through a jarring event that causes them to question racism.

Pseudo-Independence marks the beginning of a journey toward a healthy White racial identity. This status is often described as the "White liberal" phase and is characterized by large amounts of intellectualization accompanied by a reluctance to discuss feelings about race/ethnicity (Helms, 1993). Although people in this stage begin to acknowledge the responsibility of White people for perpetuating racism, they still have not succeeded in altering their worldviews to be more inclusive. Students might take action; yet their efforts often focus on helping African Americans act more like White people, rather than on changing the ways in which White people practice exclusion and racism.

Such a focus does not occur until the student transitions into the fifth status of Immersion/Emersion. In this status, students actively seek out White role models to help as they redefine a positive White identity for themselves. Many immerse themselves in biographies of anti-racists, while others join White consciousness-raising groups. The critical focus in this status is on taking action in the White community. Those who reach the final status, Autonomy, are committed to acting for racial justice. They recognize the pervasiveness of racism, abandon it in their own lives, and actively work to dismantle racism in society. In addition to working to end racism, students in Autonomy often work to challenge other forms of oppression (Helms, 1995).

As discussed earlier, Helms (1995) amended her model to refer to all stages as statuses. She contends that many interpret stage models as static, meaning that students cannot simultaneously draw upon the core assumptions of each stage. In contrast, Helms posits that when people find themselves in uncomfortable situations, they often revert to the coping mechanisms with which they are most familiar. For example, when a student who has transitioned into Pseudo-Independence finds her or his identity threatened, she or he may revert to employing reasoning that characterizes Reintegration. As such, institutions should offer a range of activities to help students actively examine their racial/ethnic identities and challenge their stereotypes. By offering students repeated opportunities to engage in self-exploration, there is a greater likelihood that they will utilize the most advanced reasoning available to them. Racial identity development is not the only factor that impacts when and how White students will interact with students of other races/ethnicities. As Chickering and Reisser (1993) explain, students' psychosocial development also influences their readiness for engaging in cross-cultural friendships.

Theory of Psychosocial Development

In the second iteration of Chickering's classic theory of psychosocial development among college students, Chickering and Reisser (1993) maintain that students progress through the following seven vectors: Developing Competence, Managing Emotions, Moving through Autonomy toward Interdependence, Developing Mature Interpersonal Relationships, Establishing Identity, Developing Purpose, and Developing Integrity. Although Chickering has been cited less frequently in recent years because of the limitations of his sample (White men at a selective institution), his theory can help explain the needs of White undergraduates. When considering the challenges of engaging White students in multicultural programming, the fourth vector—Developing Mature Interpersonal Relationships—offers insight into students' unwillingness to become involved with students of other races/ethnicities.

To resolve challenges in this vector, students need to develop an appreciation for intercultural and interpersonal differences as well as the capacity to develop close relationships with friends and partners. (The original language asserts that students need to develop a tolerance for difference; we actively reject the word "tolerance," as it implies that a person must only co-exist with these differences. In contrast, the words "appreciation" or "understanding" of differences imply that a person not only learns to co-exist with these differences, but also recognizes how intercultural differences can strengthen her or his own life.) Although students can simultaneously work on several vectors at once, they must resolve the first three vectors before they can tackle the developmental challenges of the fourth vector. Students must have mastered Developing Competence, Managing Emotions, and Moving through Autonomy toward Interdependence before they can successfully form healthy relationships with students from different backgrounds.

Chickering and Reisser (1993) claim that developing an appreciation for differences requires that people learn not to judge others based on differences and "not to leap to a negative interpretation of others' behavior based on ignorance" (p. 150). The authors further argue that appreciating differences moves beyond an intellectual understanding of diversity. To develop the capacity for intimacy, students need to be authentic with each other and appreciate people for who they are, not for who they want them to be. For many students, this vector involves breaking unhealthy relationships from their past. Many students come to college still attached to their parents and espousing the beliefs they were taught at home. If Stacy's parents raised her to believe that White people should not interact with African Americans, she will have a difficult time forming meaningful cross-racial relationships until she succeeds at breaking those ties and beginning to establish her own belief system.

White identity development depends on psychosocial development. According to Helms' (1993) model, a White student will be unable to form meaningful cross-cultural friendships until she or he has successfully worked through the first three statuses to arrive at Pseudo-Independence. Furthermore, students who have not yet resolved the first three vectors of Chickering and Reisser's model are more likely to be in the first three statuses (i.e., Contact, Disintegration, Reintegration) of Helms' model. In a study of 320 African American and White female undergraduates, Taub and McEwen (1992) found a significant correlation between racial identity development and psychosocial development. Using two sets of assessment tools, one to measure racial identity development and another to measure psychosocial development, the authors found a negative correlation (at the .001 level) between students in Helms' stages of Disintegration and Reintegration and their score on the Mature Interpersonal Relations Attitude Scale. Students in Disintegration and Reintegration were less likely to have worked through the Developing Mature Interpersonal Relationships vector.

Chickering and Reisser (1993) assert that there are ways to help students develop an appreciation for differences, but offer the following caveat. "Merely coming into contact with students from different cultures may not improve tolerance and empathy" (p. 154). Simply increasing the number of racial/ethnic minority students on a campus will not help students resolve this vector or progress through Helms's (1993) model of White racial identity development. Educators need to take concerted action to create conditions that support racial identity development and the reduction of prejudice. As such, we now turn to a discussion of one theory that can facilitate White students' development.

Deconstructing Whiteness

Any discussion of diversity and racial differences must include a discussion of Whiteness. Too often, White students have accepted the universalization of White culture and when asked to discuss the impact of their racial/ethnic identities on their lives, are unable to formulate a response. Ortiz and Rhoads (2000) offer a five-step model that helps students of multiple races/ethnicities deconstruct Whiteness as part of a multicultural educational framework. They believe this model can serve as a precursor to the exploration of racial identity through Helms' (1993) model, arguing that solely focusing on racial attitudes ignores other critical elements of White identity. Students must learn to recognize the way in which White persons have used their power and dominance to shape what many consider the universal American culture.

Ortiz and Rhoads' (2000) framework is designed to help move students from having a basic understanding of culture to developing a multicultural outlook. The five steps of the framework are as follows: (1) Understanding Culture; (2) Learning about Other Cultures; (3) Recognizing and Deconstructing White Culture; (4) Recognizing the Legitimacy of Other Cultures; and (5) Developing a Multicultural Outlook. The primary goal of Step 1 (Understanding Culture) is to help students recognize how culture shapes their lives, but also how they shape culture through their daily interactions. Step 2 calls for students to learn about other cultures; this can occur through attending various cultural events and subsequently reflecting on these experiences. In the opening vignette, Stacy pondered visiting the Multicultural Student Center. Had she done so, she might have chosen to attend an event sponsored by the Center. However, unless she was able to process the experience with a peer or, better yet, a trained facilitator, she might have failed to grasp some valuable lessons.

Step 3, Recognizing and Deconstructing White Culture, is a critical, and often ignored, component of understanding White privilege. The primary goal in this step is "helping students to see that Whites have culture, and that White culture has become in many ways the unchallenged, universal basis for racial identity" (Ortiz & Rhoads, 2000, p. 88). For White students, this is a difficult process, but as the authors note, coming to such an understanding is crucial for the creation of a multicultural society. In Step 3, White students should have acquired an understanding of Whiteness and its importance to their own identities. Students in Step 4 learn to see the ways in which other people's cultures are important to understanding their own identities. As a result, students should begin to understand the importance of multiple cultures in U.S. society. In the final step, students learn that the various cultures shape each other and that "the inclusion of all cultures requires the reconstruction of U.S. society" (Ortiz & Rhoads, 2000, p. 89). Students in this step strive to take action to help with the creation of a multicultural society and understand the societal consequences for the marginalization of various cultures.

The steps of this model do not represent tasks that can be accomplished in a one-day workshop. Rather, these elements should be incorporated into multiple aspects of campus life. Discussions about diversity, White racial identity, and privilege are effective only if they are sustained over time. Educators at colleges and universities need to create the conditions to allow these discussions to take place. The combination of these five steps has the potential to enable White students to examine their White identities and participate in multicultural programming.

Engagement Strategies

We now offer a set of strategies that postsecondary educators can adopt to help students engage in discussions about diversity and encourage White students to become involved in creating a multicultural campus. Although many of our strategies build upon the establishment of a racial justice alliance (itself the first strategy described), institutions can modify any strategies to fit campus structures already in place.

Racial Justice Alliance for Students

Establish a racial justice alliance under the umbrella of Multicultural Student Services or the campus entity that houses other racial/ethnic offices. The racial justice alliance should serve to encourage White students to explore their racial/ethnic identities and accompanying privileges as well as promote their involvement in multicultural activities across campus. The office should be staffed by a minimum of one full-time professional, though we recommend hiring a greater number of educators. The office should also rely on a large network of students to work in the office and perform campus outreach. A significant portion of the Alliance's work will come through campus education. In particular, student allies will give presentations to students in residence halls, sororities and fraternities, athletic teams, student government, and other student organizations that could benefit from their services. Presentations will focus on encouraging students to become involved in multicultural campus events, to enroll in White identity development or race relations courses, and to develop an understanding of how their skin color shapes their experiences on campus and in society at large.

Racial Justice Alliance for Faculty and Staff

Establish a parallel racial justice alliance office for faculty and staff. The office should be staffed by a minimum of one full-time professional with oversight by one faculty member. Since faculty must have a strong sense of their own racial/ethnic identities to guide students through their own journeys of awareness of privilege, oppression, and racial consciousness (Torres, Howard-Hamilton, & Cooper, 2003), this office will provide White identity development workshops for faculty and staff. The office can also promote the use of release time for faculty and staff to attend multicultural campus events to provide opportunities for interactions with diverse colleagues and students. Annual performance reviews for faculty and staff could be modified to include criteria that would evaluate individual participation in the workshops and multicultural events.

Racial Justice Alliance in Orientation

Make the racial justice alliance a significant presence at new student orientation. Offer presentations to incoming students describing the services and programs that the office provides. Introduce the different racial/ethnic and cultural offices on campus and encourage students to become involved. Offer a racial justice workshop during orientation to facilitate opportunities for students to think about racial/ethnic relations on campus and in U.S. society. As part of the workshop, facilitators can note the campus racial/ethnic disparities, with a particular focus on issues of privilege, racism, and oppression. Other additions to the workshop might include a viewing and facilitated discussion of the race relations depicted in the film *Higher Learning* (Singleton, 1995) or a discussion of McIntosh's (2004) chapter "White Privilege: Unpacking the Invisible Knapsack."

Racial Justice Alliance and Service-Learning Partnerships

Create a partnership between the racial justice alliance and the office of service-learning on campus. Well designed service-learning programs combine course content and service in the community with a critical element of reflection (Eyler & Giles, 1999). Colleges and universities should take advantage of the surrounding community to learn about local multicultural populations. Students should be placed for an extended period of time, generally a quarter or a semester, at a service site in which they can provide service to the community while simultaneously learning through their interactions. Some possible placements include serving as tutors for children in schools or in after-school programs, working with children at a Boys and Girls Clubs, or volunteering at a community center. Students should be encouraged to reflect on the impact that their race/ethnicity has on their interactions with the community as well as on their own life experiences. Reflections can take the form of weekly journals submitted to an instructor and through weekly meetings with other students serving in the community. Through well designed reflections, White students can be encouraged to learn about multicultural populations and reflect on the privileges their skin color affords them.

White Racial Identity Development Courses

Offer White racial identity development courses for students. Just as many campuses offer ethnic studies courses that help students learn about their positions in

U.S. society, campuses should also offer courses that help White students come to an understanding of their race/ethnicity. Specifically, campuses should offer a White racial identity development course (not a "White studies" course), which would include readings and workshops about confronting racism and addressing White privilege. The courses would be designed to facilitate White students' questioning and analyzing of racial identity development within a framework that positions White identity development alongside a consideration of other racial/ethnic identities. Works by authors such as McIntosh (2004), Helms (1993, 1995), and Tatum (1992, 2003) would serve as the intellectual framework for the curriculum of the White racial identity courses.

Race Relations Courses

Offer a race relations course. Since students of different races/ethnicities have varying college experiences, campuses should encourage students to participate in a race relations course. This course would examine the social problems behind race relations and provide a forum for students of various races/ethnicities to come together to share their differing perceptions and experiences of campus and society. It would examine these differences in perceptions and foster discussions of how students, faculty, and administrators are injured by a negative racial climate on campus. In addition to considering race relations in a college environment, the curriculum should include an investigation of the changes in American culture with explicit attention to the growing divergence between the definitions of White culture and American culture.

Faculty Exchange Program

Establish a faculty exchange program to send faculty members from predominantly White institutions to teach for a semester or a year at an institution with a sizable population of racial/ethnic minority students. Some possible partner institutions include historically Black colleges and universities and Hispanic-serving institutions. Faculty who have participated in the racial justice alliance and are interested in creating a multicultural campus would be encouraged to apply. The exchange program would give faculty an opportunity to teach and experience campus life while immersed in a culture different from their own. As a result of their participation, faculty members may become more sensitive to issues of diversity, which would affect their performance in the classroom and their relationships with students. Faculty may also return to their home institutions with innovative ideas for multicultural pedagogy to share with their colleagues and students. The receiving institution should be encouraged to send one of their faculty members to the predominantly White institution. These faculty members could offer skills for engaging students, both in and outside the classroom. Visiting faculty members should be encouraged to give presentations to faculty and administrators on campus.

Summer Reading Program

Establish a summer reading program that explores a variety of racial/ethnic backgrounds for students, faculty, and student affairs educators. Each year, constituents within the campus should read one or two books that explore varying racial/ethnic and intercultural experiences. The institution can advertise the summer reading list on the campus website homepage with links to the multicultural center and racial justice alliance web pages. At the beginning of the academic year, campuses might offer a one-unit seminar or a series of workshops to discuss each book and its implications for the campus community. In addition to the seminar or workshops, the campus can also establish an online chat room or listserv to pose questions and facilitate discussion of the readings. Faculty members or graduate students can monitor chat rooms to help guide discussions or answer concerns. After several years, the campus would have an archive of questions and discussions that instructors might incorporate into their own courses. Possible books for the list include *The Spirit Catches You and You Fall Down* by Anne Fadiman (1997), *The Namesake* by Jhumpa Lahiri (2003), *Black Like Me* by John Howard Griffin (1960), *Long Walk to Freedom* by Nelson Mandela (1994), and *I Know Why the Caged Bird Sings* by Maya Angelou (1970). Institutions might look at the Campus Community Book Project established at the University of California, Davis (http://occr.ucdavis.edu/ccbp) as an example of an effective program.

Cross-Cultural Speaker Series

Establish a cross-cultural speaker series. Invite leaders from the local and national community who can address a range of topics to expose students to a broad spectrum of cross-cultural presentations. The speakers should come from a variety of backgrounds, with a special emphasis on those who work for social justice. The speaker series should draw on expertise from numerous academic disciplines in the humanities, social sciences, and professional fields. Institutions should make a special effort to include White anti-racist speakers in the series.

Immersion Experiences

Take White students on an immersion experience to racial/ethnic events. Although this activity can be used on any campus, it is particularly salient for those campuses that have few racial/ethnic minority students and, therefore, few multicultural activities. We recommend that institutions focus on the races/ethnicities or cultures that are most represented in their geographical area. For example, colleges and universities in the South might send students to events in the African American community whereas universities located in the Plains states might send students to a Native American reservation. The length of the immersion can vary from a few hours to a few days. Facilitators should process the event with students, discussing students' perceptions of the culture they experienced and the impact that the experience had on them.

Ethnographic Experiences

Send White students on an ethnographic experience to an area of White culture with which they are not familiar in order to help students recognize the diversity within White culture. Some events that institutions might use for this activity include a NASCAR race, a monster truck rally, a country music festival, the opera, or a Renaissance fair. As Ortiz and Rhoads (2000) contend, White students must understand the pervasiveness of White culture before they can commit to creating and living in a multicultural society. Often, it is easier for students to analyze aspects of culture with which they are not familiar. As such, we encourage institutions to select immersion experiences for students that may not necessarily be a natural fit. Students should be given a list of elements to look for while attending the event and, upon return, be engaged in reflection about their experiences. Some possible topics for discussion include how the students felt in this different environment as well as any similarities they saw between the community at this event (e.g., dress, patterns of speech, and ways of interacting) and the community with which they most strongly identify. The primary goal for this activity is to help students recognize the existence of White culture and its different subcultures. This event should be open to students of all races/ethnicities in order to benefit from recognizing the diversity within White culture as well as the similarities that connect White people regardless of preferred pastimes.

Partnerships between Student Representatives and Resident Advisors

Provide opportunities for student representatives from racial/ethnic organizations to partner with resident advisors. Given Reason, Roosa Millar, and Scales' (2005) findings that White students often do not engage in multicultural activities unless they have been invited, institutions should encourage White students to become involved in multicultural programming. Educators can facilitate this by providing opportunities for representatives of racial/ethnic student groups and clubs to partner with resident advisors and attend weekly residence hall meetings to promote their organizations and upcoming events to White students. Student representatives could target the commuter student population by publicizing events in the commuter lounge or on a commuter information board as well as by attending commuter club meetings. In addition, representatives from racial/ethnic student organizations can make presentations to sororities and fraternities and other student organizations on campus. Institutions also can offer a one-credit course for students who assume leadership roles and plan activities for multicultural groups.

Living-Learning Floors

Establish living-learning floors in the residence halls dedicated to fostering multicultural understanding. Activities can include cultural nights that emphasize sharing different aspects of students' cultural backgrounds through films, storytelling, dance, and art. Students on these floors should attend an orientation program before the halls officially open to begin the process of building community among residents. Resident advisors and professionals in residence life should facilitate weekly meetings that include reflection, journaling, and dialogue on a variety of issues related to racial identity and race relations in the United States. Resident advisors should collaborate regularly with the racial justice alliance and the multicultural student services office to coordinate programs and events to expose and immerse residents in various cultural experiences on and off campus. Residents of the living-learning community should partner with the residence life educators in planning programs that welcome the entire population of their residence hall. Bulletin boards in central locations should be updated weekly to share news, promote events, and recruit new participants into the program. The same information should be placed on the residence life page of the institution's website to allow prospective students and their families to become more familiar with the program as they explore their housing options. As each term nears an end, residence life staff should create and distribute an assessment that addresses the goals of the program. The assessment could be either electronic or in print and should be used by staff to evaluate and improve the program and its offerings.

Days of Dialogue

Establish "Days of Dialogue" (following a model created by the City of Los Angeles), an event that facilitates structured dialogues about race/ethnicity in all residence halls. The racial justice alliance or other allies for diversity should coordinate discussions among residents at least once a term. Those campuses that have a significant non-resident or commuter population can offer similar forums for these students. Topics for dialogue might include issues in the news on campus and in the city or country. Discussion topics should be uniform across campus and determined in advance by a group of students, student affairs educators, and faculty. Ideally, these dialogues should take place in each residence hall on the same date and time. To minimize scheduling conflicts, the dialogues should be held in the evening hours after classes have ended. The dialogues should be facilitated by representatives from the Racial Justice Alliance or other trained student leaders, including resident advisors. A professional staff or faculty member should also be present to offer support to the student facilitators. Occasionally, the staff member may need to intervene to challenge students' stereotypes and to provide support for any noticeably upset students.

Changes in Pedagogy and Materials

Assess the current curriculum to ensure that it is racially/ethnically balanced. If not, take measures to institute a more balanced curriculum. In addition, ensure that instructors are using inclusive pedagogy. Include input from student leaders and staff from the office of multicultural affairs when revising the curriculum. Develop materials (e.g., admissions brochures and orientation materials) that convey the campus commitment to promoting racial justice. If a racial justice alliance exists, offer a link to the site from the campus homepage. To ensure consistency, these materials should have the same wording, perhaps developed by the racial justice alliance or the office of multicultural affairs.

Web-Based Assessment

Develop and administer a web-based assessment of students' perceptions of race/ethnicity and privilege. During orientation, White first-year or transfer students will receive an email inviting them to participate in a quantitative web-based survey asking them to evaluate their perceptions of race/ethnicity and privilege. Institutions lacking the resources to develop their own survey could use the White Racial Identity Attitudes Scale (WRIAS) developed by Helms (1993). (However, to use the scale, they must be willing to submit all collected data to Helms for use in her research.) At the end of each academic year, the institution should reassess the surveyed population of students using the same assessment tool in order to track students' racial identity development over the course of their college careers. The purposive sample should include students who have taken the race relations course and students who have taken the White racial identity development course, as well as students who have completed neither. For campuses where a race relations or White racial identity development course has not been established, faculty should identify courses from the existing curriculum that serve to promote White racial identity development or the recognition of White privilege. Institutional members should use these data to determine whether specific courses and/or specific faculty members facilitated White racial identity development. The academic senate, faculty committees, and academic departments can use these data to modify programming and provide recommendations for curricular change. The administration of the web-based survey should fall under the purview of the racial justice alliance or a similar campus office.

Conclusion

Our proposed strategies are some of the many ways to engage White students in multicultural programming. We acknowledge that it will be particularly difficult for predominantly White institutions to challenge common assumptions about White privilege in order to push students, faculty members, and staff forward in their understanding of Whiteness. An institution's history with segregation and racism will undoubtedly influence the timeline of the implementation of the suggested strategies. However, regardless of campus climate or institutional history, we maintain that every college and university can successfully implement at least one of our strategies to begin to move the campus community toward actively engaging White students in creating a multicultural community.

References

Allport, G. W. (1954). *The nature of prejudice*. Reading, MA: Addison-Wesley.

Ancis, J. R., & Szymanski, D. M. (2001). Awareness of white privilege among white counseling trainees. *The Counseling Psychologist, 29*(4), 548–569.

Angelou, M. (1970). *I know why the caged bird sings*. New York: Random House Publications.

Astin, A. W. (1993). Diversity and multiculturalism on the campus: How are students affected? *Change, 25*(2), 44–49.

Bensimon, E. M., & Tierney, W. G. (1992/1993). Shaping the vision for a multicultural campus: Strategies for administrators. *College Board Review, 166*(Winter), 4–30.

Cabrera, A. F., Nora, A., Terenzini, P. T., Pascarella, E., & Hagedorn, L. S. (1999). Campus racial climate and the adjustment of students: A comparison between White students and African-American students. *Journal of Higher Education, 70*(2), 134–160.

Chang, M. J. (1999). Does racial diversity matter?: The educational impact of a racially diverse undergraduate population. *Journal of College Student Development, 40*(4), 377–395.

Chang, M. J. (2002). The impact of an undergraduate diversity course requirement on students' racial views and attitudes. *Journal of General Education, 51*(1), 21–42.

Chang, M. J., Astin, A. W, & Kim, D. (2004). Cross-racial interaction among undergraduates: Some consequences, causes, and patterns. *Research in Higher Education, 45*(5), 529–553.

Chickering, A. W., & Reisser, L. (1993). *Education and identity* (2nd ed.). San Francisco: Jossey-Bass.

Engberg, M. E. (2004). Improving intergroup relations in higher education: A critical examination of the influence of educational interventions on racial bias. *Review of Educational Research, 74*(4), 473–521.

Eyler, J., & Giles, D. E., Jr. (1999). *Where's the learning in service-learning?* San Francisco: Jossey-Bass.

Fadiman, A. (1997). *The spirit catches you and you fall down*. New York: Farrar, Straus, & Giroux.

Garcia, B., & Van Soest, D. (2000). Facilitating learning on diversity: Challenges to the professor. *Journal of Ethnic & Cultural Diversity in Social Work, 9*(1/2), 21–39.

Goodman, D. J. (2001). *Promoting diversity and social justice: Educating people from privileged groups*. Thousand Oaks, CA: Sage.

Griffin, J. H. (1960). *Black like me*. London: Penguin Books.

Gurin, P., Dey, E. L., Hurtado, S., & Gurin, G. (2002). Diversity and higher education: Theory and impact on educational outcomes. *Harvard Educational Review, 72*(3), 330–366.

Harper, S. R., & Hurtado, S. (2007). Nine themes in campus racial climates and implications for institutional transformation. In S. R. Harper & L. D. Patton (Eds.), *Responding to the realities of race on campus. New Directions for Institutional Research* (No. 120, pp. 7–24). San Francisco: Jossey-Bass.

Helms, J. E. (1993). Toward a model of white racial identity development. In J. E. Helms (Ed.), *Black and white racial identity: Theory, research, and practice* (pp. 49–66). Westport, CT: Praeger.

Helms, J. E. (1995). An update on Helms's white and people of color racial identity models. In J. G. Ponterotto, J. M. Casas, L. A. Suzuki, & C. M. Alexander (Eds.), *Handbook of multicultural counseling* (pp. 181–198). Thousand Oaks, CA: Sage.

Hogan, D. E., & Mallott, M. (2005). Changing racial prejudice through diversity education. *Journal of College Student Development, 46*(2), 115–125.

Hu, S., & Kuh, G. D. (2003). Diversity experiences and college student learning and personal development. *Journal of College Student Development, 44*(3), 320–334.

Hurtado, S., Milem, J., Clayton-Pedersen, A., & Allen, W. (1999). *Enacting diverse learning environments: Improving the climate for racial/ethnic diversity in higher education.* ASHE-ERIC Higher Education Report (Vol. 26, No. 8). Washington, DC: The George Washington University, Graduate School of Education and Human Development.

Lahiri, J. (2003). *The namesake.* Boston: Houghton Mifflin.

MacLeod, J. (1995). *Ain't no makin' it: Aspirations & attainment in a low-income neighborhood.* Boulder, CO: Westview Press.

Mandela, N. (1994). *Long walk to freedom: The autobiography of Nelson Mandela.* Boston: Little, Brown, & Company.

Manning, K., & Coleman-Boatwright, P. (1991). Student affairs initiatives toward a multicultural university. *Journal of College Student Development, 32*(4), 367–374.

McIntosh, P. (2004). White privilege: Unpacking the invisible knapsack. In M. L. Andersen & P. H. Collins (Eds.), *Race, class, and gender* (5th ed., pp. 103–108). Belmont, CA: Wadsworth/Thomson Learning.

Milem, J. (2003). The educational benefits of diversity: Evidence from multiple sectors. In M. J. Chang, D. Witt, J. Jones, & K. Hakuta (Eds.), *Compelling interest: Examining the evidence on racial dynamics in colleges and universities* (pp. 126–169). Palo Alto, CA: Stanford University Press.

Mueller, J. A., & Pope, R. L. (2001). The relationship between multicultural competence and white racial consciousness among student affairs practitioners. *Journal of College Student Development, 42*(2), 133–144.

National Center for Educational Statistics (2002). *Profile of undergraduates in U.S. postsecondary institutions: 1999–2000.* Washington DC: U.S. Department of Education.

Orfield, G., & Lee, C. (2004). *Brown at 50: King's dream or Plessy's nightmare?* Retrieved August 20, 2007, from University of California, Los Angeles Civil Rights Project website: www.civilrightsproject.ucla.edu/.

Ortiz, A. M., & Rhoads, R. A. (2000). Deconstructing Whiteness as part of a multicultural educational framework: From theory to practice. *Journal of College Student Development, 41*(1), 81–93.

Pascarella, E. T., Edison, M., Nora, A., Hagedorn, L. S., & Terenzini, P. T. (1996). Influences on students' openness to diversity and challenge in the first year of college. *Journal of Higher Education, 67*(2), 174–195.

Rankin, S. R., & Reason, R. D. (2005). Differing perceptions: How students of color and White students perceive campus climate for underrepresented groups. *Journal of College Student Development, 46*(1), 43–61.

Reason, R. D., Roosa Millar, E. A., & Scales, T. C. (2005). Toward a model of racial justice ally development. *Journal of College Student Development, 46*(5), 530–546.

Reason, R. D., Scales, T. C., & Roosa Millar, E. A. (2005). Encouraging the development of racial justice allies. In R. D. Reason, E. M. Broido, T. L. Davis, & N. J. Evans (Eds.), *Developing social justice allies. New Directions for Student Services* (No. 110, pp. 55–66). San Francisco: Jossey-Bass.

Scheurich, J. J., & Young, M. D. (2002). White racism among white faculty: From critical understanding to antiracist activism. In W. A. Smith, P. G. Altbach, & K. Lomotey (Eds.), *The racial crisis in American higher education: Continuing challenges for the twenty-first century* (Revised ed., pp. 221–242). Albany: State University of New York Press.

Singleton, J. (Writer/Director) (1995). *Higher learning* [motion picture]. United States: Columbia Pictures.

Springer, L., Palmer, B., Terenzini, P. T., Pascarella, E. T., & Nora, A. (1996). Attitudes toward campus diversity: Participation in a racial or cultural awareness workshop. *Review of Higher Education, 20*(1), 53–68.

Tatum, B. D. (1992). Talking about race, learning about racism: The application of racial identity development theory in the classroom. *Harvard Educational Review, 62*(1), 1–24.

Tatum, B. D. (2003). *"Why are all the black kids sitting together in the cafeteria?" And other conversations about race.* New York: Basic Books.

Taub, D. J., & McEwen, M. K. (1992). The relationship of racial identity attitudes to autonomy and mature interpersonal relationships in Black and White undergraduate women. *Journal of College Student Development, 33*(5), 439–446.

Torres, V., Howard-Hamilton, M. F., & Cooper, D. L. (2003). *Identity development of diverse populations: Implications for teaching and administration in higher education.* ASHE-ERIC Higher Education Report (Vol. 29, No. 6). San Francisco: Jossey-Bass.

Wellman, D. T. (1993). *Portraits of white racism* (2nd ed.). Cambridge, UK: Cambridge University Press.

Zúñiga, X. (2003). Bridging differences through dialogue. *About Campus, 7*(6), 8–16.

Chapter 12
Meeting the Needs of Commuter, Part-Time, Transfer, and Returning Students

Scott C. Silverman, Sarvenaz Aliabadi, and Michelle R. Stiles

It is 3:30 p.m. on Wednesday afternoon, six weeks into the fall semester. Anna, a student affairs program advisor at Shell Rock University (SRU), has just returned from a student retention meeting where she received information about three students, Kevin, Angie, and Mary, who are struggling in their courses. Anna is going to contact the students to find out how she can help them in reaching their goals. As she contemplates the information she just received, she cannot help but wonder what these students are doing at the moment.

Kevin looks anxiously at his watch. It is 3:30 p.m., and he has been stuck in slow-moving traffic for the last 15 minutes. He is not sure if he can get to campus, find a parking space, and make it to class by the 4:00 p.m. start time. As the minutes tick by, he becomes more impatient and agitated. He knows he cannot ask his boss to leave earlier in the day. Just getting his boss to agree to this small adjustment in his work schedule was a tense negotiation process. Kevin knows that most of the students in his classes commute to school and work full- or part-time jobs off-campus. He wonders why SRU administrators do not understand the difficulties of students, like him, attending classes that start before the end of the workday. If there were classes on weekends or the evening, he could have enrolled in a full course load each term. As he continues his slow drive to campus, he thinks that maybe SRU is unresponsive because it does not want students like him; maybe the institution desires full-time, residential students. As this thought crosses Kevin's mind, he wonders if he should give up and drop out.

Angie was so excited to transfer to SRU after two years at a local community college. The transfer meant that she was close to completing her undergraduate education. However, six weeks have passed since she transferred, and she is beginning to doubt herself. She is still struggling to find her way around campus. She feels as lost as a first-year student, even though she knows how college is supposed to work. The environment is so different at SRU than it was at the community college she attended, and she does not feel like she really belongs. She is struggling in one of her courses. Her instructors are not very approachable, and she cannot figure out how to get help. She asked other students if they know where she can go to get assistance, but they also did not know of any resources. As she walks across campus, she tries to muster the determination needed to succeed at SRU on her own.

Mary is hurrying across campus completely preoccupied. She just dropped her two-year-old son, John, off at her mother's house across town before coming to campus. Although John enjoys staying with Grandma, he starts to cry when Mary leaves. She cannot help but wonder if she made the right decision to return to SRU to finish her undergraduate studies. Mary first attended SRU right after high school 10 years ago. She attended classes for two years and enjoyed the experience. Many of her high school friends also attended SRU, and the university offered many opportunities for full-time students to enhance their educational experiences. She had been immersed in the campus community and was devastated when life circumstances made it necessary for her to drop out. When the opportunity arose for her to return to SRU, Mary was excited and jumped at the chance. However, her student experience is different now. The campus has changed much in the last eight years. She does not have any friends on campus and because of life demands, she cannot take advantage of most of the opportunities offered to enhance her educational experience. Additionally, she is frustrated in her courses. She believes her input and participation in class discussions are not valued as highly as that of other students in her courses. As a result, she stopped participating in class discussions. She counts the minutes until class sessions end. As she rushes to her 4:00 p.m. class, she wonders if she made the right decision in returning to SRU.

In this chapter, we review the needs, concerns, and issues that impact students such as those described in these stories. We provide theories to further explain the issues and conclude with strategies to help meet the needs of and engage these students, as well as enhance their learning outcomes.

Realities Faced by Commuter, Part-Time, Transfer, and Returning Students

There are four populations at institutions of higher education that have been historically underserved in comparison to traditional students: commuter, part-time, transfer, and returning (CPTR) students. "Nontraditional" is usually the term used to describe these students as a whole, but such a term fails to recognize the distinct realities CPTR students face (Borden, 2004). Each of these groups has needs that are different from those referred to as "traditional students" (i.e., residential, full-time, and first-year enrollees directly out of high school). Commuter, part-time, transfer, and returning students customarily contend with logistical factors associated with getting to campus (transportation, traffic, road conditions, weather, parking, and security) and multiple life roles (family obligations and full-time jobs) (Banning & Hughes, 1986; Jacoby, 2000b; Wilmes & Quade, 1986). Below, we explore further the issues with which CPTR students contend.

Engagement Issues

Transfer and returning students often have a higher level of maturity than students entering directly out of high school (Jacoby, 2000b). However, the most involved and engaged students on campus have historically been traditional students because they live on campus, are enrolled full-time, and enrolled directly out of high school. Consequently, traditional students often develop a sense of engagement and community (Astin, 1973, 1984; Borden, 2004; Cheng, 2004). Commuter, part-time, transfer, and returning students need to be equally engaged on campus as traditional students; the classroom is one of the most important venues in which to establish this engagement (Chickering, 2000). Colleges and universities have historically failed to recognize the frustrations, anxieties, and challenges of commuting to campus, being enrolled part-time, transferring from another institution, or returning to school after a long hiatus. Institutions must provide options that help bridge the gap between the CPTR and traditional student experiences (Pascarella & Terenzini, 2005). By implementing key strategies designed to engage CPTR students, colleges and universities can enhance CPTR student participation in their campus communities (Banning & Hughes, 1986; Berger & Malaney, 2003; Lundberg, 2004; Ottaway, 1989; Pascarella et al., 1993; Pascarella, Bohr, Nora, Desler, & Zusman, 1994; Pascarella, Edison, Nora, Hagedorn, & Terenzini, 1998; Pascarella & Terenzini, 1981, 2005; Schlossberg, Lynch, & Chickering, 1999).

Some of the engagement challenges have a more profound effect than others depending on the particular population. For example, returning students will have increased familial obligations, and commuting students will have to contend with not being willing or able to stay after class to get involved in campus activities. In many cases, CPTR students' lack of involvement is not due to a lack of interest, but, rather, an information gap and perception that the return on time invested for participation is minimal (Hagedorn, 2005). That is, the students are often unaware of the available activities and the benefits of participating in those activities. Moreover, CPTR students often hold the prevalent assumption that none of the co-curricular experiences the institution offers are more important than their other obligations (Astin, 1984).

Competing needs compel students to allocate their limited time and energy based on their priorities and their perceptions of the return on time invested. For CPTR students, familial obligations are a top priority along with their rigorous course loads and employment commitments (which are typically off campus) (Baxter Magolda & Terenzini, 1999; Kodama, 2002). The other priorities might be related to friends, hobbies, and other activities in which the student engaged before enrolling at the college or university. As a result, there is little time for campus-based, out-of-class student activities. The net result is that unengaged students pose the greatest risk of not being retained by choosing intermittent study or dropping out (Baxter Magolda & Terenzini, 1999; Kodama, 2002).

In terms of the role that student affairs professionals play in the development of each student, the profession has been largely unsuccessful when it comes to CPTR students. At most institutions, few efforts are made to design events that will interest students in these populations. As Torres, Howard-Hamilton, and Cooper (2003) note, "Assessing the level of readiness and providing a safe environmental setting provide the best balance of challenge and support to promote growth and learning among students" (p. 38). The cognitive, moral, and identity development of students from these populations is affected mainly by their lack of availability to interact with other students, staff, and faculty on campus. Increasing exposure of these students to their peers and to the college or university environment, including co-curricular activities, will stimulate progress along developmental pathways (Zamani, 2001). By analyzing the underlying factors involved in the underserving of CPTR students by their college or university environments, student affairs educators can create and implement effective strategies to support the developmental needs of each CPTR student.

Multiple Life Role Issues

Another unique challenge for CPTR students is that they often have multiple life roles. In addition to being students, they usually work either full-time or part-time and are parents or caregivers who are responsible for supporting others (Bundy, 2004; Lundberg, 2004). Having children to support, especially for single parents, poses a large burden on students' already busy lives. Students with children have to divide their time between their children's education and their own, as well as providing childcare, food, and safety for the children. In order to provide for their families, these students often have to work a full-time job while completing their courses. Working full-time increases the likelihood that students will drop out of college (Astin, 1998). The key to CPTR student success is, therefore, learning how to strike a balance. For example, if a student works moderate hours on campus, then she or he will be able to maintain meaningful relationships with students and faculty (Lundberg, 2004). The multiple life roles these students have result in the constant competition of different demands on their time and attention. Students have to prioritize according to their own perceptions of the return-on-time invested for each demand in their lives.

Given the multiple life roles of CPTR students, they have limited time to form relationships with their peers. According to Chickering (2000), establishing a close working relationship with other students provides emotional support and strengthens educational gains from the curriculum. As Clark, Walker, and Keith (2002) found, "The research suggests that the influence of peers is the most significant variable that impacts out-of-class experiences" (p. 826). Limited opportunities to form these relationships with their peers negatively impact the engagement experiences of CPTR students.

Student–faculty interaction outside of class is also an important factor in student outcomes, though Kuh (1995) showed that these relationships impact outcomes at a lower rate for certain populations. The off-campus jobs CPTR students hold often limit the time they are available for academic and social engagement (Gortner, Mahler, & Nicholson, 1997; Lundberg, 2004). For example, at the University of California, Riverside, "59.5 percent of commuter students reported that they are not involved in any student organizations," and most student–faculty interaction occurred right before or after classes (University of California, Riverside [UCR] Student Life, 2005). Between attending class, studying, and working anywhere from 20 to 40 hours per week, students may not have the opportunity to interact with faculty in order to enhance their engagement on campus. Kuh, Kinzie, Schuh, Whitt, and Associates (2005) also explored the significance of these faculty–student interactions.

Perhaps the best-known set of engagement indicators regarding student–faculty interactions is the "Seven Principles for Good Practice in Undergraduate Education" (Chickering & Gamson, 1987). These indicators include student–faculty contact, cooperation among students, active learning, prompt feedback, time on task, high expectations, and respect for diverse talents and ways of learning (p. 8). Astin (1984) argued that finding ways to encourage student involvement with faculty is a productive activity. This interaction is essential to CPTR student success and cannot be overlooked by either the student or the faculty member.

Not only are student–faculty relationships important, but also participating in enriching educational experiences, such as study abroad programs, summer internships, and research programs with faculty, is critical to the success of CPTR students. Unfortunately, given their limited availability on campus, CPTR students will have limited opportunities to engage in these activities. Academic success, on the other hand, is often predicted by the student's level of participation in classroom discussions, amount of time spent studying, and meaningful connections with faculty and other students, all three of which are potential pitfalls for CPTR students.

Since CPTR students tend to be less available for out-of-classroom activities, it is important for student affairs professionals to find ways to connect these students with co-curricular activities. Such activities may include student organizations, internships, community service, applications for scholarships, and study abroad opportunities (Kuh et al., 2005; Likins, 1991). Commuter, part-time, transfer, and returning students are discouraged from participating actively in campus activities, as well as in classroom settings. They are seeking validation from their fellow students, and their active participation is instead typically met with disapproval (Kilgore & Rice, 2003). Therefore, to meet the needs of these students, it is critical that student affairs professionals seek opportunities for them to form connections with multiple people at their institutions (Kuh et al., 2005).

Environmental Issues
Although the personal challenges of being a CPTR student can be daunting, the most insurmountable challenges for this population are often created by the educational environment itself, which typically does not recognize the existence of multiple life roles or provide students with options that will help them manage shifting priorities and needs. As a result, institutional members often believe that CPTR students are uninterested in the educational experience (Jacoby, 1989; Likins, 1991; Rhatigan, 1986). The differences between residential and commuter students are not always recognized by educators, who have often assumed that commuter students are like residential students except they live off campus, and that programs and services are equally appropriate for all students (Jacoby, 1989; Likins, 1986). Additionally, student affairs professionals and administrators have assumed that strategies that work for traditional students will also

work for CPTR students (Jacoby, 2000a). The campus community often sees commuter students as being on the campus, but not of the campus; therefore, commuter students can be overlooked in the educational environment (Jacoby, 2000a; Rhatigan, 1986).

Commuter, part-time, transfer, and returning students are expected to function in an environment where policies are created and maintained for the traditional population. According to Borden (2004):

> The traditional "linear-matriculation" image of the college student still influences policy formulation and educational practice at all levels, despite the reality that the majority of 18- to 24-year-olds, not to mention older students, do not experience a college education in a linear fashion. (p. 12)

The necessities of education—registering for classes, applying for financial aid, attending classes, participating in group projects, and meeting with faculty—can be overwhelming tasks if they can be accomplished only during specific times. Educators often do not realize that institutional policies, practices, and decisions affect students' time spent and effort expended on academic pursuits (Astin, 1984). The co-curricular and social activities associated with developing campus support systems may be impossible for commuter students to attend if these events are planned only with residential students' schedules in mind. The traditional campus culture of these activities and events can make it challenging for commuter students to integrate their already established off-campus support systems—families, friends, and co-workers. Therefore, these students feel compelled them to further divide their time (Borden, 2004).

Courses offered on schedules convenient for full-time residential students further detract from commuter students' sense of belonging (Chickering, 2000). Additionally, because commuter students must go to the campus, the commute itself can sometimes contribute to them not feeling connected to their institution (Banning & Hughes, 1986). Combined, these factors make CPTR students feel isolated, unimportant, and invisible on campus. They must struggle to determine where they belong and how they fit into the campus environment. Commuter, part-time, transfer, and returning students need to be able to easily negotiate policies in order to participate fully in the campus community and feel important and valued (Likins, 1991).

Commuter Student Issues

One of the fastest growing populations on college and university campuses is commuter students. These students do not live in campus housing and are not residing in a fraternity or sorority house or in off-campus housing in an area immediately surrounding the campus (Jacoby, 1989; Rhatigan, 1986). Thus, they have unique needs and challenges that are different from their residential counterparts. In 1998, 86 percent of United States' college students were commuter students (Horn & Berktold, as cited in Jacoby, 2000b), and there is no indication that commuter enrollments will decline in the future. For commuter students, the college or university campus is a place to visit, sometimes for a very short time. Conversely, for residential students, the college or university campus is home (Likins as cited in Jacoby, 2000b). Life circumstances among commuter students are diverse, and this diversity creates many important distinctions between them and residential students (Jacoby & Garland, 2005). These differentiations and distinctions create unique challenges and needs for students who commute to campus.

Being a student is only one component of commuter students' lives. In addition to being a student, they might be married, in a long-term relationship, single, or divorced. Most work full-time or part-time and may be responsible for supporting and caring for others. As additional life roles are assumed by students, the complexity of their lives increases (Wilmes & Quade, 1986). Multiple life roles result in several different factors constantly competing for students' time and attention, and the amount of time that commuting students invest in other life roles reduces the time and energy they can devote to their education (Astin, 1984).

Part-Time Student Issues

Part-time students face challenges during the course of their education, many of which are related to their family and employment circumstances (Dey & Astin, 1989; Dollar, 1991). A significant portion of students—anywhere from 36 percent to 63 percent—have to work to at least some extent during their time in college in order to pay for their tuition and stay in school (Pascarella et al., 1998). Off-campus employment negatively affects year-to-year persistence in college and baccalaureate degree completion (Astin, 1993; Pascarella et al., 1998). Moderate employment on campus may not have these negative effects, but the need to work takes away time that could be spent on academic or out-of-class activities (Lundberg, 2004).

Factors such as family and employment obligations may have led to these students' decision to enroll part-time. Those influences compete with the rigors of their course load and the many out-of-class opportunities that vie for their participation (e.g., student organizations, internships, and social activities). Intermittent study is increasing as family, work, and financial issues impact students' abilities to attend school on a continuous basis (Baxter Magolda & Terenzini, 1999). This may result in part-time students taking time away from their studies, and ultimately result in drop out (failure of the institution to retain that student) or re-enrollment at a later date as a returning student (Lundberg, 2004).

Transfer Student Issues

Transfer students compose almost half of the student body at some four-year institutions (Elmers & Mullen, as cited in Kodama, 2002). The issues transfer students face include the college or university's negative attitude toward them, admissions, registration, academic advising, housing, financial aid, and difficulties with involvement in student activities (Eggleston & Laanan, 2001). Some transfer students have a level of maturity that is different from their full-time counterparts since they have previously attended another institution (Berger & Malaney, 2003). They have a level of insight into college or university life that a first-year student enrolling in higher education directly from high school might not have (Kippenhan, 2004; Laanan, 2001). Eggleston and Laanan (2001) found that nearly 50 percent of transfer students, although they have college experience, actually come from technical programs in community colleges, a factor which greatly influences their preparation and adjustment to senior-level college work. These students may have only accomplished their general education requirements at community colleges, and faculty within their four-year institutions expect them to be ready to complete their major requirements and other upper-division work while they are still unfamiliar with the campus (Cejda, Rewey, & Kaylor, 1998).

Berger and Malaney (2003) found that many students do not make a successful transition from two- to four-year colleges, and for those who are able to successfully transfer, the adjustment is difficult and often described as "transfer shock." Three sets of factors impact transfer student success in the four-year college setting: individual student characteristics, community college experiences, and college or university experiences (Berger & Malaney, 2003). Administrators and faculty members must try to establish techniques that will minimize the potentially negative issues facing transfer students by addressing them accordingly (Rhine, Milligan, & Nelson, 2000). Unfortunately, these students typically have only two years at the four-year institution, which is a short time frame in which to acclimate to their new environment and be engaged in campus experiences (Laanan, 2001). In a survey conducted at the University of California, Riverside, during the 2004–2005 academic year, transfer students reported that there was a need for a more comprehensive orientation program and peer mentors to aid them from the time of their orientation throughout their first year at the institution (UCR Student Life, 2005).

In many cases, transfer students have experienced many of the initial phases of cognitive, moral, and identity development that traditional first-year students have not yet gone through (Laanan, 2001). However, despite transfer students' level of insight, since they are still new to the institution, they may be challenged by the transition to their new campus life. Educators should strive to engage transfer students in the many academic and out-of-class activities and opportunities on campus (Laanan, 2001). Oftentimes the hurdle for student affairs professionals is that transfer students are more academically focused than other students, and in many cases, the student wants to focus on completing his or her education and is much less interested in co-curricular activities (UCR Student Life, 2005).

Returning Student Issues

Returning students face similar issues of taking care of family obligations and maintaining full-time or part-time employment in order to support their families. Returning students have to renegotiate their role as a student in order to succeed. Making the transition back to life as a student can be difficult, considering that these students have not had to function in a student capacity for some time (Evans, Forney, & Guido-DiBrito, 1998; Ottoway, 1989; Schlossberg et al., 1999; Schlossberg, Waters, & Goodman, 1995).

They may have to improve those skills that are expected of them as college students, such as critical thinking, problem solving, and writing (Ottoway, 1989).

In addition, some traditional-age undergraduates (18- to 24-year-olds) will not involve returning students in their peer groups, may try to avoid them, devalue their opinions and feedback in class, and discourage their participation in out-of-classroom activities (Schlossberg et al., 1989). Traditional-age students are not likely to go out of their way to actively recruit returning students as members of their student organizations and will tend to make returning students feel uncomfortable if they try to participate (Schlossberg et al., 1989). These experiences result in returning students feeling invalidated and unable to participate in co-curricular activities (Schlossberg, 1984; Schlossberg et al., 1989).

In 2000, over 45 percent of undergraduate students were 24 years old or older (Horn & Berktold as cited in Jacoby, 2000b). Marstain and Smart (as cited in Rhatigan, 1986) identified six factors that encourage adults to pursue an education: social relationships, external expectations, social welfare, professional advancement, cognitive interest, and escape/stimulation. Social norms emphasize that formal education is for the young, which may partially explain the exclusionary behavior traditional-age students tend to exhibit toward returning students. This results in returning students contending with problems relating to access, success, retention, and institutional accommodation (Hagedorn, 2005; Kilgore & Rice, 2003).

Theoretical Framework

As discussed in the previous section, CPTR students face a myriad of difficulties given their unique experiences as college students. They must contend with competing demands due to their family obligations, time constraints, and employment circumstances. Given the issues explored in the previous section, we present theories to further clarify the needs of this group. In so doing, we concentrate on Student Involvement Theory and Transition Theory.

Theory of Student Involvement

Astin's (1984) Theory of Student Involvement links traditional pedagogical theory components, such as subject matter, resources, individualization of approach, and desired learning outcomes. The theory is concerned with behavioral processes that facilitate learning, rather than developmental outcomes. The overarching argument of the theory is that in order for student learning and growth to take place, students must be engaged in their environments (Evans et al., 1998). Astin (1984) defines involvement as the amount of physical and psychological energy that the student devotes to the academic experience. Involvement is viewed as what the student actually does (his or her behavior), rather than his or her feelings, thoughts, or motivations.

According to Astin (1984), involvement requires the investment of physical and psychological energy into the activity, whether it is classroom-related or out of class. A necessary component of involvement is time commitment. CPTR students have less time to allocate toward involvement; therefore, it is a more valued resource for them than for traditional students (Borden, 2004). Student Involvement Theory proposes that the most precious institutional resource may be student time, and that students' achievement of developmental goals is a direct function of the time and effort they devote to activities designed to produce these gains. The theory acknowledges that the psychological and physical time and energy of students are limited, and that educators compete with other forces in students' lives for a share of their time and energy (Astin, 1984).

The level of involvement that CPTR or traditional students may experience will fluctuate over time and from one activity to another. The extent of a student's involvement in academic work, for instance, can be measured quantitatively (how many hours she or he spends studying) and qualitatively (whether she or he reviews and comprehends reading assignments). The same differentiation can be applied to out-of-classroom involvement. Astin's (1984) theory also argues that the effectiveness of any policy or practice for students is directly related to the capacity of that policy or practice to increase student involvement, and that the amount of student learning and personal development associated with any educational program is directly proportional to the quality and quantity of student involvement in that program.

Transition Theory

Schlossberg (as cited in Evans et al., 1998) describes Transition Theory as a lens for analyzing the human response to transition. For student affairs professionals like Anna (introduced at the outset of this chapter), this theory facilitates examination of a student's progress through the transition process. The theory also discusses the provision of support for transitions and the opportunity to eliminate barriers to transitions, whether a student is preparing for transition, moving through it, or ending the transition and looking toward what is next. Life transitions are often the reason an individual seeks learning (Aslanian & Brickell as cited in Jacoby, 1989; Schlossberg, 1984), and Transition Theory can be applied to learners of any age, gender, or ethnicity, but is typically categorized as a theory of adult development (Evans et al., 1998). Schlossberg (1984) defines a transition as "any event or nonevent that results in change in relationships, routines, assumptions, and/or roles within the settings of self, work, family, health, and/or economics" (p. 43) and stresses that a transition is not the change itself, but the individual's perception of the change. As the student moves through the transition, a key challenge for that student is finding a way to balance new activities with other parts of life. Transition Theory is a useful resource in enabling student affairs professionals to challenge and support CPTR students.

According to Transition Theory, in order to understand a transition's meaning for an individual, the type, context, and impact of the transition must be considered. To assess an individual's readiness for a transition, the framework of situation, self, support, and strategies should be used and the resources available in each component should be evaluated to determine how the individual will cope with the transition (Schlossberg et al., 1995). Transitions can be categorized as predicted, unpredictable/unscheduled, or non-events—events that were expected but did not occur. The context is the individual's relationship to the transition or its setting, and the impact is the degree that the transition alters the individual's daily life (Schlossberg et al., 1995).

Commuter, part-time, transfer, and returning students have historically faced transitions without the support and infrastructure characteristic of the traditional student experience (Borden, 2004; Schlossberg et al., 1999). CPTR students are undergoing one or more types and levels of transition. For example, they may be transitioning from living in the residence halls one year to commuting the next or making the transition of living at home while commuting farther away for college. Part-time students generally do not have the option of being part-time students in high school and are, therefore, making a transition in college when they choose to complete their studies part-time. The barrier to transition that transfer students typically face is the difficulty of getting accustomed to the culture of the four-year institution after the community college. Returning students have to overcome the transitional barrier associated with being out of school for several years.

Engagement Strategies

The combination of Student Involvement Theory and Transition Theory contributes to understanding the particular circumstances faced by CPTR students. Having limited time to involve themselves on campus can further exacerbate their already diminished roles on campus. In addition, the transition period can be quite difficult without meaningful support mechanisms to help these students cope with their new life challenges. Both theories provide knowledge of ways to think about how to better engage CPTR students in the many transitions they face at four-year institutions. In this section, we propose recommendations for improving the experiences of CPTR students in higher education.

Commuter Student Strategies

Commuter Student Lounge

Establish a lounge in the student union building for commuter students. By congregating, commuter students might be able to form study groups with students living near them as well as car pools for classes and campus events. The space would include a bulletin board to keep the commuter students informed of campus-wide issues and activities. This could help students discover what is happening on campus and identify other students with whom they can carpool. The lounge can also enable students to establish meaningful out-of-classroom bonds and friendships and improve their affective dispositions toward their college or university experiences.

Commuter Student Organization

Form a student organization for commuter students with at least one staff person who advises the organization and keeps these students connected to the institution. Transfer students would also benefit from a transfer-themed student organization. Such organizations can help students such as Kevin and Angie connect with commuter and transfer students like themselves. In addition, involvement in these organizations will provide students with specific opportunities to be engaged in program planning and take leadership roles within the organization. At the University of California, Riverside, for example, this organization is named Commuters Around Riverside (CAR).

Daytime Co-Curricular Activities

Increase co-curricular activities during the day in order to engage students while they are on campus. Programs that occur during the lunch hour will attract a large crowd who may not stay on campus in the afternoon or evening. In addition, providing information on the highlights of a program during the typical breaks between classes might encourage students to remain on campus for the program. This strategy can be used to encourage students to participate in evening activities at the college or university by exposing them to programming during the day.

Campus Guidebook

Develop a campus guidebook exclusive to commuter students that includes ways to improve their chances of survival. The guidebook would comprise techniques to help these students successfully navigate the college or university context. Commuter students have less time available than traditional students to get the help they need. A guide specific to each of the populations described in this chapter will serve as a scaffold for them during their studies and enable them to achieve greater successes, both during college and beyond.

Adoption of Commuter Students

Invite members within residence halls to "adopt" commuter students. This strategy provides a way for the college or university to connect commuter students with elements of the residential experience that they otherwise miss. Commuter students could visit their assigned hall during specific programs, such as hall dinners, movie nights, or ice cream socials during midterms week. The institution could also develop some ways of allowing commuter students to stay overnight on the evenings in which a program is expected to run late so that those students will not need to worry about driving home too late. This can be modeled after programs that give prospective students a campus tour and have them stay in the residence halls in order to understand the experience of living on campus and being a student. This program can help connect commuter students with their residential counterparts, thus broadening their social networks for in- and out-of-class interactions.

Part-Time Student Strategies

Block Scheduling for Courses

Coordinate with the registrar's office and academic personnel of the college or university to create a schedule that enables part-time students to take courses in a time block. This approach provides more flexibility for students in terms of timelines and graduation requirements. Part-time students will potentially be able to enroll in more courses each term if the classes better fit their availability. If courses are scheduled as a block, part-time students may be able to schedule more convenient work hours, potentially on campus, and devote more time to college-related activities, like studying or co-curricular events. For example, Angie might have class scheduled from 4:00 to 6:00 p.m. and from 7:00 to 9:00 p.m. This leaves a one-hour time block for her to eat dinner before going home at night.

Online Message Board

Develop an online message board for part-time students that will enable them to maintain close contact with the institution. Staff from various student affairs or academic departments can also be given access to post to the message board in order to notify part-time students of the opportunities available to them. This strategy will enable these students to remain connected with student affairs professionals and their peers as they navigate the campus environment.

Assessment

Develop mechanisms, such as surveys or focus groups, for systematically collecting data from commuter students about their commute, multiple life roles, schedules, and interests. Data can include commuting points of origin and routes used to reach campus, modes of transportation, range of times and days that are most convenient to attend classes, work hours, outside support structures, familial responsibilities, and general interests. Such data are invaluable in providing campus support for commuter students. For instance, the data may indicate that many students use the bus system as their mode of transportation to campus, which might encourage the institution to explore special fare pricing for students. Analysis of commuting points of origin and routes might reveal optimal locations for holding off-campus courses. Similarly, information about when students prefer to attend classes given their work schedules allows for course scheduling that better suits students' busy lives. Information about outside support structures and familial responsibilities can assist in planning out-of-class activities that will be meaningful. In addition, a focus group of part-time students may reveal that most students' work schedules would allow three- or four-hour blocks for classes. That might lead the college or university to consider greater flexibility in course requirements to enable students to structure their schedules accordingly.

Transfer Student Strategies

Transfer Student Orientation

Develop a mandatory new student orientation specifically designed for transfer students. Students should be required to attend an orientation session prior to the start of their first term at the college or university. There could be specific sections of this orientation that address the particular needs and realities faced by transfer students. The program should be offered at various dates and times—evenings, weekends, and daytime hours during the week—so that students can attend an orientation that is convenient to their schedules. The topics should be chosen by experienced student affairs professionals and should demonstrate to students that educators understand the competing demands on their time and their multiple life roles. Topics should include general information about campus, such as the location and hours of offices that students will need, as well as information about financial aid, parking, transportation, food services, student advising, campus childcare, student organizations, and tutoring. Team-building activities that group students according to their academic programs or by their student population should be part of the orientation. Each team should also include a faculty member or administrator. This will enable students to begin building institution-related support systems. Some unstructured time should also be included in the orientation to allow for informal networking opportunities.

Peer Mentors

Organize a program of peer mentors for transfer students. The peer mentors will themselves be transfer students who have already successfully completed a minimum of one year at the college or university. Each transfer student can be assigned a peer mentor who will help ease her or his transition to the institution. For instance, a mentor could help Angie decide how to register for classes as well as how to find a job on campus. More importantly, the peer mentor system will provide a means for Angie to make a friend on campus and connect with others through informal gatherings between mentors and mentees.

Student Organization Fairs

Hold a student organization fair during which student organizations recruit transfer students into their organizations. This can be held on a particular evening separate from fairs that typically draw only traditional students. This fair may also attract part-time, commuter, and returning students as well, if the scheduling is convenient. With some support, each student organization might be able to make itself more appealing to students like Kevin, Angie, and Mary. The students and each organization as a whole would benefit.

Transfer Student Theme Floor

Establish a transfer student theme floor in the residence halls. This will enable a cohort of transfer students to develop friendships and bonds with others who share similar experiences. Given that transfer students have attended another institution, they are confronted with transitional challenges that are different from their non-transfer peers. Living together and forming peer networks will help this group of transfer students make the transition from their community colleges or other contexts to their current institution.

Returning Student Strategies

Childcare Facilities

Establish a childcare facility that is available for students' use and easily accessible on campus. Returning students need access to childcare facilities that are not only conveniently located near or on the campus, but are also specifically designed for families in which one or both parents are attending the college or university. If such facilities existed at SRU, Mary would be able to provide childcare for her children while attending classes. This would stabilize her hectic life and ensure that she would be able to focus on her studies and graduate.

Returning Student Advocacy Group

Create a returning student advocacy group on campus. Involving returning students in advocacy by encouraging them to share their experiences will enable administrators, faculty, and other students to be aware of the special needs of this group. As returning students articulate their concerns and desires, they become not only more visible but also more engaged in campus and in their educational success. Advocacy can facilitate changes to help the campus better reflect returning students' perspectives in policies, course offerings, and co-curricular activities. Most notably, these students will help institutional leaders identify key areas in which the transition from a working life back to the school setting is particularly challenging and ways in which institutional leaders can help these students bridge that gap. Informal and formal advocacy activities can involve serving on committees, meeting with faculty and student groups, working on policy recommendations, and volunteering to help in social activities or community events. These practices demonstrate to returning students that their experiences and needs are recognized and validated.

Educational Enhancement Activities

Offer educational enhancement activities for returning students. Those who plan and facilitate these activities should be cognizant of returning students' multiple life roles and out-of-school experiences and expertise. For example, student affairs educators can partner with community businesses and organizations to coordinate community-learning opportunities that will help these organizations fulfill their desires to be responsible members of the community. These partnerships will help returning (as well as part-time and commuter) students overcome some of the obstacles and anxieties they might face when asking their employers for release from work and enable them to participate in activities to further connect them to campus.

Other Strategies for Engaging CPTR Students

Websites and Portals

Create sections on college and university websites and portals that are specific to commuter, part-time, returning, and transfer students. Information about campus logistics, student advising, childcare, and other student support services and resources should be posted. Increasing the accessibility of this information to CPTR students will enable them to navigate the institutional context and increase their engagement. Services and programs that strengthen student attachment to campus should be included, such as employment opportunities, study group information, and out-of-class activities and events. Portals will enable students to have individualized, interest-specific interactions each time they use the site. For instance, all of the students Anna has seen would benefit from this form of 24-hour access.

CPTR and Traditional Students

Since there is a lack of understanding between traditional and CPTR students, institutional members should support both groups in finding common ground. Gathering cohorts of students together and asking them to reflect on their multiple identities is likely to encourage relationship-building between students. This can be done as part of the Welcome Week activities that occur in the days preceding the start of classes or even during the first-year and transfer orientation programs. This suggestion is intended to help break down the divisions between traditional students and CPTR students. As they learn of each other's particular experiences, they can develop empathy and a willingness to challenge their stereotypes and assumptions about each other.

Employment Policies

Establish a policy of employment at the institution that would require at least 20 percent of on-campus employment opportunities to be reserved for commuter, part-time, and returning students. This policy would encourage students to stay on campus rather than leave to go to their respective jobs, thereby increasing campus involvement for these students. More employment opportunities on campus for commuter, part-time, and returning students means more of them will be exposed to the campus environment for longer periods of time and will be more available for engagement in campus activities.

Staff Training

Train administrators and faculty on practical ways to make themselves more accessible to CPTR students. By including in training the information reviewed in this chapter on the needs of and challenges faced by CPTR students, campus administrators and faculty can be more knowledgeable about the experiences of CPTR students. This training can occur during the administrator and faculty orientation programs. If the college or university does not already have one, establishing such an orientation will help the institution better serve students of various backgrounds.

CPTR DVD

Develop a DVD for students that includes detailed information on the realities CPTR students face and on how a CPTR student can be successful in college and beyond. This will help traditional students acknowledge and validate their CPTR counterparts, as well as help CPTR students find out what resources they may need in order to thrive at their postsecondary institutions. The DVD can be an invaluable resource for helping CPTR see the various ways in which they can become involved on campus despite their different schedules and experiences.

Conclusion

The challenges faced by CPTR students are as diverse as the populations themselves, and each CPTR student is likely to change his or her position as a CPTR student during his or her educational experiences. In addition, traditional students may sometimes find themselves in the same situations as CPTR students; therefore, broad-based education about the needs of CPTR students is important. This education will not only increase awareness among traditional students, but also prepare them should they ever be in a CPTR student's situation.

Interventions must be implemented by postsecondary faculty, staff, and administrators that respect the diversity of the needs of CPTR students while strengthening the institution's position to engage these students more actively in campus life and activities. Continuous monitoring of CPTR students will help institutions continue to serve these populations adequately. Commuter, part-time, transfer, and returning students are four of the many populations that make colleges and universities diverse, unique, and vibrant. Developing intentional policies and practices on campus to better serve CPTR students will improve retention and the engagement of these students on campus.

References

Astin, A. W. (1973). The impact of dormitory living on students. *Educational Record, 54*, 204–210.

Astin, A. W. (1984). Student involvement: A developmental theory for higher education. *Journal of College Student Personnel, 25,* 297–308.

Astin, A. W. (1993). *What matters in college? Four critical years revisited.* San Francisco: Jossey-Bass.

Astin, A. W. (1998). The changing American college student: Thirty-year trends, 1966–1996. *Review of Higher Education, 21*(2), 115–135.

Banning, J. H., & Hughes, B. M. (1986). Designing the campus environment with commuter students. *NASPA Journal, 24*(1), 17–24.

Baxter Magolda, M., & Terenzini, P. T. (1999). Learning and teaching in the 21st century: Trends and implications for practice. In C. S. Johnson & H. E. Cheatham (Eds.), *Higher education trends for the next century: A research agenda for student success.* Washington, DC: American College Personnel Association.

Berger, J. B., & Malaney, G. D. (2003). Assessing the transition of transfer students from community colleges to a university. *NASPA Journal, 40*(4), 1–23.

Borden, V. M. H. (2004). Accommodating student swirl: When traditional students are no longer the tradition. *Change, 36*(2), 10–17.

Bundy, A. P. (2004). Nontraditional students. *Journal of College Counseling, 7*(1), 3–49.

Cejda, B. D., Rewey, K. L., & Kaylor, A. J. (1998). The effect of academic factors on transfer student persistence and graduation: A community college to liberal arts college case study. *Community College Journal of Research and Practice, 22*(7), 675–686.

Cheng, D. X. (2004). Students' sense of campus: What it means and what to do about it. *NASPA Journal, 41*(2), 216–234.

Chickering, A. W. (2000). Creating community within individual courses. In B. Jacoby (Ed.), *Involving commuter students in learning. New Directions for Higher Education* (No. 109, pp. 23–32). San Francisco: Jossey-Bass.

Chickering, A. W., & Gamson, Z. (1987). Seven principles for good practice in undergraduate education. *AAHE Bulletin, 39*(7), 3–7.

Clark, R. K., Walker, M., & Keith, S. (2002). Experimentally assessing the student impacts of out-of-class communication: Office visits and the student experience. *Journal of College Student Development, 43*(6), 824–837.

Dey, E. L., & Astin, A. W. (1989). *Predicting college student retention.* Los Angeles: Higher Education Research Institute.

Dollar, R. J. (1991). College influence on analytical thinking and communications skills of part-time versus full-time students. *College Student Journal, 25,* 273–279.

Eggleston, L. E., & Laanan, F. S. (2001). Making the transition to the senior institution. In F. S. Laanan (Ed.), *Transfer students: Trends and issues. New Directions for Community Colleges* (No. 114, pp. 87–97). San Francisco: Jossey-Bass.

Evans, N. J., Forney, D. E., & Guido-DiBrito, F. (1998). *Student development in college: Theory, research, and practice.* San Francisco: Jossey-Bass.

Gortner, H. F., Mahler, J., & Nicholson, J. B. (1997). Work motivation. In H. F. Gortner, J. Mahler, & J. B. Nicholson (Eds.), *Organization theory: A public perspective* (2nd ed., pp. 269–303). Orlando, FL: Harcourt Brace College.

Hagedorn, L. S. (2005). Square pegs: Adult students and their "fit" in postsecondary institutions. *Change, 37*(1), 22–29.

Jacoby, B. (1989). *The student-as-commuter: Developing a comprehensive institutional response.* ASHE-ERIC Higher Education Report (Vol. 7). Washington, DC: School of Education and Human Development, The George Washington University.

Jacoby, B. (2000a). Involving commuter students in learning: Moving from rhetoric to reality. In B. Jacoby (Ed.), *Involving commuter students in learning. New Directions for Higher Education* (No. 109, pp. 81–87). San Francisco: Jossey-Bass.

Jacoby, B. (2000b). Why involve commuter students in learning? In B. Jacoby (Ed.), *Involving commuter students in learning. New Directions for Higher Education* (No. 109, pp. 3–12). San Francisco: Jossey-Bass.

Jacoby, B., & Garland J. (2005). Strategies for enhancing commuter student success. *Journal of College Student Retention, 6*(1), 61–79.

Kilgore, D., & Rice, P. J. (Eds.). (2003). *Meeting the special needs of adult students. New Directions for Student Services* (No. 102). San Francisco: Jossey-Bass.

Kippenhan, H. (2004). Recommendations for the recruitment and retention of transfer students. *College and University, 80*(1), 13–17.

Kodama, C. M. (2002). Marginality of transfer commuter students. *NASPA Journal, 39*(3), 233–250.

Kuh, G. D. (1995). The other curriculum: Out-of-class experiences associated with student learning and personal development. *Journal of Higher Education, 66,* 123–155.

Kuh, G. D., Kinzie, J., Schuh, J. H., Whitt, E. J., & Associates. (2005). *Student success in college: Creating conditions that matter.* San Francisco: Jossey-Bass.

Laanan, F. S. (2001). Transfer student adjustment. In F. S. Laanan (Ed.), *Transfer students: Trends and issues. New Directions for Community Colleges* (No. 114, pp. 5–13). San Francisco: Jossey-Bass.

Likins, J. M. (1986). Developing the commuter perspective: The art of advocacy. *NASPA Journal, 24*(1), 11–16.

Likins, J. M. (1991). Research refutes a myth: Commuter students do want to be involved. *NASPA Journal, 29*(1), 68–74.

Lundberg, C. A. (2004). Working and learning: The role of involvement for employed students. *NASPA Journal, 41*(2), 201–215.

Ottaway, R. N. (1989). Improving learning for adult part-time students. In A. F. Lucas (Ed.), *New Directions for Teaching and Learning* (No. 37, pp. 61–69). San Francisco: Jossey-Bass.

Pascarella, E. T., Bohr, L., Nora, A., Desler, M., & Zusman, B. (1994). Impacts of on-campus and off-campus work on first year cognitive outcomes. *Journal of College Student Development, 35*(5), 364–370.

Pascarella, E. T., Bohr, L., Nora, A., Zusman, B., Inman, P., & Desler, M. (1993). Cognitive impacts of living on campus versus commuting to college. *Journal of College Student Development, 34*(3), 216–220.

Pascarella, E. T., Edison, M. I., Nora, A., Hagedorn, L. S., & Terenzini, P. T. (1998). Does work inhibit cognitive development during college? *Educational Evaluation and Policy Analysis, 20*(2), 75–93.

Pascarella, E. T., & Terenzini, P. T. (1981). Residence arrangement, student–faculty relationships, and freshman year educational outcomes. *Journal of College Student Personnel, 22,* 147–156.

Pascarella, E. T., & Terenzini, P. T. (2005). *How college affects students: A third decade of research* (Vol. 2). San Francisco: Jossey-Bass.

Rhatigan, J. J. (1986). Developing a campus profile of commuting students. *NASPA Journal, 24*(1), 4–10.

Rhine, T. J., Milligan, D. M., & Nelson, L. R. (2000, July). Alleviating transfer shock: Creating an environment for more successful transfer students. *Community College Journal of Research and Practice, 24*(6), 443–453.

Schlossberg, N. K. (1984). *Counseling adults in transition: Linking practice with theory.* New York: Springer.

Schlossberg, N. K., Lynch, A. Q., & Chickering, A. W. (1989). *Improving higher education environments for adults.* San Francisco: Jossey-Bass.

Schlossberg, N. K., Waters, E. B., & Goodman, J. (1995). *Counseling adults in transition* (2nd ed.). New York: Springer.

Torres, V., Howard-Hamilton, M. F. & Cooper, D. L. (2003). *Identity development of diverse populations: Implications for teaching and administration in higher education.* ASHE-ERIC Higher Education Report (Vol. 29, No. 6). San Francisco: Jossey-Bass.

University of California, Riverside, Department of Student Life. (2005). *Commuter and transfer student survey and focus group results.* Riverside, CA: Author.

Wilmes, M. B., & Quade, S. L. (1986). Perspectives on programming for commuters: Examples of good practice. *NASPA Journal, 24*(1), 25–35.

Zamani, E. M. (2001). Institutional responses to barriers to the transfer process. In F. S. Laanan (Ed.), *Transfer students: Trends and issues. New Directions for Community Colleges* (No. 114, pp. 15–24). San Francisco: Jossey-Bass.

Chapter 13

Creating a Pipeline to Engage Low-Income, First-Generation College Students

Jarrett T. Gupton, Cristina Castelo-Rodríguez, David Angel Martínez, and Imelda Quintanar

John is a first-generation, low-income, first-year college student raised in a single-parent home in South Central Los Angeles. He scored exceptionally well on his SAT and received a scholarship to attend an Ivy League school on the east coast. John's high school student body was primarily Latino and African American, so college is his first experience being part of a racial/ethnic minority group. He has never lived away from home and has no family or friends that live on the east coast. Furthermore, most of John's friends did not graduate from high school. Although the financial aid and scholarships he received are substantial, they are still not enough to cover all of his expenses. John also needs to send money home to help his mother support his siblings. Therefore, he will have to work part-time to make ends meet. John feels lost and isolated in college because it seems that no one understands the challenges he faces. He has no idea whom he can turn to for advice about college life or his future aspirations of attending graduate school.

Marie is a first-generation, low-income, third-year college student who is an undocumented immigrant. At a young age, she was brought by her parents to the United States. After graduating from high school with honors, she was granted admission to a public state university with an affidavit that exempts her from paying non-resident tuition fees as a long-term immigrant student. However, because of her undocumented status, Marie is not eligible to access any form of financial aid nor is she able to participate in programs that are funded through state or federal grants. For example, even though Marie is an excellent candidate, she is not eligible to apply for programs such as the McNair Scholars Program, which increases the number of low-income students in doctoral programs.

Marie demonstrated academic excellence by maintaining a 3.8 grade point average with a minimum of 15 units per semester. Recently, she expressed feeling tremendous frustration because she works 30 hours per week to meet her financial obligations. Marie is the oldest sibling of five and is required to contribute financially to meet household expenses. She claims to feel overly extended between schoolwork and meeting home expectations. As the constant pressure at home becomes more pressing, she is considering dropping out of school to increase her work hours. She believes that leaving school would not be a difficult decision as she feels disconnected with the campus life environment. Her common experience on the campus consists of running between classes and work. She rarely participates in any school activities owing to lack of time and personal awareness of campus life activities. Marie finds herself in a desperate state of mind and does not know what to do or how to identify possible options.

First-generation students are defined as students whose parents have not earned a bachelor's degree (Thayer, 2000). Low-income students are defined by the description provided by the United States Department of Health and Human Services, in which approximately $20,000 for a family of four constitutes poverty (Federal Register, 2005). Although we have defined low-income and first-generation students under separate criteria, there is a fair amount of overlap in the issues each group experiences with regard to access, engagement, and developmental outcomes. Research has shown that two-thirds of low-income students are also first-generation students (Corrigan, 2003). Further, McSwain and Davis (2007) point out that students from working-poor families (e.g., families whose income is 101 to 200 percent of the poverty level) have experiences akin to first-generation college students. Given the similarities between these two populations we examine issues and strategies that relate to both of them. Our intent is not to suggest that low-income and first-generation students are a homogeneous group; rather, we provide recommendations and strategies that work across groups and that may be tailored to address the specific needs of multiple student populations.

In this chapter, we offer a clear articulation of the issues, a theoretical framework that is linked to praxis in the university, and strategies for engaging low-income, first-generation college students. First, we identify issues and barriers these students encounter. Next, we propose a theoretical framework for improving the academic and interpersonal experiences of this subpopulation. Finally, we suggest strategies for improving the engagement and success of first-generation, low-income students.

Developmental Needs and Issues of First-Generation and Low-Income Students

In a democratic society that values education, there should be access to higher education for all students. Yet low-income, first-generation students still do not have equitable access. The National Education Longitudinal Study found that only 65 percent of high school students whose parents had not attended college enrolled in college themselves, in contrast to 87 percent enrollment among students whose parents had gone to college (Choy, 2001). First-generation students are also twice as likely as their counterparts to attend public two-year institutions instead of four-year colleges and universities (Choy, 2001).

While in college, first-generation, low-income students constantly face financial roadblocks that limit the extent to which they engage themselves in the campus culture. The amount of financial aid a student receives has a major impact on both the persistence and work schedule of the student. In addition, first-generation, low-income students face obstacles to their personal development due to their isolation, placement in developmental courses, and a lack of familial support. Ultimately, these obstacles can have a major impact on the academic performance of first-generation, low-income students. Consistent and concentrated efforts must be made to ensure that these students are aware of resources that can enhance their academic achievement. Based on our literature review, four primary issues are of concern when it comes to low-income, first-generation students: (1) access to college; (2) barriers to engagement; (3) their own personal development while in college; and (4) academic success.

Access to College

Low-income, first-generation students face many barriers to college access that affect their higher education experience. First, they experience difficulty preparing academically and socially for college. Low-income, first-generation students lack sufficient support networks such as family, peers, or mentors that understand the various challenges that college students face (Phinney & Hass, 2003). In particular, these students may lack the knowledge and skills needed to obtain educational resources, scholarships and advice (Olivérez & Tierney, 2005). Parents who have gone to college tend to transfer such knowledge to their own children, such as information about school or the types of credentials needed for specific careers (Brewer & Landers, 2005). Tierney and Auerbach (2004) point out that families play a crucial role as a support network as students prepare for college. Since first-generation students may not be able to request help from their families, they lack this resource and must look for alternative forms of support. When students do not have a family support network that helps them prepare for college, then the information burden shifts from the adults as givers to the students as collectors, a role that low-income and first-generation students are ill equipped to play. The immediate challenges of collecting information on colleges and financial aid can force them to place their educational plans on hold (McDonough, 1997; Hagedorn & Fogel, 2002).

In lieu of parental support, these students must turn to college counselors, teachers, and student peers to help them navigate the process of applying to college. Although these substitutes for parental support are useful in guiding students through college and financial aid, they cannot fully address issues of college aspirations. A lower level of aspirations for college forms another barrier for low-income and first-generation students. Finally, for low-income and first-generation students it is difficult to build a sense of self-efficacy regarding academic performance and the college and financial-aid application process.

Barriers to Engagement

The barriers that low-income and first-generation students experience is a function of the financial burden they face upon entering higher education. If low-income and first-generation college students are forced to work to meet the cost of attending college, then they lose valuable opportunities to engage with students, faculty, and staff on their campuses. Lack of financial aid information and awards are also key barriers to engagement. Low-income, first-generation college students face other challenges in terms of financial aid as well, related to understanding the financial aid process, the type of aid received, and the effects of the underawarding of aid and the need to work on students. According to the National Center for Education Statistics (1996), in the mid-1990s 49 percent of low-income students were awarded Pell Grants. However, two-thirds of these students still had unmet financial need despite this grant (O'Brien & Shedd, 2001). Financial aid is important for low-income students, as it is a key factor in determining whether or not a student will continue to pursue higher education (Fitzgerald, 2003; O'Brien & Shedd, 2001; Olivérez & Tierney, 2005).

Flint (1992) found that students and their families experience difficulties understanding the financial aid process. For example, Richardson and Skinner (1992) found that first-generation students lack knowledge of college finances and budget management. Non-English-speaking parents face an additional barrier when they receive financial aid information that is not in their native language, which limits their access to information (Oliveréz & Tierney, 2005). The type of financial aid students are awarded also affects their higher education experience. According to a study conducted by the Higher Education Coordinating Board (1995), grants have the largest impact on students, especially when they are significant renewable amounts. For example, a study by the U.S. General Accounting Office (1995) found that providing grant money to low-income students decreased their probability of dropping out, whereas loan aid resulted in an increased probability of students leaving college without finishing.

Students face even more challenges when financial aid does not meet the costs of higher education. The federal government made significant changes in financing higher education by shifting from grants to loans as the primary method of promoting postsecondary prospects (Paulsen & St. John, 2002). According to St. John and Starkey (1995), these changes in federal student aid policy were particularly challenging for low-income students in comparison to more affluent students. Underawarding of financial aid also affects students' decisions to enter and to stay in college (Fitzgerald, 2003; O'Brien & Shedd, 2001; Olivérez & Tierney, 2005).

Many low-income students work in order to make up for underawarded financial aid. Research has found that low-income students work more hours on average than other students who work (Corrigan, 2003). In a study conducted by Walpole (2003), over half of low-income students reported working over 16 hours per week or even working full-time in comparison with only 37 percent of students from higher socioeconomic backgrounds. Working more hours leaves less time to dedicate to study or participation in precollegiate activities (e.g., college visits, college fairs, and financial aid information sessions) outside of school (Walpole, 2003). For example, Marie is being pulled in two directions by work and school, and John has to determine where he will work to meet his unmet financial need.

To be sure, many low-income and first-generation college students find employment and work-study positions on campus; yet those who do not face a tenuous balance between being engaged in their college experience and meeting the demands of a job and a life away from campus. The primary issue to consider when engaging a low-income and first-generation student is how to remedy the financial burden a student might be experiencing. Once their financial burden has been alleviated, low-income and first-generation students can engage with the resources in their campus community that allow them to maximize their human potential.

Personal Development in College

Low-income, first-generation college students face many personal development challenges once they enter college. Students are given the intellectual and social capital to succeed in their professional careers and become productive members of society. In terms of personal development, low-income and first-generation students learn how to be members of a social network and how to interact with people of diverse backgrounds and opinions. The special hurdles that first-generation, low-income students must overcome can have a negative impact on their personal development, however. A lack of support to enhance personal development can result in decreased academic performance and social interaction.

As previously described, one challenge that many students face is the need to work to pay for college-going expenses, such as books and supplies, that financial aid has been inadequate to cover (Fitzgerald 2003; O'Brien & Shedd, 2001; Olivérez & Tierney, 2005). Family obligations, such as caring for younger siblings, as well as providing financial assistance to parents also inhibits academic performance (Rendón, 2002). For example, Marie feels overwhelmed choosing between the need to support her family and her desire to complete her degree. When these distractions limit academic achievement, they are likely to lead to academic probation and eventual expulsion from the institution.

The transition to college is difficult for low-income and first-generation college students. According to Pascarella, Edison, Hagedorn, Nora and Terenzini (1996a, 1996b), first-generation students are less likely to encounter a welcoming campus environment. Saufley, Cowan, and Blake (1983) found that these students "enter an alien physical and social environment that they, their family, and their peers have never experienced." This transition is a culture shock and creates a cultural conflict between the home and college communities based on socioeconomic status (Thayer, 2000). Culture shock is an experience that arises from straddling two or more cultures. First-generation students are subject to it as they face numerous challenges in their attempts to move from the culture of home to the culture of higher education (Hsiao, 1992). John, for example, experiences culture shock between his home environment and the Ivy League university, as many of the norms and values at an Ivy League institution do not reflect John's own cultural values. For instance, many Ivy League universities base their reputations on exclusivity and competition, whereas some cultures value inclusivity and collaboration. Resolving the potential disconnect between personal and institutional values is an important aspect of personal development in higher education for low-income and first-generation students.

Social integration is linked to a higher likelihood of persistence in higher education (O'Brien & Shedd, 2001). Building relationships with university professionals and students on campus is a challenge when students work many hours or have family pressures that prohibit them from establishing these relationships. According to Tinto (1987), such students experience feelings of isolation and do not feel connected to the institution. Some of them may transfer to other institutions or drop out of school altogether because of the dissonance they experience. For example, Marie feels disengaged with the campus life environment at the university she attends and contemplates leaving because of these feelings.

Academic Achievement and Persistence

Warburton, Bugarin, and Nunez (2001) found first-generation students were more likely to leave college and not return the following semester than were their peers whose parents possessed a bachelor's degree. Similarly, Terenzini, Springer, Yeager, Pascarella, and Nora (1996) found that degree completion rates are lower for first-generation students in comparison with their counterparts whose parents were college graduates. Furthermore, few first-generation students enroll in doctoral and post-baccalaureate degree programs (Hahs-Vaughn, 2004). Specifically, over half of high-income students attended graduate school in comparison with just over a third of low-income students (Walpole, 2003).

In addition, studies show that first-generation students are less academically prepared (Choy, 2001; Hahs-Vaughn, 2004). Kaufman and Chen (1999) found that first-generation students do not use their high school experience to prepare for college. For example, first-generation students took less rigorous coursework than their peers whose parents attended college (Warburton et al., 2001). This lack of preparation affects academic performance in college. This is evident in the increase in the number of students required to take developmental courses at institutions of higher learning (Warburton et al., 2001). In fact, 67.6 percent of four-year universities offer developmental courses because of the substantial number of students coming to college unprepared for college-level coursework (National Center for Education Statistics, 2003).

Theoretical Framework

In light of the issues low-income and first-generation students experience in terms of access, engagement, personal development, and academic success in college, we apply three theories—social capital, validation theory, and social identity theory—as lenses through which to view the needs of low-income, first-generation students. This framework allows for a comprehensive view of first-generation, low-income college students.

Social Capital

Based on social capital theory, students have limited access to the information that will enable them to succeed in college, such as knowledge of the benefits of degree completion and of various resources, such as tutoring or graduate mentoring programs. Ricardo Stanton-Salazar (1997) describes the concept of social capital in terms of access to mentors and resources to encourage and educate students. Middle-class students reap the benefits of family- and school-based networks for academic support (Stanton-Salazar, 1997). However, low-income students do not have equal social capital and do not benefit from these relationships.

Social capital is defined as the various social networks one belongs to that provide access to resources within these networks. Putnam (2000) writes that, "whereas physical capital refers to physical objects and human capital refers to the properties of individuals, social capital refers to connections among individuals—social networks and the norms of reciprocity and trustworthiness that arise from them" (p. 19). Portes (1998) expands on this idea of social capital when he states that to "possess social capital, a person must be related to others, and it is those others, not himself, who are the actual source of his or her advantage" (p. 7). Social capital has to do with the amount and quality of resources individuals have access to within their social networks. Bourdieu (1986) noted:

> The volume of social capital possessed by a given agent . . . depends on the size of network connections he can effectively mobilize and on the volume of the capital (economic, cultural, or symbolic) possessed in his own right by each of those to whom he is connected. (p. 249)

In contrast to economic capital, social capital is intangible, as it "inheres to the structure of relations between and among persons" (Coleman, 1990, p. 302). Students like Marie and John are not socially connected, which prohibits them from accruing more social capital.

Although social capital is intangible, it has the ability to be productive and to facilitate action within the social structure. Networks must be constructed and maintained through strategic investment of capital, whether economic, human, cultural, or social. For instance, a second-generation or multigenerational college student may construct a social network of family members that have attended college. The student can then gain advice about issues such as the benefits of early application, how and when to apply for financial aid, college choice, or how to write a compelling college essay. A first-generation student lacks this type of network based on the absence of anticipatory socialization (Pike & Kuh, 2005). Simply put, first-generation students do not have networks that acculturate them to the college environment or how to successfully engage while in college.

The formation of social capital is linked to a student's socioeconomic background. Lareau (2003) explored how socioeconomic class impacts the accumulation of social capital in child-rearing. She indicates that middle- and upper-income children go through a process termed "concerted cultivation," in which they are purposefully placed in environments and structured activities that increase their social capital. This exposure to multiple social situations allows them to develop the necessary social networks prior to college. These children also develop tacit knowledge on how to generate future social capital. On the other hand, children from lower-income families undergo a process of natural development, meaning that the children are in charge of how they spend their leisure time. Therefore, lower income children have fewer structured interactions with peers and professionals. Although natural development may lead to greater responsibility, it hinders the amount of social capital networks the children develop, as well as their ability to create future social capital. Based on Lareau's (2003) work, there is sufficient evidence to contend that first-generation, low-income students are lacking the sufficient social capital networks to succeed in higher education due to natural development.

Validation Theory

Rendón (1994) first articulated the term *validation theory*. At the time, she was researching how to create an inclusive and affirming campus climate for non-traditional students in community college. We contend her model applies to low-income, first-generation students at four-year institutions. In this case, validation is defined as "an enabling and confirming and supportive process initiated by in- and out-of-class agents that fosters academic and interpersonal development" (Rendón, 1994, p. 4). Rendón identifies two forms of validation. The first is academic validation, which is to "trust their innate capacity to learn and to acquire confidence in being a college student" (Rendón, 1994, p. 40). Interpersonal validation is the second form, and that occurs when in- and out-of-class agents take action to foster students' personal development and social adjustment. Interpersonal adjustment is important for first-generation, low-income students; as Rendón (2002) writes,

> Students from low-income backgrounds and who are the first in their family to attend college usually find it difficult to get involved on their own. These students want to get involved but often do not know what questions to ask and may be reluctant to ask questions that make them appear stupid or lazy. (p. 645)

Although multiple studies indicate that validating experiences support college student development (Belenky, Clinchy, Goldberger, & Tarule, 1986; Rendón, 1994; Terenzini et al., 1994), its practice has yet to become an institutionalized ethos in the academy. Rendón (2005) argues that the current ethos in higher education is part competition and part separation between student and teacher, which leads to the invalidation of the student's experience. We contend that if students have lower levels of social capital, then they will need stable validating communities to foster academic and interpersonal support. The main point is that low-income, first-generation students require multiple validating communities of support. Communities of validation serve as social networks for students, thereby meeting the students' multiple needs to develop social capital and receive validation. Validation from the institution is necessary but not sufficient to foster holistic student development. First-generation, low-income students require multiple validating communities that are inclusive of family, peers, and professionals. By including the diverse communities with which a student may identify, the university can take into account the whole student.

Social Identity

As the second form of validation is interpersonal, we use the theory of social identity (Turner, Hogg, Oakes, Reicher, & Wetherell, 1987). Social identity theory suggests that a person has several selves that correspond to different circles of group membership. For example, an individual has multiple "social identities" based on aspects such as socioeconomic class, gender, ethnicity, nationality, and sexual orientation. Some social identities are salient, whereas others are non-salient. For instance, we can see race/ethnicity in many cases, whereas socioeconomic status and sexual orientation are not visible. The theory suggests that a new social context, such as the college environment, may trigger individuals to think, feel, and act on the basis of their respective social identities (Turner et al., 1987). There are three aspects of social identity. First, students tend to categorize themselves based on how they choose to self-identify. Over time, students can receive overt and covert messages regarding their social identity. Second, students then interpret and may internalize the messages and form their social self-view. Third, based on their social self-view, students develop their social self-esteem (Hogg & Vaughan, 2002).

Social identity theory contends that group membership creates in-group/out-group dynamics based on self-categorization. For example, a first-generation student like John may feel excluded by multigenerational college students. Students' social self-view is based on a process of social comparison with contrasting social identities. African American students may compare their social status with that of White students. If the results are positive, the student will feel affirmed and validated. On the other hand, if the result is negative, the student may feel unvalued and alienated. In relation to first-generation, low-income students, negative messages, both covert and overt, about their socioeconomic class and first-generation status will likely lead to lowered social self-esteem. Negative messages about an individual's social identity create an invalidating academic and interpersonal climate.

Borrowing Lareau's (2003) terminology, we argue that a "concerted cultivation" approach be taken with regard to low-income and first-generation students. Given the theoretical framework detailed above, we suggest that institutions of higher education engage first-generation, low-income students in building social capital networks through multiple validating communities that are inclusive of the student's social identity.

Engagement Strategies

◇ Establish a collaborative effort between the entity that oversees graduate studies and the division of student affairs to ensure that tailored programs are intentionally designed for first-generation, low-income students. For example, institutions should focus on the McNair Scholars Program that purposefully targets low-income undergraduate students to increase their representation in Ph.D. programs. Among other graduate school preparation activities, this program funds student participation in undergraduate research during the summer and academic school year to prepare them for academic research careers. The goal for this collaborative effort is to create a pipeline to graduate programs for students who may lack knowledge and access to professional role models in their communities. The exposure of graduate possibilities should begin early and increase with more frequency as the students reach their junior year and beyond. Primarily, students would be exposed to the possibility of continuing in graduate programs after acquiring their baccalaureate degrees. Ideally, the programs offered would consist of exposing students to distinguished guest lecturers, recruitment and informational fairs for various graduate programs, informational sessions on admissions entrance exams, and informational panels of current graduate students who openly identify as being first-generation and low-income students.

◇ Establish a community resource center that primarily engages first-generation, low-income students by offering a supportive environment that promotes personal exploration and continuous persistence towards the completion of a degree. A primary goal for the center would be to facilitate a sense of belonging for students and to validate their academic and social experiences. The center would sponsor events, such as fund raising for tuition scholarships for immigrant students who might not be able to access financial aid and informational resource sessions such as bilingual workshops for parents of first-generation, low-income students. The services offered would be made available for all students. Ideally, the center would be situated in the middle of campus or in the student union where it would have the most visibility and accessibility. Ultimately, this visibility would lead to campus participation and engagement not only by students, but by faculty, staff, parents, and community members. On account of the high volume of activity expected, the center would be made available for both day and evening students and would host events on weekends to meet the needs of the various targeted constituencies, such as working parents of first-generation, low-income students.

◇ Create an opportunity for first-generation juniors and seniors to co-teach courses with faculty members. Juniors and seniors would be selected based on academic merit and interest in working with students as role models. The identified role models would be offered a stipend for their services and for assisting faculty with the development of the courses. Additionally, the courses would incorporate the exploration of diversity issues by requiring students to engage in critical thought processes by participating in experiential exercises and simulation of case studies that would promote the exploration of their own multiple social identities.

◇ Develop a practicum course that would expose students to various opportunities outside of the classroom as they transition to the culmination of their degree. In particular with regard to first-generation, low-income students, the experience would not only build their social capital, but also expose them to different perspectives that will help them determine their next career and/or educational goals. A practicum course for juniors and seniors would provide them with an opportunity to build their résumés and to earn service-learning credit and units that count towards degree completion. In addition, students would have to complete a fieldwork experience in their chosen field of interest. An ultimate outcome of the practicum would be to empower students to explore their areas of interest. It would also expose students to guest speakers, research, and opportunities that encourage academic and social involvement. The practicum would culminate with the creation of a comprehensive portfolio of the student's academic career that can be distributed to their professional counterparts.

◇ Build a peer tutoring program for first-year students who are required to take developmental English and math courses. The implementation of this program would also benefit upper-class students by increasing their social and academic capital as they work towards the completion of their degrees. Junior and senior year students would be hired through their college work-study awards to serve as tutors and lead as supplemental instructors for developmental courses. Each tutor would be assigned to a specific course, to assist students in successfully completing the coursework. The selected tutors would be required to attend a summer training session that would not only prepare them with instructional knowledge, but also build their ability to assist first-year students as they transition into the college setting.

◇ Collaborate with first-year experience programs and identify resourceful staff, such as academic and career advisors, psychologists, and human resource professionals, to assist first-generation, low-income students. The skilled professionals would be responsible for initiating and implementing a team strategy approach between the student and faculty to monitor wellness and transitioning issues that relate to the balancing of multiple social identities. In addition, the team would agree to work toward successfully monitoring an early warning system to prevent academic failure. The team would support students in identifying possible majors for exploration and a developing time-line for degree completion.

⬥ Offer structured-interaction programming based on issues of socioeconomic class related to systems of power and privilege in the university and local community. Such programs would bring together students from multiple socioeconomic class backgrounds to discuss their views on socioeconomic class in society. This would allow students a safe environment to share that aspect of their identities. All structured-interaction programs should target low-income, first-generation students to be participants in these events. For example, when selecting participants for a fishbowl discussion on first-year experiences, the group should include first-generation, low-income students. Beyond structured interaction, institutions should conduct trainings with faculty and staff regarding the unique issues first-generation, low-income students experience and how they can help to create a more inclusive and vali-dating campus climate for this subpopulation.

⬥ Create programs and partnerships that socially embed the university into sec-ondary school settings to target low-income, first-generation students. These partnerships can help to ensure that students are academically prepared to handle the rigors of university coursework. The programs can include col-laboration with faculty to ensure that university-sponsored academic tutoring in local elementary and secondary schools is adequately preparing students for entrance exams and university coursework. In addition to preparing stu-dents academically, implementation of college preparation seminars at these schools will address the unique issues faced by low-income, first-generation college students. For low-income students, seminars can demystify the finan-cial aid and college admissions process, give students access to scholarship databases, clarify the intricacies of loan repayment, and inform students about how to survive on a limited budget. First-generation students often must learn how to cope with a different level of diversity at university in comparison with their secondary school experience. In terms of self-esteem, discrepancies in the amount of spending money one has can alienate low-income students from their more affluent peers. In addition, a longer transition period for first-generation students to college life can lead to a decrease in self-esteem. Four-year institutions can implement a student ambassador program in which college students serve as representatives of the university to assist in precollege tutoring, university recruiting events, and presenting college life or transition seminars.

⬥ Develop a summer immersion program on the university campus to give prospective students a preview of college experiences and expectations. First-generation students may have no idea of what to expect once they arrive on the college campus as first-year students. A summer immersion program can acquaint the students with the geographic layout of the campus, the university classroom culture, and the skills to improve their writing and mathematics performance. It is recommended that the immersion program be at least a two-week residential program in which students are housed in university residence halls. Intensive writing and mathematics workshops will prepare first-generation, low-income students in the core subjects that they tend to struggle with upon arrival on campus. Field trips during the immersion program to various professional settings can increase student motivation by giving them glimpses of the types of careers available to them upon graduation. An aspect of community service should be incorporated into the immersion program to tap into this subpopulation's unique bond to the local community. In addition, computing workshops can provide extra training with online resources of which low-income, first-generation students may have limited experience.

◇ Involve parents in the precollege engagement process. As a student's family plays an important validating role in the college experience, universities should make a concerted effort to include parents by informing them about the adjustments that both they and their children must make in the coming years. A publicity campaign focusing on the participation of parents should include targeted phone calling, television advertisements, and mailers. Parents will become engaged through a parent orientation CD and a specially designed parent handbook. These resources will provide specific information and telephone numbers for support offices on campus. We suggest that schools offer evening and weekend workshops at alternating times to accommodate the work schedules of low-income parents. One possible workshop can cover the rigors of coursework that students will undertake, so that parents get a sense of the demands that college places on students. This is very important since the families of first-generation students in higher education have a tendency to expect students to continue to meet family obligations such as family parties, holidays, or weekend housework, especially if their hometowns are local. A financial aid workshop is a must for the subpopulation's parents since most, if not all, do not have the means to support their child in college without aid in the form of grants, loans, and scholarships.

◇ Create a parent center that focuses on empowering parents to support their children. Although many college campuses have parent centers, assessments should be tailored to evaluate the accessibility of services offered for the parents of first-generation, low-income students. It is necessary to offer various services to help parents of these students understand the college process. For example, the parent center could host workshops based on meeting the needs of low-income, first-generation families. Workshops on topics such as graduation requirements, financial aid, the Family Education Rights Protection Act (FERPA), and how parents can support their child in his or her pursuit of higher education should be offered. In addition, the parent center could maintain a website and create a monthly newsletter to inform parents of upcoming events and important deadlines, such as financial aid or exam schedules. It is imperative that these workshops and written correspondence be offered in the native languages of the parents to ensure they have meaningful access to the information.

◈ Implement an alumni training program to inform college graduates of the effective techniques that engage low-income, first-generation students. Alumni can attend university-sponsored conferences that inform participants of the various issues that the students encounter throughout their academic career. Methods to combat isolation, low self-esteem, lack of direction, and lack of motivation will be discussed at conferences and workshops held throughout the year. A job database should be created and supplied by trained alumni specifically for low-income, first-generation students to inform them of opportunities to work alongside committed alumni. Through an alumni–student mentoring program, the students could be matched up by major with the profession of a mentor to create buddy groups. The groups should meet at least once a month to socialize and discuss academic and career aspirations. Low-income, first-generation alumni should be asked to conduct workshops for all mentoring program participants on their personal journey through their academic and professional career.

◈ Form an organization of university professionals dedicated to enhancing and supporting the college experience of low-income, first-generation students. This organization would provide university members with an opportunity to build relationships with students with whom they may not typically work on a daily basis. Many university professionals may have an interest in the issues that low-income, first-generation students face. The university professionals can directly provide numerous resources and valuable information for these students. This organization will engage students by organizing informational and social events on campus for this subgroup. Events such as a coffee study break or ice cream social directed towards these students can ease student stress, for example, during finals week. The staff organization can also conduct workshops that teach university professionals and alumni about how to engage low-income, first-generation students.

◈ Create a peer-to-peer mentor program that pairs up first- and second-year low-income, first-generation students with third- and fourth-year students. These students require consistent motivation and validation towards persistence in college. A peer-to-peer mentor relationship based on social background benefits both the student and the mentor. This particular mentor program should be student-organized and -operated through the identification of key student leaders who are themselves first-generation, low-income students. These students support the need to provide more directed resources for this subpopulation.

◇ Provide work-study opportunities and programs for first-generation, low-income students. Low-income students should be provided with on-campus work-study opportunities to help defray the costs of their education and promote social integration on campus. However, owing to possible low wages and the limited number of open positions on campus, students may opt to work off campus. This creates a major inconvenience for a student's study schedule. The university should ensure that work-study opportunities exist for all first-generation, low-income students, and that the opportunities deter students from working in off-campus jobs. Students who do participate in work-study must be given mandatory training on how to manage their work and study schedules. Students should have the option to change working hours to accommodate the demands of their class schedules.

Conclusion

Colleges and universities have existed for over three and half centuries in the United States; yet with all their advances in equity, many institutions still primarily serve as centers of social reproduction for middle- and upper-income families. If postsecondary institutions are to improve engagement and success for low-income, first-generation students, then they need to appropriately respond to the stories of John and Marie. Furthermore, there is need for some fundamental changes in order for higher education to be inclusive and to validate low-income, first-generation students.

First, the institution must be socially embedded within the K–12 system. Tierney (2003) states the following:

> The sharp divide that exists between K–12 and postsecondary education has to be overcome. Rather than look the other way or wash our hands of the problems of public education, we must create a sustained systemic involvement between postsecondary institutions and public schools. Of necessity such involvement needs to work through dialogue based on humility and respect. (p. 12)

Second, we must change the ethos around engagement so that the responsibility is shared between the student and the university. As Rendón (2005) states, "We need to change the agreement that good teaching and learning evolve from a model that distances teachers from students and that separates teaching from learning" (p. 4). The university has to take ownership of its role in the engagement relationship process. Once both parties have a sense of ownership, then the institution can move forward in creating an inclusive and positive campus climate for the diverse social identities of students.

Third, we need to lift as we climb. While access to higher education creates social mobility, the focus must be directed towards those who will follow after us. This ethos will create bonds of interconnectedness among the campus community, which will serve to generate social capital, validation, and the development of a student's multiple social identities. Finally, we have to take notice of the unseen. Socioeconomic class is a non-salient characteristic that has a dynamic impact on students' perceptions of the university. If higher education is to be inclusive, then we need to approach issues of class without a blindfold to ensure that first-generation, low income students are engaged and successful.

References

Belenky, M., Clinchy, B., Goldberger, N., & Tarule, J. (1986). *Women's ways of knowing: The development of self, voice, and mind*. New York: Basic Books.

Bourdieu, P. (1986). The forms of capital. In J. G. Richardson (Ed.), *Handbook of theory and research for the sociology of education* (pp. 241–258). New York: Greenwood Press.

Brewer, E. W., & Landers, J. M. (2005) A longitudinal study of the Talent Search Program. *Journal of Career Development, 31*(3),195–208.

Choy, S. (2001). *Students whose parents did not go to college: Postsecondary access, persistence, and attainment* (NCES-2001-126). Washington, DC: National Center for Education Statistics.

Coleman, J. (1990). *Foundations of social theory*. Cambridge, MA: Harvard University Press.

Corrigan, M. E. (2003). Beyond access: Persistence challenges and the diversity of low-income students. In J. E. King, E. L. Anderson, & M. E. Corrigan (Eds.), *Changing student attendance patterns: Challenges for policy and practice. New Directions for Higher Education* (No. 121, pp. 25–34). San Francisco: Jossey-Bass.

Fitzgerald, B. (2003). The opportunity for a college education: Real promise or hollow rhetoric? *About Campus, 8*(5), 3–10.

Flint, T. A. (1992). Parental and planning influences on the formation of college choice sets. *Research in Higher Education, 343*(6), 689–708.

Hagedorn, L. S., & Fogel, S. F. (2002). Making school to college programs work: Academics, goals, and aspirations. In W. G. Tierney & L. S. Hagedorn (Eds.), *Increasing access to college: Extending possibilities for all students* (pp. 169–193). Albany, NY: SUNY Press.

Hahs-Vaughn, D. (2004). The impact of parents' education level on college students: An analysis using the beginning postsecondary students longitudinal study 1992/94. *Journal of College Student Development, 45*(5), 483–500.

Higher Education Coordinating Board (1995). *The impact of student financial aid on persistence: A summary of national research and literature*. Olympia, WA: Author.

Hogg, M. A., & Vaughan, G. M. (2002). *Social Psychology* (3rd ed.) London: Prentice Hall.

Hsiao, K. (1992). *First-generation students*. Report No. EDO-JC-00-04. Washington, DC: Office of Education Research and Improvement. (ERIC Document Reproduction Service ED 351079)

Kaufman, P., & Chen, X. (1999). *Projected postsecondary outcomes of 1992 high school graduates* (NCES Working Paper No. 1999-15). Washington, DC: U.S. Department of Education, Nation Center for Education Statistics.

Lareau, A. (2003). *Unequal childhoods: Race, class, and family life*. Berkeley: University of California Press.

McDonough, P. (1997). *Choosing colleges: How social class and schools structure opportunity*. Albany, NY: SUNY Press.

McSwain, C., & Davis, R. (2007). *College access for the working poor: Overcoming burdens to succeed in higher education*. Washington, DC: Institute for Higher Education Policy.

National Center for Education Statistics (1996). *National postsecondary student aid study, 1996* (*NPSAS: 96*). Washington, DC: U.S. Department of Education.

National Center for Education Statistics (2003). *Percent of degree-granting institutions offering remedial services, by type and control of institution: 1988–89 to 2002–03*. Washington, DC: U.S. Department of Education.

O'Brien, C., & Shedd, J. (2001). *Getting through college: Voices of low-income and minority students in New England*. Washington, DC: Institute for Higher Education Policy.

Oliveréz, P., & Tierney, W. (2005). *Show us the money: Low-income students, families, and financial aid*. Los Angeles: University of Southern California Center for Higher Education Policy Analysis.

Pascarella, E., Edison, M., Hagedorn, L., Nora, A., & Terenzini, P. (1996a). Influences on students' internal locus of attribution for academic success in the first year of college. *Research in Higher Education, 37*, 731–756.

Pascarella, E., Edison, M., Hagedorn, L., Nora, A., & Terenzini, P. (1996b). Influences on students' openness to diversity and challenge in the first year of college. *Journal of Higher Education, 67*, 174–195.

Paulsen, M. B., & St. John, E. P. (2002). Social class and college costs: Examining the financial nexus between college choice and persistence. *Journal of Higher Education, 70*(1), 1–26.

Phinney, J. S., & Hass, K. (2003). The process of coping among ethnic minority first-generation college freshmen: A narrative approach. *Journal of Social Psychology, 143*(6), 707–726.

Pike, G., & Kuh, G. (2005). First- and second-generation college students: A comparison of their engagement and intellectual development. *Journal of Higher Education, 76*(3), 276–300.

Portes, A. (1998). Social capital: Its origins and applications in modern sociology. *Annual Review of Sociology, 24*, 1–24.

Putnam, R. D. (2000). *Bowling alone: The collapse and revival of American community*. New York: Simon and Schuster.

Rendón L. I. (1994). Validating culturally diverse students: Toward a new model of learning and student development. *Innovative Higher Education, 19*(1), 33–50.

Rendón, L. I. (2002). Community college puente: A validating model of education. *Educational Policy 16*(4), 642–667.

Rendón, L. I. (2005). Realizing a transformed pedagogical dreamfield: Recasting agreements for teaching and learning. *Spirituality in Higher Education Newsletter, 2*(1), 1–13.

Richardson, R., & Skinner, E. (1992). Helping first-generation minority students achieve degrees. In L. Zwerling & H. London (Eds.), *First-generation students: Confronting the cultural issues. New Directions for Community Colleges* (No. 80, pp. 29–43). San Francisco: Jossey-Bass.

Saufley, R., Cowan, K., & Blake, H. (1983). The struggles of minority students at predominantly white institutions. In J. H. Cones III, J. F Noonan, & D. Janha (Eds.), *Teaching minority students. New Directions for Teaching and Learning* (No. 16, pp. 3–15). San Francisco: Jossey-Bass.

Schroeder, C. (2003). How are we doing at engaging students? *About Campus, 8*(1), 9–16.

St. John, E. P., & Starkey, J. B. (1995). An alternative to net price: Assessing the influence of prices and subsidies on within-year persistence. *Journal of Higher Education, 66*(2), 156–186.

Stanton-Salazar, R. D. (1997). A social capital framework for understanding the socialization of racial minority youth. *Harvard Educational Review, 67*(1), 1–40.

Terenzini, P., Rendón, L. I., Upcraft, L., Millar, S., Allison, K., Gregg, P., & Jalamo, R. (1994). The transition to college: Diverse students, diverse stories. *Research in Higher Education, 35*(1), 57–73.

Terenzini, P., Springer, L., Yeager, P., Pascarella, E., & Nora, A. (1996). First-generation college students: Characteristics, experiences, and cognitive development. *Research in Higher Education, 37*(1), 1–22.

Thayer, P. B. (2000). *Retention of students from first-generation and low income backgrounds*. Washington, DC: Council for Opportunity in Education. (ERIC Document Reproduction Service No. ED 446 633)

Tierney, W. G. (2003). Remembrance of things past: Trust and the obligations of the intellectual. *Review of Higher Education, 27*(1), 1–16.

Tierney, W. G., & Auerbach, S. (2004). Toward developing an untapped resource: The role of families in college preparation. In W. G. Tierney, J. Colyar, & Z. B. Corwin (Eds.), *Preparing for college: Nine elements of effective outreach* (pp. 29–48). Albany, NY: SUNY Press.

Tinto, V. (1987). *Leaving college: Rethinking the causes and cures of student attrition.* Chicago: University of Chicago Press.

Turner, J. C., Hogg, M. A., Oakes, P., Reicher, S. D., & Wetherell, M. (1987). *Rediscovering the social group: A self categorization theory.* Oxford: Blackwell

U.S Department of Health and Human Services (2005). 2005 U.S. Department of Health and Human Services poverty guidelines. *Federal Register 70*(3), 8373–8375.

U.S. General Accounting Office (1995). *Higher education: Restructuring student aid could reduce low-income student dropout rate.* HEHS-95-48. Washington, DC: Government Printing Office.

Walpole, M. (2003). Socioeconomic status and college: How SES affects college experiences and outcomes. *Review of Higher Education, 27*(1), 45–73.

Warburton, E. C., Bugarin, R., & Nunez, A. (2001). *Bridging the gap: Academic preparation and postsecondary success of first-generation students* (NCES-2001-153). Washington, DC: National Center for Education Statistics.

Chapter 14

Improving Transfer Trajectories for First-Year, First-Generation, Minority Community College Students

Ramona Barrio-Sotillo, Kaneesha Miller, Kuro Nagasaka, and Tony Arguelles

José is a 17-year-old Latino student from a low-income family in an urban area. His parents emigrated to the United States in order to provide their children with opportunities not afforded to them in Mexico. His family has lived in the United States for 20 years in government housing, but neither of his parents speaks English. Since José's first language is Spanish, he has had difficulty with reading, writing, and verbal comprehension of English. Because of his parents' inability to understand English, they have not been able to assist him with his school work. Consequently, José performed poorly in high school and lacks the academic preparation needed to pursue higher education.

José has two older brothers, both of whom work in the construction field. They ridiculed him when he began thinking about higher education, saying that he would not be offered admission to any colleges. A few of José's friends are planning to attend the local community college, so he plans to join them and eventually transfer to a four-year school to pursue his dream of becoming a writer. Most of his friends, however, either dropped out of school, work full-time, or attend a local adult school to complete their high school credits or take the General Educational Development tests. Thus, José will most likely find himself alone on the college campus.

After school, José works at a local restaurant. Since his family does not have the means to pay for college, he is working to finance his education. Working a minimum-wage job and having to help his family with the bills make it difficult for him to save money. As a first-generation student from a historically underrepresented population, José lacks the experiential support and knowledge necessary to succeed in college. He will begin his first year trying to navigate his way through the new college environment. Achieving his goal will be contingent upon the resources and services the community college can offer him.

Educators and administrators in community colleges see students like José every day. Some of these students make it to their goal; others do not. The question is, how do educators help students like José to become engaged and to achieve academically in the community college setting in order to transfer to four-year institutions? When considering the needs of community college students, the first challenge is defining these students. Students attending a community college have varying reasons for matriculating. Many see community college as a low-cost, open-access institution of higher education that provides the opportunity to obtain a variety of skills, including learning English as a second language, to earn a vocational certificate or associate of arts degree, and to transfer to a four-year college or university.

In this chapter, we focus on the needs of first-year, racial/ethnic minority, first-generation students who intend to transfer to a four-year postsecondary institution. We define racial/ethnic minority students as those persons from historically and educationally disadvantaged groups, such as Latino/a, African American, and Native American populations. We accomplish three goals in this chapter: (1) identify the developmental issues impacting first-year, first-generation, racial/ethnic minority community college students; (2) provide existing theories as a framework for addressing the needs of this group; and (3) propose strategies to improve the engagement and transfer of these students to four-year colleges and universities.

Issues in the Context of Community Colleges

According to Phillippe and Valiga (2000), 60 percent of students who attend community colleges are first-generation students, meaning neither parent has any college experience (McConnell, 2000). First-generation students experience challenges to college access and achievement due in part to their minority status, being older, and having English as a second language (Phillippe & Valiga, 2000). Lee, Sax, Kim, and Hagedorn (2004) identify additional barriers of first-generation students, including low-income status, personal doubts, and lack of college involvement, institutional connectedness, family support, and academic and social integration. In the following section, we address these issues in further detail in three categories: (1) demographic characteristics, (2) academic and engagement experiences, and (3) psychosocial issues (Pascarella, Pierson, Wolniak, & Terenzini, 2004).

Demographic Characteristics

Demographic characteristics including age, gender, race/ethnicity, and socioeconomic status are relevant factors in the psychosocial development of first-generation community college students and can influence their persistence and transfer to four-year institutions (Phillippe & Valiga, 2000). Compared with other groups, first-generation students are more likely to be female, older, Hispanic, married, and low-income (Inman & Mayes, 1999; Phillippe & Valiga, 2000). Although each characteristic is important on its own, it is important to note that they do not exist in isolation, but are interconnected.

Age

Forty-six percent of community college students are over 25 years old, with an average age of 29 (Phillippe & Patton, 2000). These students arrive in the community college setting with a distinctly different set of experiences, expectations, issues, and concerns from traditional-age students. According to McConnell (2000), community college students are more likely to delay enrollment into higher education, to work off campus, and to work full-time. These outside responsibilities affect the amount of time available to dedicate to their academic work. Students often enroll on a part-time basis and are unable to fully integrate themselves into the fabric of community college life (McConnell, 2000).

Gender

National Center for Education Statistics (1998) figures show an increase in the number of women attending community colleges. Women account for over 50 percent of community college students and face different obstacles than their male counterparts. Women often assume multiple roles as caregiver, mother, student, and/or spouse. These multiple roles affect their abilities to manage successfully the demands of college coursework and can compel them to delay their pursuit of higher education in order to fulfill these other obligations. Women also face high levels of stress from parenting, financial constraints, and health concerns, particularly single mothers (Bryant, 2001; McConnell, 2000).

Women from underrepresented racial/ethnic backgrounds face additional barriers as they navigate the higher education system (Saenz, 2002). For example, in a Latino/a household, the woman may be expected to contribute to the daily household responsibilities, including caring for other children in the home, cleaning, and cooking for the family. Despite these challenges, researchers have shown women's persistence rates towards transfer to be as high as or higher than the rates of men (Mutter, 1992).

Race/Ethnicity

In addition to age and gender, belonging to a racial/ethnic minority group presents another challenge for first-year, first-generation community college students. From 1984 to 1998 the total number of White undergraduates at four-year institutions increased by 5.1 percent. During the same time frame, the number of Asian American, Hispanic, African American, and Native American undergraduates increased by 61 percent (McConnell, 2000). As the rates of racial/ethnic minority students pursuing higher education degrees continue to rise, community colleges continue to enroll a large proportion of these students. In 2001, approximately 50 percent of all Hispanic, African American, and Native American college students nationwide were enrolled in community colleges (Kim, 2002).

In a study examining transfer rates, researchers at the Center for the Study of Community Colleges found that there was considerable variation in the transfer rates of various racial/ethnic groups: 24 percent for Asians, 23 percent for Caucasians, 13 percent for African Americans, and 12 percent for Hispanics (Cohen, 1996). Tinto (1988) asserts that racial/ethnic minority community college students experience dissonance as they transition to college, especially when "their past experiences are unlikely to have prepared them for the new life of the college in the same way as have those persons who come from families that are themselves college educated" (p. 445). Latino/a students represent 9 percent of all undergraduate students in higher education and 60 percent of enrollments in community colleges (Martinez & Fernandez, 2004). Between 50 and 87 percent of Latino/a community college students identify transfer to a four-year institution and baccalaureate degree attainment as a goal (Martinez & Fernandez, 2004); however, their transfer rates are among the lowest in the country. In addition, low-income African American and Hispanic students have lower transfer rates than their White counterparts (Zamani, 2002).

Socioeconomic Status
The experiences of first-generation students vary depending on their level of income and can be further affected by race/ethnicity. Racial/ethnic minority students identify financial stressors more often than do their non-minority peers (Phinney & Haas, 2003). First-generation students are more likely to have lower incomes and dependent children (Brown & Burkhardt, 1999). Phillippe and Valiga (2000) found that 51 percent of single-parent household incomes were below $20,000, in comparison with 18 percent of two-parent homes. They also found that first-generation students reported the use of public assistance to help offset the cost of their college education. Pascarella et al. (2004) found that in comparison with their peers, first-generation students worked more hours per week during college.

The experiences and transfer rates of first-generation, racial/ethnic minority students varied based on their level of income and the community college they attended. Cohen (1996) found that the rate of transfer was 20 percent for African American students and 23 percent for Hispanic students. White students had the highest rate at 32 percent, followed by Asian Americans at 27 percent. First-generation students from middle-income backgrounds had higher rates of transfer and adjusted better to their new college settings than students from racial/ethnic minority or low-income backgrounds (Thayer, 2000).

Academic and Engagement Experiences
First-year, first-generation, racial/ethnic minority community college students face a myriad of academic challenges that can negatively affect their engagement. Given that they are the first in their families to attend college, there are few models for them to follow in achieving academic success. Consequently, these students struggle with academic preparation, academic integration, and social integration.

Academic Preparation

First-generation students are often underprepared academically for college (Inman & Mayes, 1999). They enter college with lower reading, math, and critical-thinking skills based on placement test scores for developmental English, math, and/or reading coursework (Amey & Long, 1998). Additionally, they graduate with lower high-school grade point averages (GPAs), lower SAT scores, and lower participation rates in honors programs (Inman & Mayes, 1999). This lack of academic preparation requires many first-generation students to enroll in remedial courses as a means to transfer to four-year institutions (Inman & Mayes, 1999).

In considering the number of students needing to take basic skills or remedial courses, Schuetz (2002) describes the challenges facing community college educators in responding to the academic needs of first-generation, racial/ethnic minority community college students:

> Almost half of all students entering community colleges enroll in at least one remedial course. One recent study indicated that 60 percent of this remedial population is traditional-age students enrolling in college immediately after high school graduation (as cited in Oudenhoven, p. 39). The other 40 percent are adult students who may be pursuing personal interests, preparing for transfer, upgrading job skills, or preparing to change careers. While many students require some remediation, 80 percent of the remedial population needs only one or two courses, with math the most common area of remediation. (p. 2)

Another example of the high need for remediation for community college students is seen in a Baltimore City Community College study by the Abell Foundation (as cited in Venezia, Kirst, & antonio, 2003) in the fall of 2000:

> 95 percent required remediation in math, and 65 percent of entering students needed remediation in math, English, and reading. At BCCC, nearly one-half of all entering students were assigned to the lowest level of remedial math in the year 2000—a placement that would require a student to take as many as nine courses (27 credits) before being able to begin credit level work in math. (p. 8)

The need to take several remedial courses prior to enrolling at a four-year institution can delay the transfer of community college students. Since these students are underprepared for postsecondary education, this is a challenge they must overcome in order to succeed in college.

In addition to remedial education, first-generation, racial/ethnic minority community college students face different dropout rates. Researchers and educators continue to find that community college student dropout rates are significantly higher than those of four-year institutions (Mohammadi, 1994). Two primary factors contribute to these dropout rates: placement into remedial/developmental coursework and lack of a clearly defined educational objective or educational plan on the part of the student (Grosset, 1991; Striplin, 1999). According to Summers (2003), from 1998 to 2001, only 45 percent of first-time, full-time community college first-year students who intended to earn a degree or certificate graduated. Moreover, 32 percent of students failed to return for their second year of community college or enroll in another institution. Students who were able to clearly identify their enrollment goal and maintain a high level of commitment were less likely to drop out (Mohammadi, 1994; Mutter, 1992; Summers, 2003). Rendón (1995), however, found that first-generation students receive poor counseling and advising. The lack of academic preparation of this population affects their level of academic integration into the community college setting.

Academic Integration

Academic integration involves the development of a strong affiliation with the college academic environment both inside and outside of the classroom through interactions with faculty, staff, and peers in an academic nature (e.g., study groups) (Kraemer, 1997). Academic integration plays a significant role in the persistence of community college students. Astin (1984) asserts that the amount of energy invested into the academic experience, such as hours spent studying, effort in classes, and effective study habits are directly related to student learning and development. Tinto (1988) identified GPA and hours spent on homework as academic predictors of student persistence. Mohammadi (1994) also found a strong correlation between the number of credit hours per semester, credit hours completed, and GPA as significant predictors of student retention. In a study of the academic integration of Latino students, Kraemer (1997) found that the three most important factors of academic integration were formal faculty–student interaction, informal faculty–student interaction, and study behaviors. Researchers continue to identify academic integration as influential for community college students who intend to transfer (Grosset, 1991; Halpin, 1990).

Social Integration

Students must persist through academic, institutional, and personal challenges in the community college setting in order to reach the four-year setting. Social integration is similar to academic integration; however, the focus shifts to interactions between students, faculty, staff, and peers in social contexts, such as peer interactions, involvement in student organizations, and informal contact with faculty (Kraemer, 1997). Social integration also affects student persistence in the community college setting.

Chapman and Pascarella (as cited in Bryant, 2001) found that community college students were more likely to have friends attending the same college and had more informal social contact with faculty than did four-year college and university students. However, some students delay social interactions until they determine that they have a grasp on their academic responsibilities, in particular racial/ethnic minority students (McConnell, 2000). Rendón (1994) notes that community college students who come academically and psychologically unprepared for college are not likely to get involved on their own. This is especially true for racial/ethnic minority students who must adjust to a new cultural environment. One criticism of current social integration research is that researchers do not take into account that racial/ethnic minority students need to adapt to a different cultural context with often conflicting norms and expectations in order to achieve success (Kraemer, 1997).

Students who become actively engaged in campus organizations are more likely to persist than those who are not involved (Tinto, 1988). Student organizations facilitate relationships between students with similar interests as well as connection to the institution. Furthermore, these organizations serve as social networks, which enhances their ability to increase the likelihood of integration and student persistence (Tinto, 1988). Researchers found that involvement in organizations had relatively positive effects on student development and student learning (Hernandez, Hogan, Hathaway, & Lovell, 1999; Summers, 2003). This was found to be particularly true for African American and Asian American students (Wawrzynski & Sedlacek, 2003). Eklund-Leen and Young (1997) outline the following benefits of student involvement in co-curricular activities:

Increased retention; improved interpersonal skills including communication, teamwork, organizing, decision-making and planning; greater satisfaction with their college experience on general dimensions compared with less involved students; useful experience in obtaining a job and providing job related skills; and development in lifelong values of volunteerism and service to others as well as lifelong leisure skills. (p. 72)

Eklund-Leen and Young's research supports the importance of involvement in student organizations for the persistence of community college students.

However, Bryant (2001) found that community college students are less involved at community college campuses in comparison to students at four-year institutions. They participate less frequently in campus organizations and rarely attend campus-sponsored events. Community college students participate in student clubs at a rate of 19 percent in comparison with 49 percent of four-year public college students (Schmid & Abell, 2003). Schmid and Abell found that non-persisters were less likely to be involved in student life than currently enrolled students. This is further supported by Bryant (2001), who found that community college students participate less frequently in campus organizations and rarely attend campus-sponsored events. Whitt (as cited in Bryant, 2001) posits that this student population is not able to participate at the same levels as traditional students owing to family and career commitments and lack of time and encouragement from faculty to become involved. Therefore, these low rates of participation suggest that this population may be at risk for not being retained and not finally transferring to a four-year institution (Bryant, 2001).

Ely (as cited in Kim, 2002) found that, because of the complex lives of this student population (e.g., given their family responsibilities and work commitments), social interaction mostly takes place in the classroom; therefore, faculty members play a critical role in this process. In fact, Mutter (1992) found that students who interacted informally with college faculty, staff, and advisors were more likely to persist compared with those who had minimal interactions. Contact with faculty outside of class is a crucial component in a student's decision to remain in college (Astin, 1984; Liu & Liu, 1999; Tinto, 1988), but community college students often do not have the time or take the initiative to talk to their instructors. Schmid and Abell (2003) found that community college students were less likely to speak with faculty members outside of class. Sixty-nine percent of community college students engaged in dialogues with faculty outside of the classroom in comparison to 85 percent of public, four-year college students. Such interactions not only provide students with opportunities to better understand material presented or receive additional help with assignments, they also offer students support through difficult times (Schmid & Abell, 2003).

The problem of limited opportunities for dialogues with faculty outside of class is partly caused by the disproportionate number of adjunct faculty in comparison with full-time faculty on community college campuses. Adjunct faculty teach fewer hours and have limited access to facilities to hold office hours (NCES, 2007). In addition, student responsibilities, such as family and work commitments, limit the amount of time available to meet with instructors outside of class. Astin (1984) notes that frequent interaction with faculty is more strongly related to student persistence than any other variable. A report on staffing by the Academic Senate for California Community Colleges (2002) noted the following:

> The number of full time faculty has grown to 18,864, while part time faculty now number 36,900 or 66.2%. While this represents less than a 1% increase over the past nineteen years, the percentage of credit instruction taught by part time faculty has now climbed to 46.1%, a 15.1% increase. (p. 5)

Consequently, the lack of interactions between community college students and faculty adversely affects persistence and transfer rates to four-year institutions.

Psychosocial Issues

The importance of psychological adjustment to college has been noted in the literature (Napoli & Wortman, 1998). Students' abilities to become socially and academically integrated into the campus community influence their persistence and psychosocial development. Although attending college is considered a rite of passage for most students, it is an even more significant event for first-year, first-generation, racial/ethnic minority students, since they face unique challenges in the transition to college. One of the greatest obstacles with which these students contend is negotiating two cultures—their home culture and that of the college (Do, 1996; Hsiao, 1992). Rendón (1995) identifies some additional challenges: lack of support from parents, siblings, and friends who do not have the experience of attending college; separation from their families; and the process of identity formation. We discuss these issues in greater detail below.

Family and Friendship Support

First-generation students are more likely to have limited access to information from family and friends regarding college and face a lack of support from these people (Phinney & Haas, 2003; Thayer, 2000). Parental involvement is associated with the type and amount of information that parents have about college. Parents who have not attended college have less direct knowledge of the economic and social benefits associated with higher education (Lee et al., 2004). Parents with firsthand knowledge of the college experience have a better understanding of the benefits of higher education and are more able to help their student navigate and finance their education (Lee at al., 2004). Conversely, parents without this knowledge are more likely to encourage their child to work rather than attend college (Lee et al., 2004).

Students are often faced with the difficult decision of pursuing an education or fulfilling family expectations and obligations. For those who live at home, additional problems include creating a designated study space and receiving criticism for devoting more time to school rather than family responsibilities (Hsiao, 1992). Not only do first-generation students face opposition from their families; friends may also be unsupportive of the decision to pursue a community college education. As Inman and Mayes (1999) note, "the pressure from friends and family encouraging these students not to go to college is often intense" (p. 5). This negative feedback about the desire to attend college places increased demands on such students to please their friends and family or to separate from them (Thayer, 2000).

Separation

As students transition into adulthood, they strive to become individuals (London, 1989). Tinto (1988) identified the need for students to separate from their prior environment in order to transition to the college environment. He notes that, although students who live at home do not need to dissociate themselves completely from the local community, the more they are tied to the local community, the more they are at risk for not being able to take full advantage of the intellectual and social aspects of the college. This process is further complicated by a student's first-generation status. Indeed, separation is a challenge for most community college students, as the community college by nature is designed as a non-residential system that requires students to commute.

Currently, only 60 of the nation's 1,050 two-year colleges provide on-campus housing (Bryant, 2001). Researchers have found that community college students who lived in campus housing report increased time spent studying and fewer family distractions, which enabled them to integrate socially and academically into the campus life (Bryant, 2001). A student's race/ethnicity may complicate the separation and transition process described by Tinto (1988), especially for students whose high school and/or community is racially/ethnically homogenous and have had limited opportunities to interact with people of different racial/ethnic backgrounds.

Identity Development

Students with multiple roles (i.e., student and spouse or parent) often leave the institution not because of academic difficulties but rather because they are unable to successfully manage their work, school, and home responsibilities (McConnell, 2000). These findings support Tinto's (1988) conclusion regarding community college student departure:

"external forces pull the person away from incorporation into the communities of the college" (p. 444). Institutional factors such as lack of campus housing and individual factors such as family responsibilities make separation from the home especially difficult for community college students.

Rendón (1994) found that in order to transition successfully, some students masked or shed their cultural backgrounds in order to assimilate into the mainstream academic culture. For example, racial/ethnic minority students may present an image to their professors or peers that emulates the dominant culture of the college or university (such as in their speech, interests, and mannerisms) and then display different identities and interests in their home environments. This can be seen in the example of José at the opening of this chapter, who risked being ridiculed by his brothers for wanting to apply to college. In the future he may choose not to share his college experiences with his family again for fear of rejection or ridicule. In addition, relationships between peers and families are altered or lost as the student transitions to the college community. Tinto (1988) asserts that this separation is a critical process that will allow the student to fully integrate into the campus environment and increase persistence. However, Rendón (1994) argues that institutions need to better assist students with the transition, encourage student involvement in academic and social environments, and allow students to maintain their cultural identities.

Whether students live on or off campus, social integration is achieved through social interaction. This interaction takes place outside of the classroom in peer interactions, involvement in student clubs or organizations, and informal interactions with faculty (Astin, 1984). Of most importance is the quality of these interactions rather than the quantity (Grosset, 1991). According to Tinto (1988), student involvement is difficult to achieve at most community colleges. However, researchers consistently show that social involvement, in the form of peer interactions, participation in student clubs and organizations, and discussions with faculty members, is related to persistence (Astin, 1984; Bryant, 2001).

Theoretical Framework

As mentioned earlier, 60 percent of community college students are first-generation students (Phillippe & Valiga, 2000), and they face additional barriers not experienced by their counterparts, such as low-income status, personal doubts, and a lack of college involvement, institutional connectedness, academic and social integration, and family support (Lee et al., 2004). Since issues that this particular population faces are unique when compared with students at four-year institutions, the theories on which our strategies are based must specifically address the issues and barriers encountered by first-generation, racial/ethnic minority community college students. Four theories are used to explain the unique issues with which these students contend: attribution theory, identity development theory, possible selves theory, and the interactionalist theory of college student departure.

Attribution Theory

Attribution theorists deal with competence and explain how students attribute their successes or failures. This theory may be used to explain past events and predict future outcomes (Hewstone, 1989; Weiner, 1972). Attribution, as Omrod (2002) explains, is an "example of knowledge construction in action" (p. 410). It is a method by which students attempt to construct a sense of self and make sense of the world by synthesizing newly acquired information with previously accumulated knowledge (Omrod, 2002). Weiner posited that depending on the cause, locus (internal vs. external), stability (stable vs. unstable), and controllability (controllable vs. uncontrollable) of attributions, students' degree of effort, intensity of work, and persistence may vary (Weiner, 1972). For instance, students who perceive they have more control over their academic success and attribute their achievement to internal reasons are more likely to persist and be engaged on campus, since they deem outcomes to be the result of purposeful decisions and actions (Weiner, 1972).

Attribution theory is relevant for the design of programs to increase the rate of student participation in curricular and co-curricular activities. It is especially relevant for first-generation, racial/ethnic minority students since they enter college with lower reading, math, and critical-thinking skills, according to placement test scores (Amey & Long, 1998), and are often underprepared academically and psychologically for college (Inman & Mayes, 1999). Listening to how these students attribute success and failure is one means of increasing their level of engagement on campus.

Identity Development Theory

Identity development theory addresses the psychosocial development of college students. The underlying assumption is that students undergo developmental changes during their college years and formation of identity is largely influenced by how students resolve conflicts through seven developmental tasks or *vectors* (Chickering & Resiser, 1993; Torres, Howard-Hamilton, & Cooper, 2003). Chickering and Reisser's model recognizes the significance of conflict resolution and its impact on identity development and is neither rigid nor sequential.

A criticism of Chickering's (1969) original theory was that the data were based almost exclusively on White men of traditional college age attending a four-year college (Evans, Forney, & Guido-DiBrito, 1998). In 1993, Chickering and Reisser revised the model to be more inclusive by incorporating identity development of women, African Americans, Hispanics, and college students of various ages (Evans et al., 1998).

In this chapter, we focus on Chickering and Reisser's first three vectors—Developing/Achieving Competence, Managing Emotions, and Moving through Autonomy toward Interdependence—since these are typically experienced by first-year students (Torres et al., 2003). The first vector, Developing/Achieving Competence, focuses on intellectual, social, and physical competence. This is particularly significant for first-generation, racial/ethnic minority community college students because they often enter college academically underprepared, given their low reading, math, and critical-thinking skills

(Amey & Long, 1998; Inman & Mayes, 1999). In the example of José, he will be expected not only to acquire more knowledge and develop his English skills, but also to critically analyze, synthesize, and evaluate additional information that is needed to become a successful college student.

In order to have an enriched educational experience, the second vector, Managing Emotions, must also be addressed (Chickering & Reisser, 1993). Typically, first-year, first-generation, racial/ethnic minority community college students feel anxious and/or guilty about attending community college. They may perceive that by attending college they are neglecting their household responsibilities and social obligations (Lee et al., 2004; McConnell, 2000; Saenz, 2002). For students like José, the lack of peers in college means it is difficult to talk to friends about the struggles they may be experiencing as they try to belong. They will want to make other friends and learn to express themselves in a different manner in order to be able to assume a new identity as a college student.

In the third vector, Moving through Autonomy toward Interdependence, students establish their new identities as college students and learn to seek out the assistance that they need to achieve their goals. As José's college identity develops, his need for approval from his brothers, friends, and family may begin to diminish as he moves toward autonomy and self-regulation in his environment. This autonomy and interdependence need to occur in order for José to reach his goal of transfer to a four-year institution.

Possible Selves Theory

Possible selves theory, as defined by Markus and Nurius (1986), derives from the representation of self in both the past and future. Possible selves can be thought of as a hypothetical, cognitive image of the future self in order to activate motivation towards achieving one's goal (Oyserman & Markus, 1990; Oyserman, Terry, & Bybee, 2002). This theory addresses the "conceptual link" between cognition and motivation (Oyserman et al., 2002). Hypothetically, people are free to create various possible selves; however, their choice of who they envision themselves to be in the future is largely influenced by the sociocultural and historical backdrop, which can be influenced by images portrayed by the media (Markus & Nurius, 1986). For example, in a Latino/a household, a young woman may be expected to contribute to the daily household responsibilities, including caring for other children in the home, cleaning, and cooking for the family (Lee et al., 2004; McConnell, 2000; Saenz, 2002). Therefore she may have difficulty envisioning herself as a professional, such as a doctor, professor, or engineer, in the future. Possible selves theory holds that one can construct a sense of self from past events and experiences that subsequently can guide one's expectations. This new self can act as an incentive for future behavior and provide a method of evaluating one's current self in relation to the past and future.

A criticism of the theory is that, compared with other psychosocial theories, it is the most vulnerable and susceptible to changes in the environment, since the theory is not rooted in students' social experiences (Markus & Nurius, 1986). For example, since first-year, first-generation, racial/ethnic minority community college students are often not emotionally and academically ready for college and are at higher risk of dropping out, obtaining a poor grade on a test may result in the student seeing his or her possible self as a "failure" (Inman & Mayes, 1999). This may further increase their risk of dropping out (Markus & Nurius, 1986). Possible selves theory can guide student affairs educators in developing feasible strategies to help students acquire the skills necessary to become self-directed and able to make plans for reaching goals that would lead to their academic and personal success.

Interactionalist Theory of College Student Departure

According to Tinto (1993), by the end of their first year, almost one-half of incoming students attending community colleges permanently leave the institution. Tinto's interactionalist theory of college student departure focuses on institutional impacts on a student's development. Tinto posited that an increase in social and academic integration will increase students' commitment to their goals as well as towards the institution, thus subsequently increasing the rate of retention.

Tinto (1993) asserts that institutional commitments, such as co-curricular activities and interactions with faculty and peers, are crucial to enabling students to achieve academic goals. However, Lounsbury, Saudargas, and Gibson (2004) caution researchers to consider the individual personality traits of students attending college before accepting Tinto's assumption. Lounsbury et al.'s advice is important for this group of students since their characteristics differ from students who attend four-year institutions. Tinto's (1993) theory focuses mainly on the institution's impact on the development of students. Institutional barriers can largely influence a student's decision to remain in school and persist or to drop out. Therefore, when considering the success of these students in achieving their goal of transfer, feasible strategies should focus on removing barriers that may deter students from reaching their goals.

The purpose of this section was to provide the theoretical underpinnings for the strategies recommended in the following section for improving the collegiate outcomes of first-year, first-generation, racial/ethnic minority students. To develop effective, practical strategies, it is important to utilize theories that specifically address the issues and barriers experienced by this group. The designs of these strategies are based on the developmental issues and the four theories outlined above.

Strategies for Improving Transfer Trajectories

Thus far, we have laid the groundwork for understanding the developmental needs of and issues faced by first-year, first-generation, racial/ethnic minority students. When formulating effective strategies for these students, it is important to integrate what is known about institutional barriers experienced by this group, along with their needs and the issues they face as they develop their new identities as college students. The following approaches can be used by community college faculty and administrators when working with these students.

Ambassador Programs

Offer a high school outreach ambassador program to those students who successfully complete their first year of full-time studies with a GPA of 2.0 or better. These programs will offer paid positions that afford college students an opportunity to mentor prospective first-generation students from local high schools about their college choices. These positions will give the student an opportunity to earn an income as well as become part of the campus community. These positions can be paid through the federal financial aid work-study program or the college's monies. In addition to the financial benefit, students will also enhance their personal development, such as by increasing self-confidence. Finally, the ambassador program will help to socially integrate college students into the institution, since it increases their interactions with peers in the program as well as their contacts with faculty, staff, and administrators.

Counselor Caseloads

Assign a caseload of first-year, first-generation, racial/ethnic minority students to each staff counselor. Counselors working with this group of students can use the caseload format to target students who could use information about special programs and services, and to address the questions they may have. Students participating in specialized services, such as disability services, will continue meeting with their assigned counselor for that particular program. At present, counselor caseload assignment is not a consistent practice at community colleges; therefore, many students matriculate not knowing who their counselor is or with whom they can speak. Establishing a relationship with a counselor will make it easier for students to begin their interaction with faculty at the community college. This is especially critical because of the connection between student–faculty contact and student retention. Caseloads will also give counselors the opportunity to contact students through email or standard mail to invite them to make an appointment to talk or to let them know of upcoming events or important information that might be critical to their success.

Student Educational Plan

Institutionalize a Student Educational Plan (SEP) by the middle of the first semester in college. The SEP should include mandatory English and math assessment tests and classes. The SEP will be developed by counselors along with students to help students achieve their goals, and is an academic roadmap that enables students to complete required courses for transfer to four-year institutions. The SEP can change depending on the needs of the student. For example, if a student begins with a goal of transfer as a biology/pre-med major and then decides to become an elementary school teacher, the SEP will be modified in cooperation with the counselor to reflect the new curriculum required. It is important that students maintain regular contact and dialogue with their counselor or advisor at the college.

Learning Communities

Develop cohorts and learning communities for English and math basic-skills courses. These learning communities will enable students to redress their lack of academic preparation in high school and work in a supportive environment to gain the skills needed to succeed in transferring courses to a four-year institution. This supportive environment will enable students to learn by interacting with their peers inside and outside of the classroom, thus creating friendships and additional support networks that will also help them advance and matriculate successfully to a four-year college or university.

Peer Mentoring Program

Create and sponsor a peer mentoring program through student organizations on campus such as the Pre-Med Club, Psychology Club, or Future Teachers Club. It is important that, early in students' academic careers, they be exposed to information and organizations that are actively involved in their field of interest. Often, students will indicate their desire to transfer in a particular major or field, but are unsure of the necessary steps to reach that goal or the job responsibilities of a person in their field of choice.

In the example of José, he knew he wanted to study and go to college, but was not familiar with the steps he needed to take in order to do so. He would benefit from this type of program, as it would enable him to meet other future writers or students who are interested in transferring and majoring in English. Interacting with students who are pursuing the same major will provide him with the opportunity to ask questions, emulate his peers, and build the necessary social and cultural networks to engage in internships or volunteer opportunities. There is also a benefit to the organization offering the mentoring, as students will become empowered through helping their peers achieve their goals.

Faculty Mentors

Assign faculty mentors aligned with students' area of interest during the second year of college. The administration can encourage and support this strategy by offering mentoring as part of faculty members' professional development opportunities or by requiring that it be a part of faculty job responsibilities. The college could also offer small stipends to the faculty for participating in this program. When possible, a faculty member of the same race/ethnicity and with similar interests should be assigned.

Speaker Series

A speaker series can be developed that will include former first-generation, racial/ethnic minority community college students who have graduated with their undergraduate or graduate degrees in various fields. The speakers can discuss not only their experiences but aspects of their majors and how they decided to pursue that field. First-generation students can ask these former students questions and use the knowledge gained to improve their own educational experiences. Moreover, these college graduates can show first-generation, racial/ethnic minority students that success is possible even though they began college unprepared.

Workshops

Offer biweekly workshops on assertiveness training, motivation, student success skills, gender and racial/ethnic issues, and how to navigate through college. Workshops can also be presented by members of different colleges and universities on what a student needs to transfer to particular institutions. These workshops can be targeted specifically to first-generation, racial/ethnic minority students. They will not be mandatory but attendance can be encouraged by making them count as a counselor contact. The workshops will be offered at different times during the day, in the evenings, and/or on weekends to accommodate student schedules.

Orientation

Adopt a college policy that mandates a student orientation class for incoming community college students. Included in this course should be study skills, time management, career information, and goal-setting strategies. College orientation classes are meant to help students gain the skills necessary to become informed and competent college students. A study completed at Sacramento Community College examined the success of college orientation courses for students. Barefoot (as cited in Chaves, 2003), found that "students who participated in a freshman orientation seminar at Sacramento Community College in California completed courses at a 50 percent higher rate than those students who had not participated" (p. 2). In other words, orientation is vital to students' academic achievement.

Partnerships with Career Services

Forge a partnership with the office of career services to offer on-campus jobs to students from this population. These students could be given priority consideration for these positions. By enabling students to be a part of the college community and environment, on-campus jobs make students more likely to persist during college. This should increase the likelihood of their retention and ultimate transfer to a four-year college or university.

Partnerships with Community Colleges and Four-Year Institutions

Identify and establish partnerships and relations with other community colleges. The community college can work with neighboring colleges to develop partnerships, such as the Los Angeles Regional Intersegmental Advisory Board (LARIAB). This advisory board, which includes a collaboration of community college representatives from the on-campus transfer center, as well as public and private colleges and universities, can work together to facilitate and coordinate transfer programs that will assist this group of students. Members can include admissions staff, transfer center directors, and representatives from other programs and services that target this group of students. Programs such as the Educational Opportunity Program at the various California State University institutions can help strengthen partnerships with community colleges and increase their ability to advocate and assist this group of students.

Types of cooperative efforts could include writing collaborative grants that will benefit these students. For instance, members can write a grant proposal for the coverage of transportation costs for students to visit different campuses. Members of the colleges in LARIAB wrote a grant to take students from the Los Angeles region's seven community colleges to visit campuses in northern California. This grant paid the airfare to visit such universities as the University of California, Berkeley, the University of California, Davis, San Francisco State University, and the University of San Francisco. The community colleges partnered with the universities to provide ground transportation and a program once the students reached the campuses. These partnerships can enable students to learn more about the transfer process and decide which four-year institutions will best meet their needs.

Alignment of Existing Programs

Align existing programs meant to serve first-generation, low-income, and racial/ethnic minority students at the community college. Having one multicultural office that coordinates all of these programs in one location means that students have one place to go that will enable them to get their needs met holistically. Programs such as Puente, Extended Opportunity Programs and Services, MESA (Mathematics Engineering Science Achievement), Alliance for Minority Participation, and various student organizations share the same goal of successful transfer outcomes for racial/ethnic minority students. This alignment is important for students because they may be confused by the variety of programs and may not realize that they qualify for more than one. A multicultural center also provides students with a location where they can feel comfortable asking for assistance.

Incentives and Rewards

Offer semester incentives and rewards for the completion of 12 units with a GPA of 2.5 or better. Incentives can include book vouchers, parking passes, or food vouchers for a semester. These rewards can be coordinated through various programs and supported by institutional monies and/or grants. The programs targeting these students can jointly make a commitment to set aside a certain amount of money from their budgets each year to fund these incentives.

Supplemental Instruction Programs

The purpose of Supplemental Instruction (SI) programs is to offer peer-facilitated tutoring sessions for students in courses that are historically difficult or challenging for students. Areas of particular emphasis should be English, math, and sciences. These workshops will focus on critical thinking and problem-solving exercises related to course material. Students will not receive a grade by participating in SI study sessions; however, involvement in SI can be a requirement for enrolling in a specific class or in a class taught by a specific instructor.

Assessment and Evaluation

Initiate a structured and integrated plan of evaluation utilizing quantitative and qualitative measures at the beginning of the first year of program implementation. These data should target areas or indicators known to improve the outcome of transfer for students. Areas covered can include persistence, success in completing basic-skills English and math courses, progress toward completion of the student's educational plans, contact with a counselor, and students' perceptions of the campus. Data collection of students who have successfully transferred will enable institutional members to determine benchmarks and work toward closing any gaps. This information should be reviewed annually to gauge whether the programs implemented are successful in the retention and persistence of students. An example of a program that could be evaluated would be the previously mentioned partnership grants with neighboring community colleges and four-year institutions that pay for travel costs for first-generation students to visit various institutions. A longitudinal evaluation of the data will be presented after five years to determine whether the students were successful in obtaining their outcome of transfer after the strategies were implemented.

Conclusion

The purpose of this chapter was to illuminate the challenges faced by first-year, first-generation, racial/ethnic minority community college students that may impede their transfer to four-year institutions. Our goal was to provide strategies to help student affairs educators, faculty, and administrators facilitate these students' engagement and successful transfer to a four-year college or university. Assisting these students is particularly challenging because of the diversity within the groups. First-year, first-generation, racial/ethnic minority students attending community colleges are not a monolithic group, but they present general themes and trends that should be addressed. Administrators and faculty must begin to understand and respond to the personal development issues, such as isolation and self-doubt, experienced by these students. This understanding can enable educators to implement programs and services to help students like José successfully navigate the community college. Doing so will increase the numbers of students transferring to four-year institutions and ultimately graduating with a four-year degree.

References

Academic Senate for California Community Colleges (2002). *Part time faculty: A principled perspective.* Sacramento, CA: Academic Senate for California Community Colleges. (ERIC Document Reproduction Service No. ED 471640)

Amey, M. J., & Long, P. N. (1998). Developmental course work and early placement: Success strategies for underprepared community college students. *Community College Journal of Research and Practice, 22*(1), 3–10.

Astin, A. W. (1984). Student involvement: A developmental theory for higher education. *Journal of College Student Personnel, 25*(4), 297–308.

Brown, H. E., & Burkhardt, R. L. (1999). *Predicting student success: The relative impact of ethnicity, income, and parental education.* Paper presented at the annual meeting of the Association for Institutional Research, Seattle, WA. (ERIC Document Reproduction Service No. ED 433793)

Bryant, A. N. (2001). ERIC review: Community college students: Recent findings and trends. *Community College Review, 29*(3), 77–93.

Chaves, C. A. (2003). *Student involvement in the community college setting. ERIC Digest.* Los Angeles: ERIC Clearinghouse for Community Colleges. (ERIC Document Reproduction Service No. ED477911)

Chickering, A. W. (1969). *Education and identity.* San Francisco: Jossey-Bass.

Chickering, A. W., & Reisser, L. (1993). *Education and identity* (2nd ed.). San Francisco: Jossey-Bass.

Cohen, A. M. (1996). Orderly thinking about a chaotic system. In T. Rifkin (Ed.), *Transfer and articulation: Improving policies to meet new needs. New Directions for Community Colleges* (No. 96, pp. 25–34). San Francisco: Jossey-Bass.

Do, V. T. (1996). Counseling culturally different students in the community college. *Community College Journal of Research and Practice, 20,* 9–21.

Eklund-Leen, S. J., & Young, R. B. (1997). Attitudes of student organization members and nonmembers about campus and community involvement. *Community College Review, 24*(4), 71–81.

Evans, N. J., Forney, D. S., & Guido-DiBrito, F. (1998). Chickering's theory of identity development. In U. Delworth (Ed.), *Student development in college* (pp. 35–52). San Francisco: Jossey-Bass.

Grosset, J. M. (1991). Patterns of integration, commitment, and student characteristics and retention among younger and older students. *Research in Higher Education, 32*(2), 159–178.

Halpin, R. L. (1990). An application of the Tinto model to the analysis of freshman persistence in a community college. *Community College Review, 17*(4), 22–32.

Hernandez, K., Hogan, S., Hathaway, C., & Lovell, C. D. (1999). Analysis of the literature on the impact of student involvement on student development and learning: More questions than answers? *NASPA Journal, 36*(3), 184–197.

Hewstone, M. (1989). *Causal attribution: From cognitive processes to collective beliefs.* Cambridge, MA: Blackwell.

Hsiao, K. P. (1992). *First-generation college students. ERIC Digest.* Los Angeles: ERIC Clearinghouse for Junior Colleges. (ERIC Document Reproduction Service No. ED351079)

Inman, W. E., & Mayes, L. (1999). The importance of being first: Unique characteristics of first generation community college students. *Community College Review, 26*(4), 3–22.

Kim, K. A. (2002). ERIC review: Exploring the meaning of "nontraditional" at the community college. *Community College Review, 30*(1), 74–89.

Kraemer, B. A. (1997). The academic and social integration of Hispanic students into college. *Review of Higher Education, 20*(2), 163–179.

Lee, J. J., Sax, L. J., Kim, K. A., & Hagedorn, L. S. (2004). Understanding students' parental education beyond first-generation status. *Community College Review, 32*(1), 1–20.

Liu, E., & Liu, R. (1999). An application of Tinto's model at a commuter campus. *Education, 119*(3), 537–541.

London, H. B. (1989). Breaking away: A study of first-generation college students and their families. *American Journal of Education, 97*(2), 144–170.

Lounsbury, J. W., Saudargas, R. A., & Gibson, L. W. (2004). An investigation of personality traits in relation to intention to withdraw from college. *Journal of College Student Development, 45*(5), 517–534.

Markus, H., & Nurius, P. (1986). Possible selves. *American Psychologist, 41*(9), 954–969.

Martinez, M., & Fernandez, E. (2004). Latinos at community colleges. In A. Ortiz (Ed.), *Addressing the unique needs of Latino American students. New Directions for Student Services* (No. 105, pp. 51–62). San Francisco: Jossey-Bass.

McConnell, P. J. (2000). ERIC Review: What community colleges should do to assist first-generation students. *Community College Review, 28*(3), 75–87.

Mohammadi, J. (1994). *Exploring retention and attrition in a two-year public community college.* Martinsville, VA: Patrick Henry Community College, Institutional Planning and Research Information Services. (ERIC Document Reproduction Service No. ED382257)

Mutter, P. (1992). Tinto's theory of departure and community college student persistence. *Journal of College Student Development, 33*(4), 310–317.

Napoli, A. R., & Wortman, P. M. (1998). Psychosocial factors related to retention and early departure of two-year community college students. *Research in Higher Education, 39*(4), 419–455.

National Center for Education Statistics. (1998). *Digest of education statistics, 1997.* Washington DC: U.S. Department of Education, Office of Educational Research and Improvement.

National Center for Education Statistics (2007). *Digest of education statistics, 2006.* Washington DC: U.S. Department of Education, Office of Educational Research and Improvement.

Omrod, J. E. (2002). Cognitive factors in motivation. In J. E. Omrod (Ed.), *Educational psychology: Developing learners* (4th ed., pp. 388–426). Upper Saddle River, NJ: Merrill.

Oyserman, D., & Markus, H. (1990). Possible selves and delinquency. *Journal of Personality and Social Psychology, 59,* 112–125.

Oyserman, D., Terry, K., & Bybee, D. (2002). A possible selves intervention to enhance school involvement. *Journal of Adolescence, 25,* 313–326

Pascarella, E. T., Pierson, C. T., Wolniak, G. C., & Terenzini, P. T. (2004). First-generation college students. *Journal of Higher Education, 75*(3), 249–284.

Phillippe, K. A., & Patton (2000). *National profile of community colleges: Trends and statistics* (3rd ed.). Washington, DC: Community College Press.

Phillippe, K. A., & Valiga, M. J. (2000). *Faces of the future: A portrait of America's community college students. Summary findings.* Washington, DC: American Association of Community Colleges. (ERIC Document Reproduction Service No. ED439760)

Phinney, J. S., & Haas, K. (2003). The process of coping among ethnic minority first-generation college freshmen: A narrative approach. *Journal of Social Psychology, 143*(6), 707–726.

Rendón, L. I. (1994). *Beyond involvement: Creating validating academic and social communities in the community college.* University Park, PA: National Center on Postsecondary Teaching, Learning, and Assessment. (ERIC Document Reproduction Service No. ED374728)

Rendón, L. I. (1995). *Facilitating retention and transfer for first generation students in community colleges.* University Park, PA: National Center on Postsecondary Teaching, Learning, and Assessment. (ERIC Document Reproduction Service No. ED383369)

Saenz, V. B. (2002, September). *Hispanic students and community colleges: A critical point for intervention. ERIC Digest*. Los Angeles: ERIC Clearinghouse for Community Colleges. (ERIC Document Reproduction Service No. ED477908)

Schmid, C., & Abell, P. (2003). Demographic risk factors, study patterns, and campus involvement as related to student success among Guilford Community College students. *Community College Review, 31*(1), 1–16.

Schuetz, P. (2002). *Emerging challenges for community colleges*. Los Angeles: Eric Clearinghouse for Community Colleges. (ERIC Document Reproduction Service No. ED477829)

Striplin, J. J. (1999). *Facilitating transfer for first-generation community college students. ERIC Digest*. Los Angeles: ERIC Clearinghouse for Community Colleges. (ERIC Document Reproduction Service No. ED430627)

Summers, M. D. (2003). ERIC review: Attrition research at community colleges. *Community College Review, 30*(4), 64–84.

Thayer, P. B. (2000). *Retention of students from first generation and low income backgrounds*. Washington, DC: National TRIO Clearinghouse. (ERIC Document Reproduction Service No. ED446633)

Tinto, V. (1988). Stages of student departure. *Journal of Higher Education, 59*(4), 438–455.

Tinto, V. (1993). *Leaving college: Rethinking the causes and cures of student attrition* (2nd ed.). Chicago: University of Chicago Press.

Torres, V., Howard-Hamilton, M. F., & Cooper, D. L. (2003). *Identity development of diverse populations: Implications for teaching and administration in higher education. ASHE-ERIC Higher Education Report* (Vol. 29, No. 6). San Francisco: Jossey-Bass.

Venezia, A., Kirst, M. W., & antonio, a. l. (2003). *Betraying the college dream: How disconnected K–12 and postsecondary education systems undermine student aspirations*. Retrieved June 1, 2005, from the Stanford Institute for Higher Education Research website: www.stanford.edu/group/bridgeproject/betrayingthecollegedream.pdf.

Wawrzynski, M. R., & Sedlacek, W. E. (2003). Race and gender differences in the transfer student experience. *Journal of College Student Development, 44*(4), 489–501.

Weiner, B. (1972). Attribution theory, achievement motivation, and educational process. *Review of Educational Research, 42*(2), 203–215.

Zamani, E. M. (2002). Institutional responses to barriers to the transfer process. In F. S. Laanan (Ed.), *Transfer students: Trends and issues. New Directions for Community Colleges* (No. 114, pp. 15–24). San Francisco: Jossey-Bass.

Chapter 15
Redefining Championship in College Sports
Enhancing Outcomes and Increasing Student-Athlete Engagement

Brandon E. Martin

University of Southern California, the institution at which I currently work as an athletics administrator and faculty member, has an impressive legacy of winning championships. Throughout its 128-year history, USC student-athletes and coaches have won a cumulative total of 107 national titles. Between 2002 and 2007 alone, the university was crowned national champion one time each in women's water polo, men's tennis, women's golf, and women's soccer, and twice each in football, men's water polo, and women's volleyball. Clearly, the institution has a culture of winning in which we take tremendous pride. Despite all the trophies, recognition, and bragging rights that come along with such an extraordinary reputation in college sports, I present an alternative conceptualization of "winning" in this chapter. Specifically, I argue here that real champions graduate from college having accrued all the benefits, gains, and outcomes associated with engagement in educationally purposeful activities, inside and outside the classroom beyond athletics.

Student-athletes are winners when their communication and critical-thinking skills improve from one year to the next; when they graduate and enter the workforce with competencies that enable them to be effective; and when they have had opportunities to develop holistic identities—essentially, the same outcomes identified by Harper and Quaye in Chapter 1 of this book. For the institution, the active engagement of all student-athletes in rich educational experiences outside of athletics is the ultimate indicator of a championship season. That is, when those who play sports are able to cultivate friendships beyond their teammates, balance athletic and academic commitments, participate in internships and service-learning, work with faculty on research projects, and assume leadership positions in student organizations, an athletics department can truly brag about having won.

In this chapter, I provide a snapshot of what the published literature says about the challenges faced by college student-athletes. My discussion defaults primarily (though not exclusively) to Division I sports programs as a context because these have been the focus of most prior research. I then offer some theoretical perspectives on the identity challenges that student-athletes face. The chapter concludes with a set of strategies for increasing student-athlete engagement beyond athletics departments and their sports teams.

Issues and Challenges of Division I College Student-Athletes

Much has been published about the experiences of college student-athletes, particularly those participating at Division I institutions. Some researchers have investigated various issues related to the career planning, academic motivation, and post-college outcomes (e.g., Adler & Adler, 1987; Benson, 2000; Lapchick, 2003; Meyer, 1990; Miller & Kerr, 2002; Pascarella & Smart, 1991; Simons, Van Rheenen, & Covington, 1999), while others have focused on the psychosocial and non-cognitive challenges faced by student-athletes (Astin, 1993; Howard-Hamilton, & Watt, 2001; Pinkerton, Hinz, & Barrow, 1989; Sedlacek, 1987, 2004; Sedlacek & Gaston, 1992). Described below are the academic, social, and career development challenges faced by college student-athletes, as well as their troublesome relationships with faculty.

Academic Issues

There has been much debate regarding the effects of college athletics on student-athletes' academic performance and persistence. It is unfairly assumed, particularly at institutions with laudable athletic reputations, that student-athletes are academically inept and incapable of performing well in the classroom (Howard-Hamilton & Watt, 2001). Unfortunately, this results in many student-athletes being stereotyped and treated unfairly on college campuses. In addition to their being stigmatized as academic underachievers, other issues are presented in the literature regarding the educational effects of athletic participation on college students. First, student-athletes are typically drawn from secondary schools and socioeconomic backgrounds that are significantly different from those of non-athletes (Hood, Craig, & Ferguson, 1992; Pascarella & Smart, 1991; Shulman & Bowen, 2001). Secondly, the literature has revealed that college athletics may not constitute a single subculture in terms of their effects on students' intellectual and personal development during college. For example, Pascarella, et al. (1999) found evidence that participating in revenue-generating sports (e.g., football and men's basketball) placed students in a subculture with different academic expectations and practices. Unlike those participating in non-revenue-generating sports (e.g., golf, tennis, and swimming) student-athletes in revenue-generating sports are often under enormous pressure to satisfy the goals of the athletic department. Unfortunately, this pressure usually affects their academic performance in negative ways.

Social Challenges

Researchers investigating the social challenges faced by college student athletes have found they are often isolated from other students and faculty on campus. According to Hyatt (2003), isolation from non-athletic activities can have detrimental effects on a student-athlete's ability to integrate into both the social and academic environments of a college or university. One reason why student-athletes are often isolated on campus is because of their demanding athletic obligations. This inevitably creates various time constraints and leaves these students with a limited amount of time to fully integrate into the campus community. Sellers, Sellers, and Damas (2002) refer to this issue for student-athletes as "role conflicts," because the student role interferes with the athlete role and its pressures and demands. As explained by Briggs (1996), "as student-athletes become overwhelmed with their athletic roles, educational aspirations and campus involvement tend to suffer" (p. 12). Thus, many become engulfed, and satisfied with only fulfilling their athletic commitments to the institution. This in turn causes isolation and disassociation from others on campus who can possibly assist them with balancing their dual roles.

Using the football culture as an example, Nishimoto (1997) posits that student-athletes construct their individual and collective identities by the "football student-athlete culture," because they are functionally, psychologically, and physically separated from the general student body. He further asserts:

> Athletes are trapped in a self-perpetuating system set in motion early in their lives. They have a special commodity that separates them from the rest of the [college] population—athletic talent. Unfortunately, while they benefit from the special attention, they are also blocked from "normal" development by being segregated on college campuses. (p. 628)

These findings suggest that social disengagement can prevent student-athletes from maximizing their development and growth as students. In some cases this can also negatively affect their lives after college, as their interpersonal communication and relationship-building skills remain underdeveloped.

Adler and Adler (1987) studied the social relations of a major Division I men's basketball program at a large private institution. Their findings indicate that the participants' social experiences on campus were primarily with other student-athletes. The participants expressed comfort and a preference for living, dining, and taking classes with fellow student-athletes. Adler and Adler found this peer subculture conflicted with their academic roles in three ways: (1) discouraging them from exerting effort in academics, (2) engendering distractions that made it difficult for them to study, and (3) influencing them to not seek out and associate with other students who could have provided greater academic role modeling. These findings confirm the importance of student-athletes socializing with non-athletic peers and integrating into the larger campus community.

Career Development and Transition

There remains a paucity of research in the area of student-athlete career development and transition. However, exciting studies have reported that athletic identity—the degree to which an individual identifies with her or his athletic role—could influence student-athletes' development and the actualization of their career aspirations (Brewer, Van Raalte, & Linder, 1993). According to this, those with strong athletic identities place great importance on being involved in their sports. Although this identity may be highly beneficial for student-athletes in the athletic domain, it could exert an effect on post-collegiate career identification and development in this group.

Martens and Lee (1998) found that college athletes often do not access sources of occupational information, such as the university career center. College athletes generally have more time constraints and pressures than non-athletes (e.g., practices and games, film sessions, rehabilitating injuries, and rigorous travel schedules). Furthermore, their lives are often highly structured and monitored, with many important decisions being made by coaches and other athletic personnel. Taken together, these factors may cause a student-athlete to feel that she or he is lacking in terms of tangible and practical occupational information.

Smallman and Sowa (1996) found that male student-athletes in revenue-generating sports scored in the bottom 25th percentile of norms on the Career Development Inventory (CDI), a standardized measure of career maturity and development. Athletic termination and transition issues are extremely significant for student-athletes participating in revenue-generating sports. According to a 2006 NCAA report, 1.8 percent of college football players are drafted in the National Football League (NFL), and 1.2 percent of men's basketball players are drafted in the National Basketball Association (NBA). Given these statistics, it is important that these student-athletes are encouraged by coaches, administrators, and faculty to pursue and development interests outside their respective sports.

Faculty Attitudes toward Student-Athletes

Fear, conscious and unconscious prejudicial attitudes and behaviors, and stereotyping toward student-athletes all are perpetuated by members of the campus community (Engstrom & Sedlacek, 1993; Engstrom, Sedlacek, & McEwen, 1995). Leach and Conners (1984) speculated that professors may hold more negative attitudes toward college student-athletes than do other students, administrators, and alumni. In a study of 201 faculty at a large public research university, Engstrom et al. (1995) found that faculty held prejudicial attitudes and stereotypes about revenue-generating and non-revenue-generating student-athletes alike. Engstrom and Sedlacek (1993) also reported that faculty were surprised when student-athletes earned A's on term papers and exams. This signifies skepticism that student-athletes can be academically prepared for the rigors of college-level coursework.

In their quantitative study of male student-athletes at Division I universities, Comeaux and Harrison (2007) found that for both African American and White student-athletes in revenue-generating sports, academic success was to some extent dependent on their interaction with faculty. For example, faculty who provided encouragement and support for graduate school made a strong contribution to both the White and African American student-athletes' academic success. Overall, they found faculty were more likely to provide assistance with study skills and exam preparation to White student-athletes.

An article in the *Chronicle of Higher Education*, titled "Black Athletes and White Professors: A Twilight Zone of Uncertainty," reported that African American student-athletes feel marginalized and not taken seriously by White professors (Perlmutter, 2003). This feeling of being devalued academically is supported by Steele's (1997) Stereotype Threat Theory, according to which, when African American students are continually faced with the threat of being judged or viewed as academically incapable, they may gradually come to devalue school performance. If African American student-athletes are constantly prone to feelings of academic inadequacy, they may be less likely to interact with faculty at predominantly White institutions. They may also extricate themselves from situations in which they could perform well in the classroom to protect their self-esteem.

A major criticism by Hurley and Cunningham (1984) was that "colleges and universities are sacrificing their academic integrity in order to develop competitive athletic teams" (p. 51). As such, institutional stakeholders, particularly faculty members, have serious concerns about the unethical behavior that has recently been manifested in academic scandals involving plagiarism, grade changes, and other unfair academic practices (Gaston-Gayles, 2003). These negative perceptions and expectations of student-athletes have undoubtedly precluded many university and college faculty members from collaborating with athletic officials on improving academic outcomes for student-athletes. This lack of input from educators and administrators outside of athletics can potentially hinder academic support programs for student-athletes and limit opportunities for these students to develop healthy identities.

Theoretical Perspectives on Identity

Psychological identity as an athlete has been related to one dimension of self-concept (Brewer et al., 1993). Markus and Wurf (1987) explain that individuals choose to participate in activities that are consistent with more highly developed and central aspects of their self-concepts. As a result, these individuals will be more satisfied with relationships that confirm or validate their self-concept. This suggests that having an athletic identity will inevitably affect the development of self-concept—influencing social relationships, the activities one seeks, and the way one's experiences are processed. Before exploring the identity conflicts among college student-athletes, it is imperative to underscore the significance of adolescent athletic experiences.

Several scholars have expressed concern that the psychological centrality of athletics within an adolescent's social system and the community's value system may contradict educational goals and the psychological development of the adolescent (Goldberg & Chandler, 1995). Moreover, young athletes must cope with the stresses of choosing peer groups with different value expectations. Sellers (1992) and Nelson (1982) both examined the crucial period of identity-versus-role conflict and its effects on the adolescent athlete. Nelson found that the issue with adolescent and high school athletes is that role engulfment (i.e., high participation in athletics) reduces the motivation to explore alternative roles. He further contends that a role conflict can lead to "identity foreclosure," which can impede the development of skills needed to deal with challenges and new situations in college. Unfortunately, the demands of college athletics, particularly revenue-generating sports, perpetuate these role imbalances for student-athletes.

According to Howard-Hamilton and Sina (2001), college athletes typically form an ego identity based on how well they perform in a particular sport. Student-athletes receive positive reinforcement and rewards from family members, coaches, and the media based on their performance in athletic events. This support might appear to be positive, but when recognition comes only for athletic competence, a person's entire sense of self-worth hinges on making big plays and winning the game (Howard-Hamilton & Sina, 2001). This type of recognition can be problematic, because it often impedes a student's overall development throughout her or his years in college. As noted by Pearson and Petitpas (1990), ego identity can become fragile when society defines a developing personality according to superficial values.

Although current reports suggest that student-athletes struggle with identity conflicts more than their non-athletic peers (Pinkerton, Hinz, & Barrow, 1989), an even more alarming issue is the underutilization of campus counseling services by student-athletes. One explanation for this is the lack of exposure to and knowledge of campus resources by this population throughout their collegiate careers. In most cases, athletic personnel do not encourage student-athletes to use services outside of the athletic department domain. Most athletic departments offer a host of services and accommodations for student-athletes, so other campus services are considered secondary at best. In addition, some head coaches view psychological distress as a sign of weakness. This is problematic because coaches are not equipped with the skills to determine if a student-athlete is suffering from problems related to alcohol, drugs, depression, eating disorders, or other psychological ailments. Failure to connect student-athletes with the appropriate counseling resources can result in long-term mental and physical challenges for student-athletes.

Engagement Strategies

Below are some strategies that coaches and athletic administrators, faculty, and student affairs educators can employ independently and collaboratively to enhance outcomes and resolve identity conflicts among college student-athletes.

Exposure to Leadership and Engagement Opportunities

Many student-athletes do not see the value of college experiences beyond the academic and athletic domains. They should be informed that they are less likely to discontinue their pursuit of a baccalaureate degree if they are involved in out-of-class activities and student organizations. Having student-athletes explore leadership roles outside of athletics positively influences their overall perceptions of the university and their roles as students. A student-athlete who is the president of a fraternity or sorority would likely attract more student-athletes to these campus organizations. Additionally, participation in student government and service opportunities allows student-athletes to interact with non-athletes, student affairs educators, and faculty on campus. This level of meaningful engagement inevitably aids student-athletes in maximizing their non-athletic college experiences.

Utilizing Offices and Support Services Outside of Athletics

Depending solely on the resources and services provided by the athletic department can be detrimental to the overall well-being and growth of student-athletes. Campus orientation sessions are critical for educating and assisting student-athletes with navigating the campus terrain. During orientation sessions, student affairs professionals should inform student-athletes of the different offices and services available for students (e.g., the career center, counseling services, ethnic cultural centers, disability services). As student affairs educators work with student-athletes, it is important for them to be flexible and creative when offering programming, counseling, and advising. In many cases, student-athletes are deeply engulfed in negotiating their academic and athletic roles. Meeting with student-athletes after practices and games, conducting meetings in residence halls, and counseling and advising via telephone are specific examples of ways to work within the time demands of this population.

Connecting Classroom Learning to Other Experiences

Lessons learned from athletic participation should not be undervalued. Teamwork, sacrifice, and discipline are just a few examples of what student-athletes learn from being actively involved in athletics. Student-athletes should be encouraged to apply the principles of teamwork in various non-athletic endeavors—collaborating with classmates on academic projects, working with students in clubs and organizations, and developing meaningful alliances with professors and staff on campus. Partnering with other groups not only expands student-athletes' campus networks, but also provides them with life-long interpersonal skills that are essential for post-collegiate professional success.

Enhancing the NCAA's CHAMPS/Life Skills programs (which exist in athletics departments across the country) would enable student-athletes to gain practical competencies that can be transferred to other environments. For example, a sexual awareness component added to a CHAMPS/Life Skills program can educate student-athletes about responsible sexual behaviors and sexually transmitted diseases/infections; this type of educational component can make student-athletes better equipped to make prudent decisions about their sexual conduct. A host of other topics can also be addressed: alcohol and substance abuse, gambling, communication skills, stress management, and financial planning. Although these programs are typically administered by athletic department personnel, student affairs educators and faculty should also be involved with the curriculum, implementation, and evaluation.

Self-Reflective Opportunities for Identity Development

Defining one's self-concept and identity are key tasks for college students at large. For student-athletes, a healthy identity is marked by recognition of various roles and responsibilities, such as student, athlete, friend, son, and engineer. Athletic department personnel, faculty, and student affairs staff should facilitate courses and seminars that focus exclusively on self-exploration and identity development. Creating spaces for student-athletes to assess their values, purpose, religious beliefs, and personal interests enables student-athletes to better understand themselves beyond the domain of college athletics. Discussions by former student-athletes to discuss some of their identity challenges, hardships with injuries, decision making, and overall maturation process through college would garner the attention and respect of student-athletes. This may be especially beneficial for ethnic minority student-athletes. Identifying a former African American student-athlete to talk about his or her experiences at a predominantly White institution would provide much-needed insight for African American student-athletes challenged with self-concept and identity conflicts. The presenters might also be available to serve as one-on-one mentors.

Enhancing Readiness for Future Roles

Student-athletes possess many attributes important to their success in future employment: commitment, confidence, team-building skills, and determination. However, a student-athlete career symposium can assist student-athletes with supplementary career guidance. This symposium should include a wide array of panels, presentations, and workshops conducted by former student-athletes, student affairs staff, representatives from various companies and professional organizations, and coaches. Résumé building, interviewing skills, and other professional skills should be addressed throughout the symposium. This event should be heavily marketed to all student-athletes, irrespective of sport or class standing. Additionally, faculty members should reach out to student-athletes to educate them about graduate school opportunities. A large majority of student-athletes are ignorant of GRE and graduate program application deadlines, financial resources, and the potential for assistantships. Awareness of this information, coupled with sound faculty mentorship, will enable more student-athletes to pursue postbacca-laureate academic opportunities.

Increasing Engagement with Diverse Others

Many student-athletes are comfortable with developing friendships, networks, and alliances only with their athletic peers. In most cases, student-athletes are not encouraged by coaches to integrate into the "mainstream" of the college or university—social networks, student-led clubs and organizations, faculty and staff functions, and various other forms of campus life. Athletic departments should mandate that student-athletes live in residence halls during their freshman and sophomore years. Student-athletes spend a significant amount of time together during practice, games, athletic-sponsored events, and study hall. Therefore, they should have exposure to other student groups and populations more frequently. Isolation from these other students encourages student-athletes to neglect their primary role as students. Exposure to diversity is an integral part of a student-athlete's overall growth and development. Leaders from Student-Athlete Advisory Councils (SAACs) should connect with leaders from other student groups to cre-ate forums, programs, and social gatherings that bring together student-athletes with students from the larger campus community. Including athletic administra-tors, faculty, and student affairs staff as active participants in these collaborations would also create a space for these groups to make meaningful professional connections.

Systematic Assessment

More research is needed regarding the emerging issues, trends, and outcomes pertaining to college student-athletes. Surveys, focus groups, and individual interviews should be conducted frequently by student affairs professionals, fac-ulty, and athletic department personnel. Survey respondents may report limited knowledge of various involvement opportunities on campus. Latina focus group respondents, for example, may indicate that a lack of diversity in student organiza-tions discourages their participation in out-of-class activities. Collecting these data is paramount to extending knowledge about student development and learning, engagement issues, barriers to retention, student welfare influences, and program-matic effectiveness. These data are also vital to the overall credibility of practice and policy.

Conclusion

Athletes are often told that sports participation is not just about winning and losing. However, I argue here that it is impossible to be a championship college or university if strategic efforts are not employed to ensure that every student-athlete has a winning season filled with developmental outcomes. Coaches, student affairs educators, and faculty must be willing to become teammates for success and collaborate in ways that confirm for spectators that student-athletes are in fact students first. The literature makes clear that these students often struggle to balance athletic, academic, and out-of-class engagement commitments. Therefore, institutional efforts must be enacted to create a culture of engagement within athletics departments that conveys high expectations for student participation in enriching educational experiences beyond their sports teams. Losers are the institutions that deprive student-athletes of the opportunities to acquire the skills and experiences that will enable them to compete successfully in roles after college. Even with its 107 national titles, the best championship that USC can ever win is that which ensures its student-athletes graduate with the most robust set of educational outcomes and competencies.

References

Adler, P., & Adler, P. A. (1987). Role conflict and identity salience: College athletics and the academic role. *Social Science Journal, 24*(4), 443–455.

Astin, A.W. (1993). *What matters in college? Four critical years revisited*. San Francisco: Jossey-Bass.

Benson, K. (2000). Constructing academic inadequacy: African American athlete's stories of schooling. *Journal of Higher Education, 71*(2), 223–246.

Brewer, W. B., Van Raalte, J. L., & Linder, D. E. (1993). Athletic identity: Hercules' muscles or Achilles' heel? *International Journal of Sport Psychology, 24*, 237–254.

Briggs, C. L. (1996). *Differences in degree aspirations and attainment outcomes between football and basketball players and other intercollegiate athletes*. Unpublished manuscript, Association for the Study of Higher Education, Memphis, TN.

Comeaux, E., & Harrison C. K. (2007). Faculty and male student athletes: Racial differences in the environmental predictors of academic achievement. *Race, Ethnicity and Education, 10*, 199–214.

Engstrom, C. M., & Sedlacek, W. E. (1993) Attitudes of residence hall students towards student-athletes: Implications for training, programming, and advising. *Journal of College and University Student Housing, 23*(1), 28–33.

Engstrom, C. M., Sedlack, W. E., & McEwen, M. K. (1995). Faculty attitudes toward male revenue and non-revenue student-athletes. *Journal of College Student Development 36*(3), 217–227.

Gaston-Gayles, J. (2003). Advising student athletes: An examination of academic support programs with high graduation rates. *National Academic Advising Association Journal, 23*(1), 50–57.

Goldberg, A. D., & Chandler, T. (1995). Sports counseling: Enhancing the development of the high school student-athlete. *Journal of Counseling & Development, 74*, 39–42.

Hood, A., Craig, A., & Ferguson, B. (1992). The impact of athletics, part-time employment, and other activities on academic achievement. *Journal of College Student Development, 33*, 447–453.

Howard-Hamilton, M. F., & Sina, J. A. (2001). How college affects student athletes. In M. F. Howard-Hamilton & S. K. Watt (Eds.), *Student services for athletes. New Directions for Student Services* (No. 93, pp. 51–58). San Francisco: Jossey-Bass.

Howard-Hamilton, M. F., & Watt, S. K. (Eds.) (2001). *Student services for athletes. New Directions for Student Services* (No. 93). San Francisco: Jossey-Bass.

Hurley, R. B. & Cunningham, R. L. (1984). Providing academic and psychological services for the college athlete. In A. Shriberg & F. R. Brodzinski (Eds.), *Rethinking services for college athletes. New Directions for Student Services* (No. 28, pp. 51–58). San Francisco: Jossey-Bass.

Hyatt, R. (2003). Barriers to persistence among African American intercollegiate athletes: A literature review of non-cognitive variables. *Journal of College Student Development, 37*(2), 260–276.

Lapchick, R. (2003). *Sweet sixteen men's teams fail to make the grade.* Orlando: University of Central Florida.

Leach, B., & Conners, B. (1984). Pygmalion on the gridiron: The Black student-athlete in a white university. In A. Shriberg & F. R. Brodzinski (Eds.), *Rethinking services for college athletes. New Directions for Student Services* (No. 28, pp. 31–49). San Francisco: Jossey-Bass.

Markus, H., & Wurf, E. (1987). The dynamic self-concept: A social psychological perspective. *Annual Review of Psychology, 38,* 299–337.

Martens, P., & Lee, F. (1998). Promoting life-career development in the student athlete: How can career centers help? *Journal of Career Development, 25,* 123–134.

Meyer, B. (1990). The academic performance of female collegiate athletes. *Sociology of Sport Journal, 7*(1), 44–57.

Miller, P. S., & Kerr, G. (2002). The athletic academic and social experiences of intercollegiate student-athletes. *Journal of Sport Behavior, 25*(4), 346–365.

National Collegiate Athletic Association (NCAA) (2006). *Report on careers in professional sports.* Indianapolis, IN: Author.

Nelson, E. S. (1982). The effect of career counseling on freshman college athletics. *Journal of Sport Psychology, 4*(1), 32–40.

Nishimoto, P. A. (1997). Touchdowns and term-papers: Telescoping the college student athlete culture. *College Student Affairs Journal, 16*(2), 97–103.

Pascarella, E. T., & Smart, J. C. (1991). Impact of intercollegiate athletic participation for African American and Caucasian men: Some further evidence. *Journal of College Student Development, 32,* 123–130.

Pascarella, E. T., Truckenmiller, R., Nora, A., Terenzini, P. T., Edison, M., & Hagedorn, L. C. (1999). Cognitive impacts of intercollegiate athletics participation. *Journal of Higher Education, 70*(1), 1–26.

Pearson, R. E., & Petitpas, A. J. (1990). Transitions of athletes: Developmental and preventive perspectives. *Journal of Counseling and Development, 69*(1), 7–10.

Perlmutter, D. (2003). Black athletes and White professor: A twilight zone of uncertainty. *Chronicle of Higher Education,* B7–B9.

Pinkerton, R. S., Hinz, L. D., & Barrow, J. C. (1989). The college student-athlete: Psychological considerations and interventions. *Journal of American College Health, 37,* 218–225.

Sedlacek, W. E. (1987). Black students on White campuses: 20 years of research. *Journal of College Student Personnel, 28*(6), 484–495.

Sedlacek, W. E. (2004). *Beyond the big test: Noncognitive assessment in higher education.* San Francisco: Jossey Bass.

Sedlacek, W. E., & Gaston, J. A. (1992). Predicting the academic success of student-athletes using SAT and non-cognitive variables. *Journal of Counseling & Development, 70,* 724–727.

Sellers, I. H., Sellers, R. M., & Damas, A. (2002). One role or two? The function of psychological separation in role conflict. *Journal of Applied Psychology, 87*(3), 574–582.

Sellers, R. M. (1992). Racial differences in the predictors of academic achievement for student-athletes in Division I revenue producing sports. *Sociology of Sport Journal, 9*(1), 48–60.

Shulman, J., & Bowen, W. (2001). *The game of life: College sport and educational values.* Princeton, NJ: Princeton University Press.

Simons, H. D., Van Rheenen, D. V., & Covington, M. B. (1999). Academic motivation and the student-athlete. *Journal of College Student Development, 40*(2), 151–161.

Smallman, E., & Sowa, C. J. (1996). Career maturity levels of male intercollegiate varsity athletes. *Career Development Quarterly, 24,* 236–239.

Steele, C. M. (1997). A threat in the air: How stereotypes shape intellectual identity and performance. *American Psychologist, 52*(6), 613–629.

Chapter 16

The Changing Landscape of Higher Education

Developmental Approaches to Engaging Emerging Populations

Kenechukwu (K.C.) Mmeje, Christopher B. Newman, Dennis A. Kramer II, and Mark A. Pearson

Over the past decade there has been a dramatic shift in the composition of undergraduate students attending college in the United States. Beginning in the late 1990s, and continuing into the early twenty-first century, the college student population is as diverse as it has ever been. Today, almost 25 percent of students are coming from underrepresented (African American, Latino/a, Asian American, and Native American) or disadvantaged backgrounds and more than 40 percent of the entire student enrollment is over the age of 24 (Saunders & Bauer, 1998). The increase of diversity in higher education has created new dynamics between and within student groups. More stringent admissions standards have resulted in decreased access and affordability for minority groups (Osei-Kofi & Rendón, 2005). This has forced many students to consider alternative educational settings.

The increase in White students at historically Black colleges and universities (HBCUs), the ongoing emergence of Hispanic-serving institutions (HSIs), and the proliferation of proprietary institutions has led to the emergence of new populations in higher education. The growth and prominence of these populations have placed a premium on understanding the cultural and environmental barriers preventing their engagement. These populations are in need of effective ways to enhance their postsecondary experience through social and academic engagement. Over the past 10 years, these three groups have solidified their place in higher education by continually increasing their presence (Hall & Closson, 2005; Conrad, Brier, & Braxton, 1997; Kinser, 2007; Stearns, Watanabe, & Snyder, 2002). The uniqueness of these populations warrants the formation of innovative engagement strategies—approaches that are not currently widely utilized in higher education. This chapter presents a summary of the existing literature on these student populations, an examination of each population within its unique institutional context, a theoretical framework for bringing about institutional change, and practical strategies for increasing student engagement.

White Students at HBCUs

> While both White and Black students overall expressed a level of comfort and support, White students lacked a sense of connection to the university and struggled with a sense of exclusion.
>
> (Hall & Closson, 2005, p. 40)

HBCUs have played a vital role in higher education, particularly as they relate to providing access and opportunity to higher education for the nation's disenfranchised African American community. Today, there are a total of 103 degree-granting HBCUs in the United States and many remain committed to their founding principles of educating a socially conscious and active African American citizenry. According to the U.S. Department of Education, HBCUs conferred 21.2 percent of all baccalaureate degrees awarded to African American students, 11.0 percent of all master's degrees, and 10.75 percent of all doctoral degrees in 2003 (National Center for Education Statistics, 2007). In recent years, HBCUs have experienced an increase in White student enrollment. In 2001, over 289,000 students were enrolled in the nation's HBCUs and White students accounted for 12 percent of the HBCUs' total enrollment (National Center for Education Statistics, 2001).

The increase in White student enrollments at HBCUs has prompted these institutions to re-examine their missions, curricula, programs, and delivery of services to ensure they meet the needs of all students. Specifically, White students at HBCUs face unique challenges associated with their "temporary minority status" that must be addressed if they are to become fully engaged in the college experience. These challenges include, but are not limited to, the following: academic, social, and cultural integration into an environment designed specifically for African American students; identification of positive role models/mentors that may or may not share their racial or ethnic background; overcoming feelings of exclusion and isolation; and understanding that their enrollment at an HBCU is a convenient means to earning a degree.

Enrollment Factors

In order to properly address the barriers that prevent White students from becoming fully engaged in the academic experience at HBCUs, it is important to understand the unique characteristics of this population and the factors that lead them to enroll at HBCUs. Elam (1978) and Hazzard's (1988) studies found the following characteristics to be common among White students at HBCUs: they were older than the traditional student age of 18 to 24 years, had dependents, had completed military obligations, were often transfer students, were employed, and attended part-time as commuters. Recent studies (Conrad, Brier & Braxton, 1997; Hall & Closson, 2005; Hazzard, 1988; Levinson, 2000) explore the factors that lead White students to enroll at HBCUs. According to the existing literature, White students enroll at HBCUs for the following reasons: cost, convenience, increased recruitment efforts by HBCUs, and availability of academic programs.

The cost of education continues to be an important consideration for most students when determining which college or university to attend. In today's market of high tuition and fees, HBCUs are becoming an increasingly cost-effective alternative to predominantly White institutions (PWIs), particularly for White low-income and first-generation college students (Wenglinsky, 1996, 1997). In addition to the low tuition set by many HBCUs, some HBCUs offer minority scholarships for White students.

Given that most White students enrolling at HBCUs are older than traditional college students, have dependents, and are employed (Hazzard, 1988), convenience is particularly important to this population when selecting a college or university. Most White students at HBCUs live in close proximity to their campus and they are often commuter students (Levinson, 2000). Typically, the perception is that White students at HBCUs come to campus simply to take classes and earn a degree as quickly as possible; rarely is this population engaged in other aspects of campus life.

In recent years, HBCUs have been the target of lawsuits challenging the practice of actively recruiting solely African American students. Most notably, the 1992 Supreme Court ruling in the *United States* v. *Fordice* sought to end the two-tiered (Black and White) higher education system that existed in many southern states. Many public institutions, particularly the nation's 38 public HBCUs, interpreted this ruling as a mandate to diversify their enrollment. Consequently, public HBCUs implemented desegregation compliance plans that included scholarships for White students, recruitment plans geared towards increasing White student enrollment, and minority support programs and services similar to those found for African American students enrolled at PWIs (Brown, 2002). The existence of special minority programs and services for White students at HBCUs has fueled the rise in White student enrollment.

The availability of a desired academic program is a significant factor in selecting a college or university for any student, and it is among the leading reasons White students are choosing to enroll at HBCUs (Conrad, Brier & Braxton, 1997; Hall & Closson, 2005). Conrad, Brier, and Braxton's 1997 study found that offering programs in high-demand fields was the single most important factor attracting Whites to HBCUs, especially among White graduate students at HBCUs. White students tend to enroll in the following academic programs at a higher rate: business, education, engineering, nursing, and public administration. In addition, White students cited alternative program delivery systems (weekend courses, evening courses, and off-campus courses) as a reason they chose to enroll at a HBCU. This finding is consistent with other research that suggests convenience is a driving factor for this population when deciding to enroll at HBCUs.

Barriers to White Student Engagement

Given what is known about White students who enroll at HBCUs, there are numerous potential barriers, such as parenting and work, that prevent them from becoming fully engaged in the student experience. The research cited above tells us that, in addition to being students, this population juggles other obligations that compete for their limited time. In many instances, they choose to enroll at an HBCU over a PWI simply because the HBCU offers them the convenience needed to earn a degree while managing other obligations. As a result, their circumstances do not afford them the opportunity to become fully engaged in the academic and co-curricular experience.

In Hall and Closson's 2005 study examining the experiences of Black and White graduate students at an HBCU, they found that despite overall feelings of comfort and support, White students lacked a sense of connection to the university. White respondents struggled with a sense of exclusion; however, they attributed their exclusion to social differences rather than racial differences. Research shows that if minority students are experiencing feelings of exclusion, or perceive the campus environment to be unwelcoming, they are less likely to persist towards degree completion or become involved in co-curricular activities (Nettles, 1991).

As mentioned earlier, HBCUs were founded specifically for the purposes of educating African American students, and therefore many of their services and programs were designed with that particular population in mind. In light of the recent influx of White student enrollment at HBCUs, support programs and services must be modified to meet the needs of the changing student population while also honoring the institutions' rich history and culture (Brown, 2002). Until the necessary changes are made, White students will not reap the full benefits of the collegiate experience.

Latino/a Students at HSIs

> The support and comfort that students experience while attending an institution where they feel at ease with other Latino students is commonly understood to be a benefit to students' college achievement.
>
> (Dayton, Gonzalez-Vasquez, Martinez, & Plum, 2004, p. 33)

Latino/a student enrollments at U.S. colleges and universities increased from 4 percent in 1980 to 10 percent of all students in 2002 (National Center of Education Statistics, 2007). This substantial increase in enrollment can partially be attributed to a demographic shift that occurred between the years of 1990 and 2000. The U.S. Latino/a population grew by nearly 10 million people in that time period (Llagas & Snyder, 2003). This demographic shift substantiates the relevance and importance of institutions seeking the federal designation of "Hispanic-Serving" under Title V, which the U.S. Department of Education defines as a non-profit institution that has at least 25 percent Latino/a full-time equivalent enrollment, 50 percent of which students must be considered low-income, as determined by the Census Bureau.

Often unintentionally, colleges and universities that were not founded to serve minority students qualified to apply for the classification of Hispanic-Serving. Stearns, Watanabe, and Snyder (2002) report that Latino/a college student enrollment increased from about 782,000 in 1990 to 1.3 million in 1999. As Latino/a student enrollment continues to grow, HSIs will play an increasingly significant role in providing not only equitable access to higher education, but also meaningful engagement.

Barriers to Latino/a Student Engagement

Cultural norms may create a ubiquitous conflict in Latino/a students' engagement. More specifically, the Hispanic ideology of putting the family before the individual may inhibit engagement (Dayton et al., 2004). This barrier is heightened by the fact that HSIs are typically located in areas with highly concentrated Latino/a populations such as California, Texas, New Mexico, and Puerto Rico. On one hand, it is very convenient for Latino/a students to remain in their parents' home while attending college; on the other hand, doing so may entail strict familial obligations (Saunders & Serna, 2004). Students often have to take care of siblings, grandparents, or children and work full-time or part-time to make a financial contribution to the household, which often impedes their ability to perform academically.

In addition, Latino/a students are often the first person in their family to go to college. These first-generation college students frequently do not receive adequate parental support. Latino/a parents typically lack social capital and are sometimes hesitant to apply for financial aid because of the intrusive nature of the required financial documentation; this phenomenon is especially true for parents whose official legal residency may be in question. Some HSIs have tried to alleviate this barrier by funding programs that support parental involvement of Latino/a students and provide financial aid resources and information. Laden (2001) asserts that "bilingual-bicultural counselors and faculty, outreach recruiters, and other program specialists" (p. 82) are very effective at bridging the gap with Latino/a parents by helping them "understand what a college education is and how it can increase their children's economic mobility" (p. 82). As a result of these programs, parents often become college advocates who motivate their children to go to college and provide the support needed for matriculation (Laden, 2001).

Aside from first-generation and parental support challenges, Latino/a students still must adjust to the unfamiliar social context of the ivory tower. Sidanius, Van Laar, Levin, and Sinclair (2004) state that minority ethnic organizations serve as "ethnic enclaves," which are characterized as a safe haven within a foreign or hostile environment. Many scholars have studied the correlation between ethnic organizations and the sense of institutional belonging (e.g., Hurtado & Carter, 1997, Sidanius et al., 2004). Research in this area has demonstrated that ethnic organizations support minority students as they negotiate adverse campus climates. Sidanius et al. (2004) found that "joining a minority ethnic organization in college was related not only to the degree of one's ethnic identity and intergroup bias, but also to the degree that one identifies with the larger, superordinate institution of the university" (p. 101). Students can avoid feelings of isolation and maintain their ethnic identity by joining the new social networks provided by ethnic organizations.

Ethnic organizations may indirectly give Latino/a students a sense of belonging to an institution, but engaging Latino/a students through educational role models is arguably the most effective strategy to realize success in the academy. Across many decades of research, communication scholars have identified several negative stereotypes of Latinos/as depicted in the mass media, where they are portrayed as poor, uneducated, criminals, buffoons, or hypersexual Latin lovers (Mastro & Greenberg, 2000). These stereotypes inevitably have a negative psychological impact on Latino/a students' self-perceptions. In serving as a counterbalance, Dayton et al. (2004) see the role of Latino/a faculty and staff as "ambassadors of comfort" for Latino/a students. This suggests that there should be substantially more role models in the classrooms and administrative offices who reflect the students themselves. These faculty and administrators are more likely to have a genuine understanding of and commitment to meeting Latino/a students' academic, cultural, and personal needs (Laden, 2001).

In contrast to HBCUs, where African Americans are the majority student population, Latino/a students at HSIs are typically not the majority on their campuses. Studying 2003 data from the National Survey of Student Engagement (NSSE), Nelson Laird, Bridges, Holmes, Morelon, and Williams (2004) found that Latino/a students at PWIs and HSIs had self-reported similar feelings of "supportive campus environments and satisfaction with college." One may conclude that the environments, experiences, climates, and opportunities that HSIs make available to their students are not distinctly different from those of a PWI. In examining the mission statements of HSIs, Contreras, Malcom, and Bensimon (2008) uncover a number of institutions' mission statements that do not contain "symbolic representation that call attention to their Hispanic-Serving identity," which may be a subconscious lack of commitment by the institution. The authors suggest that some HSIs may still be in the early developmental stages of their Hispanic-serving identity and that more time is needed for these institutions to fully embrace it. As Marin-Kennen and Aguilar (2005) suggest, institutions must go beyond being just "Hispanic enrolling institutions" to earn the title Hispanic-serving institutions.

Looking forward, researchers at the National Center for Education Statistics project that by the year 2050 the Latino/a population in the United States will reach nearly 100 million. This dramatic growth will result in Latinos/as making up 25 percent of the U.S. population, which is more than three times their population in 2003 (Llagas & Snyder, 2003). Furthermore, the 2006 *Digest of Education Statistics* reported that HSIs enrolled over 2.1 million students in 2005, of which 42.1 percent (approximately 912,675) were Latino/a. As Latino/a student populations steadily increase over the coming years, HSIs must continue to take positive steps toward fulfilling the needs of Latino/a students through purposeful planning and action.

> Digital technology is reshaping the nature of university outreach, extension, and engagement, providing the new opportunities and new challenges. (Duderstadt, Atkins, & Houweling, 2002, p. 74)

Historically, proprietary institutions have provided trade and occupational or vocational education to specialized student populations. The transformation of these privately controlled, for-profit entities into degree-granting institutions has prompted the emergence of a non-traditional student population. The combination of recent technological advances and the growing need for access to higher education has created a need for the convenience offered by proprietary institutions. Differences between for-profit institutions and a traditional college or university are easily visible when one examines the educational philosophy and business mission of each institutional type. Hawthorne (1995) states that traditional universities accept money to provide education and possess a mission to provide a quality education, whereas proprietary institutions are in the business of providing an education in order to receive money. Proprietary institutions have also been defined as "direct providers of learning opportunities for students" (Ryan, Scott, Freeman, & Patel, 2000, p. 2), which exist entirely in cyberspace without a physical location (Goldman & Hiltz, 2005). This lack of a physical space has been the largest contributor to the rapid increase in student enrollment. It is difficult to pinpoint the origin of these mass producers of online education (Weigel, 2002), but mention of corporate universities can be found as early as Fulton's (1969) study on corporate involvement in higher education. The most widely accepted version of the inception of the current proprietary model was the creation of DeVry University in 1991 (Ruch, 2001). This institution revolutionized corporate involvement in higher education and created a culture in which monetary gain was accepted in exchange for student learning.

The start of proprietary institutions instantly created an alternative access point to higher education for a large number of non-traditional students. The growth of for-profit education in the first decade of the twenty-first century is made evident by the half-million increase in student enrollment figures and the creation of more than 350 new virtual and physical campuses (Kinser, 2007). In addition, the National Center of Education Statistics (2001) reports that over 3.1 million students were enrolled in online universities in 2001, and the numbers continue to grow. Morey (2001) identified a fundamental shift in the educational paradigm as moving away from a teaching-centered model to one focused on learning. This shift has resulted in a decreased emphasis on courses and credits and placed more emphasis on student assessment. This change has weakened the reliance on class hours and progress towards degrees and, combined with the new technology, created forms of measuring student progress and teaching (Levine, 1997).

Institutional Barriers to Student Engagement

The core difference between proprietary institutions and traditional colleges and universities is that goal of the former is to obtain a better fiscal bottom line whereas the mission of the latter is the general acquisition and application of knowledge. In discussing the missions of proprietary institutions, Kelly (2001) quoted a proprietary institution's chief executive officer who stated that the purpose of his or her institution was to "number one, train them for careers; number two, get them jobs." With this mission in mind, proprietary institutions are marketing to a population that is career-driven and does not have the luxury of a flexible schedule that allows them to attend campus-based courses. Apling (1993) found that students attending proprietary institutions are significantly less likely to receive sufficient financial aid to cover the cost of tuition. This was later confirmed by Lingenfelter and Voorhees (2003). Inadequate financial assistance by the proprietary institutions has created a pressure-filled environment that promotes rapid degree completion. The combination of students looking to rapidly increase their earning potential (Collison, 1998), a shortened academic curriculum, and a lack of student services has led many to question the quality of education that students receive (Apling, 1993).

Finally, the levels of services integrated in the online student learning environments are continually proven to be deficient compared with their more traditional counterparts. Not only are there few student services present for online students, but these services fail to adequately meet students' needs (Westfall, 1991; Mehrotra, Hollister, & McGahey, 2001). For a positive online learning experience, it is imperative that fundamental training and access to the online teaching environments are provided. Areas that need improvement within the online learning environment are instructional support, communication, and institutional experience in designing effective online support mechanisms (Maor & Volet, 2007). In addition to variations in specialized services for online student learners, a study by May (2002) found that significant demographic differences (e.g., age, gender, socioeconomic status) exist between online student learners and traditional college students; however, the perceived need for services that would affect the collegiate experience was the same in both groups. Despite differences in student characteristics, there are fundamental services that are essential for a positive and meaningful postsecondary experience, and online learning environments are currently not providing them.

Social, Cultural and Interpersonal Barriers to Student Engagement

Marketing by proprietary institutions has been successful in recruiting students from disadvantaged backgrounds, the working population, and minority students who see these institutions as a way to gain employment (Collison, 1998; Levine 1997). Many of these students are first-generation college students who internalize the task of supporting their families financially (Collison, 1998). The combination of the institutional culture and internal pressures has led to the redefining of the relationships within proprietary learning environments. Evidence of the difference in engagement and role definition is seen in a study conducted by Levine (1997), which found that students attending proprietary institutions preferred their relationship with their course instructors to mirror the relationships they have with their banks, supermarkets, and quick service companies—convenient, accessible, high-quality, low-cost, and available on weekends and evenings.

Bolliger and Martindale (2004) found that traditional higher education students desire an interplay among student characteristics, faculty relationships, student life, support services, and instruction. In contrast, students at proprietary institutions who have difficulty making connections with their instructors and student services administrators are completely dependent on the reliability of online matter and access (Bolliger & Martindale, 2004; Apling, 1993). The lack of connection with faculty and interaction with peers has led to a decrease in educational effectiveness, student persistence, and overall student satisfaction (Zirkin & Sumler, 1995).

As access to higher education increases so will the prevalence of an online student population. Corporations will continue to market the opportunities that proprietary institutions provide, while not providing a traditional college experience. It is important to understand that many online learners are not looking for a traditional college experience, nor do they have the ability to alter their daily routine to engage in these activities. The tools for engaging this population will be found outside the traditional model. Research on engagement strategies and online student desires is limited. In order to create a platform of meaningful engagement strategies, empirical research is needed.

Theoretical Framework

To further understand the situation of White students at HBCUs, Latino/a students at HSIs, and distance learners in proprietary institutions, we frame our understanding by examining a specific organizational change theory, cultural change. The previous sections have described the rapid growth of these populations in different higher education settings. However, higher education institutions have not yet adapted to meet the needs of these emerging populations. It may be helpful to analyze cultural change theories in order to get a better understanding of how to meet the needs of these groups. This will shed light on the ability of higher education to address the needs of these emerging populations in an expeditious manner.

Theoretical Perspectives on Cultural Change

Cultural change theories help explain the organizational complexities of institutions, such as colleges and universities. They were initially developed to clarify the role of culture in organizations (Morgan, 1997). In later years, cultural change was used to elucidate organizational achievement (Chaffee & Tierney, 1988). Specific cultural change models have been created and integrated by scholars to explore complex issues facing higher education institutions (Berquist, 1992; Dawson, 1994; Kezar & Eckel, 2002; Tierney, 1991).

In general, higher education institutions focus on the advancement of institutional goals, education and research for the greater good, and progression for all humankind; attributes such as these distinguish higher education. These institutional attributes are ingrained in higher education and are at the core of cultural organizational values. In addition to values, higher education institutions are rich in traditions, beliefs, rites, myths, and rituals (culturally based institutional attributes). Organizational change within higher education institutions requires adjustments to values, traditions, beliefs, rites, myths, and rituals (Schein, 1985). As a result, conflict is inherent in cultural change; the various higher education constituencies that have been created to encompass culturally based institutional attributes can delay change through polarized views and conflicting perspectives. This struggle provides the discourse for change; it also reflects higher education's prodding nature and the political and social constructivist ideals that accompany cultural change. This dialectical component explains a cultural process that eventually elicits change. In turn, cultural change tends to be slow and long-term (Kezar, 2001). This notion can explain the phenomenon of higher education institutions' inability to expeditiously address the needs of emerging populations. In this regard, higher education institutions' culturally-based institutional attributes are a hindrance to the change process. Even though the dialectical process can hamper the progression of change, there are even greater obstacles to change in higher education institutions, including organizational history and leadership.

Similarly to culturally based institutional attributes, organizational history can also serve as an obstruction to change. Higher education institutions emphasize qualities that differentiate themselves from peer institutions. This is seen through culturally based institutional attributes, the most significant being the history of an institution. History not only details the significance of a particular institution, but also represents the process of change over time (Kezar, 2001). History equates to the linkages of stages in an organization's development (Clark, 1972). Consequently, the ability to implement change may be stifled by the same dialectical struggles that serve as a hindrance to expediting a change process or that cause regression in an organization's development. Additionally, institutional history contextualizes common experiences, perspectives, reflections, and rationales as well as worldviews and creates shared meaning for a specific group of people (Berquist, 1992). In this regard, a specific group of people can hinder change if the change is regarded as non-contiguous with the ideologies developed from institutional history. If the change process violates the cultural norms that have been created throughout an institution's history, the change may be viewed as inappropriate and the change process may be halted (Kezar & Eckel, 2002). It is important to understand that people affect and implement change. The multiple and diverse constituencies that make up a higher education institution function as change agents. If these change agents are unwilling to accommodate and implement change, it is often regarded as a failure in leadership; this is another impediment to the change process.

Leadership plays a vital role in expediting and implementing a change process. For a change to be effective and permanent, it is essential that it filter through all levels of an organization. From a cultural change perspective, culturally based institutional attributes can be manipulated to encourage organization-wide change (Kezar, 2001). Deep changes within higher education institutions require in-depth modifications to culturally based institutional attributes; leaders can positively or negatively affect this process. It is critical for leaders to interpret change into metaphors and culturally based language that is palatable for change agents and encourages the change process (Feldman, 1991). Leaders who focus on the spirit of an organization and the deeper organizational realities will help rechannel the energies of change agents. It is essential for people to relate to the reshaping of an institution's identity; higher education leaders must ensure that this relationship between the individual and the institution is brokered properly. Not doing so will result in unsuccessful change processes.

Cultural change theories share many suppositions about change with social cognition theories such as change being unfounded, unexpected, unintentional, continuing and dynamic (Smircich, 1983). Shared assumptions like these, combined with elements of dialectical change theories, create the sophistication of cultural change theories. It is difficult for one theory to explain the myriad of complexities and critical issues that higher education institutions face. However, cultural change theories have managed to evolve and incorporate integrated organization theory approaches that appropriately explicate critical issues of change, or lack thereof, in higher education institutions. If nothing else, cultural change theories serve as a lens for higher education institutions to examine and rethink current paradigms and practices in order to properly address and accommodate the emerging populations such as those mentioned in this chapter.

Cultural change theorists (Schein, 1985; Smircich, 1983; Morgan, 1997) assert that change is hindered by an organization's own customs, rites, culture, routines, systems, and values. It is these institutional barriers to change that are entrenched in the foundation of the organizations and explain the undercurrent of why organizations are the way they are. Change strategies aimed at encountering these organizational, philosophical, structural, and procedural issues are forward-thinking in nature; this resonates well with planned change strategies. These strategies have roots in organizational development and are currently used as "scientific management" techniques and measures. To this end, we offer in the next section recommendations through five distinct planned change lenses: (1) focus on the vision, mission, and desired outcomes of the institution, (2) encouragement of creative and supportive leadership, (3) retraining of individuals on an ongoing basis or implementation of systemic individual professional development, (4) data-driven decisions, and (5) the ensuring of collaboration (Kezar, 2001).

Engagement Strategies

Focus on the Vision, Mission and Outcome of the Institution

⬦ HBCUs must perform a comprehensive review of their mission statements, curricula, delivery of services, and publications to ensure they are inclusive, welcoming, and representative of all students. HBCUs' mission statements should clearly state their commitment to providing educational access and opportunity to African American students while also acknowledging their commitment to educating all students regardless of race (and other protected identities). If HBCUs fail to acknowledge White students' existence in the campus community, White students are less likely to feel a connection to the campus, and therefore are less likely to become fully engaged in the collegiate experience.

◇ HSIs must reframe their mission statements to include serving Latinos/as and minorities. Additionally, an "evaluative metric of equity in educational outcomes for Latinos/as" is needed to ensure that HSIs are fulfilling their commitment to serve Latino/a students (Contreras et al., 2008).

◇ As stated in Hawthorne (1995), the difference between a proprietary institution and a traditional college or university is that traditional universities accept money to provide education and have a mission to provide a quality education, whereas proprietary institutions provide an education in order to receive money and are in the business of providing education. Corporate-owned educational entities are concerned with fiscal profit and not with the overall educational enjoyment their students receive. In order to better engage proprietary students, it is important for federal governmental subsidies to ease the pressures on these institutions to make a profit. Such subsidies can also be utilized to institute regulations that mandate student support services, professional development, and continual assessment of faculty, student, and social interactions.

Creative and Supportive Leadership

◇ HBCUs must develop minority affairs offices designed to serve White students. Among this office's priorities should be the following: providing culturally relevant academic and co-curricular programming for White students; providing ongoing campus-wide diversity education, specifically as it relates to promoting multicultural awareness and cross-cultural interaction/dialogue; and last, but certainly not least, providing individual advising/intervention for White students as needed. Ideally, this type of office would be situated within the division of student affairs, but would work collaboratively with faculty and student organizations. It is important to also acknowledge that not all White students might feel comfortable accessing a minority affairs office or minority services.

◇ In an effort to promote White student involvement in co-curricular activities, HBCUs should provide alternative programming designed to meet their needs. Considering that most White students at HBCUs commute to campus, and typically do not stay on campus during the evening hours, HBCUs should offer more programming options during the day. Unlike traditional co-curricular offerings, alternative programming for White students at HBCUs should be academic and career-oriented. Additionally, HBCUs should encourage and support White students in the development of culturally based student organizations.

◇ Administrators at HSIs must encourage students to participate in ethnic organizations and must provide mentorship for these organizations. This involvement not only will increase students' sense of belonging to the institution, but will strengthen the community the organizations serve.

◇ Bilingual financial aid counselors are needed to bridge the gap between Latino/a parents and their children who are first-generation college students. The financial aid process is intimidating, but a caring and sensitive counselor can help demystify procedures.

◇ HSIs should increase parental involvement beyond the first-year parent orientation. The more parents understand their children's collegiate experience, the better equipped they will be to support and encourage them through their journey.

◇ Kelly (2001) shows that the majority of the leaders of proprietary institutions are members of the corporate environment. Educational administrators, and student affairs administrators in particular, are often absent from management teams that decide the desired outcomes for online learning environments. It is important to begin bridging the gap between proprietary and traditional institutions and to create dialogue between student affairs divisions and the management of proprietary institutions. This dialogue can lead to the dissemination of information regarding the importance of engaging student populations and the exchange of ideas.

Professional Development and Ongoing Training

◇ HBCUs should provide ongoing diversity training for faculty and staff to ensure that they are well equipped to deal with the unique challenges facing White students. Given that the majority of faculty and staff at HBCUs are African American, it is especially important that they are willing to mentor and advise White students.

◇ Dayton et al. (2004) note that, whatever the racial makeup of faculty and staff, the "ethic of caring" is of greater importance. This suggests that HSIs can enact positive change by providing diversity training for both faculty and staff, which will help both groups understand the lives of Latino/a students.

◇ Maor and Volet (2007) found that insufficient technical knowledge and a low level of preparedness have a significant effect on course completion in an online setting. It is important for proprietary administrators and course facilitators to assess students' technical abilities and tailor the course requirements to ensure assignments are within the realm of the students' abilities. Additionally, students entering proprietary online settings should be mandated to complete a "training course" as a prerequisite before registering for subsequent online courses. This fundamental training will allow students to focus on learning the subject matter instead of learning how to operate the online apparatus.

Data-Driven Decision Making

◇ HBCUs must recruit, hire, and retain White faculty, staff, and administrators. In order for White students to feel fully integrated in the campus community, they must see themselves represented at all levels of the institution, particularly the classroom. White faculty are particularly well positioned to serve as mentors and role models for White students at HBCUs. In addition, White students are more likely to disclose feelings of isolation and exclusion to White faculty and staff. Oftentimes, such diversity initiatives must be supported by the highest levels of leadership within the institution (usually the president or provost) in order to have any validity.

◇ Latino/a faculty members can have positive impacts on the retention and matriculation of Latino/a students. Therefore, it is a matter of paramount importance that HSIs seek to recruit and hire diverse faculty. In addition, a sustainable "pipeline" of Latino/a students interested in eventually becoming faculty themselves is needed, so we recommend shifting resources to promote undergraduate research projects and graduate school preparation programs and workshops.

Ensure Collaboration

◇ The most essential collaboration needed within the HSI community is for four-year institutions to strengthen their involvement with local two-year institutions by maintaining communication and outreach efforts, which will ensure access to four-year colleges and universities through the successful transfer of two-year college graduates.

◇ Four-year HSIs must also reach out to regional high schools by sponsoring visits to school campuses and sending institutional representatives and current students to share pertinent information and their experiences. Such outreach demonstrates an active commitment by the institution; as a result, the high school students will feel welcomed by the college or university and will be more likely to seek admission.

◇ HSIs should use their federal funding to sponsor initiatives similar to the California State University, Northridge, Latino/a Library Collection Project. This project was founded to increase Latino/a students' library use and to sharpen students' research skills by expanding its collection of library materials related to "Latino history, social sciences and culture" (Solis & Dabbour, 2006).

◈ Social networks have become a popular way for the college population to connect with their peers (Bugeja, 2006). Utilizing the same technology, proprietary institutions need to create access points where virtual students can gather and student organizations can form. Muilenburg and Berge (2005) found that a lack of social interaction was a barrier not only to course enjoyment but also to course completion. Providing students at proprietary institutions with the opportunity to network virtually will allow them to create social connections, which will increase their overall satisfaction with their educational experience and increase the likelihood of persistence.

◈ Building on the access to social networking, it is imperative that the ability to collaborate and connect also occur during academic activities. Nicol, Minty, and Sinclair (2003) found that online communication is *asynchronous* (having breaks in the conversations or interactions), which leads to a significantly lower level of social learning and a decrease in pressure to participate in discussion. Online facilitators must provide "real-time" collaborative learning opportunities, in which online students' dialogue can be continuous for a sustainable amount of time. This will allow online communication to resemble a face-to-face conversation and increase participation in online discussions. Sharon (1990) found that collaborative learning has led to an increase in material mastery and retention along with transference of knowledge and strategies for reasoning.

Conclusion

Understanding newer and emerging populations in higher education will enable administrators, faculty, and staff to produce an environment that is conducive to positive student development. Even though these emerging populations exist in distinct environments, they share many commonalities in the barriers they face. Members of these populations often face educational engagement barriers, such as being the first member of the family to attend college, being an older student, or working a job off campus while trying to navigate a way through college. Each of these populations is new to the system of higher education and has emerged as a direct result of a need for increased access to higher education. The overall student desire for admission into higher education has grown exponentially in the past decade, and it is more important than ever before for postsecondary institutions to provide a quality education that fosters both academic intellect and personal growth.

The system of higher education can no longer ignore the needs of these populations. A fundamental need exists for academic and career services. In addition, these populations share the need for faculty, staff, and administrators who understand the unique barriers to their engagement. It is important that universities begin to refine their campus cultures in such ways that they provide understanding for all populations. Such adaptations of culture can result when universities take the initiative to reshape their educational missions and values to include a dedication to engage all populations on campus. In addition, universities must display a devotion to this new mission through the hiring of faculty, staff, and administrators who can serve as role models for these populations. These role models will serve as agents for connecting students to campus entities that offer opportunities for dialogue and support.

As illustrated in this chapter, there is an inherent need for additional research to be conducted on these emerging populations and on effective strategies for engaging them in their educational environments. Although these populations are relatively new within the higher education system, it is important that universities begin the process of planned change to ensure that they are engaged effectively. Using the cultural change framework, higher education administrators will be able to use the effective strategies currently in place and continue to develop efficient programs through constant assessment. The goal of all institutions of higher education should be the ability to provide a postsecondary experience that engages all student populations. Effective engagement strategies will increase not only students' academic persistence, but also their overall satisfaction with their collegiate experience. As higher education opens its doors to an increasingly diverse population it is important that its programs service effectively the increasing diversity of student needs.

References

Apling, R. N. (1993). Proprietary schools and their students. *Journal of Higher Education, 64*(4), 379–416.

Berquist, W. (1992). *The four cultures of the academy.* San Francisco: Jossey-Bass.

Bolliger, D. U., & Martindale, T. (2004). Key factors for determining student satisfaction in online courses. *International Journal of E-Learning, 3*(1), 61–68.

Brown, C. (2002). Good intentions: Collegiate desegregation and transdemographic enrollments. *Review of Higher Education, 25*(3), 263–280.

Bugeja, M. (2006). Facing the facebook. *Chronicle of Higher Education, 52*(21), C1.

Chaffee, E., & Tierney, W. G. (1988). *Collegiate culture and leadership strategies.* New York: Macmillan.

Clark, B. (1972). The organizational saga in higher education. *Administrative Science Quarterly, 17*(2), 178–184.

Collison, M. N. K. (1998). Proprietary preference. *Black Issues in Higher Education, 15*(10), 31–32.

Conrad, C., Brier E., & Braxton, J. (1997). Factors contributing to the matriculation of White students in public HBCUs. *Journal for a Just & Caring Education, 3*(1), 37–62.

Contreras, F. E., Malcom, L. E., & Bensimon, E. M. (2008). Hispanic serving institutions: Closeted identity and the production of equitable outcomes for Latino/a students. In M. Gasman, B. Baez, & C. S. V. Turner (Eds.), *Understanding Minority Serving Institutions* (pp. 71–90). Albany, NY: SUNY Press.

Dawson, P. (1994). *Organizational change: A processual approach.* London: Paul Chapman.

Dayton, B., Gonzalez-Vasquez, N., Martinez, C. R., & Plum, C. (2004). Hispanic-serving Institutions through the eyes of students and administrators. In A. Ortiz (Ed.), *Addressing the unique needs of Latino American students. New Directions for Student Services* (No. 105, pp. 29–40). San Francisco: Jossey-Bass.

Duderstadt, J., Atkins, D., & Houweling, D. (2002). *Higher education in the digital age: Technology issues and strategies for American colleges and universities.* Westport, CT: Praeger.

Elam, A. (1978). Two sides of the coin: White students in black institutions. *Journal of the NAWDAC, 16,*

57–61.

Feldman, M. (1991). The meanings of ambiguity: Learning from stories and metaphors. In P. J. Frost, L. F. Moore, M. R. Louis, C. C. Lundberg, & J. Martin (Eds.), *Reframing organizational culture* (pp. 146–156). Newbury Park, CA: Sage.

Fulton, R. A. (1969). Proprietary schools. In R. L. Ebel (Ed.), *Encyclopedia of Educational Research* (4th ed., pp. 1022–1027). New York: Macmillan.

Goldman, R., & Hiltz, S. (2005). Asynchronous learning networks: Looking back and looking forward. In S. Hiltz & R. Goldman (Eds.), *Learning together online: Research on asynchronous learning networks* (pp. 261–280). Mahwah, NJ: Lawrence Erlbaum Associates.

Hall, B., & Closson, R. (2005). When the majority is the minority: White graduate students' social adjustment at a historically Black university. *Journal of College Student Development, 46*(1), 28–42.

Hawthorne, E. M. (1995). Proprietary schools and community colleges: The next chapter. In D. A. Clowes & E. M. Hawthorne (Eds.), *Community colleges and proprietary schools: Conflict or convergence? New Directions for Community Colleges* (No. 91, pp. 93–98). San Francisco: Jossey-Bass.

Hazzard, T. (1988). *Attitudes and perceptions of White students attending Historically Black Colleges and Universities.* Unpublished manuscript, Florida State University.

Hurtado, S., & Carter, D. F. (1997). Effects of college transition and perception of the campus racial climate on Latino college students' sense of belonging. *Sociology of Education, 70*, 324–345.

Kelly, K. F. (2001). *The rise of for-profit degree-granting institutions: Policy considerations for states.* Denver, CO: Education Commission of the States.

Kezar, A. J. (2001). *Understanding and facilitating organizational change in higher education: Recent research and conceptualizations.* ASHE-ERIC Higher Education Report (Vol. 28, No. 4). San Francisco: Jossey-Bass.

Kezar, A. J., & Eckel, P. D. (2002). The effect of institutional culture on change strategies in higher education: Universal principles or culturally responsive concepts? *Journal of Higher Education, 73*(4), 435–460.

Kinser, K. (2007). Dimensions of corporate ownership in for-profit higher education. *Review of Higher Education, 30*(3), 217–245.

Laden, B. V. (2001). Hispanic-serving institutions: Myths and realities. *Peabody Journal of Education, 76*(1), 73–92.

Levine, A. (1997). How the academic profession is changing. *Daedalus, 126*, 1–20.

Levinson, A. (2000). As different as day and night: Missouri's historically Black Lincoln University, now predominantly White, searches for a way to bring its two divergent populations together. *Black Issues in Higher Education, 16*(23), 30.

Lingenfelter, P. E., & Voorhees, R. (2003). *Adult learners and state policy.* Denver: SHEEO/CAEL.

Llagas, C., & Snyder, T. D. (2003). *Status and trends in the education of Hispanics.* Washington, DC: U.S. Department of Education, National Center for Education Statistics.

Maor, D., & Volet, S. (2007). Engagement in professional online learning: A situative analysis of media professionals who did not make it. *International Journal of E-Learning, 6*(1), 95–118.

Marin-Kennen, E., & Aguilar, W. (2005). Defining Hispanic-serving institutions and living up to the definition. *Hispanic Outlook in Higher Education, 15*(21), 27–35.

Mastro, D. E., & Greenberg, B. S. (2000). The portrayal of racial minorities on prime time television. *Journal of Broadcasting & Electronic Media, 44*(4), 690–703.

May, M. (2002). A comparative study on student satisfaction with the provision of student services in traditional and web-based environments. Doctoral dissertation, Kent State University. *Dissertation Abstracts International, 60*, 3129.

Mehrotra, C. M., Hollister, C. D., & McGahey, L. (2001). *Distance learning: Principles for effective design, delivery and evaluation.* Thousand Oaks, CA: Sage Publications.

Morey, A. (2001). The growth of for-profit in higher education. *Journal of Teacher Education, 52*(4), 300–317.

Morgan, G. (1997). *Images of organization* (2nd edn.). Thousand Oaks, CA: Sage.

Muilenberg, L. Y., & Berge, Z. (2005). Student barriers to online learning: A factor analytic study. *Distance Education, 26*(1), 29–48.

National Center for Education Statistics (2001). *The condition of education 2001.* Washington, DC: U.S. Department of Education.

National Center for Education Statistics (2007). *Digest of education statistics, 2004.* Washington, DC: U.S.

Department of Education.

Nelson Laird, T. F., Bridges, B. K., Holmes, M. S., Morelon, C. L., & Williams, J. M. (2004). African American and Hispanic student engagement at minority serving and predominantly White institutions. Paper presented at the annual meeting of the Association for the Study of Higher Education, Kansas City, MO.

Nettles, M. T. (1991). Racial similarities and differences in the predictors of college student achievement. In W. R. Allen, E. G. Epps, & N. Z. Haniff (Eds), *College in Black and White: African American students in predominantly White and in historically Black public universities* (pp. 95–110). Albany, NY: SUNY Press.

Nicol, D. J., Minty I., & Sinclair, C. (2003). The social dimensions of online learning. *Innovations in Education and Teaching International, 40*(3), 270–280.

Osei-Kofi, N. & Rendón, L. (2005). Latinos, higher education, and the "needs" of the market. *Latino Studies, 3*, 249–260.

Ruch, R. S. (2001). *The rise of for-profit university.* Baltimore: Johns Hopkins University Press.

Ryan, S., Scott, B., Freeman, H., & Patel, D. (2000). *The virtual university: The internet and resource-based learning.* London: Kogan Page.

Saunders, L. E., & Bauer, K. W. (1998). Undergraduate students today: Who are they? In K. W. Bauer (Ed.), *Campus climate: Understanding the critical components of today's colleges and universities. New Directions for Institutional Research* (No. 98, pp. 7–16). San Francisco: Jossey-Bass.

Saunders, M., & Serna, I. (2004). Making college happen: The college experiences of first-generation Latino students. *Journal of Hispanic Higher Education, 3*(2) 146–163.

Schein, E. (1985). *Organizational culture and leadership: A dynamic view.* San Francisco: Jossey-Bass.

Sharon, S. (Ed.) (1990). *Cooperative learning: Theory and research.* New York: Praeger.

Sidanius, J., Van Laar, C., Levin, S., & Sinclair, S. (2004). Ethnic enclaves and the dynamics of social identity on the college campus: The good, the bad, and the ugly. *Journal of Personality and Social Psychology, 87*(1), 96–110.

Smirich, L. (1983). Concepts of culture and organizational analysis. *Administrative Science Quarterly, 28*(3), 339–358.

Solis, J., & Dabbour, K. S. (2006). Latino students and libraries: A U.S. federal grant project. *New Library World, 107*(1/2), 48–57.

Stearns, C., Watanabe, S., & Snyder, T.D. (2002). *Hispanic serving institutions: Statistical trends from 1990–1999* (NCES 2002-051). Washington, DC: National Center for Education Statistics, U.S. Department of Education.

Tierney, W. G. (1991). Organizational culture in higher education: Defining the essentials. *Journal of Higher Education, 59*(1), 2–21.

Weigel, V. (2002). *Deep learning for a digital age: Technology's untapped potential to enrich higher education.* San Francisco: Jossey-Bass.

Wenglinsky, H. H. (1996). Educational justification of historically black colleges and universities: A policy response to the U.S. Supreme Court. *Educational Evaluation and Policy Analysis, 18*, 91–103.

Wenglinsky, H. H (1997). *Students at historically black colleges and universities: Their aspirations and accomplishments.* Princeton, NJ: Educational Testing Service.

Westfall, B. (1991). *The development and implementation of an academic and non-academic support system for distance learners at Brandon University.* Unpublished doctoral dissertation, Nova University.

Zirkin, B., & Sumler, D. (1995). Interactive or non-interactive? That is the question: An annotated bibliography. *Journal of Distance Education, 10*(1), 95–112.

Afterword

Occasionally an idea comes along that clarifies complicated matters and suggests approaches for managing fundamental problems in higher education: Student engagement is one of those ideas. The engagement premise is straightforward. The more students study a subject, the more they learn about it. Similarly, the more students practice and get feedback from faculty and staff members on their writing, speaking, and collaborative problem solving, the more adept they become at those skills. Being engaged in a variety of educationally productive activities also builds the foundation of skills and dispositions people need to live a productive, satisfying life after college. In other words, engagement helps students to develop habits of the mind and heart that enlarge their capacity for continuous learning and personal development.

The importance of engagement has been documented in the literature for decades, with its meaning evolving over time. One of the earliest iterations was the pioneering work of the eminent educational psychologist Ralph Tyler, which showed the positive effects of time-on-task on learning. In the 1970s, drawing on 30 years of his own research, C. Robert Pace developed the College Student Experiences Questionnaire, which framed the construct as quality of effort. Alexander Astin popularized the concept with his theory of involvement. Many other scholars, such as Ernest Pascarella, Patrick Terenzini, and Vincent Tinto, have contributed scores of papers addressing different dimensions of the engagement concept and its relationship to various desired outcomes of college. And, as noted by the contributors to this volume, in recent years the term *engagement* has been firmly established in the higher education lexicon, in large part because of the widespread use of the National Survey of Student Engagement (NSSE) (Kuh, 2003). The relevance of engagement has been noted by the popular media as well, and it is often mentioned in stories about selecting a college and about the accountability and assessment movement.

Although it is gratifying that the importance of engagement is now widely embraced (this timely volume is additional evidence), like other constructs it can be misused and misinterpreted. Indeed, popular concepts often lead to a hegemonic, one-size-fits-all way of thinking. For example, a one-size-fits-all mentality has had a stranglehold on our theorizing and research about student development and success. For years, researchers and policymakers tended to focus on large-scale studies because the results were thought to be generalizable across institutions and students. As the contributors to this volume make plain, given the increasing diversity of college students today, it is erroneous to presume that what works in one setting for certain students will have the same effects in other settings for different types of students. Because institutional contexts differ, students' experiences will differ, as will what they get out of college.

To illustrate, from an analysis of NSSE data, we found that at Hispanic-serving institutions where Hispanics made up at least 10 percent of the faculty, Hispanic students interacted more often with faculty members and participated more frequently in active and collaborative learning activities and enriching educational experiences, such as community service, compared with their counterparts at HSIs with lower percentages of Hispanic faculty or at predominantly White institutions (Bridges, Kinzie, Nelson Laird, & Kuh, 2008). This finding is consistent with other research showing that minority faculty members are more likely to use effective educational practices than are White faculty members (Kuh, Nelson Laird, & Umbach, 2004). It is also reminiscent of Outcalt and Skewes-Cox's (2002) observation of the importance of "reciprocal engagement"— the idea that student involvement and campus environmental conditions coexist in a mutually shaping relationship to support student success at HBCUs.

In addition, there is mounting evidence that although engagement in effective educational practices generally benefits all students, the more pronounced effects tend to be conditional and sometimes compensatory (Cruce, Wolniak, Seifert, & Pascarella, 2006; Kuh, Cruce, Shoup, Kinzie, & Gonyea, in press; Pascarella & Terenzini, 2005). Conditional effects represent differences in the amount of change or development or learning of one group of students relative to other groups. As Pascarella and Terenzini (2005) explained about conditional effects, "Finding that, say, women change significantly in one direction or another while men do not is different from determining whether the differences in the *degree of change* for women and men are statistically significant" (p. 324).

Research on compensatory effects indicates that students who may start college underprepared in one or more areas benefit even more than their relatively advantaged peers by participating in certain programs or practices. For example, Kuh et al. (in press) found that taking into account a global measure of engagement (a composite score based on 18 items from the National Survey of Student Engagement) boosted to a small degree the first-year GPA of students who entered college with lower levels of academic achievement. Specifically, students with an ACT score of 20 realized an increase in GPA of 0.06 for every standard deviation increase in their participation in educationally purposeful activities, net of background characteristics. Students with an ACT score of 24 realized only about 0.04 point GPA advantage for the same increase in engagement; students with a 28 ACT score had an advantage of only 0.02 points. Similarly, a one standard deviation increase in student engagement resulted in about 0.11 advantage in first-year GPA for Hispanic students compared with only 0.03 benefit for White students.

Engagement has conditional effects on persistence as well. Here, too, the more engaged a student is, generally speaking, the more likely the student is to return to the same school for the second year of study, net of background characteristics including previous academic achievement. But African American students seem to benefit more than White students from increasing their engagement in educationally effective activities (Kuh et al., in press). That is, although African American students at the lowest levels of engagement are less likely to persist than their White counterparts, as their engagement increases to within about one standard deviation below the mean, they have about the same probability of returning as Whites. As African American student engagement reaches the average level, those students became more likely than White students to return for a second year.

These are but two examples (Pascarella & Terenzini, 2005, discuss many more) of areas in which the impact of college as represented by differing levels of participation in educationally purposeful activities has conditional effects. How and why these practices work in different institutional settings with different types of students is discussed by others (Chickering & Gamson, 1987; Chickering & Reisser, 1993; Dayton, Gonzalez-Vasquez, Martinez, & Plum, 2004; Education Commission of the States, 1995; Fleming, 1984; Kuh, Douglas, Lund, & Ramin-Gyurnek, 1994; Kuh, Kinzie, Schuh, Whitt, & Associates, 2005; Kuh, Schuh, Whitt, & Associates, 1991; Outcalt & Skewes-Cox, 2002; Pascarella & Terenzini, 2005; Watson et al. 2002). Other promising practices specific to particular groups or activities are also available, such as working with adult learners (Cook & King, 2005), undergraduate teaching and learning (Sorcinelli, 1991), developmental education for underprepared students (Boyland, 2002), and student affairs work (Blimling & Whitt, 1999). We will almost certainly learn more about these matters from such initiatives as Achieving the Dream, an initiative funded by the Lumina Foundation for Education that is focused primarily on the enrollment by two-year and community colleges of large numbers of students from low-income and racial/ethnic minority backgrounds.

The results of the research I briefly summarize here, along with the other chapters in this volume, strongly suggest that faculty and staff should continue to refine as well as develop additional promising approaches to channel student energy toward educationally effective activities. This is especially important for those students who start college with certain "risk" factors—such as being academically underprepared, or first in their families to go to college, or from low-income backgrounds. Even though some students may benefit more than others from exposure to certain effective educational practices, it behooves faculty and staff to create opportunities for all students to participate in what research from NSSE and other quarters indicate are "high impact" practices (Association of American Colleges and Universities, 2007).

These include learning communities, student–faculty research, service-learning, internships, study abroad, and capstone seminars or other culminating experiences. These practices tend to have greater effects because they require students to take responsibility for activities that require daily decisions and tasks; as a result, students become more invested in the activity and more committed to the college and their studies. The use of these and other effective educational practices more frequently throughout the institution may help compensate for shortcomings in students' academic preparation and help create a culture that fosters student success (Allen, 1999).

Similarly, advisors, counselors, and others who are in routine contact with students must persuade or otherwise induce them to get involved with one or more of these kinds of activities or with a faculty or staff member. Academic advisors can use some of their time with students to explain the advantages of engagement and encouraging them to become involved with peers in campus events and organizations and invest effort in educational activities known to promote student learning and development (Braxton & McClendon, 2002; Kuh et al., 2005; Kuh, Kinzie, Buckley, Bridges, & Hayek, 2007). However, simply offering programs based on promising practices does not guarantee that they will have the intended effects on student success; institutional programs and practices must be of high quality, customized to meet the needs of students they are intended to reach, and firmly rooted in a student success-oriented campus culture (Kuh et al., 2005). Therefore, colleges and universities must ensure that interconnected learning support networks, early warning systems, and safety nets are in place and working as intended.

There is, of course, much more to learn about how engagement of different groups of students in different educational settings affects student success. As with between- and within-institution differences on measures such as NSSE, the variance within any group of students, such as men and women or African Americans and Latinos/as, is almost certainly going to be greater than variation between the groups. That is, although it may appear that on average students in one group seem to benefit more from certain practices or experiences, it is also the case that many students within the group that appears to have the advantage benefit much less than the average student in the lower-performing group. Our penchant for focusing on what are often small, albeit statistically significant, differences between groups ignores this fact. It would be especially instructive if scholars would focus on within-group differences to the same extent as they do between-group differences in order to determine whether there are other variables that help explain why such differences exist and attempt to tease out the elements of programs and practices that are particularly effective with lower-performing students. Only then are we likely to increase the numbers of students who engage at meaningful levels in purposeful educational activities, attain their educational and personal objectives, and acquire the skills and competencies demanded by the challenges of the twenty-first century.

I salute the editors and contributors to this volume for focusing on ways to engage students from historically underserved backgrounds. As is almost always the case, learning more about the undergraduate experiences of different types of students raises additional questions and points to issues that, if properly addressed, will yield insights that can be adapted to enhance student learning and personal development for all students. I hope the scholars and experienced administrators whose thoughtful work appears in this volume and those who read it direct some of their time and expertise toward these important ends.

George D. Kuh

Chancellor's Professor and Director, Center for Postsecondary Research,

Indiana University

References

Association of American Colleges and Universities (2007). *College learning for the new global century.* Washington, DC: Association of American Colleges and Universities.

Allen, D. (1999). Desire to finish college: An empirical link between motivation and persistence. *Research in Higher Education, 40,* 461–85.

Blimling, G. S., & Whitt, E. J. (1999). Identifying the principles that guide student affairs practice. In G. S. Blimling & E. J. Whitt (Eds.), *Good practice in student affairs: Principles to foster student learning* (pp. 1–20). San Francisco: Jossey-Bass.

Boyland, H. R. (2002). *What works: A guide to research-based best practices in developmental education.* Boone, NC: Appalachian State University, Continuous Quality Improvement Network and the National Center for Developmental Education.

Braxton, J. M., & McClendon, S. A. (2002). The fostering of social integration and retention through institutional practice. *Journal of College Student Retention: Research, Theory & Practice, 3*(1), 57–71.

Bridges, B. K., Kinzie, J., Nelson Laird, T. F., & Kuh, G. D. (2008). Student engagement and student success at Historically Black and Hispanic serving institutions. In M. Gasman, B. Baez, & C. S. V. Turner (Eds.), *Understanding minority serving institutions* (pp. 217–36). Albany, NY: SUNY Press.

Chickering, A. W., & Gamson, Z. F. (1987). Seven principles for good practice in undergraduate education. *AAHE Bulletin, 39,* 3–7.

Chickering, A. W., & Reisser, L. (1993). *Education and identity.* San Francisco: Jossey-Bass.

Cook, B., & King, J. E. (2005). *Improving lives through higher education: Campus programs and policies for low-income adults.* Washington, DC: Lumina Foundation for Education and American Council on Education Center for Policy Analysis.

Cruce, T., Wolniak, G. C., Seifert, T. A., & Pascarella, E. T. (2006). Impacts of good practices on cognitive development, learning orientations, and graduate degree plans during the first year of college. *Journal of College Student Development, 47,* 365–83.

Dayton, B., Gonzalez-Vasquez, N., Martinez, C. R., & Plum, C. (2004). Hispanic-Serving Institutions through the eyes of students and administrators. In A. Ortiz (Ed.), *Addressing the unique needs of Latino American students. New Directions for Student Services* (No. 105, pp. 29–39). San Francisco: Jossey-Bass.

Education Commission of the States (1995). *Making quality count in undergraduate education.* Denver, CO: ECS Distribution Center.

Fleming, J. (1984). *Blacks in college: A comparative study of students' success in Black and in White institutions.* San Francisco: Jossey-Bass.

Kuh, G. D. (2003). What we're learning about student engagement from NSSE. *Change, 35*(2), 24–32.

Kuh, G. D., Cruce, T., Shoup, R., Kinzie, J., & Gonyea, R. M. (in press). Unmasking the effects of student engagement on college grades and persistence. *Journal of Higher Education.*

Kuh, G. D., Douglas, K. B., Lund, J. P., & Ramin-Gyurnek, J. (1994). *Student learning outside the classroom: Transcending artificial boundaries.* ASHE-ERIC Higher Education Report (No. 8). Washington, DC: The George Washington University, Graduate School of Education and Human Development.

Kuh, G. D., Kinzie, J., Buckley, J., Bridges, B. K., & Hayek, J. C. (2007). *Piecing together the student success puzzle: Research, propositions, and recommendations.* ASHE Higher Education Report (Vol. 32, No. 5). San Francisco: Jossey-Bass.

Kuh, G. D., Kinzie, J., Schuh, J. H., Whitt, E. J., & Associates (2005). *Student success in college: Creating conditions that matter.* San Francisco: Jossey-Bass.

Kuh, G. D., Nelson Laird, T. F., & Umbach, P. D. (2004). Aligning faculty and student behavior: Realizing the promise of Greater Expectations. *Liberal Education, 90*(4), 24–31.

Kuh, G. D., Schuh, J. H., Whitt, E. J., & Associates. (1991). *Involving colleges: Successful approaches to fostering student learning and personal development outside the classroom.* San Francisco: Jossey-Bass.

Outcalt, C. L., & Skewes-Cox, T. E. (2002). Involvement, interaction, and satisfaction: The human environment at HBCUs. *Review of Higher Education, 25*(3), 331–47.

Pascarella, E. T., & Terenzini, P. T. (2005). *How college affects students, Vol. 2: A third decade of research.* San Francisco: Jossey-Bass.

Sorcinelli, M. D. (1991). Research findings on the seven principles. In A. W. Chickering & Z. F. Gamson (Eds.), *Applying the seven principles for good practice in undergraduate education. New Directions for Teaching and Learning* (No. 47, pp. 13–25). San Francisco: Jossey-Bass.

Watson, L., Terrell, M. C., Wright, D.J., Bonner, F. Cuyjet, M. J., Gold, J., Rudy, D. & Person, D. R. (2002). *How minority students experience college: Implications for planning and policy.* Sterling, VA: Stylus.

Index

academic advisors: explaining importance of engagement to students 316; training in LGBTQ issues 75–76

academic barriers: for disabled students 42, 47–48; for first-year, first-generation, minority community college students 265–266; ill-considered engagement strategies as 9; for low-income, first-generation students 248; for racial/ethnic minority students 185; for student-athletes 284–285; for transfer students 230

academic freedom (*Lernfreiheit*) 83

academic identification 159

academic integration 266, 273

academic support services, for disabled students 44

academic validation 250

accessibility, for disabled students 45–47

accommodations for disabled students: academic support services 44; challenges of providing 41, 43; faculty and staff ignorance about 44–45, 55, 56; legal requirements for 40; percent of disabled receiving 41; student satisfaction with 44; theoretical frameworks 49–52

active learning, and effective educational practice 5

admissions criteria, co-curricular activities as 140

admissions data, disaggregation of 33–34

"adopt a commuter student" programs 234–235

advisors *see* academic advisors

advocacy groups, for returning students 237

affirmative action, negative stereotypes of 160

African American(s), income *vs.* Whites 139

African American faculty, as percentage of faculty 161

African American female student engagement 142–143

African American male student engagement: benefits of 139–140, 141–142; case for addressing 138–142; enrollment, retention, and persistence 138–139, 141; explanations for trends in 144; institutions' commitment to improving 137–138, 149–150, 153; institutions' responsibility for 138, 144–146, 149–150; mentors and role models 144; strategies for improving 149–153; theoretical frameworks for 144–149; trends in 142–144

African American student(s): engagement and persistence in 315; percentage receiving degree from HBCUs 296; as percent of student population 201; rate of community college enrollment 263; in STEM fields 120; and stereotype threat 125; student-athlete marginalization 287; *see also* racial/ethnic minority students

African American student organizations 152, 182

alcohol: abuse, in men 102, 103–104; religious minority students and 82, 93–94

alumni, training in support for first-generation students 256

ambassador programs 254, 274

in 183; for Latino/a students at Hispanic service institutions 307; leadership training and 185; for LGBTQ students 71; and persistence 267; promoting racial/ethnic minority organizations to White students 216–217; for racial/ethnic minority students 184–185, 193; recruitment of racial/ethnic minority students 193; recruitment of transfer students 236; student organization fairs 236; for White students at HBCUs 307; for women in STEM fields 130

co-curricular activities: as admissions criteria 140; African American males and 139–140, 152; barriers to racial/ethnic minority students' participation in 179–186; and career success 43; CPTR students and 225, 226, 228, 230, 234; engagement strategies for racial/ethnic minority students 188–194; importance of 10, 180, 185, 194, 267; international students and 22, 29; participation rates of men *vs.* women 103; and persistence 273; theoretical framework for engagement of racial/ethnic minority students in 186–188; for White students at HBCUs 306; *see also* clubs and organizations

cognitive development theories, sexism in 123
cognitive identity development 166–167
cohorts, for women in STEM fields 127
Coleman-Boatwright, P. 205
collaboration between/within organizations: community college partnerships with other institutions 277, 308; to encourage African American male engagement 150–152; to meet needs of religious minorities 91–92; to set goals for racial/ethnic minority student involvement 193–194

collaborative learning: and effective educational practice 5; racial/ethnic minority students and 171

college student(s), demographics 201
College Student Experience Questionnaire (CSEQ) 103, 142, 313
common sense, critical race theory on 163
communication(s): awareness of religious diversity in 94; of institution's racial equality goals 149; with international students 32; LGBTQ student inclusiveness 72, 74; racial/ethnic minority inclusiveness 189

communities of validation 250–251
community college(s): graduation rates for 266; partnerships with other institutions 277, 308

community college students: transition to four-year college 230, 262, 264, 308; women as 263; *see also* first-year, first-generation, minority community college students

community resource centers, for low-income, first-generation students 252

commuter, part-time, transfer, and returning (CPTR) students: challenges faced by 223–231;

engagement issues 224–226; engagement strategies 233–239; monitoring of 239; theoretical frameworks for engagement 231–233

commuter student(s): challenges faced by 223, 228–229; engagement strategies 233–235; *see also* commuter, part-time, transfer, and returning (CPTR) students

commuter student lounge 233
compensatory effects of engagement 314–315
concerted cultivation approach, to low-income, first-generation students 251
conditional effects of engagement 314–315
connected knowing 123
connected teaching 123, 128–129
consultants, for assessment of engagement 169
conversation partners, for international students 33
counseling services: for first-year, first-generation, minority community college students 274; international students and 23, 30, 32; student-athletes and 288; *see also* academic advisors

course clustering, for women in STEM fields 127
course scheduling, for part-time students 235
CPTR students *see* commuter, part-time, transfer, and returning (CPTR) students
critical consciousness 163–164
critical race theory (CRT) 147–148, 162–165
cross-cultural mentoring 27
cross-cultural speaker series 215
CRT *see* critical race theory
CSEQ *see* College Student Experience Questionnaire
cultural capital theory 124–125
cultural centers 186
cultural change theory 303–305
Cultural Environment Transitions Model 205
cultural exclusivity, in campus environment 181–183, 184
culturally responsive pedagogy: incentives and rewards for 173; need for 162; requiring from faculty 218; training in 172
culture shock 21–22, 31, 247
curriculum: culturally responsive 161, 174, 175; ingrained racism in 205; racial/ethnic balance in 218; for racial/ethnic minority students 163

D'Augelli, A. R. 67–68
Days of Dialogue 217
diet: accommodation of 29–30, 81, 82, 85; international students and 24, 29–30; religious minority students and 81, 82, 85
disability services offices 43, 54
disability specialists 56
disabled students: applicable law 40; challenges faced by 39–40, 42–49; definition of disabled person 40; demographic data 40–42; engagement strategies 52–57; right not to report disability 40; self-perception 47–48, 52; social

barriers 39–40, 42–43, 45, 46–47, 48–49, 56, 57;
theoretical frameworks for engagement 49–52;
types of disabilities 41; *see also* accommodations
for disabled students

discrimination: by campus police 182; in classroom,
responding to 172; against disabled, legal
constraints against 40; and engagement 181;
international students and 22; against LGBTQ
students 61–62, 63, 64–66, 69; against Muslim
students 84; perception of, by racial/ethnic
minority students *vs.* Whites 160–161; in
residence halls 183; types of, in social justice
theory 87–88; against women in STEM fields
122

distance learning *see* for-profit training/educational
institutions

diversity: as buzzword 12; and engagement 1–2;
increasing racial/ethnic diversity on campuses
295; increasing religious diversity on campuses
84

diversity, respect for: and aggregation of admissions
data 34; educational institutions' responsibility
for 22, 207; educational institutions' rhetoric *vs.*
reality 12, 183; in student staff 75

Diversity Scorecard 169

diversity training and programs: in accessibility
to CPTR students, for faculty and staff 239;
educational institutions responsibility for 212;
for faculty and staff at HBCUs 307; faculty and
staff workshops 192; in gender equity, for faculty
128; in gender identity development 110–111;
for graduate assistants 192; impact of 203; in
LGBTQ issues 75–76; for student leaders 73–74;
summer reading programs 215; and White
identity development 203, 204; White student
resistance to 11, 199–207

domestic students, orienting to international
students' needs 29, 30

dominant group, strategies for maintenance of
hegemony 124, 163

double-loop organizational learning 145–146

eating disorders, in women 101

educational institutions: changes required to serve
emerging populations 303–305, 309–310;
commitment to improving African American
male student engagement 137–138, 149–150,
153; contemporary religious climate 83–84;
and CPTR students 228; culture of, and change
304–305; diversity rhetoric *vs.* reality 12, 183;
embedding of programs in secondary schools
254, 257, 308; faculty exchange programs 214–
215; history of religious involvement 82–83;
programs to combat racism 203; resistance
to multicultural programming 205–206;
responsibility for creating engagement 6–8, 138,
144–146, 149–150, 257–258; responsibility for

diversity training 212; responsibility for success
of at-risk students 12; responsibility for success
of international students 27; responsibility to
celebrate diversity 22, 207; shift from teaching-
centered to learning-centered paradigm 301;
and student identity development 99–100;
unresponsiveness to cultural needs 182

employment: for CPTR students 238; for first-year,
first-generation, minority community college
students 274, 276; international students and 25;
for low-income, first-generation students 243–
244, 246–247, 253, 257; and persistence 229; *see
also* career services

engagement: benefits of xxiii–xxv, 313;
compensatory effects 314–315; conditional
effects 314–315; definition of 1–2; history of
concept 313–314; institutions' responsibility for
creating 6–8, 138, 144–146, 149–150, 257–258;
misuse of term 314; outcomes of xxii–xxiii, 3–4;
and persistence 3–4, 180, 315; power of concept
313; varying cultural standards for 168; *vs.*
involvement 5, 6

engagement plans, individual 151

engagement strategies: customizing, to meet
student needs 316; further research avenues
316–317; necessity of 7; overview 315–316;
preparation for implementing 8–10; student
input into 9–10, 90–91; theory as guide in 10–
11; value of 3; *see also specific groups*

engagement teams, for African American male
students 151

engineering *see* women in STEM (science,
technology, engineering, and mathematics)
fields

Enriching Educational Experiences benchmarks
140

enrichment experiences: CPTR students and 227;
and effective educational practice 5–6; for
returning students 237–238

environmental climate assessments, for women in
STEM fields 132

environmental press, and African American
engagement 146–147

epistemological racism 205

Equity Scorecard process 150–151

Ethnic Identity Development, Phinney's Model of
186, 187

ethnic minority students *see* racial/ethnic minority
students

ethnographic experiences, for White students 216

European students, academic issues and needs 20

evaluation *see* assessment

Evans, N. J. 3, 13, 42, 52, 63, 65, 68, 77, 79, 123, 134,
159, 176, 188, 195, 230, 231, 232, 240, 271, 279

exit surveys, for women in STEM fields 132–133

experiential knowledge, validation of 163, 167–168,
171

HSIs *see* Hispanic-serving institutions
Hurtado, S. 7, 12, 13, 14, 22, 35, 54, 58, 160, 171, 177, 180, 181, 182, 184, 185, 196, 202, 205–207, 219, 220, 299, 311

I-20s 23–24, 30
identity development: in African American males 142; in disabled students 52; in first-year, first-generation, minority community college students 269–270, 271–272; in LGBTQ students 63–64, 65, 66–69, 71, 95; in racial/ethnic minority students 186, 188; in religious minority students 86, 94–95; research on 99; and social justice attitudes 90; in student-athletes 285, 287–288, 290; in women 122–123; *see also* cognitive identity development; ethnic identity development; gender identity development; psychosocial development theory; racial identity development; White racial identity development
Identity Development and Sexual Orientation Model (D'Augelli) 67–68
identity development theory 99–100, 166–167, 271–272
identity disclosure, by LGBTQ students 63, 67–68, 70, 75, 76
identity foreclosure 288
immersion experiences, for Whites 215–216
immigrants: educational challenges 243–244; scholarships 252
imposter phenomenon, women and 126–127
incentive programs: for faculty 173; for students 189–190, 278
Inclusive Model of Lesbian, Gay, and Bisexual Identity Development (Fassinger) 67–68
inclusiveness: as buzzword 12; educational campaigns for 74; of language on forms 73, 94; training student leaders in 73–74
individual discrimination, definition of 87
insider knowledge: benefits of access to, for graduate students xxiii–xxiv; first-generation students' lack of 245, 246, 268–269
institutional barriers, for disabled students 43–45
institutional discrimination 87
Integrated Threat Theory of Prejudice 24
interactionalist theory of college student departure 273
interest conversion, in critical race theory 147–148
international services office 31
international students: challenges faced by 17–25; definition of 18; engagement strategies for 20, 27–34; orientation programs 26–27, 28, 30–31; psychological issues faced by 19–20; theoretical frameworks for engagement 25–26; tuition costs and 23
internships: African American students and 139–140; benefits of 316
interpersonal validation 250

involvement: definition of 4–5, 186, 231; Theory of Student Involvement (Astin) 186–187, 231–232; *vs.* engagement 5, 6
Involving Colleges (Kuh *et al.*) 1–2

Jewish students, challenges faced by 81–82, 85
Jones, S. R. 66–67

knowing, gendered ways of 123
Kuh, G. D. 1, 3, 4, 5, 6, 7, 9, 13, 14, 22, 35, 43, 59, 85, 97, 103, 104, 115, 119, 135, 139, 155, 180, 196, 201, 202, 220, 226, 227, 241, 249, 259, 314, 315, 316, 317, 318

language: and construction of gender 105; inclusive, on applications and forms 73, 94
language barrier, for international students 20, 27, 33
Latino/a faculty 161, 300, 308
Latino/a Library Collection Project 308–309
Latino/a population, projected growth of 300
Latino/a students: college enrollment 263, 264, 298; as percent of student population 201; women in STEM fields 120; *see also* racial/ethnic minority students
Latino/a students at Hispanic-serving institutions: challenges faced by 299–300; engagement strategies 299–300, 305–306, 307, 308–309; engagement *vs.* Latino/as at other institutions 314; theoretical frameworks for engagement 303–305
Lavender/Rainbow graduation ceremonies 70–71
leadership: for change in educational institutions 304–305; collaboration and xxiv–xxv; student-athletes and 289
leadership training 73–74, 93, 185, 190
learning, ACPA/NASPA definition of 10–11
learning communities: benefits of 183, 316; cultural exclusivity in 183; ensuring appeal of, to racial/ethnic minority students 194; for first-year, first-generation, minority community college students 275; for women in STEM fields 129
learning disabilities 41, 50
Learning Partnerships Model (LPM) 166–167
Learning Reconsidered (ACPA & NASPA) 9, 10–11
learning styles, tailoring instruction to 162
lesbian students *see* LGBTQ (lesbian, gay, bisexual, transgender and questioning) students
LGBTQ resource centers 62, 63, 71, 72–73, 76
LGBTQ (lesbian, gay, bisexual, transgender and questioning) students: challenges faced by 61–66; engagement strategies 69–76; heterosexist culture and 61–62, 63, 65–66; homophobia and 62, 63–65, 69; identity development and conflicts 63–64, 65–69, 70, 71, 75, 76, 95; internalized homophobic ideologies 65, 67;

students 26–27, 28, 30–31; for LGBTQ student
parents 73; for LGBTQ students 76; for racial/
ethnic minority students 191; racial justice
alliance participation in 213; for religious
minority students 92; for student-athletes 289;
in support of women in STEM fields 130; for
transfer students 236
Ortiz, A. M. 211
out-of-class activities *see* co-curricular activities

Pace, C. R. 313
parent centers 255–256
parents or guardians: breaking ties to belief system
of 210; first-year, first-generation, minority
community college students and 268–269; of
Latino/a first generation students 299, 307;
of low-income, first-generation students 255;
orientation for Latino/a first generation student
parents 299; orientation for LGBTQ student
parents 73
part-time students: challenges faced by 229;
engagement strategies for 235–236; *see also*
commuter, part-time, transfer, and returning
(CPTR) students
Pascarella, E. T. 3, 4, 6, 7, 13, 15, 22, 36, 54, 58, 103,
116, 160, 176, 181, 195, 202, 203, 206, 219, 220,
225, 229, 241, 247, 248, 259, 262, 264, 266, 280,
284, 293, 313, 314, 315, 317, 318
Patriot Act, international student documentation
issues 23–24
peer mentors and mentoring 236, 256–257, 275;
family-style 27
peer networks 170, 174–175, 309; *see also*
networking
peer relationships: of CPTR students 226, 227,
231; of first-year, first-generation, minority
community college students 268–269
peer tutoring programs 253
Pell Grants 246
personal development: of low-income, first-
generation students 247–248; validation and 250
Phinney's Model of Ethnic Identity Development
187
physical barriers, for disabled students 45–47, 53
pluralism: as buzzword 12; and engagement 1–2
positionality, identity development and 106
possible selves theory 272–273
practicum courses, for low-income, first-generation
students 253
predominantly White institutions (PWIs):
culturally exclusive climate of 181–183; first-
year racial/ethnic minority students at 179–195;
overwhelming Whiteness at 183–184
pre-orientation, for international students 26–27,
28, 30
procedural knowledge, types of 123
proprietary institutions *see* for-profit training/
educational institutions

proving process 160
psychosocial development theory 209–211
psychosocial issues: in first-year, first-generation,
minority community college students 268–270;
for international students 19–20
publications, campus, including racial/ethnic
minority students in 189
PWIs *see* predominantly White institutions

questioning students *see* LGBTQ (lesbian, gay,
bisexual, transgender and questioning) students

race relations on campus: courses on 214; current
status of 7; *see also* discrimination; racial
tension; racism
racial climate: positive, characteristics of 163; White
vs. minority perception on 206; *see also* racial
tension
racial/ethnic minority faculty 161, 172
racial/ethnic minority students: assimilation and
181, 183, 270; challenges faced by 157–162,
179–186; cross-cultural mentoring and 27;
definition of 262; discrimination perceived by
160–161; educator's responsibility to engage
158, 175; engagement strategies for classrooms
158, 168–174; engagement strategies for co-
curricular activities 188–194; isolation of
157–159, 160–161, 179–180, 183, 188; mentors
and role models for 161, 170–171, 173, 189;
rate of college enrollment 263; and scientific
culture 124–125; theoretical frameworks for
engagement in classrooms 162–168; theoretical
frameworks for engagement in co-curricular
activities 186–188; validating experiential
knowledge of 163, 167–168, 171; *see also* first-
year, first-generation, minority community
college students; race relations on campus
racial identity development 159–160, 166; *see also*
White racial identity development
racial justice alliances 212–213
racial tension: and academic success of minority
students 160; multicultural programming and
160; undergraduate peer groups and 206–207
racism: critical race theory on 147–148; definition
of 202; epistemological 205; microaggressions
163; as pervasive element of U.S. society
202–203, 203–204, 205, 211–212; programs to
combat 203; in residence hall staff and student
leaders 183; White students' need to confront
202–203
RAs *see* resident assistants
reflective practice: in development of engagement
strategies 8; learning to adopt xxiv
Rehabilitation Act of 1973, Section 504 40, 42
Reisser, L. 209–211, 271–272
religion, in educational institutions: contemporary
climate 83–84; history of 82–83

Transition Theory 25–26, 232–233
tutoring programs, for low-income, first-generation students 253
two-year college students *see* community college students
Tyler, R. 313

United States: defacto segregation in 201; necessity of reconstructing culture of 211; racism as pervasive element in 202–203, 203–204, 205, 211–212
United States v. *Fordice* (1992) 297
universal design theory, on disabled students 51, 55–56

validation 250; communities of 250–251
validation theory 250–251
visas, international students and 23–24, 25, 30

Web resources: communication guidelines for LGBTQ awareness 72; for CPTR students 238; LGBTQ resource center sites 72–73
White Male System 121–122
Whiteness: deconstruction of 211–212; overwhelming, of PWIs 183–184, 189
White privilege: White students' acknowledgment of 200, 203–205; White student's education on 170, 172, 211–212
White Racial Identity Attitudes Scale (WRIAS) 218
White racial identity development: courses in 213–214, 218; diversity training and 203, 204; educational institutions' role in 206; psychosocial development and 210–211; theory of 207–209; tracking of, in students 218; White Racial Identity Attitudes Scale (WRIAS) 218
Whites, income *vs.* African Americans 139
White students: acknowledgment of White privilege 200, 203–205; education on White privilege 170, 172, 211–212; impact of multicultural contact 202; lack of exposure to racial/ethnic minorities 201–202; and learning disabilities 41; as percent of student population 201; perception of discrimination *vs.* minority student perceptions 160–161; resistance to multicultural programming 11, 199–207;

strategies for engagement in multicultural programming 212–218; theoretical frameworks for engagement in multicultural programming 207–212
White students at HBCUs: challenges faced by 296, 298, 308; engagement strategies 305–306, 306–307, 308; increase in 296; reasons for enrolling 296–297; theoretical frameworks for engagement 303–305
women: African American, levels of engagement 142–143; athletes, eating disorders in 101; community college attendance 263; eating disorders in 101; enrollment rates *vs.* men 101; gender identity development in 101–102, 104–106, 112–113; and imposter phenomenon 126–127; income *vs.* men 102; institutional discrimination against 87; levels of engagement 103; minority, challenges faced by 263; Muslim, social barriers 85; segregation into traditionally feminine disciplines 101–102; social activism orientation of 103, 120; stereotypes of 120, 121, 125–126; and stereotype threat 125; *see also entries under* gender
women in STEM (science, technology, engineering, and mathematics) fields: assessment of institutional progress 131–133; campus climate for 121–122, 128–131, 132–133; enrollment, retention, and persistence 118–120, 125, 132–133; experiences of 120–122; mentors and role models 121, 129, 130–131; needs and issues 118–122; stereotypes of 125; strategies for meeting needs of 127–133; Summers (Lawrence) on 117–118; theoretical frameworks for engagement 122–127
women's athletics 65, 101
women's centers 130
women's studies programs 128
workshops: on diversity, for faculty and staff 192; on skills development, for first-year, first-generation, minority community college students 276; on social justice, disabled students and 53; on White privilege 170
work-study opportunities 257
WRIAS *see* White Racial Identity Attitudes Scale
writing, insights gained from xxiv